MAKING
DARKNESS
LIGHT

Joe Moshenska is professor of English at the University of Oxford, where he teaches early modern literature. He is a BBC New Generation Thinker and his essays and reviews have appeared in the *Times Literary Supplement*, the *White Review*, the *Financial Times*, and the *Observer*. He received his PhD from Princeton and lives in Oxford, UK.

Also by Joe Moshenska

Feeling Pleasures:
The Sense of Touch in Renaissance England
A Stain in the Blood:
The Remarkable Voyage of Sir Kenelm Digby
Iconoclasm as Child's Play

MAKING DARKNESS LIGHT

A Life of
JOHN MILTON

Joe Moshenska

BASIC BOOKS

New York

Basic Books
Hachette Book Group
1290 Avenue of the Americas, New York, NY 10104
www.basicbooks.com

Printed in the United States of America

First Edition: December 2021

First published in Great Britain in 2021 by Basic Books London, an imprint
of John Murray Press, an Hachette UK company

Published by Basic Books, an imprint of Perseus Books, LLC, a subsidiary
of Hachette Book Group, Inc. The Basic Books name and logo is a
trademark of the Hachette Book Group.

The Hachette Speakers Bureau provides a wide range of authors for speaking events.
To find out more, go to www.hachettespeakersbureau.com or call (866) 376-6591.

The publisher is not responsible for websites (or their content)
that are not owned by the publisher.

Typeset in Janson Text by Palimpsest Book Production Ltd, Falkirk, Stirlingshire

Library of Congress Control Number: 2021943268

ISBNs: 9781541620681 (hardcover), 9781541620698 (ebook)

LSC-C

Printing 1, 2021

For Rosa, Alejandro and Beatriz,
who 'bring with thee / Jest and youthful jollity, /
Quips and cranks, and wanton wiles, / Nods, and becks,
and wreathed smiles'.

And for Sean, who taught me what it means to read,
and accompanied my 'wandering steps and slow'.

Contents

CONTENTS

Introduction: The Two John Miltons

To begin, a man in a chair; *Take One*. The chair is of medium height, fashioned from dark wood, tendrils of ornamentation carved across its top and sides – a set of cartouches, and in the centre a flower that digs into the nape of the man's neck. He too is of moderate stature, in his mid fifties, light brown hair tending now to grey as it frames his oval face; the skin pale and surprisingly delicate, its smoothness belying his years. Only the hands, gripping the arms of the chair harder than they need to, betray the suffering that the calm exterior works to suppress. The knuckles, rough with calluses, twitch and lock in response to the lances of pain that zigzag up through the body from his gouty legs. No sign of this suffering registers in the brown eyes that stare ahead, undistracted by any shadows or flickers of movement at the window or wainscot. Though their whites and irises look perfectly clear, it is a decade since first the left eye and then the right began to register blank spots and whole areas of fuzzy indistinction before giving way to darkness altogether.

As always at such times, he sings a quiet song to himself beneath his breath, forcing his gnarled knuckles to move and tap along to the tune. This is the hard part – the everyday paradox of *trying* to go to sleep, knowing that the only way is not to try at all, to let one's mind wander in the secret hope that sleep will itself sneak up and pounce. It's nine o'clock in the evening – long gone are the schooldays when he would stay up into the early hours, often until midnight or one o'clock, feverishly scribbling. He has eaten little since a light dinner, concerned that cramming his belly will lead to more of the violent rumblings that used to grip his gut after the evening meal in the years before he went blind. Never one to eat much, his appetite has now dwindled almost to nothing. Impossible to make oneself sleep, to draw an end by force of will to the stream of sensations and associations slipping by. Dangerous, too: every schoolchild knows that sleep is when the recumbent body is most vulnerable to threats from without and within, from hags and imps that suck the breath from babies, from lustful thoughts that bubble up and tarnish even the most carefully managed mind. Gradually, imperceptibly, wakefulness gives way.

At first it seems to him that there is nothing, then, suddenly, something – a crackling and sparking at the edge of the mind. Later, when he wakes, it will be impossible to remember just how it happened. Time would seem – not to stop, but never to have started; words like 'before', 'after', 'now' seemed flatly irrelevant. Sometimes it would seem like it had been a fissure in the darkness, a glimmer of red or lilac light; sometimes akin to a taste, sweet and salt at once, that would tingle the tongue not altogether pleasantly, a taste new and tart like the lurid fibres of a pineapple. Most often, though, it would seem to begin as a sound, first a far-off rumbling like the trembling skin of a beaten bass drum or of brewing thunder, that would gradually, without it being possible to decide when the tremors had resolved themselves into words, form itself into a sort of speech.[1] These were the best nights, when the words arrived, picking up the thread that had been cut that morning at the moment of waking.

When his clear unseeing eyes opened, the words would seem to vanish – but he would instantly know whether they were still there, waiting to be found and fashioned. Gone for now from the mind, they had settled in the belly, as if restricting himself to a meagre dinner the previous night had been necessary to leave room for them to come. But, just like sleep itself, the words themselves could not be sought by force of will, no matter how tempting it was to try. By now he knew it was better to sit and wait. He could not see the darkness in the room beyond the window at this early hour – probably four or five o'clock, the usual time of his return to the waking world – but he called out into it, waiting for the slap of footsteps in response that would announce the approach of his servant or one of his daughters. On bad days the call would go unanswered. Pressing his hands on the arms of the chair, he would force himself to rise and stand upright on his agonised legs, barking out his favourite joke for such an occasion, the one at which his daughters grimaced with distaste hearing it for the tenth time, that he was 'full, and wanted to be milked'.[2] But this was a better morning: his manservant swiftly on hand, and after the curtest of morning greetings he heard a smaller chair being pulled from the wall and a rump being lowered onto it, the pages of a book ruffling as it was opened. The sixth psalm, read in the language in which it had been given to King David by God. Had David's nights been like his, he wondered, when the words were given to him? Had the King of Israel's inexpressible tastes and textures and sounds taken the same form that his took? *Yagati v'anchati ascheh v'chol-laylah mitati b'dimati arsi amseh.* He had taught his assistant how to extract the sounds from the Hebrew letters but nothing of their meaning, and his amusement at this fact made up for the stumbles and the slips to which he had to listen. Or half listen, for he knew the words all too well, and that was the point. The sounds of the holy, long-dead language, at once familiar and alien, seemed to clear a space in his mind – to carve out an enclosed area, empty but thrumming with readiness, into which the words in his belly, now beginning to churn anew, could rush. And, suddenly, there they were in their hundreds, no longer in the distantly heard voice of the night-time – a woman's voice, he was sure, even though he could never remember its tone or pitch – but now in his own. He held up a hand and the halting Hebrew verses instantly ceased; more paper flapped as his servant set down the chunky Bible, picked up yesterday's sheet and poised the freshly inked pen. It had been, somehow, both so hard and so easy to get to this point, impossible to make it happen but now impossible to imagine it not happening. His mouth opened: 'Silence, ye troubled waves, and thou deep, peace, / Said then th' omnific word, your discord end'.[3]

Take Two. The scene is similar, almost identical. The chair, in fact, is exactly the same – the same hefty wood and careful carvings.

The man also looks similar, but there are differences. This time he is dressed not in a flowing grey coat but in tighter-fitting clothes of black. Despite his unseeing eyes, there is a small sword with a silver hilt tucked through the band at his waist – and the eyes themselves are equally clear and unblemished in their shine, but they are no longer brown, rather a cooler blue-grey. He's the same height as before but considerably stockier, which makes him look rather less tall – short and thickset would be an unkind way to put it, but at least some of the bulk is muscle, suggesting that before he lost his sight and his hands curled into painful knots he would have known well how to use the sword. He again eats little, and enjoys his pipe and cup of water before settling into the chair for the evening, but rather than pursuing sleep he puts it off, enjoying the small noises of quiet and solitude, the gentle rustling of the green hangings that cover the walls. Time to think. The great work that he has known, for longer than he can remember, he was destined to achieve is finally underway, flowing freely each morning when he has had time to ruminate upon its latest part. The quiet between the hubbub of the day and the dimly punctuated blankness of sleep is when it happens. He can return to where he left off as easily as if it were a speech that he had paused momentarily for a sip of water or to clear his throat. There it is: 'and with the Center mix the Pole'. What does he need for what comes next? He knows that it will be there when he turns to look for it.

Without letting his eyelids screen his still and sightless eyes, he allows the small surrounding sounds to congeal into a single background hum and retreats inward. His memory-place. He'd been taught from the time he was a boy to think of it in many different ways: as a vast hall, a palace with many rooms, a storehouse crammed with caskets and barrels waiting to be opened and relieved of their contents, a theatre on whose stage figures from the past could be compelled to prance and perform. What amazes him still, after a lifetime of sifting and searching the world behind the eyes, is that one way or another whatever he wants can be found there. Not always in the same way, mind you. At times he has to do no more than aim a glance inward and what he seeks will appear, ready and waiting. At other times he will know where to find it but then discover that it has stuck fast in the receptacle where he placed it. Usually if he pulls at it with the taut muscles of his mind then it will pop forth like a cork in a bottle, before too long. At yet other times an attempt to recall one word or fact or face will lead to a whole gaggle of possibilities leaping from their storage places, clamouring for his attention. An inner wave of the hand will send the unbidden recollections scampering back to their hiding places, leaving the one required memory emerging from the mist of indistinction.[4] And there it will be. Phrases, lines, torrents of words – some from the writers he loves the most, that seem more comfortably couched and rooted in their mental resting places, polished by years of frequent recall. Others from works perused only once or in part, that emerge less like a cork wrenched from a bottle and more like a butterfly or a dandelion puff snatched from the air as it floats past. Words from books, letters, and official documents in half a dozen or more languages, living and dead, absorbed and at hand – but other words too, snatches of conversation that echo on command in the hall of memory, turns of phrase and tones of voice. His father, singing and playing the viol; his boyhood friend Charles, laughing in a field; the distinct tenor of voice of each of his three wives. The melodious calls of swans, echoing from the dark shadows of night on the Thames, audible from the first London home that he remembers. And not just sounds: the stinging lash of a teacher's switch on flesh; the rank stench wafting unexpectedly from a verdant, flower-strewn mountainside.[5]

Somehow, slowly, it gives way to order. The moment sometimes recalls the now impossible process of scanning a crowd of strangers for the one comfortingly familiar face; sometimes sifting a bowl of flour and fat through the fingers, feeling for lumps and rubbing them to smoothness. It is never sheer cacophony in his inner hall; with sufficient patience, something will emerge. The right ones will be found – the words that echo and resonate with those within, that carry with them the memory of his own journey inward, that bear the burden of their past even as they announce themselves as absolutely new. He calls his servant and hears the man tramp in, knows that he holds the usual book, catches the sound of pages pre-emptively opened. No time for that today, he snaps – the Word of God will have to wait. Set this down: 'Silence, ye troubled waves, and thou deep, peace, / Said then th' omnific word, your discord end'.

Take three. No man, no chair, no flashes of divine light or memory-halls. Words appear on a black screen; the bare facts are recited in voice-over:

> *John Milton was born on 8 December 1608. In the early 1650s he gradually went completely blind. In 1667 he published his epic poem* Paradise Lost, *which retold the biblical story of the fall of humankind. In it he suggested that he believed himself to have been inspired by a divine muse, who would visit his slumbers nightly. He died on 8 November 1674, a month shy of his sixty-sixth birthday. Cut.*

◆

There have always been two John Miltons. The prophet and the scholar; the radical and the know-it-all. In fact that's not quite true, or at least it's somewhat too simple. Better to say that, since I first read *Paradise Lost* and began to think about his poetry, I have had these two John Miltons in mind. I don't necessarily love or like or admire or respect one of them, the prophet or the scholar, more than the other, and I don't exactly find it easier to imagine one than the other, though I do have times and moods when one dominates, and distracts me from his curious doppelgänger. I don't want to let go of either of them, and yet I have no idea how to keep them together – whether to place them side by side, or try to make them occupy the same place in my mind.

Part of the problem with trying to place the two Miltons is that both are, as I find myself imagining them, utterly *out* of place. Distinct though they are from one another, both are in different ways, to use one of Milton's own favourite words, *transported* – literally carried beyond the confines of themselves, whether by divine forces or by bubblings of recollection.[6] Seated at home in their respective chairs in the Buckinghamshire village of Chalfont St Giles, whether sleeping or waking, the two Miltons are at the same time profoundly displaced, exploring the realms of inspiration or of memory. And, if the two Miltons are in different ways both in and out of place, they are no less in and out of time: on the one hand quite precisely located, at this point, in the early 1660s; on the other hand, locked in ecstatic communion with somewhen else altogether – with the remembered past, with the words of ancient writers dead for centuries, or with the timeless and eternal Divine.

How to understand, or write about, a life divided in this way? Is it possible to write a biography of these various Miltons? Conventional wisdom would say no: if an account of a life should stick to its known or sensibly inferred facts, then the facts of Milton's life are well documented, unusually interesting, and have often been related. Already in 1779, just over a century after Milton's death, Samuel Johnson felt compelled to begin his rather bad-tempered and brilliantly readable biography by admitting that '[t]he life of Milton has already been written in so many forms, and with such minute enquiry', that he wondered whether he might limit himself to 'the addition of a few notes' to these previous biographies rather than writing his own from scratch.[7] If this was true in 1779 then it is truer still nearly two and a half centuries later, with every aspect of Milton's life and the traces he left having been meticulously pored over. If Milton seems like a dream for a biographer, it is partly because – unlike the protean and elusive Shakespeare – he is so prominently and obviously *in* his works. When, in *Paradise Lost*, the narrator places himself 'In darkness, and with dangers compassed round, / And solitude', surely we can only understand these lines if we know that 'darkness' refers to Milton's own blindness, and that 'dangers' reflect the genuine peril in which he was placed by the restoration to the throne of King Charles II, whose father's execution Milton had thunderously justified in public.[8] This Milton, who vividly presents himself to us, seems to know exactly who he is, and wants us to know too. The constant demand that we keep in mind the person behind the works if we want to understand them would seem to make some knowledge of Milton's life necessary for reading him, and so it's little wonder that there have been many attempts to tell his life story. But, I would suggest, the urge to retell Milton's life is not only a response to his prominent presence in his writings, nor a reflection of his stature as a great poet, nor of the fact that he lived a peculiarly interesting life in particularly interesting times. It cuts deeper than this. He is a tempting subject for biography because he has seemed to many of his readers like a powerful example of what it means not only to be a poet, but to live a human life. He seems to remain consistently aware of who he is and what he is doing, and he develops in clear and distinct stages while nonetheless remaining recognisably and unmistakably himself.

Viewed in this way, I'm inclined to see Milton not just as a tempting subject for biography but as the embodiment of the biographical temptation itself: his life seems to be eminently writable because it is so thoroughly knowable, by him and therefore by us. It's perhaps for this reason that Milton's name sometimes appears on lists of great men who exemplify the allure of biographical narrative. The renowned American essayist Ralph Waldo Emerson, praising the 'perfect sympathy that exists between like minds', a sympathy that biography makes possible across time and space, wrote that 'Socrates, St Paul, Antoninus, Luther, Milton have lived for us as much as for their contemporaries if by books or by tradition their life & words come to my ear'.[9] Emerson captures here something of Milton the prophet's desire to escape time, to be perennially contemporary. In order to demonstrate this timeless greatness it would be enough to relate the facts of Milton's life, of which there are plenty. And there are certainly ways of bringing my two Miltons, the scholar and the prophet, into the realm of fact. We know lots of things about the many books Milton read, and some things about the particular ways in which he read them, as we'll see. And we know as a fact that he believed himself to be (or wanted us, his readers, to believe that he believed himself to be – see how slippery this quickly becomes) something akin to a prophet. Even taking this belief seriously is not easy for us to do, now that prophets and seers are generally associated with superstition and quackery, but this is by no means a new problem. When the poet and artist William Blake, another of Milton's greatest and most complicated admirers, read the painter Joshua Reynolds's claim that taking a poet's account of inspiration literally was absurd, he angrily scribbled in the margin of his copy: 'Plato was in Earnest: Milton was in Earnest. They believed that God did Visit Man Really & Truly.'[10] Whether or not Milton truly was inspired, Blake suggests, we must take his belief in his prophetic inspiration seriously; the *belief* was a fact, and a fact that infuses Milton's poetry, even if the nightly visits by a divine muse were not. But what would it mean to take it seriously?

One approach would be to ask, what did it mean to present oneself as a prophet in the seventeenth century? Milton was only one of many figures who shared this conviction about themselves and their writings in this remarkable period of history, and so we can ask what he meant by it or hoped to achieve by it, and what it might have meant to his contemporaries. I have come to feel, however, that while historical questions of this sort are absolutely necessary for understanding Milton – and I'll ask plenty of them in the chapters that follow – they are not sufficient. They can too easily become a way for me not to understand Milton, but to explain him away, to consign him to a safely distant past. This is what I have in many ways been taught to do, and taught myself to do, over my years of studying and teaching literature, and I by no means want to abandon this striving to inhabit a lost historical moment, to respect the distance and the difference of the past. A lot about Milton only makes sense to me when I find ways of placing the fine textures of his writing in relation to the equally granular details of the seventeenth-century world. I've come to realise, however, that doing this also means shutting out, refusing to answer, some of the questions that keep crowding my mind as I read his writings: weirder, less respectable questions, such as what would it feel like to be divinely inspired? What would it be like to inhabit a mind capable of recalling nearly everything that it had experienced? What is it like to compose more than ten thousand lines of intricate verse while blind? Because these questions cannot be answered, because they cannot even be asked without seeming to transgress upon the mystery of the creative act itself, learning to read properly – seriously, *professionally* – often means learning not to ask them. But I do keep asking them, and I've come to believe that one job of art in general, a job that Milton's poetry performs upon me with particular intensity, is to encourage us to indulge in impossible questionings and wild imaginings of this sort. Precisely *because* we can never know exactly what it would feel like to create any given artwork, one question that artworks nonetheless raise with peculiar and teasing tenacity is this: what would it have been like to make this thing? Continuing to ask this question that we can never fully answer is one of the ways in which works of art that matter to us get woven into the texture of our lives. This book is, then, founded on a wager, a growing conviction: that it's impossible to separate the place of Milton's writings in his lifetime from the questionings and imaginings that they can provoke in ours.

For these reasons this book is not only a biography. Milton fascinates me in part because his writings display to an unusually intense degree the desire shared by many, perhaps all, writers of literature: to intertwine his words and thoughts with the words, thoughts, and lives of his readers; to change them. This is undoubtedly a hubristic ambition, and the idea that books alter who we are can sound overblown or sentimental to modern ears. Certainly few would now dare to argue that art or literature straightforwardly make us better people: SS officers in the Second World War enjoying Bach or Goethe in their breaks from mass murder have put paid to this lofty hope. And yet there is still room for the more everyday fact that works of art and literature do *help to make us the people we are*, even if they don't necessarily make us better ones. They form part of the curious medley of ideas and associations that knock around our minds. In the case of a poet or other kind of writer, the ways in which they use words can seep into our patterns of thought and speech without us even realising. Milton is often considered as part of 'the Canon', the roster of great writers, but his writings also exist as part of *my* canon of valuable writings, the set of things that matter to me and that form and frame my thinking, which might include other poems but also include a strange medley of song lyrics, television shows, novels, and the other bric-a-brac of memories and associations with and within which I perpetually live. In this way, whenever we read or watch or hear or experience something new we are quite literally modifying who we are, often in tiny and imperceptible ways, by altering the stock of stuff in our minds. Choosing to spend longer in the company of a given writer who matters to us, to return to his or her writings repeatedly and over a long period of time, is choosing to be changed more and for longer, and in ways that are likely to become more apparent to us as time goes on. To reread a book or poem that matters to us, to rewatch or listen again to a favourite song or film, is not only to experience it in a new way but also to encounter both the person we were when we last encountered it and the changes that have transpired since.

The way in which Milton matters to me is now, whether I like it or not, entangled within the whole of my life, and this means that to write about him, to make any kind of sense of him, is partly to think about his place within this whole. I don't have a single, crucial experience with Milton that defines his importance to me – a decisive and life-changing journey I undertook with *Paradise Lost* in my pocket, a trauma or rite of passage he helped me to navigate. I have travelled, at times, with Milton, as a way of trying to keep up with or make sense of or be responsive to his constant restlessness and self-displacements; but these journeys, a number of which will feature in the following chapters, have often ended in disappointment or bafflement, albeit of a kind that has added in new ways to my understanding. I don't think that reading Milton will necessarily make you a better or more interesting or more intelligent person. Yet I remain convinced that reading Milton is something worth doing, something worth expending time and energy upon. Convinced too that I can only write about Milton's life in his times by reckoning along the way with his place in my own life, in my times. This will mean bringing Milton's life and his writings into contact with the personal and public worlds that he inhabited, but also showing along the way how his writings have come alive for me, the things that they illuminate and that have come to illuminate them: locations, landscapes, later writers who admired and sometimes reviled him. If this means staying less than fully focused on the facts of Milton's life and work, I hope it will be truer to what I see as one of his deepest preoccupations: the place of literature in a life.

I have begun instinctively to use the language of illumination to speak of Milton's works, and this leads me to my title, *Making Darkness Light*. It is adapted from a phrase that, like many of Milton's most intriguing lines in *Paradise Lost*, is spoken by one of his devils. In this instance it's the smooth-tongued Belial, who tries to persuade his fellow fallen angels that life in Hell isn't all that bad. It could be worse – they could be overwhelmed with 'cataracts of fire' or 'Caught in a fiery tempest'. They might even get used to it, and 'receive / Familiar the fierce heat, and void of pain; / This horror will grow mild, this darkness light'. Although the narrative voice quickly scolds Belial for his 'words clothed in reasons garb' and encouragement of 'ignoble ease, and peaceful sloth', what complicates this dismissal, as is so often the case in *Paradise Lost*, is how similar Belial's words sound to some of Milton's own deep convictions and ambitions.[11] Belial may encourage inaction because he is lazy and craven, but the imperative not to rush in hastily, and instead to wait and seize the moment of greatest possibility, was one upon which Milton insisted. More complicatedly still, Belial's hope that darkness will before long grow light comes just a few hundred lines after the poem's famous opening invocation, in which Milton implores his muse: 'What in me is dark / Illumine'.[12] The inspired poet and the damned devil hope for a remarkably similar change: darkness giving way to light.

When I began to connect this yoking of light and dark to Milton's account of the poetry of *Paradise Lost* arriving to him at night, I became more fully preoccupied with his experiences of poetic creation. Where this led me, as my two Miltons suggest, is not so much to the experience of the inspired dream itself as to the dark–light moment of waking, the stage when consciousness is still returning to itself. The point when one is neither oneself nor another, awake nor asleep, neither securely in nor entirely outside of time and space. This is, for me, the interval of *Darkness Light*; the writing of *Paradise Lost* is the *Making* that becomes possible at such a moment. It did not escape me that this is exactly the kind of in-between state which begins the only modern novel to rival *Paradise Lost* in the intense emphasis on the experience of its own making, Marcel Proust's *À la Recherche du Temps Perdu*. Its narrator, Marcel – who is and is not Proust in something like the way the narrator of *Paradise Lost* is and is not Milton – begins that vast work by describing the experience of falling asleep while reading without realising that he has done so, and half-waking to a 'mind, which hesitated on the threshold of times and shapes'. This same hesitating, wavering point is where I want to place Milton's creating mind. The experience is, for Marcel, likewise bound up with light and its absence:

> everything revolved around me in the darkness, things, countries, years . . . when I woke in the middle of the night, since I did not know where I was, I did not even understand in the first moment who I was; all I had, in its original simplicity, was the sense of existence as it may quiver in the depths of an animal.[13]

This total dispossession in and by darkness, this quivering simplicity, is necessary for the light of illumination to come. The hesitating at the threshold of experience that Proust describes has helped me approach Milton's own making, between darkness and light.

There are still other ways to hear these words, however, which bring out their political as well as their poetic resonances, and which have taken on an increased urgency in the current historical moment. At the outset of her seminal book *Things of Darkness*, Kim F. Hall cites the contrast that Milton draws in one of his early prose works between the 'sober, plain, and unaffected style of the

Scriptures' and 'the knotty Africanisms, the pamper'd metaphors, the intricat, and involv'd sentences of the [Church] Fathers'. This contrast is, Hall argues, typical of the ways in which 'descriptions of light and dark, rather than being mere indications of Elizabethan beauty standards or markers of moral categories, became in the early modern period the conduit through which the English began to formulate the notions of "self" and "other" so well known in Anglo-American racial discourses.'[14] *Paradise Lost* does not link the language of darkness and light so explicitly to divine clarity and African obscurity, but with the luminescence of Milton's Heaven and the murky opacity of his Hell it certainly participates in this process by which lightness and darkness, of bodies as well as souls, come to be associated with good and evil. If I keep the language of light and dark prominent in my title, this is in part because I see Milton as both invested in the creation of these simple and damaging kinds of opposition (quite literally, insofar as he worked for a government under whom the enslavement of Africans in the Caribbean increased exponentially), and as providing resources for alternative ways of thinking about identities and the ways in which they are formed. One of the paradoxes of his writings that I set out to understand is that Milton is both the poet of clear and brutal contrast, content to set up poles of light and dark, and the poet of the shades and gradations that lie between those poles.

I am still not quite done with these words, however, and will close my account of my title by suggesting one final way of hearing them. When Belial suggests that the darkness of Hell may grow light, in a punning way (and the sins of Milton's devils often manifest in a fondness for puns) he simultaneously suggests that they'll grow lighter in the sense of being less heavy, easier to shoulder. I'm further encouraged to hear the line this way by the fact that, in one of his much earlier poems, Milton made probably the most famous poetic use of the word 'light' in this other sense, when the carefree speaker of 'L'Allegro' calls out: 'Come, and trip it as ye go / On the light fantastic toe'.[15] This is lightness of a different sort: a fluid ease of movement and of gait, the dexterity and oblivious-ness of a virtuosic dancer. It's not a quality that we usually associate with Milton, but we should. Belial resembles the poet who created him not just in his desire for illumination but also in his hope to grow light like L'Allegro, to spring or to float airily despite the burdens placed upon him. The modern writer who helps me see this side of Milton is Italo Calvino, who proposed for literature 'an existential function: the search for lightness as a reaction to the weight of living'. 'It might be said', Calvino ventures, 'that two opposing literary tendencies have competed over the centuries: one that seeks to make language a weightless element that hovers over things like a cloud, or, better, a fine dust, or, better still, a magnetic field; another that seeks to imbue language with the weight and thickness and concreteness of objects and bodies and sensations.'[16] I have come to believe that Milton is distinctive and compelling because he exhibits both of the opposing tendencies that Calvino describes in unique abundance, sometimes alternating between them, sometimes straining to unify them. If I see Milton as more than the weighty, ponderous figure of grand reputation, then my aim is to describe this opposing impulse towards weightlessness: his urge to make himself, his poems, his readers, trip lightly out of the dark.

In explaining my title, *Making Darkness Light*, I've already begun connecting Milton with later writers who matter to me, and I do so in part because it's important to stress at the outset that this book is not the end point of a process of understanding Milton and his poems. My ideas and opinions about him are not fixed and final: I'm writing not because I've made my mind up about him but partly to work out what I think. This might seem like an odd thing for a biographer to admit, but I am drawn repeatedly back to Milton because various aspects of his character and his writings seem like proper puzzles to me, and so too does his place in my own life. Bluntly put, I am not sure why I have chosen to spend so much time with this particular long-dead Christian poet, and with his knotty and challenging writings. I know that I find him good for thinking with, but I don't know why I've chosen him in particular to animate my thinking.

The simplest reason for this perplexity is the aspect of Milton's writing that provides the biggest obstacle to many modern would-be readers of his work. If Milton is usually identified as one of the greatest poets in the history of England, he is certainly seen as the country's greatest *Christian* author: his writings, more than those of Chaucer or Shakespeare or Jane Austen or William Wordsworth, seem to require both knowledge of and interest in Christianity if they are to retain any power to affect and compel. Johnson, in his vivid and tetchy account of Milton's life, wrote that 'All mankind will, through all ages, bear the same relation to Adam and Eve', which makes Milton's choice of their story for his epic 'universally and perpetually interesting'.[17] Many modern secular readers – and indeed, even many modern religious readers – would beg to differ, and it's not clear that modern Christian believers will have an immediate affinity for Milton because his deeply idiosyncratic version of Christianity is likely to seem startlingly different from theirs.

As a Jew who doesn't believe in God's existence, and for whom religion is a matter of upholding some enjoyable family traditions, not a matter of either personal conviction or communal religious practice, my constant return to Milton feels even more perplexing when I reflect upon it. My grandmothers, both raised in impoverished Yiddish-speaking households in the East End of London, were raised never even to touch the New Testament; yet I spend a great deal of my intellectual and imaginative energies in studying seventeenth-century Christians and teaching their doctrines, albeit as matters of history rather than piety. My devout forebears – I only have to go back four generations to find a rabbi – would be turning in their graves. How did I get to this point?

Reflecting further on my own background has provided hints towards a few possible answers. One – which I hugely like, even if I can't bring myself to believe it – comes from a family story. Sometime in the 1960s my maternal grandmother tried to reconnect with some of her relatives with whom she had lost contact. The attempt ended with her being denied entry to the house of a distant cousin by that cousin's wife, who denounced the 'great shame' that my grandmother's branch of the family had brought upon them all. Questioned a little further, the shame in question turned out to be the fact that my grandmother's direct ancestors in Smyla (located downriver along the Dnieper from Kiev) had been followers of the charismatic Jewish leader known as Sabbatai Sevi or Shabsai Tzvi, who purported in the seventeenth century to be the Messiah. He supposedly claimed that he had visions of God, could pronounce the forbidden name of the deity, could even fly, and was an exact contemporary of Milton's.[18] This, then, must be it! Somewhere, woven into the fabric of my bones or encoded deep within my DNA, is a susceptibility to prophets, to great men and their wild claims, a willingness to take seriously the utterly unlikely. My mother recently discovered with the help of a genealogy website that as late as 1923 one of my ancestors died whose middle name was Shabbatai, so the affiliation seems to have persisted through the ages. Shabsai Tzvi, as a scholar of *kaballah* trained to understand the mystical significance of letters, might have liked the fact that Milton and I share the same initials (our birthdays are even a mere five days apart): it was clearly meant to be.

Tempting, but unconvincing. I love this story, am bamboozled by its sense of the past still dictating the present, but such explanations will never be mine. I mention it here because, even setting such mystical inheritances aside, I do still feel that my ways of relating to these personal and familial traditions are connected to my ways of relating to Milton. I suppose part of what I'm trying to convey with this piece of family lore is simply a sense of growing up with a vague and hovering awareness of being, or feeling, less than fully English, of having ties to past times and places that could suddenly feel startlingly direct – and the strangeness, in light of this continued feeling, of having then chosen to study and to teach something called 'English literature'. And, nested within this strangeness, the further oddity of having devoted a significant portion of my time to thinking about a man who was not only a committed Christian but has also often been held up as the essence of Englishness. One scholar writes that 'John Milton is something of a national institution, as much a part of the English landscape as fox-hunting or the Bank of England.'[19] When Thomas Gray wrote his much anthologised 'Elegy Written in a Country Church-Yard', with its twilit scene of glimmering English landscape, he tellingly chose to label the anonymous poet whom he imagined lying dead beneath the loam as 'Some mute inglorious Milton'.[20] This is the Milton who in his writings could issue a nationalistic clarion call to the English as 'a noble and puissant Nation rousing herself like a strong man after sleep, and shaking her invincible locks'.[21]

It's certainly possible to tell a story about John Milton, Englishman – to echo the title of an earlier biography – and present him as a Christian patriot.[22] But, as I'll try to show, it would very much be only one part of a much more complicated story. Instead, I'm interested in a Milton who helps me ask, how much of a tradition can one reject and still belong to it? Can one belong to it, in some strange sense, *by* rejecting it? My own ongoing attempt to make sense of what it means to be Jewish without believing in God or sharing much feeling of kinship with an abstract religious community is entangled in some way with my sense of Milton as a person who could only remain a Christian through extraordinary acts of mental effort and contortion. Who, as we'll see, radically rethought the central Christian doctrine of the Trinity, and rejected its orthodox versions in ways that many have found shocking and sought to deny. Who could barely bring himself to stare on the spectacle of the suffering Christ, which is central to so much Christian devotion. Likewise, my sense of myself as both inescapably English – formed by my upbringing in this country, professionally involved in teaching its 'great literature' – and at the same time as entirely out of sync with so much that I associate with England, and detesting any claims to national or linguistic exclusiveness, maps onto another double sense of Milton. If Milton can seem synonymous with fox hunting or twilit country church-yards, to others he has repeatedly seemed not quite English enough. In fact, Tom Paulin characterised 'the dominant English attitude to Milton' as 'a type of begrudging embarrassment': 'Unlike Dante in Italy or Joyce in Ireland, he is not venerated – respected and admired, yes, but not everywhere, and not always.'[23] This ambivalence reflects other sides of Milton, sides less easy to label as English – the Milton who wrote and thought in multiple languages, sometimes all at once, with such intensity that the distinctions between them began to break down. Whose imagination was not narrowly nation-bound but profoundly international (even interstellar, pan-universal). The same Milton who elsewhere saw England as less distinctively noble and puissant, and insisted that 'the Sun which we want [i.e. lack], ripens Wits as well as Fruits; and as Wine and Oil are Imported to us from abroad: so must ripe Understanding, and many civil Virtues, be imported into our minds from Foreign Writings.'[24] This is Milton not as insular but as emphatically and gloriously porous. And these mixed inclinations define the man who interests me throughout *Making Darkness Light*: Milton as a writer who can seem both integral to certain categories – man, Christian, poet, Englishman – and to undercut our very sense of where these categories begin or end. He can seem both culturally central and never fully to belong.

When the Jewish philosopher and theologian Franz Rosenzweig wrote his magnum opus, *The Star of Redemption*, at the very end of the First World War, he claimed in it that 'so far as his language is concerned, the Jew feels always he is in a foreign land, and knows that the home of his language is in the region of the holy language, a region everyday speech can never invade.'[25] I'm drawn to, and will return to, this image of language as a foreign land in which one can be lost. But I want to approach my time spent with Milton by asking, what if you feel lost in this way but the holy language provides no refuge?

Since in the chapters that follow I am going to be considering how my own specific experiences inform my relationship to Milton, and more generally how our experiences affect the connections we form with artworks, I need to provide a little more personal background. My great-grandparents' Yiddish was filtered out across the generations, and during my childhood it was not a separate language I spoke at home but rather something with which my family seasoned our English with a flavour of frequent, everyday difference. Certain actions, objects, people, were referred to automatically with Yiddish words. My sense that this was a family affair was augmented by the fact that I grew up and went to school in an overwhelmingly non-Jewish area. Yiddish has never been absorbed into the wider consciousness in the United Kingdom with the kind of nostalgic affection that has occurred in the United States, and I learnt a form of low-level code-switching from a young age: it was only at home that a flannel was a *shmatter*, a knick-knack a *shmonsy*, to be openly proud was to *kvell*, someone who stole a bite of your ice cream was a *shnorrer* or a *chaper*, a falling-out was a *broigus*, a foolish or unworldly or unpleasant person was a *nebbish* or a *nudnik* or a *shmendrik* or a *shmerrel* or a *lobbes* or a *shlemiel*, depending on a set of fine but unarticulated distinctions. This meant that Yiddish became the linguistic manifestation of the ways in which I experienced my and my family's difference from the world around us: difference that was enjoyable – private and special – but also potentially exposing. In my experience, to respond to someone wishing you happy Christmas by explaining 'I celebrate Hanukkah, actually', was to be unnecessarily awkward. Why make a fuss? Why not just fit in? I felt this pressure, like many Jewish children, and would quietly accept Christmas and Easter wishes just as I would quietly leave my Yiddishisms at home when I stepped out of the front door.

I should also mention here that my childhood was affected by more direct and vicious kinds of antisemitism, but while these experiences were horribly traumatic, they're also relatively easy to recognise, and to condemn. They're less relevant to what I'm trying to get at here through my experience of Yiddish: a kind of antisemitism that is much more slippery, elusive, often hard to specify or to prove. It's less about being marked out as completely alien, and more a case of being perceived as a strange inflection of the norm. Of being, for want of a better phrase, a bit weird. I felt, growing up, that my family and I were anomalies, particularly difficult for others to place. The mixed language we spoke at home and the foreign name I bore contributed to a sense that my family and I didn't entirely fit in with the versions of either Englishness or Jewishness amidst which I grew up. The Jewish soundtrack of my childhood was not the kitschy, nostalgic version of my forebears' history represented by *Fiddler on the Roof* and klezmer music, neither of which I can abide; it was the folk songs of the Jewish socialist Leon Rosselson. In 'My Father's Jewish World' he sang of his family's past in a way that I could recognise, 'half belonging, half a stranger'. He seemed to be describing my and my family's experiences with uncanny closeness.

If there was an England in which Rosselson seemed more at home, then it was the world of seventeenth-century England. He sang of the True Levellers, better known as the Diggers, whose attempt to establish a paradisal community of shared land and property on St George's Hill in Kent was violently dismantled by the authorities in 1649. My favourite of his songs was the one about a Ranter named Abiezer Coppe, who scandalised English sensibilities in the 1640s and fifties by claiming that God could be praised by drinking, swearing, and fornicating, and who warned the rich that, as Rosselson's song put it, 'your property will canker / And your houses will decay / And the rust of all your silver / Will burn your flesh away'. For Rosselson, Coppe was no historical curiosity but a haunting presence, ominous and impish at once: 'History disowned him / His ghost they cannot kill / Haunts the rich and righteous / Drunk and dancing still'. These lyrics were, for me, the first form that the rhythms of the seventeenth century took in my mind.[26] Fuelled by my mother's particular enthusiasm for the period and its politics, from a young age I was building Lego models of the execution of Charles I with my brother, and writing stories about Roundheads and Cavaliers at school. I also came to realise from a young age that my bookishness, my love of reading and writing stories in this way, also marked me out as different: I don't so much mean the praise it often won from my teachers or the reputation it earned me among my peers for swottishness, so much as a pervasive sense, absorbed by cultural osmosis, that loving literature was not the sort of competitive, physically taxing activity that was appropriate for boys.

By describing my childhood in this way, as oddly filled with the seventeenth century and its politics, I might seem to be suggesting that my route to studying and teaching Milton was smooth and straightforward, predestined from a young age. In fact the opposite feels more the case. It took me many years to find my way back to the period in which Milton lived. My love of reading was almost destroyed by bad experiences at school, and only redeemed thanks to good fortune and good teaching. As I moved through my studies, however, I rarely felt there was time to stop and think about why I'd gravitated towards Milton. There certainly wasn't space in the writing that I was being trained to do to reflect on how these interests had come about and how they related to my background and my experiences. I have come to realise over the years, however, that my background does inform my decision to spend years of my time in Milton's company, but in more complicated and curious ways than I initially realised. Throughout *Making Darkness Light* one of my aims is to explore how and why Milton offers resources for making sense of ourselves that don't rely upon straightforwardly identifying or agreeing with him. He was able to be absolutely himself while remaining in some sense foreign to himself, and this strange kind of self-relation I have found rich and useful in making sense of *my*self.

I feel the need to provide this sense of my background because I'm going to be drawing in the chapters that follow on my own ex-periences with Milton. There is, however, a more specific way in which I have come to connect Milton's works with this account of myself. I've already observed that Milton has sometimes been seen as less than fully or comfortably English, not a straightforward national icon. This is partly due to his politics – his fervent repub-licanism and support for regicide. But it's also, I think, more subtly connected with the long history of responses to the strangeness of Milton's poetic language, which has divided opinion more than that of any other major English poet. His long and complicated sentences, his tendency to warp and abandon conventional word order, his avid borrowing of vocabulary and grammatical structures from other languages: all of these have led him both to be admired as sublimely virtuosic, and vilified for abandoning English altogether, even doing a kind of violence to the language. Samuel Johnson claimed that Milton 'was desirous to use English words with a foreign idiom', which led him to construct 'a *Babylonish Dialect*, in itself harsh and barbarous', meaning that in order to admire him Johnson had to 'find grace in its deformity'.[27] These criticisms were restated in the twentieth century by the pre-eminent poet and critic of modernism, T. S. Eliot, who took Milton to task for 'the deterioration – the peculiar kind of deterioration – to which he subjected the language'. To Eliot, Milton was not a monument to English greatness but one who 'violates the English language', producing a 'foreign idiom, the use of a word in a foreign way or with the meaning of the foreign word from which it is derived rather than the accepted meaning in English'.[28]

I first read and was captivated by Eliot's poems as a teenager, and, as soon as I then began to learn more about him, I quickly encountered the question of his (disputed) antisemitism. A brilliantly insightful essay by the scholar Matthew Biberman helped me understand the queasy feeling that Eliot's attack on Milton's supposed violations of English gave me in my stomach: the claim to be degrading the language, infecting it with foreignness, is precisely the claim that has been aimed at Jews over the centuries, and especially Yiddish-speaking Jews like my forebears.[29] One of countless examples, and one that Eliot likely knew, is the antisemitic screed by the composer Richard Wagner, which declared that 'The Jew speaks the language of the country in which he has lived from generation to generation, but he always speaks it as a foreigner.'[30]

I am not suggesting here some deep affinity with or essence of Jewishness on Milton's part, and his attitude towards the actual Jews of his time seems to have been ambivalent at best. Rather, I'm suggesting that these criticisms are inadvertently accurate testimonies both to what makes Milton's use of language so electrifying, and what makes it resonate with my particular linguistic experiences growing up, speaking an English seasoned with Yiddish. Milton's contortions of the language bring to the fore the way in which English exists only in a porous state, constantly changing, borrowing, adapting from elsewhere, just as he did. It's in this sense that I can understand my affinity with him: not as a monument of achieved and insular Englishness, but as a writer whose existence in and between languages constantly reveals this idea as a dubious fantasy. One way in which I've come to understand the poetic language that Milton developed is to see him as creating across the course of his life something akin to a personal Yiddish, or English made into a kind of Yiddish. His example convinces me that none of us are truly at home in any given tongue, because languages are not distinct, stable, timeless structures in which we can take up residence. They are a labyrinth of intersecting paths amidst which we wander. *Making Darkness Light* explores Milton's writings as a space in which to come to terms with and to enjoy this predicament.

In 1623, when Milton was a teenager, the First Folio of Shakespeare's works was published, a prestigious and expensive collection that was a crucial step in establishing the playwright's literary reputation. In one of the poems tagged onto the beginning of the volume, Ben Jonson proclaimed of Shakespeare: 'He was not of an age but for all time!' This sentence is famous and endlessly quoted, and I can't abide it. There are few descriptions of an author more empty than the claim that he or she is timeless – it's rarely more than a pompous way of saying 'really, really good'. It's not just the claim to timelessness that bothers me about this line, but its simplistic either/or logic. A work of literature must belong either to the time in which its author composed it, or be so great that it belongs to every time equally, and hence to no time at all.

Seven years later, in 1630, Milton penned his own poem in Shakespeare's memory; in 1632 it became his first published poem when it appeared among those prefaced to Shakespeare's Second Folio, and it begins as follows:

> *What needs my Shakespeare for his honoured bones,*
> *The labor of an age in piled stones,*

Or that his hallowed relics should be hid
Under a star-ypointing pyramid?
Dear son of Memory, great heir of fame,
What need'st thou such weak witness of thy name?
Thou in our wonder and astonishment
Hast built thyself a live-long monument.[31]

The thought behind these lines is fairly straightforward – there is no need for a grand monument to Shakespeare because his own works are more magnificent and enduring a testimony than such a structure could ever be. Paradoxically, a hefty and durable pile of stones is in fact a 'weak witness' compared to the plays and poems themselves, a point that Milton makes in characteristic fashion by playing dextrously with the words he uses in making it. I particularly like the third line, where the sonorous and slightly pretentious word 'hallowed' seems to shrink and shrivel into the tiny word 'hid', in which the same first and final letter surround a single pinched vowel. Contrary to appearances, Milton claims, to be hallowed in this way *is* to be hidden.

The irony of reading this poem today is that the fate that Milton sees Shakespeare as having fortunately escaped is arguably that which has befallen him. I don't mean this literally – there are a few busts and statues of Milton in and beyond England, but they hardly litter the landscape. Rather, he's suffered the logic of that third line, in which to be hallowed is to be hid. In his poem to Shakespeare, Milton is well aware that monuments are strangely paradoxical things. On the one hand they loom over us, imposing in their gilt and marble splendour – Nelson's Column, the Washington Monument, the Arc de Triomphe. On the other hand, as the Austrian novelist Robert Musil acutely observed, 'There is nothing in this world as invisible as a monument. They are no doubt erected to be seen – indeed to attract attention. But at the same time they are impregnated with something that repels attention, causing the glance to roll right off, like water droplets off an oilcloth, without even pausing for a moment.'[32] When a figure becomes monumental we no longer feel obliged to look at or think about them; the deciding has been done. They *matter*, but they matter in a fixed, formidable, and therefore forgettable way.

Today a limited selection of Milton the Monument's writings are found on a few school and university syllabi, and in the poetry or classic literature sections of bookshops. The fate of his works was already apparent to Mark Twain in the year 1900, when Twain gave an after-dinner speech in New York to a group called the Nineteenth Century Club in which he told the gathered company: 'I don't believe any of you have ever read *Paradise Lost*', 'and you don't want to'. The reason was simple: 'It's a classic,' Twain explained, which is to say, 'something that everyone wants to have read and no one wants to read'.[33] I find myself in a strange position when it comes to Milton the Monument or the writer of classics, because, as I've begun to suggest, a lot of what I think about him – a lot of what I find myself thinking, with his help – is totally opposed to this idea of a towering literary aristocrat. And I find it deeply painful that, when the place of poetry in modern education is explicitly discussed, my nightmare version of Milton seems to be held up as an ideal of what poetry should be and do: teach children 'proper' language as a means to inculcate 'proper' values. Children of six and seven, the website of the UK's Department for Education tells me, should be 'continuing to build up a repertoire of poems learnt by heart, appreciating these and reciting some, with appropriate intonation to make the meaning clear'.[34] This is poetry as a sculptor's mallet, which, if you whack them with it hard enough and in the right places, will help mould children into the right shape.

Don't get me wrong: there is a side of Milton that seems to want to bludgeon me or whoever reads his works into submission with his erudition and his eloquence, to take his place among the monuments of literature, but this is only one portion of him, and only one sliver of my ongoing encounter with him. Milton the Monument or the Classic does not sit at all easily alongside Milton the Prophet or even Milton the Scholar. One motive for my thinking and writing about Milton in this way – for allowing myself to imagine him in different modes and settings – is a fervent belief that tradition cannot be allowed to become the sole preserve of traditionalists; that those of us who work on literature often labelled 'great' cannot allow the fact of having read it or the ability to quote snippets of it from memory to signal only that a person has had a certain kind of elite education or belongs to a particular social class. Milton is important to me in this regard not only because he's assumed a particular place in my own life, but because his writings provide a constant provocation to shake every monument that confronts us, to see how stable they are and to ask how and why they keep standing, and whether they should.

If I don't want to see Milton as a monument, then how do I suggest we see him? At the risk of sounding irritatingly sentimental: as a friend. I mean this, however, in the quite specific sense used by the philosopher Alexander Nehamas, when he draws a parallel between finding an artwork beautiful and being friends with a person. 'My friends', he writes, 'are people from whom – no matter how familiar their character, their quirks, or their weakness – I don't yet know exactly what I want to get, because I trust them enough to let them influence what I believe and what I desire in ways I would not be able to do, or even imagine, on my own.'[35] Reading something is like befriending someone, Nehamas suggests, in that both are acts of trust; opening oneself up to a work of art or literature or to another person requires a leap of faith in that we must genuinely be unsure as to what will happen as a result, but we must be interested enough to find out to keep reading, or watching, or talking. It is unpredictable precisely because it is truly companionable.

Part of the appeal to me of this notion of approaching Milton as a friend in this sense is its obvious perversity – and not just because he's been dead for three and a half centuries, but because so many modern writers have made a point of observing just how unlikeable he seems to them. Eliot began his diatribe against Milton's corrupting of the English language with the words: 'As a man, he is antipathetic. Either from the moralist's point of view, or from the theologian's point of view, or from the psychologist's point of view, or from that of the political philosopher, or judging by the ordinary standards of likeableness in human beings, Milton is unsat-isfactory.'[36] This is delicious: whatever these 'ordinary standards of likeableness in human beings' might be, he's in no doubt that Milton falls short of them. Closer to our own time, the critic Colin Burrow felt compelled to ask a question rarely posed of long-dead poets: 'How is it possible to *like* Milton?' 'There is certainly a great deal to dislike,' he continues. 'Most people would think of him as an overlearned poet who combines labyrinthine syntax with a wide range of moral and intellectual vices.'[37] What Eliot's and Burrow's words have in common is their shared sense that there is something wrong with Milton as both person and poet, and that the personal and poetic wrongs are somehow connected.

In fact, Milton has probably provoked more dislike and antipathy than any other English poet, as well as a great deal of lavish praise, and this is part of what makes him interesting to me. When I look to the history of responses to Chaucer, or Shakespeare, or Jane Austen, I can find interesting instances of dislike or disdain, but these punctuate what is largely a torrent of approval, differing largely in what to admire rather than whether to admire at all. By contrast, as we've already begun to see, many people *hate* Milton; they hate his poetry and they hate him as a person. Or they love his poetry but hate his personality or his actions. Or, as was the case with Samuel Johnson, George Eliot, Virginia Woolf, and T. S. Eliot himself, they are divided between love and loathing, and changed their minds repeatedly. This history of deeply mixed feelings makes Milton appealing to me: there's a real argument to be had here about what sort of person and writer he was.

I'm also tempted to see the ways in which Milton has violently divided opinion as a reflection of the ways in which he himself was divided, and the ways I've been tempted to divide him: prophet and scholar, monument and shaker of monuments, bundle of facts and spur to imagination. He can in all of these respects, at times, feel itchingly close and familiar; at other times he seems utterly alien, impossible to understand on our terms. But this isn't the either/or logic of a writer being time-bound or timeless that Jonson proposes, but something more like a wild oscillation between ways of thinking, feeling, and being. And it's on this basis that I'd like to retain and adapt Nehamas's claim that artworks are like friends, in that we trust them to change us in ways that we cannot anticipate. This is not the same as saying that we must always like artworks, or their creators – just as, indeed, we do not always have to like our friends. We can be baffled, frustrated, exasperated by them; our moods change in relation to them; we can want to be with them more at certain times than at others.

In Shakespeare's *Hamlet*, when the ghost of the Prince's father appears to him, his best friend Horatio quite understandably calls it 'wondrous strange'. Hamlet replies: 'And therefore as a stranger give it welcome.'[38] This is my challenge throughout this book: not to tell the story of Milton's life as if I know in advance exactly what a life is, but to welcome Milton in the manner Hamlet urges, not by making him too familiar but by allowing him to remain strange. In perhaps the most famous sentences from his prose writings, Milton proclaimed: 'I cannot praise a fugitive and cloister'd vertue, unexercis'd & unbreath'd . . . that which purifies us is triall, and triall is by what is contrary.'[39] The challenge Milton set his contemporaries with these words – to change themselves by encountering and navigating the difficult and the strange, to be exercised by what can often seem contrary – is, throughout this book, the challenge of how properly to welcome the strangeness of his life and his writings.

Each chapter in this book begins with a particular scene or moment that is drawn from or illuminates Milton's life and work. The ensuing pages then move back and forth from this moment or circle around it, focusing on particular events in and around Milton's life, and on the works that he wrote, but also weaving in later writers and artists who responded to or resonate with Milton, as well my own evolving engagement with his works. Each chapter is, therefore, more like an essay prompted by a stage in Milton's life than an attempt to exhaustively capture a segment of that life. The book is divided into three parts, which are quite different from one another. Part I opens up the question of when a life begins and how it is measured, using the moment of Milton's birth as a jumping-off point for considering both his place in time and how his writings change our experience of time. In this first chapter I also introduce the term *rhythm* as key to understanding the shifting effects of Milton's writings, and my relationship with them. The remaining chapters in this section continue the same rhythmic movement, exploring Milton's life through his school and university years until the writing of his first great poem, the so-called Nativity Ode, in 1629. Part II is slower in its progression, covering just a few years in Milton's late twenties and early thirties, including pivotal events in his life such as the writing of his poem 'Lycidas' and his travels in Italy, which are explored more slowly and in greater detail. Part III moves more quickly through the latter half of Milton's life, and is both continuous with and distinct from what went before. The chapters it contains consider Milton's intertwined poetic, personal, and political activities, culminating in the writing of *Paradise Lost*. I end by returning via Milton's last great work, *Samson Agonistes*, to the question of whether Milton desired or deserves to be seen as a monument, and, if so, of what kind. My aim in proceeding in this fashion is to reflect both the way in which a life unfolds and the fact that this unfolding is never smooth, even, or regular. The time of any life is singular but never single, and this is emphatically true of Milton's. The same is true of *Making Darkness Light*.

PART I

I

9 December 1608: 'On Time'

Friday, 9 December 1608; a cold winter morning. It's still dark and fairly quiet on Bread Street in London, an easy ten-minute walk east of St Paul's Cathedral. The street smacks of affluence, respectability. The bakers whose trade provided its name three centuries before have long moved on, and now it is 'wholly inhabited by rich merchants', as one observer notes.[1] At its north end Bread Street hits Cheapside, one of the busiest thoroughfares in a city which seems to get more crowded with each passing month, but at this hour the merchants and their servants, the vendors and criers whose voices will compete with each other in the frosty air, are only beginning to set up shop, shuffling about on the frozen crust of the muddy roadway. From high up in one of Bread Street's impressively tall buildings, its five storeys looming over the street below, a sound can be heard; the agonised cries of a woman in labour, in a bedchamber on the third floor, where the female servants and local midwife gather around her recumbent figure.

In the empty hall immediately below, these cries form a muffled background of pain. This is the largest room in the building, almost exactly twenty feet square. Listen carefully, and you can catch another softer, more regular sound; it emanates from a small metal box that hangs on the wall. The top of it is a dome of darker iron, dully functional; the rest is shinier brass, engraved with delicate patterns. Below it is a pair of concentric circles. The inner one is scored with a loop of roses and two faces, a smiling angel at the top and a squashy-nosed devil below. The outer one is marked with dark shapes at even intervals, the Roman numerals from one to twelve: a clock. Down below it hang a pair of lengthy chains made from small links; each chain runs around a small wheel, and from the wheel dangles a dark sausage of metal, a lead weight. The clock has a single hand of black iron whose looping, ornamental prong is pointing downwards and very slightly to the left. Throughout the night and early morning, each time it has pointed straight at a number, the dome at the top has been struck by an internal hammer and a peal of sound has disturbed the darkened room, but at this exact moment it hovers equidistant between vi and vii, and, rather than the jarring bell, a softer and entirely familiar sound is heard, roughly every two seconds, as the dangling weights exert their force on the mechanism and the escapement continues to turn: *tick . . . tick . . . tick*. Upstairs, another cry, then a period of tense silence, ended by the reedy wails of a baby. John Milton has been born. *Tick . . . tick . . . tick.*

◆

Why do we care about the date on which a 'great' poet, or any reputed genius, was born? It seems self-evident that a date of birth matters; it is the obvious beginning, the point from which we begin to count the duration of a life. But there's an equally obvious sense in which his date of birth seems to tell us little about Milton the writer, the Milton in whom I'm interested. It's a trivial data point; everyone has to start somewhere.

There are reasons, however, to bear in mind not just the date but the precise time of Milton's birth. Perhaps the most obvious is that he himself knew it, and cared about it. Later in his life, on one of the blank sheets at the start of the family's Bible, Milton noted his birth in the third person: 'John Milton was born the 9th of December 1608 die veneris [Friday] half an howr after 6 in the morning.' The note is followed by a bare, unelaborated list of the births and deaths that would define his life, a poker-faced register lacking in overt joy or sorrow. His brother Christopher, seven years his junior and a man whose political views were utterly opposed to his own. His nephews Edward and

John Phillips, whom he had schooled as boys. His five children – two of whom, his son and namesake and his daughter Katherine, died in infancy, along with his first wife, Mary, and his second wife, also Katherine.

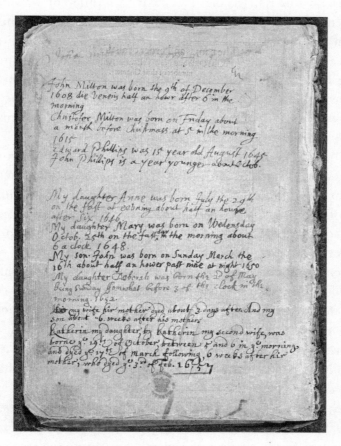

FIGURE 1: The list of births and deaths written in Milton's family Bible, now in the British Library.

If it's a touching list it's also a slightly strange one, seeming first to exert a tight grip on time, then to hold it more loosely. Milton's birth is fixed precisely to half past six; his brother's, oddly, to a highly specific time ('5 in the morning') but a much vaguer date, 'about a month before Christmass'. The nephews get still vaguer dates of birth, but each of his own children is assigned to the closest known hour on the day in question. Some deaths are more vaguely remembered than births, seemingly less important to fix in time: his first wife died 'about 3 days after' the arrival of his third daughter, his son 'about 6 weekes after his mother'. And time's passage is marked on this remarkable document in a different way. For the final entries on the list, the handwriting changes: by this time Milton was completely blind, and needed another's help to record the deaths of his own wife and children. His sight was probably fading increasingly with each entry, some scored unseen into the page using nothing more than muscle memory, though they seem remarkably neat. Milton almost certainly never saw his only son's face before the boy's death, aged two.

It's hard to know what to do with a document of this sort – what sort of response it demands, if any. It's a historical document, not a poem, even if its shape on the page tempts me to read it like one. Very often, in trying to reconstruct a life from an earlier century, we're confronted with information of this sort – mute facts or traces that seem to leave unsaid as much as they reveal. What would a life comprised merely of such traces, a simple list of dates and facts, look like? Can such a thing be imagined? The twentieth-century poet Denise Levertov, who hated the nosiness and prurience of many modern biographies, drew a contrast between their sensationalism and the restrained habits of the seventeenth century. When Milton's contemporary, the Welsh poet Henry Vaughan, was asked for details of his and his brother's life by his cousin John Aubrey, he responded 'modestly, albeit with eager courtesy', and sent a 'bare list of facts'. 'How that modesty', Levertov exclaims, 'contrasts with the egotism of writers who assume the reader wants to know that they have smelly feet or that a sibling once deliberately pissed on them.'[2] The contrast isn't entirely a fair one, however. Not only was Milton capable of an egotism to match any modern writer, as were plenty of others in the seventeenth century, but when I read Vaughan's expression of supposed humility for myself I find there's something irritatingly self-aggrandising about it, a phoniness in his gratitude for Aubrey's interest in 'such low and forgotten thinges as my brother and my selfe'.[3] It's apparently not all that easy to be sincerely modest about the facts of one's life, and there may be no such thing as a bare list of facts that speak for themselves. Indeed, no one knew this better than the adult Milton, whose poetry was often crammed with oddly ornate lists that were anything but bare, whose sonorous sounds seemed designed to be relished rather than understood: 'And all who since, baptized or infidel / Jousted in Aspramont or Montalban, / Damasco, or Marocco, or Trebisond'.[4]

Already there's a risk here that needs acknowledging. Births and deaths seem to speak immediately to us: they savour of recognisable landmarks, of facts of human existence that persist through the ages. Milton may, however, have cared about the precise time of his and his children's birth for very different and apparently peculiar reasons. Around 1650, in the very midst of the sequence of births and deaths this page records, an astrologer named John Gadbery cast Milton's horoscope, based on the precise date and time of the poet's birth. The configuration of the stars at this moment suggested a pensive and introspective person, inclined towards artistic and intellectual activities: a person just like Milton.[5] If it seems incongruous to find Milton doing something as frivolous and superstitious as having his horoscope cast, we shouldn't rush to judgement. Most learned people in the seventeenth century distinguished between wicked or deluded forms of astrology and its learned and pious manifestations. To see the stars as influencing one's life didn't mean relinquishing responsibility; it meant carefully scrutinising both the movements of the heavens and the arc of one's existence for connections and correlations between them. Strange though it might seem to us, in this way the pursuit of learned astrology contributed to the development of both astronomy (because of the technical skill with which the heavens had to be read) and autobiography (because it made the minute details of a life matter enough to be recorded). I'm less interested in Milton's horoscope for what it tells us about him – like all horoscopes, it tells a reassuring story of what one thinks one already knows – than as a lesson against historical complacency. If I take my initial bearings from Milton's own interest in the very moment of his birth, it might matter to the two of us for wildly different reasons.

Milton's horoscope suggests one reason for caring about beginnings – because to know the beginning is to know, to be able perfectly to anticipate, the rest of the story. This was, however, only one of his motives. Milton's lifelong fascination with beginnings involved both the desire to understand them and a keen awareness of the difficulty of knowing them, or pinpointing them exactly. For Milton, the questions of how and where a life begins and how and where a piece of writing begins were strangely intertwined. Do we truly begin when we're conceived, born, or become aware of ourselves? Or much earlier, with our family and forebears, who shape us in ways we can't and don't choose? Likewise, does the poem begin with the intention to create it, or even earlier, with a feeling or phrase that leaps to mind? With the first rumblings of an idea? When pen is put to paper? Or when it's finished and sent off into the world? When Milton came to write *Paradise Lost*, as we'll see, he staged these questions obsessively, and beginning seems to have been a more complicated matter for him than for almost anyone else. We can know certain facts about his life with a pretty strong degree of assurance: if by modern standards of systematic and obsessive recording it can seem like we have relatively few scraps and clues from which to build, then by the standards of seventeenth-century lives, Milton's is well documented, and has been much pored over.

We know, for example, not only the time and date of his birth but also something about the house in which he was born, its layout and furnishings, thanks to a detailed survey of the property that was undertaken when Milton was a boy. The building was owned by Eton College, and a copy of the survey survives in the archives there.

One thing we can't know, I need quickly to admit, is the kind of clock that Milton's family owned, and indeed whether they owned one at all: so why bother to put one in my imagined version of the scene? In the collection published in 1645 that contained most of his poems written up to that point, Milton included a poem titled 'On Time', which starts with an address to Time as a figure, and gradually envisages a human progression towards a 'long Eternity' when 'Attir'd with Stars, we shall for ever sit, / Triumphing over Death, and Chance, and thee O Time'.[6] The published version of the poem, however, omitted a subtitle Milton had added in the handwritten original, thought better of, and crossed out: 'To be set on a clock case'.

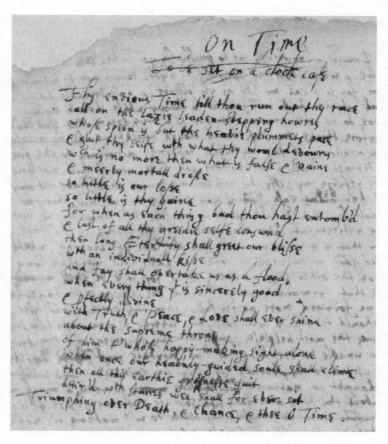

FIGURE 2: 'On Time', as written by Milton in the Trinity Manuscript.

And indeed, the poem itself gestures not just towards Heaven and eternity but also towards the clanking, jerky mechanisms of clocks as they existed in Milton's lifetime: Time is challenged to 'Call on the lazy leaden-stepping hours, / Whose speed is but the heavy Plummets pace'.[7] A plummet was the name for the lead weight that dangled below what was known as a lantern clock, gradually pulling round its cogs as time passed, the standard timepiece until the invention of the pendulum clock later in Milton's lifetime. Time in clocks like these doesn't swing back and forth but seems to fall gradually downwards – like the sand in an hourglass, but far less smoothly and silently. The language of the clock's plummet stuck in Milton's head: here's Satan, falling through the terrifying and turbulent realm of Chaos in *Paradise Lost*, when 'all unawares / Fluttering his pennons vain plumb down he drops / Ten thousand fadom deep, and to this hour / Down had been falling', if by pure chance he had not been blown back upwards by an abrupt chaotic gust.[8] Satan here, falling 'plumb down', is like a rogue meteorite careening through outer space, like a speck of matter driven through a crazed particle accelerator – but also like a plummet falling below a clock until he threatens, if only in a counterfactual act of the imagination, to touch our own time: *'to this hour'*, as if this other imagined Satan could come crashing suddenly through the ceiling as we read.

A scribbled out subtitle to a little-known poem might seem a small thing on which to hang an imagined scene, but I'm more interested in the way in which this example brings out two extremely basic but extremely important things that literature in general and Milton's writing in particular routinely ask us to do, yet which seem surprisingly absent from discussions of why or how we might choose to read at all. First of all, the detail of the poem's originally intended location, the lantern clock case, asks us to care about, and sometimes to find out more about, things that don't instinctively or obviously matter to us. To be frank, I'd never given much thought to Milton's clock, or to clocks in general, before I came across this deleted subtitle. My reading around the topic led me quite quickly to the basics of lantern clocks, but I was left with as many questions as answers. I didn't just want to know the kind of clock for which Milton might have intended his poem, but the difference it would make if I imagined him living, growing up, with a clock of this sort – time falling with a weight, not swinging with a pendulum. A visit to the History of Science Museum in Oxford – appropriately housed in a building that, by the late seventeenth century, contained the first public museum in the country, the original Ashmolean – gave me the chance to stare at an impressive range of lantern clocks: but they sat, still and mute, piled on top of one another in cases. Seeing them sit silent in this way presented me with a question that hadn't occurred to me before: what sort of *sound* did Milton's clock make? Did it go *tick-tock* like a pendulum clock? To borrow the wonderful title of the Russian-Jewish poet Osip Mandelstam's memoir, what was *the noise of time* for Milton?[9] I couldn't find an answer to this question in any discussion of the poem, or any history of clocks: it seemed too basic to ask or answer. Fortunately, the internet led me to a leading authority on lantern clocks. He confirmed for me that lantern clocks do make a ticking sound, at varying intervals depending on the nature of their mechanism, and he sent me a picture of a beautiful early seventeenth-century clock that I used as my mental image for the clock ticking away at the moment of Milton's birth. But this didn't by any means *solve* the poem, or explain it away: in fact, he told me, the notion of setting a poem on a clock case is itself an odd one, since there is little room for text; it's not entirely clear what Milton had in mind.

Now I need to acknowledge at this point that pursuing Milton's clock in this way is not entirely normal, and has little to do with the ways in which most people read. I teach sixteenth- and seventeenth-century liteature for a living – of course I'm going to be interested in obscure oddities like this. Furthermore, I'm in the immensely privileged position of having the time and the resources to go on wild goose chases of this sort, to access the resources and materials I need to do so. This fact was particularly brought home to me by the manuscript in which the original title for 'On Time' is recorded – commonly known as the Trinity Manuscript because it's held in the Wren Library at Trinity College, Cambridge, where I taught for eight years. It took several of those years for me to pluck up the courage to ask to see this manuscript first-hand because I didn't really have a good excuse to do so – and, since I'm going to retell several tales of disappointment and disillusion when it comes to tracking Milton's traces, I should say that the first time I looked at the manuscript in the company of the Wren librarian all my

FIGURE 3: Anonymous lantern clock with
angel's head and devil's head, c.1630.

cynicism about literary tourism melted away in a moment of breathless magic.

It was only later that I recalled Virginia Woolf's account of her very different attempt to view the very same manuscript in the very same place, related in *A Room of One's Own*. Woolf was inspired by one of Charles Lamb's essays to seek out Milton's handwritten words, and decided to 'follow Lamb's footsteps across the quadrangle to the famous library where the treasure is kept'. Finding herself 'actually at the door which leads into the library itself', she continued,

I must have opened it, for instantly there issued, like a guardian angel barring the way with a flutter of black gown instead of white wings, a deprecating, silvery, kindly gentleman, who regretted in a low voice as he waved me back that ladies are only admitted to the library if accompanied by a Fellow of the College or furnished with a letter of introduction.

For Woolf, this experience of exclusion, all the more brutal for being so impeccably calm and polite, became emblematic of the ways in which institutions function and police their own boundaries, typically at women's expense:

That a famous library has been cursed by a woman is a matter of complete indifference to a famous library. Venerable and calm, with all its treasures safe locked within its breast, it sleeps complacently and will, so far as I am concerned, so sleep for ever. Never will I wake those echoes, never will I ask for that hospitality again, I vowed as I descended the steps in anger.[10]

It's no coincidence that it was the thwarted attempt to view a Milton manuscript that prompted Woolf's righteous anger: the librarian, at once dustily bookish and pseudo-angelic in the enforcement of all-male purity, is clearly a version of Milton himself, often experienced by other readers and writers, and especially by women, as an embodiment of oppressive and exclusionary male power. And although the Wren Library obviously welcomes women today – and the Milton Manuscript is available on the internet in high-quality scans for all to see – the kind of bars and obstacles to encountering Milton and the high culture he often seems to represent are no less real today, even if they've mutated into new forms. Working in the institution where this manuscript is housed made me determined to try to find ways to lift these barriers or make them more porous, but also acutely aware of how silently powerful they remain. While acknowledging this, I do want to return to my two Miltons, and to the ways in which his life and his writings seem constantly to provide resources both for those who would construct and police these kinds of walls and doors and gates, and for those who would seek to break them open and make all that is known, felt, and experienced available to all.

If my potentially self-indulgent interest in Milton's clock raises questions of access and privilege, I also want to hold onto it as a route towards a second fundamental fact: that reading *takes time*, but its relationship to the way in which a clock measures time is not straightforward. Once the crossed-out subtitle is restored to Milton's poem, its title becomes a pun: it is 'On Time' in the sense that it describes or is 'about' time; but also, if set on a clock case, it is carved or pasted on to time, on to the object that seems to embody and to remind us of time's passing.

But the poem is also 'On Time' in a third sense – a sense that is true of any poem, but becomes inescapable when time is in its title. Look back at the poem in the Trinity Manuscript, and allow yourself to pause for a moment over its most obvious feature – the poem's shape, or silhouette – before you even bother trying to decipher its words. Its lines are uneven – they vary markedly in length. As it goes along, the poem's own lines, its basic way of occupying our time, dilate and contract, ask more or less of our attention: that which Time devours, the poem insists, 'is no more than what is false and vain, / And merely mortal dross; / So little is our loss, / So little is thy gain'.[11] In the act of insisting they have lost little, these lines *become* little, abruptly shrinking in length by almost half, from ten syllables to six: they stand up to Time, deny its tenacity, by taking up less of our time. We can imagine eternity, but we can't possess it: what we have in the meantime, perhaps, are words, and their own ways of making time speed up and slow down, of pausing and starting afresh; their rhythms.

It is perhaps too obvious to be worth observing that clocks and poems have this feature in common: they both make rhythms. Or at least mechanical clocks do. The rhythms of poems like this one, of course, have to be at least somewhat varied if they're to remain interesting, whereas clocks ideally sound out a regular and unchanging rhythm. Ask any English-speaking child what sound time makes and I'd guess that '*tick-tock*' is what she or he would reply. In fact, if we stop and listen hard, it's obvious that the sounds made by a mechanical clock, at least one that is running properly, are all the same: it doesn't make two kinds of sound but the very same one, again and again. The sounds of clocks and watches might be dying out today, as their mechanisms are increasingly replaced by silent digital faces, but the cliché of time going *tick-tock* remains. In Milton's own time, however, with newly portable timepieces only gradually making their way into homes, their routine background noise was a new experience, possibly even a disconcerting one. John Aubrey, in one of his *Brief Lives*, tells a story of a man for whom Milton would have had very little time, to say the least – the Roman Catholic mathematician and book collector Thomas Allen. Allen, a lover of arcane knowledge and wondrous devices, 'became terrible to the vulgar . . . who took him as a conjuror', and his spooky reputation threatened to ruin a visit to a friend in Herefordshire. Allen, Aubrey reports, 'happened to forgett his Watch in the Chamber-windowe. (Watches were then rarities).' The maids entered to clean the room, and, 'hearing a thing in a case cry Tick Tick Tick', they 'presently concluded that this was his Devill', and threw it out of the window and into the moat to drown it. Fortunately for Allen, the watch caught on a sprig of elder and so 'the good old Gentleman gott his Watch again', but for the servants this piece of good luck only 'confirmed them that 'twas the Devill'.[12]

Sadly, this is more likely to be one of Aubrey's 'excellent after dinner stories', as his editor puts it, than the truth, since the ticking clocks and watches that were becoming familiar by the time Aubrey wrote it down in the 1680s were not just 'rarities' but entirely unknown in Allen's lifetime.[13] I'm less interested in the veracity of the anecdote, however, than in what it suggests about the ways in which people can respond to changes in the measuring and experiencing of time. The rise of the mechanical clock is often hailed as one of the harbingers of the modern age – the rise of a regular, empty, one-size-fits-all experience of time that gradually flattened out the varied and homespun versions of time within which people lived their lives.[14] Aubrey's story suggests just how strange and ragged a process this might have been in practice, the ticking timepiece an embodiment not of calm and regular reason but of alien and demonic danger.

On a more mundane level, however, the story interests me because it shows that, at least at this point, the watch's beats were heard as the same: *Tick . . . Tick . . . Tick.* This is time not as a series of alternating pairs, but as the constant repetition of the same, and my hunch is that *tick-tock* as a convention gradually developed as a way of coping with, or fending off, this feeling of endless repetition, of never-ending sameness. As Frank Kermode puts it: 'We ask what [a clock] *says*: and we agree that it says *tick-tock.* By this fiction we humanize it, make it talk our language. Of course, it is we who provide the fictional difference between the two sounds: *tick* is our word for a physical beginning, *tock* is our word for an end.'¹⁵ While Kermode acknowledges that *tick-tock* by itself is 'not much of a plot', he nonetheless sees it as the basis for all of our plots: our desires to shape and organise time, to give it an order and a form that is varied but predictable. Though Kermode does not use the word, I'd again say that what *tick-tock* does, by introducing a difference of a single letter, is give time a *rhythm.*

Rhythm is my word in these opening chapters – it's not Milton's; he uses it nowhere in his writings (neither, incidentally, did Shakespeare). I need, therefore, to say a word about what I want from it – why thinking in terms of rhythms might give us purchase on Milton's early life. Although the word was known and used in England by the sixteenth century, it was still quite new to English, and sounded odd and complicated: 'This very word Rhythmus in matter of speech,' wrote one of Milton's contemporaries, 'what it is . . . would be . . . a long and difficult businesse to make it plain.'¹⁶ There's still something of this slight strangeness to the word if I stare at it for a few seconds or say it out loud a few times, rhythmically, in succession. This might be in part because it lacks all of the five principal vowels (*rhythms* is the longest English word without *a, e, i, o,* or *u* that can be played in Scrabble). A dive into the dictionary gives me various helpful definitions: 'The measured flow of words or phrases in verse . . . The measured flow of words or phrases in prose, speech, etc.'[17] Linguists disagree about the origins of the Greek word *ruthmos* from which *rhythm* derives, some arguing that it comes from the verb meaning 'to flow' and is borrowed from the movement of waves rippling the sea's surface, others insisting that it means form or organisation, the way in which the parts fit together within the whole.[18] Something that has a rhythm moves and meanders through time, but it has to be in some way organised, measured, if we're to recognise it as a rhythm. A rhythm doesn't have to be as regular as the *tick-tock* of a clock, it can ripple and vary, but it has to be regular enough for us to follow it through time, to stay with it.

We find and make rhythms in many places, and on many scales. The dictionary definitions refer to language, and it is words and music of which we think most readily when it comes to rhythm, but if a sentence or a brief cadence can have a characteristic rhythm then so too can an entire novel or a symphony. And it's not just artworks: our lives have rhythms, some that we're aware of as they're unfolding, others only in retrospect, and many not at all. Some biologists argue that rhythm is the characteristic that unites and defines all living things.[19] And, to go back to Milton's own unknowable beginnings, we're exposed to rhythms before we enter the world, in the womb: rhythm comes before individuality, long before self-awareness. 'The sound that dominates the unborn child's world is its mother's heartbeat. Other voices and familiar sounds add harmony to the already progressive composition of the uterine symphony. From the 24th week on, the unborn child listens all the time', primarily to a sound that has been described as a 'rhythmic "swooshing" of the blood as it rushes through the placental vessels'.[20] Perhaps it's partly thanks to rhythm's primacy in our experience that we can find ourselves tempted to understand non-living things, on a wide variety of scales, as having a rhythm of their own. If a minute of our day can take on a distinctive rhythm, so too can an hour or a year or a decade, even an entire century or epoch. If a river or sea can seem to possess its distinctive rhythm, so too can an entire city. Another way of putting this, to go back to my imagining of Milton's clock, would be to say that it's practically impossible for us to inhabit time of any sort in the form of *tick-tick-tick*, the ceaseless repetition of the same: we need and create difference. As soon as there's difference, there's rhythm; and as soon as there's rhythm, there's the possibility of a story.

It's probably no surprise that poets and composers tend to be the ones who've thought the hardest and pronounced the loudest about rhythm, but broadening the word in this way, allowing it to resonate on a variety of scales, permits a different way of understanding why and how poems and other artworks might matter to us, why and how they fit with a life like Milton's. A particularly beautiful way of thinking is offered by the French poet Stéphane Mallarmé, who admired Milton for his habits of linguistic mixing, and whom T. S. Eliot compared to Milton based on 'the violence that they could do to language'.[21] Mallarmé made the typically enigmatic and alluring claim that '*toute âme est un nœud rhythmique*' – 'every soul is a rhythmic knot'.[22] What I take from this opaque pronouncement is the idea that we might ask of a person – that I might ask of Milton – not what is or was s/he like or what kind of person is or was s/he, or what are or were his or her essential qualities, but rather, what were his or her rhythms? What was the particular knot of rhythms that made up Milton and that Milton made?

If I want to make sense of the knot of rhythms that made up Milton and his life, however, there's a further way of thinking about rhythm that's going to matter, and that's the rhythm of my own time spent with Milton. We don't often think of the time spent with books, other artworks, or indeed people or places or pets, as a kind of rhythm, but I'd like to suggest that this is the best way of describing the intermittent but essential role they play as we make up our own and one another's lives. Thinking of these encounters as a bundle of interlocking rhythms focuses our attention upon the most banal fact about reading: *it takes time*. We don't usually pause over this fact, and we don't have readymade ways to talk about it. If we decide to read, and if we decide to talk to one another about what we read, it's pretty acceptable to ask, what did you think of the story? What did you think of the characters? Did you enjoy the style? What did you think of the ending? But what if you told me you'd read a book and my first question was, how long did it take you to read? – this would sound aggressive, accusatory, perhaps competitive. If I asked, where did you read it? What was going on in the background when you read Chapter Four? I would probably sound nosy, invasive, weirdly fixated on irrelevant details. But this means that most of the reading experience, and much of what we carry with us in our memories from the books we read, gets left by the wayside. Thoughts and feelings prompted by a book are just about okay to discuss, in certain situations – book groups, with certain close friends, and so on – but the knot of rhythms in which our reading is situated, the web of experiences and sensations within which it is embedded, these we usually keep to ourselves.

One of the reasons Milton has come to matter in my life is that he has become for me a vital figure with whom to ponder this basic but crucial point – that reading takes time, and takes place in time. The most basic appeal artworks make to us is that we give them our time, if we are fortunate enough to have it to spare. They are coagulations of the time their creators spent making them. They offer us a particular quality of time's passing, and ask for our time in response. But how much time? What's the right amount of time to spend with a book or painting? How long to linger before each piece in a gallery? How slowly or quickly does a particular novel or poem seem – if I can put it this way – to want us to read it? There's no single or simple answer to these questions, but that's what makes them seem, to me, worth asking. Precisely what books and other artworks offer us is an opportunity to experience time's rhythms in a way that draws upon, but nonetheless profoundly differs from, the rhythms that make up the rest of our lives. A set of rhythms that can be shifting, unpredictable, comforting; that can fade into the background or draw attention to themselves. 'On Time' is far from my favourite of Milton's poems, but it stands out for me as a crystallisation of a deep preoccupation with time that runs through his works, and that encapsulates both the biggest and most abstract of questions – can we look forward to a timeless afterlife? – and the most mundane and everyday ones: what are the objects, whether plummeting clocks or poems, through which we experience the rhythms of time? To read is, on this basis, to create a new rhythmic knot: it is to intertwine our personal rhythms, those of the life we are leading and the particular day on which we do the reading, with the rhythms of whatever new thing we choose to read. This means that it matters a great deal where we read (in bed, on a bus, on the beach), what time of day, how quickly or slowly, how attentively or distractedly. It means that when we reread a particular book or poem, as I suggested in the introduction, we not only meet a set of words that we may or may not remember, but a version of our past selves: when I read one of Milton's poems that I know well, not only are my knot of rhythms and the knot that he created coming into contact, but I am meeting my own pasts at the same time that I meet his.

I'm going to approach Milton by way of his rhythms because it gives me a way to inhabit the shifting patterns, the measured flows, that made him who he was – to consider how his rhythms related to those of the seventeenth-century worlds in which he grew up. But also because these rhythms are what thrum across time to us; they are what allow us even to be tempted by the impossible idea of bringing a long-dead poet back to imagined life when we read him. If we view Milton's life and his works as, among other things, opportunities to forge new and responsive rhythms, then we can't separate them from the reactions that they have solicited; Milton always wanted to resonate across time as well as to intervene in his own. Let me give one of my favourite examples.

'I have paid much attention to Milton's rhythms': so pronounced Gerard Manley Hopkins in a letter of 3 April 1877 that he wrote to his friend Robert Bridges, offering critical comments on a number of poems that Bridges had sent him.[23] Hopkins is known as one of the great rhythmic innovators in the history of English poetry, and one of the only poets to have a particular variety of rhythmic techniques – known as 'sprung rhythm' – associated solely with him. He's also my mother's favourite poet, so I was familiar with the sound of his lines long before I remember hearing any of Milton's, and Hopkins certainly doesn't sound like anyone else. 'Cloud-puffball, torn tufts, tossed pillows | flaunt forth, then chevy on an air- / Built thoroughfare: heaven-roysterers, in gay-gangs, | they throng; they glitter in marches': so begins one of his best and best-known poems.[24] No other writer I know better captures the sense that poetry has to diverge from straightforwardness to the very threshold of nonsense in order to say something worth saying, as the almost crazed higgledy-piggledyness of these lines' patterns of sound suggests. But if Hopkins was undoubtedly an innovator, he pointed again and again to Milton as a precursor, despite reviling his beliefs, religious and otherwise: 'I think he was a very bad man,' Hopkins writes, and, since Hopkins was a devout Roman Catholic, had Milton been able to peer ahead into the nineteenth century then the feeling would very much have been mutual.[25] But Hopkins nonetheless couldn't get the sound, the rise and fall, of Milton's poems out of his inner ear. In a letter to Richard Watson Dixon, written the year after the one to Bridges, he writes: 'Milton's art is incomparable, not only in English literature but, I shd. think, almost in any . . . this is shewn especially in his verse, his rhythm and metrical system . . . I have paid a good deal of attention to Milton's versification and collected his latest rhythms.'[26] What if we thought of poets – and, in a related but distinct way, of ourselves, in and beyond our lives as readers – as collectors of rhythms?

Later in the same letter Hopkins describes the process by which he overturned his decision to abandon poetry when he became a Jesuit: the occasion for his change of heart was the drowning in the Thames of several Franciscan nuns. Following this tragedy he set to work: 'I had long had haunting my ear the echo of a new rhythm which now I realised on paper.'[27] The outcome was another of his most remarkable poems, 'The Wreck of the *Deutschland*'. Its lurches of sound, like all Hopkins's poems, have many sources: he refers to 'hints of it in music, in nursery rhymes and popular jingles', and to Bridges he wrote that his sound patterns were 'got in part from the Welsh, which is very rich in sound and imagery'.[28] It is nonetheless Milton to whom he refers as his most important precursor – but again, my point is not that Milton *influenced* Hopkins or that Hopkins *imitated* Milton. It's rather that Milton's rhythms were part of the knot that Hopkins found 'haunting my ear', reverberating around his mind and becoming one element in the creation of something entirely new. Even if we can't hope to write poems like him, he's a model for what it means to live with Milton's rhythms, to hear and feel them in and across time.

Having wandered some way from where I began – the first moment of Milton's life, his fascination with dates and times of birth and death, his interest in clocks as they make and measure time – it's now the moment, having suggested the opportunities that Milton's rhythms have created for some of his more inspired and idiosyncratic readers, to turn in the next chapter to the particular knot of rhythms that made up his early life. But before I do so, one final anecdote from a time between his and mine: a return not to the clock in the Milton household that I began by imagining as it marked the ticking moment of his birth, but another imagined Miltonic timepiece. In the 1840s the great American essayist Ralph Waldo Emerson – who saw Milton, as I mentioned in my introduction, as an ideal subject of biography – travelled across England and Scotland, and among the various encounters that he later remembered was the following:

> A gentleman in London showed me a watch that once belonged to Milton, whose initials are engraved on its face. He said, he once showed this to Wordsworth, who took it in one hand, then drew out his own watch, and held it up with the other, before the company, but no one making the expected remark, he put back his own in silence.[29]

This gentleman showed Emerson an object, both everyday and intimate, that Milton was supposed to have possessed. And he used it to tell the strange story of William Wordsworth, probably the most famous of Milton's effusive poetic admirers, striking a pose with the watch and being disappointed in his anticipation of a response. What did Wordsworth want the assembled company to say? Presumably that he much resembled Milton, or even that his watch was uncannily like Milton's? It's a strange scene, combining the ludicrous with the curiously poignant. Perhaps this is what appealed about it to Emerson, who also admired Wordsworth greatly and shared with him a sense that the deep-and-meaningful can all too easily slide into the laughable: 'Separate any part of Nature and attempt to look at it as a whole by itself, and the feeling of the ridiculous begins.'[30] The desire to be like Milton seems in this scene to be something both irresistible and silly – silly not least because it's derived from something as commonplace as the fact that they both owned watches, and sillier still since the watch in question was undoubtedly a Victorian forgery: it survives in the British Museum, the name *Ioanni Miltoni* inscribed upon it certainly a later addition.[31] And yet there is something compelling to me about this phoney object, fixing and orientating Milton in his time, Wordsworth in his, us still in ours as we read Emerson's account of it and imagine ourselves holding, and posing awkwardly with, this watch, which belongs to each of these distinct historical moments and yet ties them together through the rhythms of memory, imagination, and time itself: *tick . . . tick . . . tick.*

2

17 October 1614: 'At a Solemn Music'

B ack to Bread Street: an evening in October 1614. The house
is largely unchanged from the morning, nearly six years ago,
when John Milton was born. We're once again in the same large
hall on the first floor of the building where the family's clock might
have been ticking, and let's say it's still there, hanging on the wall,
the chains and plummet weights dangling below it, pulling time
on its way. Now, however, its mechanical voice is obscured by the
bustle of noise in the panelled room. A square wooden table has
been dragged to the centre, and around it stand a group of men,
mostly bearded, leaning over the table to get a close look at the
object that sits at the centre of it: a book. They are looking down
at it and talking in low voices about how best to proceed. They
speak English but with a mixture of accents: some sound like
Londoners; others' strongly accented English bespeaks overseas
origins; one man's subtly altered vowels suggest English beginnings
that have been shaped and stretched by years spent abroad,
absorbing a new set of cadences. They are staring down at the book
and discussing what best to do with it, how to approach it. The
volume is quite large, around thirteen inches high and nine inches
wide, and it's obviously a luxury item: bound in white vellum, it's
stamped with a gold coat of arms showing lions and a harp, and
beautifully printed, with the names of many of the gathered men
curled into an elaborately decorated circle on the title page.[1] This
book doesn't belong to these men, but they're trying it out, making
sure everything is as it should be before it's sent to its illustrious
dedicatee: Charles, Prince of Wales.

The volume contains not just words but a series of parallel lines dotted with notes: a set of musical scores, squeezed on to each page. And it's not a book that's designed to be read in just one direction, proceeding from left to right across each line and down each page in turn, but a 'part-book', designed to be viewed from four directions at once, so that each singer and player can see what he or she has to do. Nor is it a book to be read in solitude, but one to be gathered around, and for a very practical purpose.

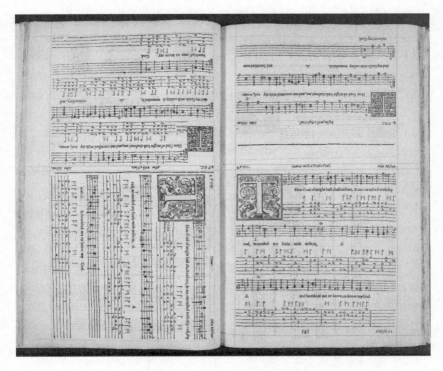

FIGURE 4: The opening of John Milton senior's
'Thou God of Might' as it appears in William Leighton's
Teares or Lamentacions of a Sorrowfull Soule.

The men finish their murmurings to one another. Some of them begin to tune instruments that they have brought with them: a wooden flute; a set of three long-necked stringed instruments, one with a body shaped like a teardrop, another with wavy contours that make its silhouette look rather like a cloud. Two men, one of whom walks with a self-assurance that suggests he is the owner of the house, move briskly to the other side of the room, passing the row of chairs lining one wall on which a number of women and children sit. The pair approach a piece of expensive-looking furniture that wasn't there in 1608 – a large cupboard fronted with double doors, which swing open to reveal a set of six compartments lined with green baize, in each of which sits a polished stringed instrument.[2] They are all roughly the same shape but sit in three pairs of ascending size; they look rather like modern violins, violas, and cellos, but with thicker necks and straighter top edges. Their owner reaches in and passes one of the middle-sized pair and its bow to his companion, who carries it back to the table and rejoins the company. He takes one of the largest instruments for himself and turns back towards his friends, then pauses, and, on second thoughts, grasps its twin and passes it on his way back to the table to a small boy of nearly six, his eldest son, who sits at the side of the room, watching keenly. The child can barely hold it, but he has to get used to its heft at some point. Coming back to the book atop the table, the man glances at his companions who surround it, mouths and instruments at the ready. It's an occasion for mixed feelings. This is a celebration of sorts – they've worked hard on this book, each of them contributing numerous pieces to its pages. For many of them, although they've long copied one another's works by hand, or paid a scribe to do so, and passed the music among themselves, this is a first chance to see their tunes and combinations in print, available to anyone willing to pay a bookseller. The man who brought them together and persuaded them all to do so, however, is conspicuous by his absence. William Leighton is languishing in prison because of unpaid debts and a decade spent backing the wrong political causes. Leighton hopes this volume of heartstring-tugging laments, many of them self-penned and dedicated to the fourteen-year-old prince, will cause an upturn in his fortunes. The men all look to the house's owner, who glances around at them and briefly at the small boy holding the large viol at the back of the room, before beating time on the edge of the wooden table as the set of instruments and voices burst into a glorious sound that fills the room and makes its panelled walls vibrate: *'Thou God of might hast chastened me, and me corrected with thy rod.'*

◆

The facts behind this scene are fairly basic. Milton's father and namesake was a talented and well-known amateur musician. Milton was born into a house full of music, and absorbed at least a fair degree of his father's passion and talent. John Milton senior, John Aubrey observes, 'was an ingeniose man, delighted in Musique, composed many songs'; Milton's nephew John Phillips (so many Johns to keep track of) likewise referred to the older Milton's 'addiction to music'.[3] Milton himself, Aubrey continues, 'had a delicate tuneable Voice and had good skill: his father instructed him: he had an Organ in his howse: he played on it most.' The love of music that his father helped foster is everywhere evident across Milton's writings. One of his early poems, 'At a Solemn Music', is a bit like 'On Time' in that it crystallises and brings into focus a subject that fascinated him at every turn. 'Blest pair of sirens,' it begins, 'pledges of heaven's joy, / Sphere-borne harmonious sisters, Voice, and Verse.'[4] In this poem music is both a heavenly fact, 'sung before the sapphire-coloured throne' of the Almighty, and an earthly one, and by its end the two worlds blur: Milton imagines God welcoming humankind into his 'celestial consort', and the word is carefully chosen. A consort was the standard term for a mixed group of musicians of the very sort that had gathered regularly on Bread Street.[5] In this poem, imagining a heavenly harmony, he not only looked ahead into a sublimely tuneful afterlife but back to the medley of sounds that had filled his childhood home.

This is certainly one way of making Milton's childhood meaningful, of drawing a line between it and his eventual works, but I've come to feel that it's not enough. Music is an obvious place to begin disentangling Milton's knot of rhythms, for these were the literal rhythms that would intermittently have filled his childhood home, but I realised that I knew little of the kind of music his father wrote and played, or of the worlds of which it formed a part. I propose to approach these worlds, however, by an unlikely route. In 2019 two things happened in my life, close together in time, that bore an awkward relation to one another. First I decided, for a variety of reasons, to start taking piano lessons. I'd been slightly, but not especially, musical as a child, having played the recorder well enough to grace a primary school assembly or two, and spent a few of my teenage years playing the tuba in a youth orchestra, a fact I now find strangely embarrassing to mention. I'd forgotten the bulk of those modest skills, however, including most of my ability to read music. I had long harboured a desire to take up the piano, and now that my children were approaching the age when they could learn I decided that it would feel less like pushy middle-class parenting if it were something that we did together. Unfortunately, a few weeks after I began learning, I managed while playing football with my daughter to kick the little finger of my own right hand and break it quite badly, a turn of events almost as embarrassing as my years of tuba playing. It's ached dully ever since – it's aching slightly as I type these words – even though the bone has healed. I've continued to play the piano, but my injury has added an unexpected element to the experience, since in order to learn I have to stretch and spread my right hand beyond a point of comfort much more frequently than other activities demand. Learning falteringly to produce new melodies and rhythms has become routinely inter-twined, for me, with low-level twinges of discomfort and pain.

I'd been thinking about learning the piano as a new skill, a chance to make new and hopefully pleasant sounds, but not as something that I was doing *to* my body rather than just with it. Charles Rosen, the writer and pianist, has written brilliantly about the ways in which learning to play the piano is a training of the body as well as the mind, but a training that can never fully be finished or complete because each composer makes a distinct set of physical demands on performers, forcing them to adapt their bodily habits in unpredictable ways each time they play. Ravel's music reflects the fact that he sat very low before the piano, and is very different from the higher stance taken by Liszt, whose 'style of octaves demands a play of the back and shoulder muscles more difficult to manage from a low position'.[6] Pianists' education is a training of the body, but it can't be too rigid since these habits need to change according to the physical demands of each new composer, of each new piece.

If trying (or rather struggling, sometimes painfully) to play music has led me to think differently about it, it's particularly made me wonder about the extent to which we routinely experience it through our bodies; and it's this question, informed both by my reading and by my painful piano playing, through which I want to approach the musical rhythms amidst which Milton grew up. The idea of music affecting us physically is a slightly odd one in that, if asked, we'd probably be able to conjure up a number of moments in our lives in which music seemed to inhabit our bodies, and yet there are also many contexts in which it would seem gauche or weird to display this fact (on the bus, at the opera). Even though in certain times and places it's acceptable, even expected, that we dance or respond physically to music, these have come to seem like the exception rather than the norm. But I'm tempted to see these extreme forms of bodily response as intensifications of some-thing that's subliminally or potentially present in every experience of music.

This latent but deep connection between music and the body was known and understood in a different way during the time in which Milton grew up, but for both our age and his the contexts in which music and the body come into closest contact are often medical ones – where the body is damaged or disordered. Remarkable effects have been described by physicians treating patients with dementia or aphasia, who often respond strikingly to music, suddenly regaining forms of speech and movement of which they are otherwise incapable for as long as the music plays. Likewise premature babies, unable yet to confer any order on their welter of experiences, can be markedly calmed by musical sounds. Some studies have suggested, however, that it is not the *melody* of the music, the part we typically think of ourselves as remembering, that triggers these responses, but its *rhythm*: that it might be the region of the brain specific to the perception of rhythm that needs to be stimulated for experience to resume or begin, to be given a shape.[7]

I lack the expertise to evaluate these accounts, but they interest me because they hint at the deep underpinnings of certain basic facts that we rarely pause to ponder: that not just musical experiences but a whole array of rhythmic experiences are deeply woven into our sense of ourselves, the memories that make us who we are. This is a set of processes that relies upon, and seems to exist at the very cusp between, our minds and our bodies. As Raymond Williams puts it, 'rhythm is a way of transmitting a description of experience, in such a way that the experience is re-created in the person receiving it, not merely as an "abstraction" or an "emotion" but as a physical effect on the organism – on the blood, on the breathing, on the physical patterns of the brain.'[8] If this physical, rhythmic response is something that we often suppress or strive to ignore nowadays, it was known in a different way in Milton's lifetime, and much earlier. It was taken for granted by ancient Greek writers and their Renaissance followers that music could have powerful bodily effects that could be harmful or salutary. Most people (including the young Milton) accepted Pythagoras's distinction between a cosmic music, the music of the universe or of the heavenly spheres, which was inaudible to mere mortal ears, and a lowly, degraded, human form of music, the mere twanging and warbling of songsters and minstrels, which appealed only to the body, and degraded it. They also envisaged a third kind of music which might mediate between these extremes, bringing soul and body into harmony with one another and thereby with the heavens. This was described by one of its best-known proponents, the Florentine Marsilio Ficino, as a '*gravis musica*' or 'solemn music', the very phrase Milton might have been translating in the title of his later poem.[9] What's notable is that most accounts of this solemn music placed a particular emphasis on its rhythms, its workings in and with the body as it existed in and through time. Plato insisted that musical harmony was akin to the revolutions of the soul, and that 'Rhythm was bestowed on us to be our helper' in restoring this ideal harmony.

St Augustine wrote an extensive treatise which, though titled *De Musica* or *On Music*, is as much about the rhythms of language and bodily movement that unfurl through time without our noticing, as it is about music itself: 'for the most part . . . we meanwhile effect temporal numbers in some bodily movement, easy and useful, by walking or singing, then they pass straight through us unnoticed.'[10] The doctor and polymath Thomas Browne, Milton's contemporary, wrote: 'I will not say with *Plato*, the Soule is an Harmony, but harmonicall, and hath its nearest sympathy unto musicke: thus some, whose temper of body agrees, and humours the constitution of their soules, are borne Poets, though indeed all are naturally inclined unto Rhythme.'[11] The poet simply tunes to a higher pitch the natural inclination to rhythm that all people share in their very souls. Through music we can sometimes become fully and intensely attuned to time itself as it passes in and through our bodies, in and through our lives.

Clocks of the sort on which Milton wrote were still rare, and they measured the hours with only wavering accuracy, providing little purchase on the smaller units of minutes and seconds into which they were divided. For this reason rhythms, both of music and of the human body, often had a very practical role in measuring time. Recipe books, if they needed to tell their readers how long to undertake a given action, would often say things like: 'Let it remain boiling, while your pulse beateth two hundred strokes' or 'The water is to remain upon it, no longer than whiles you can say the *Miserere* psalm very leisurely.'[12] Time here is not seen as it passes: its beats are felt or spoken or sung. When Galileo Galilei became intrigued by the rhythmic swing of a pendulum but had no precise way of timing its back and forth, he turned first to his own body, trying to gauge speed by the beatings of his pulse; next he sought to measure acceleration due to gravity by singing a loud and strongly rhythmic folk song as he rolled a ball down a wooden slope.[13] Musicians like the men who gathered on Bread Street were trained to think of the beats and rhythms that they produced as a form of *tempo sonoro* or 'sounding time', the sound of time itself as it passes; their music was a way of counting, and inhabiting, continuous time.[14] These kinds of rhythms, existing at once in time and in the body, were those that permeated Milton's childhood.

My first instinct in trying to make sense of Milton's early musical experiences was to read as much as I could about his father's milieu, and to listen to modern recordings of his music. These were valuable and enjoyable pursuits, but I felt I was circling around the most basic fact of the rhythms that I was trying to understand: that they take place in part in or through the body.[15] I therefore decided, before trying to understand John Milton senior's music, to attempt in a small and imperfect way to dwell within it. This is not at all the same as reconstructing it, or capturing its true essence, which would be a delusory goal, but more like an experiment to see if my experience of this music might be changed by trying to inhabit it from within, by playing some of it myself.

What became most vividly clear to me was that this music is full of voices. I don't just mean human voices, but the voices of the instruments to which I alluded above, and that made up the standard mixed consort: lute, bandora, bass viol, cittern, treble viol, flute. On the modern recordings to which I'd listened – which didn't use these instruments – the sound formed a beautifully rich texture that my untrained ear struggled to unpick. Yet playing and listening along to parts of it brought home the deftness with which these voices slipped in and out of one another, sometimes flowing together, at others standing at odds or seeming to force one another out of the music. In the piece 'O Woe Is Me for Thee', for example, whose text is adapted from David's lament over Jonathan in the Old Testament, the biblical king's single voice is split between the singers, who at times complement one another, at others drop out and enter as if picking up one another's burdens: at one point the bass singer drops out for as many as twelve bars of music, and re-enters just as the cantus, or lead voice, falls silent for eight bars, before they are finally reunited for the finale of the piece.[16] There's a sense here of restraint, of resources being used deftly and sparingly, that passed me by on first listening to this piece. Moving more slowly through it also allowed me to appreciate the ways in which the name 'Jonathan' itself is placed under pressure throughout by the manner of singing: at times the multiple voices can do things with the name that the voice of David alone could not do, often crunching into dissonance at the moment when 'Jonathan' is uttered, at one point exploiting the harsh overlap of G and G$^\sharp$ as if in a moment of choked and despairing grief.

These features gradually became clear to me in the course of my own slow and faltering encounter with these musical works. This was also an experience that had its own distinctive rhythm, one that was entirely new to me: the chance to stop and start, to ask questions and ponder possibilities that was very different from the surrender to music as it flows past to which I, like most people who have grown up with recorded music as a basic fact of life, am much more accustomed. At times, as I tried out short sections from this music on the piano and struggled to make my fingers form the unfamiliar chords of John Milton senior's 'If That a Sinner Sighs', gathering the work of three voices into my right hand and two into my left, my little finger would throb with a complaint that the shape into which I was contorting it wasn't natural; but this felt like a useful if uncomfortable reminder of the very literal way in which my body was becoming imbricated with the music's rhythms. 'It is easy', writes Richard Rastall, who has prepared the scores of Milton senior's works for modern choirs and music groups, 'to miss the flexible rhythms of this music: modern singers are encouraged to emulate their seventeenth-century counterparts and work from the texts outwards, reading the texts carefully and noting the verbal rhythms before singing the musical setting . . . This will allow the subtleties of cross-rhythms characteristic of that style to come through in the music.'[17] If Rastall's helpful account captures the slippery but central import-ance of rhythm to the music amidst which Milton grew up, it also brings home the extent to which the elements that Milton identi-fied in 'At a Solemnn Music', that 'Blest pair of sirens . . . Voice, and Verse', exist in a potentially tense relationship, one that would interest Milton in his later writings: should the rhythms of language dictate, or succumb to, those of song?

I've wanted, in approaching Milton's formative years, to start with rhythms rather than facts: to try, in a necessarily and usefully imperfect fashion, to inhabit some of the rhythms that surrounded Milton in his youth before trying to understand or account for them. Now is the time to return to some of the facts and see how these rhythms help them appear differently. By the time Milton was born, his father was part of a sophisticated circle of musicians who were based in the area around St Paul's Cathedral. It's possible, though not certain, that Milton senior's musical interests dated back to his own childhood: he was born in Stanton St John, a village just outside Oxford, and Aubrey claims that he 'was brought up at the University of Oxon: [Oxford] and Christ Church', where he may have been a chorister. Milton's grandfather, Richard, was a recusant Roman Catholic, who was excommunicated and convicted for his illegal beliefs in the decades before the poet's birth. Aubrey adds that 'his grandfather disinherited [John Milton senior] because he kept not to the Catholique religion' after 'he found a Bible in English in his chamber'.[18] Whether or not these stories are strictly true, they suggest that the younger John Milton grew up with a sense of his family having been split by their religious beliefs. The Reformation – the prolonged and ragged bundle of steps through which the Church of England had separated itself from the Roman Catholic Church – was not at all abstract or distant, but lay behind the very personal dispute that had propelled his father towards his London life. As the English Church changed, the status and worth of music was one of the many issues that was intensively debated within it. Some insisted that music could rouse the mind to pious thoughts and be a spur to holiness, others insisted that it was distracting at best and idolatrous at worst, clogging the mind with sensory pleasure. This nervousness or uncertainty about the value of music can be glimpsed at the start of Elizabeth I's reign, when the official injunctions grudgingly permitted, in addition to the normal liturgy, the use of 'modest and distinct song, so used in all parts of the common prayers in the Church'. It was made very clear, however, that this music was not *necessary* for the worship to take place or for the prayers to have their effect:

> the same may be as plainly understanded, as if it were read without singing, and yet nevertheless, for the comforting of such that delight in music, it may be permitted that . . . there may be sung a hymn, or suchlike song to the praise of almighty God, in the best sort of melody and music that may be conveniently devised, having respect that the sentence of the hymn may be understood and perceived.[19]

Music was permissible but only if it were understood as an ornament that some appreciated and others did not, but in no way should it eclipse the language of the hymns, or be understood to improve them. It belonged in that category of indifferent actions and beliefs to which Protestant theologians increasingly turned to create a buffer zone between warring parties and world views. It's possible as we read the words of this injunction to feel their formulator tying himself up in knots, striving to hold at bay a dangerous set of possibilities and yet awkwardly solder together conflicting ways of understanding not just religion but the place of the human body, its senses and its pleasures, within it. This was a conflict that would explode later in Milton's life in a different form in the English Civil Wars.

Matters changed somewhat with the death of Elizabeth I and the ascent to the throne of her successor, James I, five years before Milton's birth in 1603. James was strongly Calvinist in his theological beliefs, which would seem likely to align him with the austere sort of English Protestant who was deeply suspicious of music and its pleasures. In the event, however, he proved keen to incorporate a relatively broad range of religious, political, and artistic viewpoints within his court and the circles around it, and then to exercise and consolidate his power by acting as the balancer or mediator between these countervailing forces. This was also how he approached England's place in the wider world: he wasted no time in ending the long and expensive war that Elizabeth had waged with Spain, and sought alliances with European powers on every side of the confessional divides that split the Continent, presenting himself publicly as a new Solomon, the great biblical peacemaker. This also meant trying more aggressively to emulate the splendour and sophistication of the European courts with whom diplomatic relations became increasingly crucial, and there was a pronounced growth of interest among English aristocrats in forms of musical, artistic, and literary innovation, influenced by European taste, that would have seemed deeply dubious a generation before. The king's elder son Henry, Prince of Wales, who was the focus for all those who envisaged a renewed Protestant amalgam of piety, military might, and cultured eloquence, was a noteworthy patron of the arts until his sudden and shocking death in 1612, aged only eighteen, and several laments composed by John Milton senior and his friends mourned the prince's untimely demise. Henry's younger brother Charles, though he lacked his elder brother's charisma, had even more refined and Continental artistic leanings: hence the dedication of William Leighton's *Teares or Lamentacions* to him, two years after he had succeeded his late brother as Prince of Wales. In this milieu, the creation of artful music offered one potential route to favour and respectability.[20]

The musical gatherings in the house on Bread Street that helped form the young Milton's early rhythms were therefore, on one level, strikingly and distinctively *English* gatherings, which took their bearings from these broader developments in English society. While John Milton senior was rumoured to have created musical pieces for much larger groups of voices – 'he Composed an *In Nomine* of Forty Parts', according to Edward Phillips – none of this music has survived if indeed it ever existed, and all of what we have was written to be performed in domestic spaces; its rhythms designed to interlock with those of the home.[21] It was only in England that domestic musical performances of this sort and scale seem to have occurred with any frequency in the century during which Milton lived, since it was only in England that there had by this point emerged a sufficiently large and affluent class of people whose wealth came from commerce rather than inheritance, and who occasionally made music as a leisure activity.[22] It's not just that Milton's father happened to make music in his home: the fact that its chambers sometimes reverberated with music helped to prove it was a new *kind* of home. This was the period during which the forms of life emerged that would later produce the mixture of jingoism and chauvinism we encounter in the proverb 'an Englishman's home is his castle': a sense of the household as an ordered unit whose organisation both echoed and underpinned that of society at large. This was a patriarchal society in a very literal sense: the father was to the household as the bishop was to the church and as the king was to the state; each form of power resembled and fed off the others. The period of Milton's childhood saw an explosion of books on proper household management that made this ideal clear. One, published when he was four, pronounced:

The dutie of the Husband is to get goods: and of the wife to gather them together, and save them. The dutie of the Husband is to travell abroad, to seeke living: and the Wives dutie is to keepe the house . . . The dutie of the Husband is to deale with many men: and of the Wives to talk with few. The dutie of the Husband is, to be entermedling: and of the wife, to be solitary and withdrawne. The dutie of the man is, to be skilfull in talk: and of the wife, to boast in silence.[23]

It's certainly possible, and accurate, to see Milton's domestic rhythms as one of the ways in which these divisions were ordered and reinforced: the group of male musicians enters the household to beautify it, to confer form and order upon it. I am painfully aware that Sara Milton, the poet's mother, remains silent in my scenario, shunted to the side of the room, 'solitary and withdrawne' in just this way. While there were many incidental opportunities for women to learn and make music, this was generally a private affair, undertaken separately, and instrumental music was generally not considered an appropriate pastime for a woman.[24] In this same period, by contrast, when Henry Peacham advocated the learning of the viol in just the manner that the young Milton learned – 'I desire no more in you then to sing your part sure, and at the first sight, withall, to play the same upon your Violl . . . privately to your selfe' – he did so in a book tellingly titled *The Compleat Gentleman*.[25] This is what the mastery of music's rhythms could help an aspirational young Englishman become.

But there's another side to this story, which doesn't change or minimise this account of national and male stridency but demands to sit alongside it – precisely because the two sides would eventually collide in Milton's mind and style, and form his rhythms. If the household on Bread Street was on one level a self-consciously and respectably English one, it was also one in which the relationship between languages and nations was far from stable, the divisions between them far from clear. Likewise, the confidence of the male musical world was less total than might appear. The London of Milton's childhood was not only expanding at a rate that astounded and sometimes horrified his contemporaries, but was growing increasingly international in a number of ways. People and a wide array of commercial goods – glassware and ornaments from Venice, spices and exotic foodstuffs from North Africa and the Levant, and also slaves, people who *were* commercial goods – flowed into and out of England at a massively greater speed and volume than a century before. Bread Street lay a short distance from several locations where this confluence of peoples, languages, and commodities came together in particularly conspicuous, and indeed cacophonous, forms. Foremost among these was the Royal Exchange, the huge new commercial centre opened in the sixteenth century, which lay only five minutes' walk to the east, and where one satirist of the time proclaimed that the vendors and shoppers spoke 'in severall Languages, And (like the murmuring fall of Waters) in the Hum of severall businesses: insomuch that the place seemes Babell, (a Confusion of Tongues)'.[26]

If this was a city in which English existed only as part of a buzz of many languages, a situation that some celebrated and others feared, then this was emphatically the case with the circle of musicians of which John Milton senior was a part. Loosely clustered in the streets around St Paul's Cathedral, many of its members had either come to London from abroad in search of patronage and advancement, or were English in origin but had travelled extensively in other lands.[27] Milton senior's music often appeared, in both printed and handwritten form, alongside music by Giovanni Coprario, who later became Prince Charles's personal viol instructor.[28] Coprario, born in England as 'John Cooper', had travelled to Italy and as far as Ragusa (now Dubrovnik in Croatia) in his earlier years, and had assumed the Italian version of his name upon his return. This musical group also included Anglicised Italians who had been transformed in the opposite direction, notably Alfonso Ferrabosco the younger, one of a well-known family of Italian musicians who had been based in England since the days of Queen Elizabeth. He taught music to Prince Henry until the latter's untimely death, eventually replacing Coprario as chief court composer, and came to particular prominence writing the music for many of the court masques written by Ben Jonson, the spectacular and lavish performances in which James and his court performed and reaffirmed their centrality to the nation.[29] In addition to these very public spectacles, Ferrabosco also wrote music for Jonson's poem 'The Houre-glasse', in which the sand falling silently through this ancient form of clock – 'this small dust / here running in this glasse / by attomes moved' – becomes an emblem for the eventual fate of the human body, ashes to ashes, dust to dust: a poem that could have inspired Milton's later rumination on time's passing through a very different kind of timepiece.[30] Thanks in no small part to men from this kind of mixed background, the rhythms of Milton's youth would have been audible as a mixture of the native and foreign. This was music that owed a great deal to older English forms of secular song, but which infused it with – to borrow the title of one popular collection – *Musica transalpina*, music from across the Alps. These were Italian compositions by composers such as Luca Marenzio and, the most famous of all, Claudio Monteverdi, whose tunes and rhythms rubbed shoulders in onerously hand-copied manuscripts with those of Milton's father and his friends.[31]

This background illuminates one of the most remarkable features of Milton's early life: at some point as a young man, and before he ever set foot in the country, he learned Italian to a remarkably high degree of fluency. How he learned the language has always been something of a mystery. There were many ways that languages were learned in seventeenth-century London. Private tutors of all stripes plied their trade, and it's been pointed out that the house on Bread Street was also just around the corner from the church on Cheapside that was the centre of the exiled Italian Protestant community in London.[32] I'll have more to say about Milton's encounter with this language, and with languages in general, in the next chapter, but, if I had to hazard a guess, I'd suggest that his first and most formative encounter with the words and rhythms of Italy also came by way of his father's cosmopolitan musical friends.

It's easy, and tempting, to sentimentalise this group as a cheery example of languages and identities mingling literally in harmony with one another, but Milton's childhood world was one characterised by a curious mixture of openness to these kinds of mixtures and meldings, and deep-set paranoia. A householder such as John Milton senior was supposed to embody an ideal of the prosperous Englishman. This ideal was, however, deeply fragile – it was no more straightforwardly clear at this moment in history exactly what it meant to be English, or to be a man, than it is in ours – and this meant that its boundaries were policed with all the more fearful vigilance. A figure like Giovanni Coprario/John Cooper might, in the context of an English aristocratic world increasingly seeking to emulate Continental fashions, seem like the pinnacle of sophistication: but he was also the embodiment of a commonplace fear throughout this period that travel abroad, especially to Italy, was a corrupting influence. That it would produce hybrid figures, Italianate Englishmen, and would teach them, as one satirist put it, 'the art of atheism, the art of epicurising, the art of whoring, the art of poisoning, the art of sodomitry'.[33] But if to be un-English in one's gait and style was to be both dissolute and unmanly, this was potentially true of the musical world in general. If musical accomplishment was increasingly seen as an important facet of the complete gentleman, one recurrent form of the wider anxiety about music was the specific fear that it was effeminising; that its enjoyment made men too like women, and might even, like travel to

Italy, teach 'the art of sodomitry'. One earlier writer, summing up this fear, thundered: 'If you would have your sonne softe, woman-nishe, uncleane, smothe mouthed . . . if you would have hym, as it were transmuted into a Woman, or worse, and inclined to all kinde of Whoredome and abhomination, set hym . . . to learne Musicke, and then you shall not faile your purpose.'[34] The risks to a boy of an excessively musical childhood were apparently real, and obvious. Another minor musical figure from John Milton senior's immediate circle embodied these same risks: Tobias Hume, a talented composer and viol player who might well have attended the Bread Street gatherings, had in his earlier life been a soldier of fortune in both the Swedish and Russian armies. He presented himself to the readers of his printed music, revealingly, as a soldier first and a musician second: 'I doe not studie Eloquence, or professe Musicke,' he wrote, 'although I doe love Sense, and affect Harmony: My Profession being, as my Education hath beene, Armes, the onely effeminate part of me, hath beene Musicke.'[35] It was necessary, amidst the throb of musical rhythms, to lodge this protest: I may have travelled into foreign countries, I may love to create new music with my mind and with my body, but I am still a soldier; still English; still a man.

While I don't think that my attempts to inhabit his father's musical world allow me anything like a reconstruction of Milton's child-hood, I do think that they allow us to access something of his formative rhythms. Returning now to his father's music, several of its general features have come to seem significant to me, because they resonate with my experience of the writings that Milton would produce in his early years. I don't mean to imply that Milton was necessarily *aware* of these features – more that these were some of the assumptions he would have absorbed on Bread Street along with the rhythms of his father's music. First, the splitting and coagulating of voice that I've just been describing – the questioning of what it means to have or claim an individual voice, or whether one's voice only makes sense with others'. Second, an emphasis on death and mourning that is striking even in an age of low life expectancies: 'O Woe Is Me for Thee', which I discussed earlier, is just one of a disproportionate number of his father's surviving works that respond to, and are prompted by, death. It seems quite normal in this musical world that an expression of loss is a frequent occasion or justification for creating something in public.[36] Third, a tendency to repeat. Many of the musical genres in which Milton's father wrote – madrigal, fantasia, and so on – were built around repetition to an obsessive degree: this is a kind of music that moves forward only by looking backward. 'Fair Orian, in the Morne', for example, whose anonymous lyrics Milton senior himself may have written, is a tissue of pastoral conventions, of shepherds and nymphs who seem to spin dizzyingly round in the extreme repetitiousness of the music, pushing the boundary (at least to modern ears) between reassuring pleasure and irritating sameness.[37] And fourth, and finally, the subject of 'O Woe Is Me for Thee', David's lamentation for his beloved friend Jonathan, is an example from scripture of an intense and passionate relationship between two men that Christians in and before Milton's time struggled to keep within the limits of what might be considered acceptable. When the English King Edward II's relationship with his favourite, Piers Gaveston, was remembered during the Middle Ages, his biographer wrote: 'I do not remember having heard that one man so loved another. Jonathan cherished David, Achilles loved Patroclus; but we do not read that they went beyond what was usual.'[38] The very need to insist on this point, however, suggests that Milton senior had chosen for his music a text that raised the thorny question of exactly what was 'usual' between male friends. This passion seemed all the harder to contain when expressed in a music that seemed designed to take over not just the ears but the bodies of those making and listening to it. Each of these features, each of the questions that they raise, will turn out to pulse and echo in different ways in the poems Milton went on to write.

Perhaps the best way to summarise what I take away from my experiments with his father's music, then, is that music's rhythms seem to exist, in the period during which Milton grew up, in a set of *in-betweens*, where I also feel I need to situate myself in order to understand him. The value for me of rhythm as a way of thinking about Milton's early years is that rhythm of any sort implies movement *between* two or more states – there is no rhythm without change, without difference. Musical rhythms existed in Milton's childhood between people – they were a sociable matter, a gathering of men as makers of music. They emerged between a set of voices, greater than the sum of their parts, alternating between harmonious concord and moments of deliberately crunching discord. They moved between the soul and the body, partaking of and affecting both, but identical with neither. They drifted between the sexes, often excluding women from their making even as it threatened to make the men who made them more like women. They fluctuated between music and the words that were set to it, words that they could amplify or threaten to drown out. They fluttered between languages and nations, especially those of England and Italy.

But in order properly to attend to these various in-between states, we also need to recognise that the musical rhythms I've been trying to access also exist in another middle ground between two states that would go on to fascinate Milton in his writings – cacophonous noise and pristine silence. I take my lead here from an intriguing sentence that has stuck in my mind ever since I read it in what is still the most enjoyable account of Milton's life, the crabby and guarded narrative given by Samuel Johnson. Describing a later period, after Milton returned from his travels to Europe and set himself up as a schoolmaster, Johnson writes that he 'took a house in Aldersgate-street . . . and chose his dwelling at the upper end of a passage, that he might avoid the noise of the street'.[39] This sounds like quite a practical choice, but it lodges in my mind another possibility, one which rings true when I read his poems: Milton seems extraordinarily sensitive to sound. In fact it's not quite true to say, as I did above, that Milton's writings reveal his love of music; perhaps it's better to say that they display his acute responsiveness to noise and sound in all their forms, and that gorgeous music is always caught up, for him, in the possibility that it might be drowned out by, or deteriorate into, cacophonous noise. Whereas Thomas

Browne, to whose paean to music I referred earlier, could extract a harmonious and heavenly music from even the din of a pub – 'even that vulgar and Taverne Musicke, which makes one man merry, another mad, strikes in mee a deepe fit of devotion, and a profound contemplation of the first Composer' – Milton seems to have been much more inclined to avoid or banish noise absolutely.[40] Milton's poem 'At a Solemn Music' describes the Fall of humankind, perhaps his foremost theological obsession, as the moment when 'disproportioned sin / Jarred against nature's chime, and with harsh din / Broke the fair music that all creatures made / To their great Lord'. The human world is not just full of wickedness; it is noisily out of tune. If the rhythms of Milton's childhood were in part musical, music, for him, was always bound up with noise, with the wider din and hubbub of life; music was the best part of this world of sound, but also struggled to escape from it. Music would have been prominent for Milton in his early years, but only as part of what Roland Barthes beautifully describes as 'the familiar, *recognized* noises whose ensemble forms a kind of household symphony: differentiated slamming of doors, raised voices, kitchen noises, gurgle of pipes, murmurs from outdoors'. Barthes invokes Kafka, who called his room his 'noise headquarters'.[41] Perhaps another way to say this is that music, along with these domestic and ambient sounds, must all have been woven early into Milton's rhythmic knot.

And the neighbourhood around Bread Street was notably noisy: recall the description of the languages spoken in the Royal Exchange, 'like the murmuring fall of Waters . . . insomuch that the place seemes Babell'. There was also the actual hum of waters, the sprawling flow of the Thames much closer to the top of Bread Street than its modern, straitened form, and the cries of those travelling and doing business along it. The sounds would shift throughout the day and across the seasons, the changing hours marked in a shifting pattern of ways by the ceaseless ringing of church bells that allowed people to orient themselves in time and space.[42] Several men from the musical circle of Milton's father were sufficiently fascinated by this welter of incidental noise that they experimented with ways of working it into their music: Martin

Peerson and Orlando Gibbons, whose music appeared cheek-by-jowl with John Milton senior's, wrote pieces that incorporated non-human noises like birdsong and street vendor's cries into their music, their songs including lyrics like 'Jug jug, tereu tereu' and 'Oysters, oysters, three pence a peck'.[43]

But there would have been a less pleasant aspect to the household symphony of Milton's childhood on Bread Street, a set of more discordant notes. For while Milton's father was respected as a musician, he was never more than a talented amateur. Although some of his friends scraped a living from their music, for John Milton senior it was a hobby, a breather from his busy and lucrative career as a scrivener. This job has no straightforward modern equivalent: it involved some scribal work, as its name suggests – the reliable copying of documents was crucial, especially in a time of low literacy – but also legal and notarial tasks such as the drawing up of contracts. Above all, however, the elder John Milton was a moneylender, loaning out funds and charging interest, often via a complicated web of intermediaries and surrogates. His eldest son and namesake was inducted into his business dealings from a young age: the rhythms of household music beat alongside the rhythms of money going in and coming out; the sound of song alternated with the sound of desperate borrowers, pleading to have their debts forgiven.

We shouldn't forget in the following chapters that various aspects of Milton's life were made possible by his father's affluence, and by his own adult activities as a property owner and moneylender.[44] They allowed him to spend years vacillating over his chosen vocation, travelling to Europe, and experimenting with poetry. And his first marriage, as we'll see, was directly bound up with his status as a creditor. But his father's moneylending activities are also important because they introduced complicated, unstable currents into the seemingly respectable household on Bread Street. Whether or not usury was acceptable had been a fiercely debated question in the century before Milton's birth. On the one hand it was violently denounced as ungodly, unnatural, cruel: making money illicitly breed money, seeking to create new wealth where only God could create from nothing, making gold into an idol, alchemically transforming time itself into money. One memo-randum even denounced 'the odious name of buying and selling money for time, otherwise called usury'.[45] But, on the other hand, the increasing number and complexity of the relationships which social life in London made necessary – as the city and its popula-tion grew, consumption expanded, but cash remained relatively scarce – made complex relations based upon credit ever more required, and debt an increasingly common part of everyday life.[46] Milton grew up in a time of economic as well as cultural trans-formation, during the exact period when the very idea of a commercial *system* – of an interconnected network of trade and commerce – was first being developed and debated. Yet the economy of his youth was still notably mixed: it was not uncommon to purchase expensive items, such as jewels, using a mixture of cash, wheat, and credit.[47]

Much time and effort was put into distinguishing the appropriate extension of credit to one's fellow citizens – that which was neigh-bourly, charitable, and godly – from the heinous sin of usury, which was often aligned with sodomy as a corruption of the desire to reproduce that flew in the face of God.[48] But in practice the charging of interest was ubiquitous during Milton's early years, and his father was constantly embroiled in legal disputes with his debtors. The kind of cognitive dissonance that made this situation possible was summed up when one of the parliaments convened during Milton's youth agreed to limit the interest that could be charged specifically by scriveners to five per cent; the House of Lords approved the proposal, with the proviso that it not 'be construed or expounded to allow the practice of usury in point of religion or conscience'.[49] Usury was to be permitted so long as no one had the temerity to suggest it was being permitted.

In much the same way, life on Bread Street probably proceeded according to the collective, silent insistence that all of John Milton senior's dealings were entirely valid, and that he was a respectable and upright citizen, a pillar of the community. But Milton would have known all too well that his father's profession laid him open to hatred and derision. One writer described a scrivener as

a Christian cannibal that devours men alive. He sits behind a
desk like a spider in a cobweb to watch what flies will fall into
his net . . . his life is so black that no ink can paint it forth, he
is one of the Devil's engines to ruin others, he is a paper-worm,
or a rack for honest men.[50]

Businessmen like Milton's father strove to dispel such perceptions,
and to present themselves in the most respectable light. Double-
entry bookkeeping, which emerged in this period, was designed to
make the workings of money seemingly transparent and innate, as
if the numbers did their own modest work, creating only enough
profit to offset the lender's risk, and producing an orderliness and
simplicity sanctioned by God.[51]

In the face of these wildly opposed versions of what it meant to
be a professional moneylender, Milton's own feelings seem to have
been understandably mixed. Later, when he filled the page headed
'On Usury' in his commonplace book, he noted Dante's opinion
'that usury sins against both nature and art: against nature because
it makes coin breed coin, which is an unnatural birth, and against
art because it does not labour itself'; but he also recorded Andreas
Rivetus's approval of usury in his commentary on the Ten
Commandments.[52] This ambivalence towards his father's principal
trade is worth bearing in mind when we later encounter Milton's
mixed feelings towards a whole range of questions: the vocation
that he should follow, what it means to create and to reproduce,
whether value and worth reside in the objects that make up the
world or are created by people through their actions.[53]

But I want to end this chapter by taking seriously the possibility
that music and moneylending, Milton's father's main pastimes, were
connected, and ask whether this too might point us usefully towards
Milton's own later preoccupations. It can seem slightly vulgar,
embarrassing, to dwell on a poet's financial affairs: we want our
geniuses to be above such grubby, worldly concerns. A surprising
number of poets, however, have spent their working lives amidst
the grim minutiae of finance, manipulating money at work and

words in their spare time, including two great and ambivalent readers of Milton: T. S. Eliot, inspired by his work at Lloyd's to study 'the science of money' and 'the theory of banking' and rising to become head of the bank's Intelligence Department, and Wallace Stevens, somehow writing his radiant lines of verse in Connecticut in the gaps afforded by a lucrative job selling insurance (specialising in surety bonds), able still to generate 'The luminous melody of proper sound'.[54] 'On a good day,' writes James Longenbach, thinking of Stevens, 'money may be a kind of poetry, but poetry is not a kind of money.'[55] Maybe so, but the rhythms of the one might infiltrate, and help us understand, the other.

The philosopher Jacques Attali writes of the time in which Milton lived: 'Beginning in the seventeenth century, economic mechanisms break their silence and stop letting men speak. Production becomes noisy; the world of exchange monopolizes noise and the musician is inscribed in the world of money.'[56] For Attali, the history of music is a struggle between the organising and disorganising potentials of noise; as music becomes more and more a commodity, as composers and performers are paid for their talents, the unpredictable rhythms of sound as humans make and shape it come to be increasingly tamed and regularised. Although 'time traverses music and music gives meaning to time', once music becomes an object to be exchanged, bought and sold like any other, 'it makes the stockpiling of time possible'.[57]

For Attali, music is always prone to be regularised, packaged, bought and sold in this way, and he calls for a renewed emphasis on it as something in whose creation we can all be involved, and involved with our whole bodies, regardless of our level of talent: 'To improvise, to compose, is thus related to the idea of . . . the rediscovery and blossoming of the body. "Something that lets me find my own rhythm between the measures" (Stockhausen).'[58] That's what I've sought to do, in my own limited and painful way, when inhabiting John Milton senior's music. But I'm also reminded here that one of the standard terms in Milton's lifetime for both a set of poetic lines and a group of musical melodies was *numbers*: anything with a beat, with a rhythm, is something that we can count, and Milton himself would refer to the portions of *Paradise Lost* that came to him each night as 'harmonious numbers'.[59] Earlier, George Puttenham had defined 'accountable number' as that 'which we call arithmetical (*arithmos*), as one, two, three'. This is counting as *accounting*, the kind of measuring native to money – the determining of value, the balancing of credit and debt, that John Milton senior routinely undertook in his scrivener's shop on Bread Street. But Puttenham distinguished this arithmetical number from another kind:

> a musical or audible number, fashioned by stirring of tunes and their sundry times in the utterance of our words, as when the voice goeth high or low, or sharp or flat, or swift or slow, and this is called *rhythmos* or numerosity, that is to say, a certain flowing utterance by slipper [slippery, smooth] words and syllables, such as the tongue easily utters and the ear with pleasure receiveth, and which flowing of words with much volubility smoothly proceeding from the mouth is in some sort harmonical, and breedeth to the ear a great compassion.[60]

The number of arithmetical accounting and the number of music or poetry are both distinguished and aligned here; these arts are always entangled, in our world, with the calculations and measurements of money, but also offer the possibility of experiences – stirring, flowing, smoothly proceeding pleasure – that exceed any attempt to determine their value precisely. Rhythm, for Puttenham, is full of *numerosity* but never reducible to number; its details are countable, its effects incalculable. The rhythms of art and accounting meet, as they did in Milton's childhood, but flow off in opposite directions.

3

8 April 1624: 'The Almighty's Hand'

It's a quarter-hour after eleven on a Thursday morning. John Milton, aged fifteen, is preparing to leave his schoolhouse near the north-east corner of the churchyard of St Paul's Cathedral, for the start of the two-hour interlude that divides the long school day in half. The rules of the school specify that the boys who study there can 'bring no meat nor drink nor bottles nor use in the school no breakfasts nor drinkings in the time of learning', and so they have to come with full stomachs for a seven o'clock start, and return to their homes for lunch.[1] Now that Milton has reached the final year of his schooling, he is taught by the headmaster himself, Alexander Gil, fearsome and kindly by turns, his lessons prone to spiral off from the details of dead languages into diatribes and digressions on his various personal obsessions. These include the healing benefits of drinkable gold, the foul heresies of Turks and Jews, and especially the frustrating inconsistencies of the English language itself, for the speaking of which the boys are punished if they are heard lapsing from Latin within the school walls. Over the large chair in which Gil sits as he lectures the boys is a bust of the school's modern founder, the learned John Colet, who, they are frequently reminded, established it on the most unimpeachably modern principles: reverence for the ancients, carefully studied, as guides to fine writing and fine living. Inscribed on the walls and windows are Colet's Latin phrases, looming over them, year after year: *Doce, disce, aut discede*; teach, learn, or be gone.[2]

Gil has spent the morning working with the boys on their Hebrew, a smattering of which they're expected to acquire before they leave the school, and with the help of a grammar book they've been stumbling through Psalm 114, which describes the exodus of the Israelites from Egypt. The headmaster has been pausing to hammer home the importance of particular words: the Egyptians, he explains, are not just oppressors to the Hebrews but *lo'ez*, a people who lack language, who utter strange and meaningless grunts and hoots; barbarians.[3] When he returns after lunch they will sink into the more familiar cadences of Homer's Greek.[4]

The schoolhouse is one large open space that is divided in half by a curtain, and as Milton leaves he passes into the area in which he spent his earlier years, and where boys ranging from seven years old to their early teens are packing away their belongings. The youngest boys are finishing their Latin grammar drills with the headmaster's son, also named Alexander, who has been friendly to Milton, recognising his way with languages and occasionally slipping him copies of his cruelly witty Latin poems. This morning, however, he is all malice and no friendliness; as Milton passes on the way out of the building, Gil is looming over a small boy who is still seated on his bench at the side of the room, barred from leaving until he answers the final question correctly, gripping his Latin grammar in white-knuckled terror as tears stream down his cheeks and onto the pages of the book. '*N—n—noctem vigilas?*' the boy stammers, and as Milton exits the school building he hears the crack of the younger Gil's rod on the wooden bench, an inch from the boy's upper thigh, as the master screams into the child's face '*Ablativus temporis!*' One more mistake and the switch will meet the boy's soft flesh, not the wood; it's an everyday scene, and Milton doesn't pause to ponder it.[5]

The walk home is brief and familiar. Milton skirts the corner of the large and ramshackle cathedral, keeping his distance from the public toilet close to its north-east corner, and glancing up at its weathered sides and battered spire. The area whirrs with its characteristic sound, a 'humming or buzze, mixt of walking, tongues and feet . . . a still roare or loud whisper', occasionally broken by a voice crying '*Quid novi?*' – 'What's the news?'[6] The churchyard is dominated by the stalls of booksellers and printers who cluster there in increasing numbers, churning out volumes of their own and hawking stacks of them shipped from the great book fairs at Frankfurt and Lyon. The recent gossip suggests the threat of war with Spain will draw the royal purse strings ever tighter and leave the cathedral in its tumbledown state.

As he walks towards the arched gate that leads out of the corner of the churchyard, Milton runs into his friend Richard Pory. The two of them have grown closer in the past year, and have begun to discuss plans beyond school, perhaps even moving on together to university. Emerging from the arch, the pair part ways opposite the church of St Michael-le-Querne, dwarfed by the nearby cathedral. Pory skirts the church on its west side and heads north across Bladder Street and up St Martin's while Milton proceeds east along Cheapside, the busiest shopping street in London. At the end of the church he sees a small crowd of people holding pots and pewter jugs, crowding around the entrance to a building with a crenellated top: the local water source, known as the 'pissing conduit'. In the last few weeks he has seen a thieving servant boy locked in the pillory there, and a housewife whipped for calling a respectable citizen a 'copper-nosed drunkard', but today there's nothing more than the usual chattering, arguing, and elbowing.[7]

Cheapside is crowded with people at this hour. Carts and carriages lurch and bounce across its tattered surface, forcing shoppers to leap aside. Feet clink loudly with metal devices known as 'pattens', designed to elevate their owners' feet above the filth of the street; pigs squeal and grunt. (Milton remembers the proverb 'He that loves noise must buy a pig.')[8] The buildings on each side of the broad thoroughfare have wide windows on the ground floor, each fronted by a wooden stall-board that seals the window by night and by day is laid horizontal and covered with goods for sale: wooden trenchers and costly glassware, fine cloth woven through with veins of glinting metallic thread. Grocers' and apothecaries' tables are covered in sacks spilling out their contents, from everyday fare like carrots and sprigs of mallow to exotic delicacies like peppercorns, dried fruit, oranges, and lemons. The air rings with the cries of stall owners to passers-by: 'What do you lack?'[9]

Today, Milton doesn't pause to acquire anything, but winds his way through the crowd as the buildings to his right, on the south side of the street, get larger and more lavish: the stretch of ten houses and fourteen shops know as Goldsmith's Row after the elite craft that is practised there, said to be 'the most beautiful frame of fair houses and shops that be . . . in England'. Their four storeys loom over the street, festooned with coats of arms and carvings of wild naked woodmen riding on monstrous beasts, painted and gilded in lurid colours.[10]

Within a minute or two Milton sees the familiar landmarks which tell him that he is nearly home. First a hulking structure in the middle of the thoroughfare, towering thirty-six feet over the shoppers and passers-by, its three stone tiers studded with statues of holy figures. It's topped with the figure of a dove supposed to represent the Holy Ghost, and the gilded crucifix that gives it its common name: the Cheapside Cross. Most people trudge past without paying it special attention, but Milton is pleased to see a servant carrying a basket on his back turn his head and spit towards the cross, as he has done himself in his braver moments. In the same instant he is appalled to see several passers-by incline their heads and subtly bow their bodies as they pass while mumbling a charm to themselves, the idolatrous simpletons.

The base of the cross is surrounded by a railing, designed to repel those who have tried over the years to aim godly assaults at it. One niche contains a statue of the Virgin Mary, which was for a time replaced by the pagan goddess Diana, Thames water gushing from her stone breasts. The Virgin was restored, though her crown has been stolen, and if Milton squints he can see the knife mark left in her chest by a recent godly zealot. There have been increased rumblings and mutterings about the cross since the Prince of Wales's return from Spain the year before. There are complaints in the taverns that this landmark, 'one of the jewels of the whore of Rome', is openly revered by foreign idolaters and even by some recalcitrant English traitors. God showed his own view just a few months before, when a chapel attended by three hundred Roman Catholics in nearby Blackfriars collapsed during a sermon, killing them all in their error. Milton's own teacher, the younger Alexander Gil, wrote a Latin poem on the occasion, comparing it to the biblical fall of Dagon.[11]

Passing the Cheapside Cross, Milton sees beyond it the building that marks the corner of Bread Street, and lodged on its side the statue of a white bear that gives it its name. He turns right and leaves Cheapside behind, skirting the White Bear and passing on his left the most famous of the street's taverns, the Mermaid, known throughout London for the semi-mythical club of wits who congregate there, clustering around the coruscatingly witty and ever more corpulent Ben Jonson. Men of the theatre and of the court, they exchange stories of the club's first luminaries – its founder Walter Raleigh, playwrights like William Shakespeare and John Fletcher, even the young John Donne, himself born at the south end of Bread Street. Once a notorious tearaway, Donne is now a changed and sombre man, who Milton heard deliver a riveting but suspiciously clever sermon at St Paul's Cross eighteen months previously, imploring loyalty to God's chosen monarch on the anniversary of the heinous Gunpowder Plot. Bread Street is scarcely less busy than Cheapside itself at this hour, clogged with foot traffic making its way to and from the theatres and houses of ill repute that pepper the river-edge region of Bankside, and further worsened by the coaches that pick up and drop off passengers from as far away as Bath and Bristol at the smaller taverns that line the street. Milton elbows his way through the crowd, his ear caught by a snatch of fine Tuscan Italian spoken by two men heading north and dragging a large trunk between them, having, he guesses, probably disembarked at the Queenhithe docks.

Finally, Milton is home. He ducks sharply to the left below the sign of the spread eagle that marks the portion of the building where his family live and where his father makes his living, and steps into the narrow entryway. He makes his way towards the stairs that lead up to the living quarters, but pauses as he passes the door to his father's shop, where several voices are raised in competing fury. It's far from an unfamiliar sound: entering the house by this route, he's often heard sounds of disagreement, or the wailing and pleading of those begging to be forgiven for the debts they have incurred to his father. A high, desperate voice Milton does not know begs for more time to repay the loan; his father's lower tones, calm and menacing, insist that the day for repayment has arrived. The door opens and Milton pulls further back into the shadows to ensure that he cannot be seen. An elderly man lurches out, and, before he turns towards the hubbub of Bread Street, Milton catches a glimpse of his face – drawn, panic flashing in his eyes. Something in the drag of his legs as he stamps away suggests that this is a man not long for this world.[12] Milton turns and proceeds up the stairs, where the servants will, as usual, have his lunch ready: perhaps, today, some more of the pigeon pie laced with sugar that his mother has been urging him to eat, the warming properties of the meat and the spice supposed to lift his occasional fits of melancholy. Better, he reflects as he reaches the top of the stairs and the door to the kitchen, to eat too little than too much, even if it means returning to school and tackling Homer's Greek on an empty stomach.

✦

In July 2019 I visited Bread Street for myself, and took the modern version of the walk that I've just been describing, along Cheapside from St Paul's Cathedral, as part of a day spent circumambulating the places in London where Milton lived. There was a convenient end point for this particular part of the walk: a blue ceramic plaque on the side of Bow Bells House which reads *The Poet and Statesman John Milton was born 1608 in Bread Street*. The building's south-facing wall reveals that the narrow covered walkway that runs alongside it and beneath the adjacent building, a dark passage clad in sleek stone and metal that ends at a small churchyard, is named *John Milton Passage*. While it's nice to see Milton's name mentioned, it could hardly be in more underwhelming circumstances. The sign is next to a tall ventilation panel, above a small notice politely telling anyone who chooses to gaze at Milton's name that their every move is being recorded on closed-circuit television. It's hard to imagine a less suitable place to stand and, say, recite passages from *Paradise Lost*, or try in some other way to commune with Milton's spirit. In fact it's difficult to imagine stopping for too long at all: John Milton Passage and the entire north end of Bread Street feel determinedly featureless, aggressively blank, the sanded surfaces of the stone designed to withhold any finger or toeholds with which the imagination might seek to begin its climb.

What, I asked myself, was I doing here? On the one hand the underwhelming plaque in its banal setting seemed to corroborate the mixed feelings I've always had about literary tourism, which, I confess, springs from a kind of snobbery that's not uncommon among academics, and of which I'm not proud: the feeling that the books and the poems themselves are the real thing; that the follower of the tourist trail is, at best, naive. But it is also rooted in misgivings that I think are more significant, about the way in which, once a tourist industry springs up around a writer – Shakespeare, Austen, Wordsworth come most readily to mind – it tends to solidify a smooth and reassuring version of them that has had all of the challenging corners and splinters sanded off.

Bread Street still felt worth seeing, however, precisely for the sense of disappointment that it provided. The plaque had only been placed there in 2008, on the occasion of Milton's 400th birthday, and its newness and modesty seemed to reflect Milton's uncertain status: admired more readily than he's loved, a national monument rather than a national treasure.[13] But the very lack of fanfare, the fact that there was no Milton museum, no gift shop selling *Paradise Lost* tea towels or 'Lycidas' lollipops, freed me from any pressure to try and recapture some kernel of the authentic Milton. Instead, I could experience in one small corner of London the cycles of destruction and reconstruction through which the city has been obliterated and remade over the centuries. The sign of the White Bear that marked Milton's building was first lost to the Great Fire of London in 1666, rediscovered by chance in 1882, and then lost for good when the area was once again levelled during the Blitz in the Second World War.[14] The curious blankness of this part of London started to feel less like a true void than an inadvertent testimony to a set of absences, as if the decision over several decades to build the most antiseptic and charisma-free buildings imaginable were a crafty ploy to ensure the forgotten histories couldn't be entirely forgotten because there was nothing there to replace them; as if their glass and steel fronts were a screen onto which the imagination could project itself.

If I'd been alone and had lingered too long near the surveillance cameras, I suspect that security guards would have come to check my intentions, but I was able to enjoy the curious mixture of connection and dissociation that Bread Street provided because I had company. My friend Sean was a willing accomplice on several of the idiosyncratic Milton excursions which feature in the chapters of this book. His companionship while walking between the sites of Milton's school and his family home felt especially apt since, before we became friends, Sean was my teacher, and it's thanks to him that I persisted with the study of English literature at all. Until the age of sixteen I had seen no connection at all between reading, which I loved, and the experience of studying literature at school, which, when it wasn't actively painful, was unutterably tedious. Within a few weeks of moving to the sixth-form college where Sean taught for many years, and being taught *The Merchant of Venice* by him, I was sold: this was what, and how, I wanted to study. Sean never taught me Milton, but he changed my sense of what it means to learn from, and to teach, literature, and some years later he did read the hymn to wedded love from *Paradise Lost* at my wedding. Before my English classes with Sean, my experiences at school had made me intensely sceptical of the idea that literature was worth teaching at all, if it simply involved excavating prescribed platitudes from prescribed works whose value was not up for discussion.

Sean's lessons changed my mind because they challenged the idea that there was a single way to study great works of literature, a single set of questions that could be asked of these works or that could emerge from them, or a single set of reasons for which they mattered but that didn't need to be justified or explained. As I'd grown older and my friendship with Sean had developed, I'd also recognised certain common factors in our backgrounds that, I realised, made him the ideal companion on Bread Street, and for the odd enterprise of following Milton back to school. Although we'd both studied at Cambridge – Sean at Milton's own college, Christ's – this trip was to move us closer to our working-class London roots, albeit roots from which I was a generation or two further removed. Bread Street is only a mile or so from the parts of the East End where both my grandmothers had grown up, one of them the eldest of fourteen children born to Yiddish-speaking parents, while Sean was raised in the west of London, near Heathrow Airport, and had told me about the anti-Irish bigotry that his father experienced upon first arriving in England. Both of us, it seemed, shared a desire to spend time with the words and historical traces of a great dead writer not as an act of reverence but as an expression of continued uncertainty, a feeling of investment in Milton's life and works that's combined with a sense of distance from them, of approaching them from the outside as things that do not straightforwardly belong to us. If we'd both ended up loving, studying, and teaching English literature, we both did so from a shared sense that its traditions were not straightforwardly or unthinkingly ours, by virtue of our differing backgrounds and beliefs. But it also felt as if this awkward position, of being inside and outside at once, might be a particularly useful place from which to ask how and why a writer like Milton might matter so much.

I mention my earlier experiences because teaching, learning, and coming to decisions about how we spend our time and energies seem to me not to be smooth or linear processes. They are always affected by a wider social context, by quirks of individual personality and facts of family background, as well as by sheer happenstance. And this seemed like a good starting point for making sense of Milton's early life and education. I wanted to begin by thinking my way back into the cityscape in which his schooling was embedded, and the national and international struggles in which his city was embroiled, because while he might have been only dimly aware of these as a schoolboy, they would form the framework of his later life. For now, however, I want to focus on what

Milton would have experienced at school, and I find myself thinking, once again, in terms of rhythm. After all, though we don't necessarily construe it in these terms, what is a school if not a machine for the creating and the regularising of rhythms, an impersonal organisation demanding that each person it contains fits him- or herself into and around its regular divisions of times and spaces, the punctuated tempos at which things are done? The timetable at St Paul's, which had been re-formed at the start of the sixteenth century by John Colet, was rigid and precise. Colet's statutes outlawed all activities that involved 'foolish babbling and loss of time', and when they were amended in 1602 the timetable remained unaltered, the only change being that the masters were now subjected to it with the same strictness as the boys: 'We do ordain, that the high master, surmaster, and usher shall be tied to the same hours.'[15] Every minute of time was to be productively used across the rhythm of the school day:

> The children shall come unto the school in the Morning at VII of the Clock both winter and summer and tarry there until XI and return again at one of the clock and depart at V and thrice in the day prostrate they shall say the prayers with due tract [period of time] and pausing . . . in the morning and at noon and at evening.[16]

'Tract and pausing' is a nice phrase for the way in which such a day takes on a rhythm, the way that it pivots around these moments of pious suspension.

Milton was anywhere between seven to twelve years old when he first started at St Paul's School – the records were lost to the Great Fire. It was the most renowned school in the area since Colet was one of the closest English friends of Desiderius Erasmus, the pre-eminent educational reformer in northern Europe. Erasmus was a central figure in the movement known as Humanism, a word whose significance, however, should not be confused with its modern meaning of rational and anti-religious thought. It derived, rather, from what the ancient Romans had called *humanitas*, the values conferred upon a free man by a civilised and liberal education, known by extension as the *studia humanitatis*, from which the modern description of arts subjects as 'the humanities' derives. To be a humanist meant to devote oneself to the reading of ancient Greek and Roman works that had been lost (or known only in incomplete or mediated forms) during the Middle Ages, and to equip oneself with the linguistic skills to decode and correct these works, to restore their pure and original forms. The idea that the study of literature goes hand in hand with the inculcation of virtue is ever-present in the statutes that Colet wrote for his school. The high master is to be 'a man whole in body, honest and virtuous and learned in good and clean Latin literature and also in Greek', and his job is to teach the children 'not only good literature but also good Manners' using only 'good authors such as have the very Roman eloquence joined with wisdom, especially Christian authors that wrote their wisdom with clean and chaste Latin'.[17]

Decades later, Milton described himself as being 'devoted from boyhood to humane studies [*humanioribus . . . studiis*]', and the rhythms of the St Paul's classroom offer glimpses into the habits of his mind.[18] The schoolboys' unfolding encounter with the Latin language and its peculiarities took place in a curious meeting ground of the time-bound and the timeless. Basic Latin was required for entry to the school – each child had to be able to 'read and write Latin and English sufficiently, so that he be able to read and write his own lessons' – and all instruction took place in the language, which became a practical, living tool of expression. While rote repetition was frowned upon – 'What is the point', Erasmus asked, 'of repeating words parrot-fashion that are not understood?' – forms of repetition with creative kinds of difference were endlessly demanded of the boys.[19] They might answer a series of questions, and then be asked the same questions in a different order, 'every way forward, backward', as William Lily put it in his standard grammar, written for use at St Paul's. They might break a sentence down into its component parts, or a word down into its syllables, and then be tasked to reconstruct it in a different but equally fine form.[20] One of the most formative and widespread practices, and one that undoubtedly shaped Milton's thinking, was to encourage boys to begin keeping a commonplace book, a notebook whose pages bore thematic headings – the virtues and vices, love and hate, youth and old age, the mind and body, dwellings, food, or the divisions of time itself.[21] While reading, students would be encouraged to copy pithy, memorable, and elegant phrases and passages onto the relevant page, as a way of fixing them in their memory, and as material for future composition. Another standard exercise was so-called 'double translation', in which the student would render a Latin passage in English and then, as one of the best-known accounts put it, 'pausing an hour at the least, then let the child translate his own English into Latin again in another paper book'; for older boys the same would be done between Latin and Greek.[22] These forms of learning had their own rhythms, but these stops and starts circled invariably around an unchanging, timeless ideal.[23] Such exercises made up the rhythm of a day, which, pivoting around its pauses and shifts of activity and focus, was designed to leave few if any gaps or interstices of useless and unproductive time. There was to be no space for a void to open up between the inculcation of eloquence and the cultivation of virtue. The days slowly added up to years that increased in complexity, adding harder ancient texts and pushing beyond Latin to assail Greek and eventually Hebrew, but without changing in their essence, and ideally creating a smooth and incremental path to eloquent and virtuous adulthood.

It's also essential to these classroom rhythms that they were orchestrated by, and designed to produce, not just virtuous adults but virtuous *men*. In ancient Rome, where education in rhetorical excellence had been overwhelmingly restricted to male children, a contrasting set of terms developed to describe the ideal qualities of a *virile* style – hard, forceful, vigorous, fiery – and the loose, soft, decadent, enervating style that was invariably described as effeminate, and associated either with women themselves, or with uncivilised and feminised nations beyond Europe – what Erasmus called 'Asian exuberance'.[24] Cicero, the Roman orator who had the greatest influence on Erasmus and the entire world of Renaissance rhetoric, summed up both the general solution and its obvious limitations in his widely read *De Officiis*, where he urged his readers neither to be effeminate and soft (*effeminatum aut molle*) nor harsh and rustic (*durum aut rusticum*) in manner.[25] The eloquent, well-educated man walked a tightrope between excessive softness and elegance, which could seem feminine, and too much asperity, which risked appearing uncouth and ill-formed.

The move to intensive study of Latin at grammar school has been compared to the rites of passage that mark the complex transition between stages of life in tribal societies, and that often involve symbolically segregating men from women. One influential English humanist explicitly wrote that at the age of seven, when a boy began his formal studies, he should be 'taken from the company of women'. English was the language of home and household, quite literally and significantly the mother tongue. Latin was principally the language of educated men, found, as another writer observed, 'not in common talk but in private books'.[26] It was the language in which boys and men could understand one another without being understood more than they wanted to be. St Paul's was a world full of surrogate fathers – not just the teachers but the ancient authors themselves, who were persistently understood as fathering the eloquent Latin produced by the brains of their imitators. It becomes clear that it's no accident, when we peer into this world rife with father figures, that we know so much about Milton's father and so little about his mother, whom we can glimpse only in frustratingly fleeting and idealised forms. Milton later called her 'a woman of purest reputation, celebrated throughout the neighbourhood for her acts of charity'; his first biographers called her 'a prudent, virtuous wife' and 'a woman of incomparable virtue and goodness'.[27]

Of all the rhythms that formed this version of controlled eloquent maleness, however, I have not yet touched on the most notorious, and in many ways the hardest to judge: the rhythm of birch on flesh, of the switch wielded against palms and rumps, a rhythm of grunts of furious exertion and whimpers of suppressed agony. The stylised male body that was to be produced in the classroom was almost always a flogged body, formed by the intertwined rhythms of Latin verb conjugations, noun declensions, and elegant periodic sentences, on the one hand, and the punctuating rhythms of violence on the other. Erasmus may have denounced 'these ill-tempered, brutal drunkards who flog their pupils only in order to gratify their own instincts and who obviously possess that monstrous mentality which finds pleasure in the pain of another person', but all agreed with Proverbs 29:15 that 'The rod and reproof give wisdom': the question was how much of the rod to apply.[28] Milton's school remained particularly associated with flogging masters – the famous educator Richard Mulcaster, who was high master until the year of Milton's birth, was widely satirised as dozing through lessons and then arbitrarily beating boys for sleeping when he himself snapped awake. The same was even more emphatically true, as I suggested above, of the men who ran the school during his time there, Alexander Gil the elder and younger.[29] Even in an age when violence against the children in one's care was taken for granted, both men were notorious for the beatings they doled out, which frequently attracted both serious concern and satirical comment. In 1612 the elder Gil, whom John Aubrey later said 'had moodes, and humours; as particularly his Whipping fitts', was urged to 'moderation in his corrections' by a court order, and numerous ballads by former schoolboys and other enemies of the pair (who had a real talent for getting embroiled in furious disputes) did the rounds of literary London.[30] One, on Gil senior, began 'In Paul's church yard in London, / There dwells a noble Firker [i.e. one who flogs], / Take heed you that pass, / Lest you taste of his lash', and described him whipping a series of boys, visitors, even an unfortunate lost Frenchman who stumbled into the schoolhouse to ask for directions to the cathedral. Another poem imagined the elder Gil beating his son (who had been a pupil at the school): Gil junior is to be whipped 'for thy faults not few / In tongue Hebrew / For which a Grove of Birch is due'.[31] The younger Gil eventually graduated from being beaten to become a notorious flogger in his own right. In 1623, when Milton was still at St Paul's, Gil was publicly mocked by Ben Jonson (with whom he repeatedly crossed verbal swords) in a court masque that was performed by Prince Charles himself before King James and the French ambassador, as one who 'Hangs all his school with his sharp sentences, / And o'er the execution place hath painted / Time whipped, for terror to the infantry'.[32] These were not just malicious rumours: years after Milton left St Paul's, Gil was dismissed from his post for savagely beating a boy named Bennett, and dragging him about the school by the ears.[33] It's highly likely that father and son alike beat the young Milton on more than one occasion, scoring the rhythms of discipline and eloquence alike on his flesh. The critic Eve Sedgwick provocatively writes of her own early experiences: 'When I was a child the two most rhythmic things that happened to me were spanking and poetry.'[34] The same was likely true for many seventeenth-century schoolboys, including Milton.

It's possible to envisage a version of Milton with the most sophisticated and exaggerated kind of mind that might emerge from an educational system of this sort – one supremely confident in itself, in its ability to master the variety of the world that it encountered and to confer order and cohesion upon it. A mind secure in its separateness – especially separate in the intellectual refinement of its effortlessly elegant Latin from the working worlds of the lower orders, and of women. A mind fluent in multiple languages and able to shuttle between them. A mind forged in no small part by repeated and ritualised violence, but able to turn this violence to its own ends – to salvage from whipped flesh a way of whipping its ideas into shape, and of lashing its adversaries with the edge of a finely honed tongue. Above all, a mind comfortable within, and in charge of, time, capable of pleating together ancient centuries and the unfolding hours of the day, synchronising their rhythms within a complicated and tightly tied knot. This is the Milton to whom I've alluded on a few occasions, the Milton who seems to stand as the embodiment and proudest justification of dominant and domineering cultural forces. As one writer puts it, this is Milton as 'the embodiment of the qualities of the establishment class – a classical education, a Christian theology, a cold, unapproachable demeanour'.[35] This is a Milton who can be valorised by those who value such qualities and reviled by those who detest them, but these two sides are united in their appraisal of who and what Milton was, and the forces that went into making him that way.

I find myself perennially uncomfortable in my relationship to this establishment Milton. Part of my curiosity about Milton's classical education arises from the fact that I didn't receive one myself – by which I mean that I was never taught Latin, let alone Greek. A lot may have changed educationally since Milton's day, and the possession of Latin no longer draws such a clear and unembarrassed line between the worlds of the learned and the unlearned, but having 'done Latin at school' is still, at least in Great Britain, a sort of code or shorthand (not infallible, but pretty reliable) for having attended a private school, and the language is therefore still densely caught up with the nature of the British class system, and with how it is constructed, displayed, and concealed. I did eventually acquire functional Latin, but as a graduate student in the United States, where I was able to start with an intensive beginners' class known informally as 'Turbo Latin'. This means that I've never felt entirely secure in my abilities; even writing this down feels weirdly exposing, as if I'm outing myself as someone who doesn't have the right or the authority to write about Milton, which in itself suggests the tenacious gatekeeping role that the sort of classical education that Milton received, and its modern descendants, still has, and is intended to have.

The more I've studied and thought about Milton's education, however, the more the humanist classroom at St Paul's has come to seem, to me, like both a system for producing order and regularising the rhythms of children, and a system that constantly produced wild, subversive, and destabilising alternative possibilities that it then struggled either to acknowledge, to exorcise, or to control. In order to make sense of the person and the writer whom Milton became, we need to refuse to take the schoolroom (and, at times, refuse to take him) at face value, or to accept that elite education and traditional values mutually reinforce one another as seamlessly as their defenders and their detractors often want to believe. So again, I find myself faced with two Miltons; and the second version who emerges, for me, from St Paul's, is no less shaped by the world of the classroom, by its reverence for the classics and its commitment to organisation and to violence, than the first, but with very different outcomes.

Let's go back to the schoolroom, then, and back to where I ended my first foray, with the beatings which the Gils and countless other teachers administered. I should also confess that this is an aspect of education (and of history more broadly) I find hard to treat with equanimity and historical detachment, and that makes me wonder whether this should be the aim. We don't know the details of how and how often Milton was beaten at school, although, as we'll see, corporal punishment also shadowed his university years, and he went on to be a confirmed beater of boys when he himself was engaged in teaching. This depressing fact might seem to confirm one way of viewing the history of childhood, which sees it effectively as a history of relentless abuse, one traumatised generation passing on their trauma to the next: 'Century after century of battered children grew up and in turn battered their own children,' writes one historian morosely.[36] Rather than simply lamenting this fact, I need to acknowledge how privileged I am to find it difficult truly to recapture what this routine violence must have been like, especially in educational contexts. Unlike my parents' generation, I have never been taught by anyone who is legally permitted to inflict violence on me, and I find it haunting to think of the ease with which this possibility was accepted as routine for so long, by all involved. I have a clear memory from childhood, when my family spent two years living in Zimbabwe and we met with an acquaintance from England, a teacher, who had moved there to teach in a school which was in many respects – rules, uniform, and corporal punishment – a self-conscious throwback to the time of the British Empire. When my parents asked him how he coped with administering beatings, he smiled ruefully and said: 'It was hard at first, but you get used to it.'

Maybe this is just something I want to believe, but using violence to create orderly children, and getting used to it in this way, seems not only damaging but completely incoherent: using one form of chaos to tame another; the chaotic adult let loose on the chaotic child. This is one way to make sense of the fact that, while no one during the time of Milton's childhood seems to have doubted the virtue of beating children, there were significant anxieties about how this beating was carried out, and what it meant. Time and again the anxiety arose, often in indirect and barely expressible terms, that there was an illicit side to these beatings, a darkly sexual charge that sat uneasily with the model of manliness that it was supposed to inculcate. Later in the century Milton's friend, the journalist Marchamont Nedham, complained that excessive beating by some schoolmasters had brought infamy on the whole profession, 'not to speak of the ill use some have made of it to lewdness . . . it being a kind of uncovering of nakedness'.[37] It's easy to see why it became so easy to present the teacher's beatings, usually in teasing euphemisms, as an excuse for perverse sexual contact between man and boy. That this was the case in Milton's immediate educational environment is abundantly clear from the mocking poem describing the elder Gil flogging his son that I mentioned above, which is subtitled 'Gill's Arse uncas'd, unstript, unbound', and in which the father's threat to 'pull-down your hose' prompts the son's plea: 'In private let it be / And do not sowce me openly'. But the father ignores the son's begging words: 'Yet I will make thy Arse to sneeze / And now I doe begin / To thresh it on thy skin, / For now my hand is In, is In.'[38] It's grotesquely funny – the sneezing arse – and entirely disturbing, this scene of violent incest; beating suddenly seems less like a technique for smoothly forging boys into regulated and orderly men, and more like a strange, furtive, and disreputable practice on the threshold between public example and shady secret (is it to be done 'in private' or openly?) and between edifying, sombre ritual and anarchic, perverted pleasure. It's notable that, while a theory of what we would call sadomasochism would have to wait some centuries to be formulated, it was in 1639, when Milton himself was about to start working as a schoolteacher, that a work was published by a professor of medicine explaining that some men and women couldn't enjoy sexual relations without being whipped. Titled *De Flagorum Usu in re Veneria*, it was written in complicated Latin that made it entirely inaccessible to the unlearned.[39]

There's nothing particularly surprising about these jokes, these nods and winks. The figure of the schoolteacher as a sexual pervert hiding in plain sight, whose pedagogical erotics can be sinister or benign, has become a cultural cliché, most recently encapsulated in Alan Bennett's play *The History Boys* (2004). Yet it's precisely because it's a cliché that venturing into its earlier history can be helpful, because doing so suggests ways in which the very tools that have been designed to create and refine a certain highly important version of educated masculinity, a version that Milton himself has often been taken to embody, are potentially very unstable, or prone to undo their own ideals.

If the floggings that were supposed to help mould boys into men turned out in practice to produce much less reassuringly moral behaviour, then this was true in other ways of the less overtly violent techniques of the St Paul's classroom. In fact, while I've begun with these beatings, it's more sensible to see them as just one of the many ways in which humanist educators sought to shape not just the minds of their charges but also their bodies, their voices, the whole of their ways of understanding and carrying themselves. This, as I suggested earlier, would have made the experience of the schoolroom at least somewhat continuous, for the young Milton, with the way in which the entire body, and not just the ear, hands, or voice, were implicated in his father's musical world. When Milton was later said to have 'a delicate tuneable Voice' and 'a beautifull and well proportioned body', these would have been read as proofs of his successful early education.[40] Humanists were drawn to the writings of Roman rhetoricians precisely because they paid such careful attention to the techniques for shaping not just writing but also the body and voice; rhetorical training provided not just bookish expertise but also a preparation for the public worlds of politics and law. What's striking, however, is that the emphasis on virile, manly style that I mentioned above is constantly expressed in highly anxious, acutely defensive terms. The ideal student of rhetoric had to achieve a flexibility of style on every level – a suppleness not just of writing, but of body and voice – that allowed him to achieve *decorum*, the ability to fit himself smoothly to the demands of a situation; failure to do so was a mark of boorishness, a lack of education. And yet the orator or rhetorician was always at risk of going too far, of becoming *too* expressive, *too* flexible, *too* hyper-stylised. As the most influential pair of Roman rhetoricians, Cicero and Quintilian, put it: 'In these matters we must avoid the two extremes: our conduct and speech should not be effeminate and over-nice, on the one hand, nor coarse and boorish on the other'; the voice should be 'neither dull, rough, heavy, hard, stiff, and thick; nor thin, hollow, feeble, soft and effeminate', but rather 'easy, strong, rich, flexible, sturdy, sweet, durable, clear, pure and penetrating'.[41] The fear that students might lapse into effeminacy was specifically associated with the misuse of rhythms – as if women are simply more rhythmically excessive than men, or rhythmic in the wrong way. For Cicero, rhythms that were too frequent and too obvious became too poetic, too theatrical, too womanly: 'There must be no unmanly softness in the neck,' he warned the aspiring orator, 'and the fingers should not make delicate gestures or move in time to the rhythm', while the elder Seneca denounced his own youthful taste for 'extreme ornamentation and effeminate rhythm'.[42]

These proclamations read to me less like a straightforward account of what it means to be, and to carry oneself, as an educated man and more like an intensely anxious set of defensive manoeuvres. They reveal an awareness that the ideal of masculinity that it trumpets is deeply fragile and difficult both to define and to embody, prone to veer off in uncontrolled directions. It's easy to say under such circumstances that one should be an eloquent man, much less clear how to go about being one.[43] The matter becomes stranger still when we look again at what went on in schoolrooms like Milton's, and see that many of their practices seem designed not to hold the female at bay but precisely to require the boys to inhabit the kinds of female voice, the styles of women's appearance and their bodies, from which they were supposed to distance themselves.

The stress on the education of the entire body meant that the classroom could be highly performative, indeed theatrical. As with the more famous practices of the commercial stage for which Shakespeare wrote, boys often performed plays in school, in both English and Latin, where they dressed and spoke as women, and this had been the case at St Paul's since Colet's day.[44] Even when not performing so overtly, however, everyday classroom practice routinely asked boys, paradoxically, to develop and refine their own voices by constantly assuming and inhabiting the voices of others: their teachers, inanimate objects, and, very often, the voices and world views of women. A particularly notable example was the *Heroides*, a collection of poems by the Roman poet Ovid, which Erasmus had recommended as models 'for refining and displaying your skill', and many of which took the form of imagined speeches by the heroines of classical mythology – Penelope singing a lament for Odysseus, Dido for Aeneas, Medea for Jason.[45] Schoolboys were extensively trained to inhabit, with their minds and their imaginations, the very same voices, bodies, rhythms, and words of women that they were simultaneously warned against resembling too closely.

Again I need to pause and emphasise that I'm not suggesting this was necessarily a positive or progressive fact. It's easy to see how it could be presented in this way – that the experience of speaking, writing, performing as a woman gave Milton, or the other writers shaped and educated within this system, special sympathy with and insight into female experience, of a sort that helps explain his eventual depiction of Eve or the vivacity of Shakespeare's heroines. But it's too smug, too glib, to fall back on the idea of special geniuses whose sensibilities allow them to transcend the limits not only of their times but of their gender. The truth, I think, is stranger than this, more paradoxical. What interests me is that the same schoolroom exercises that were designed to knot together the rhythms of a confident male self constantly required that boys *become other people*, including women; that they broke down the boundaries of who they were and allowed themselves to be taken over by other voices, other rhythms, other kinds of being. Petrarch, who did so much to establish the humanist reverence for the ancients, and who, as we'll see, Milton revered in turn, wrote that he had read ancient writers

> not once but countless times . . . I have thoroughly absorbed these writings, implanting them not only in my memory but in my marrow . . . sometimes I may forget the author, since through long usage and continual possession [*longo usu et possessione continua*] I may adopt them and for some time regard them as my own; and besieged by the mass of such writings, I may forget whose they are and whether they are mine or others.[46]

Petrarch's use of *possessione*, 'through . . . possession', seems to flicker between suggesting that he owns these writings – having absorbed them so thoroughly into his very body – and suggesting that they've continually possessed *him*, as a spirit or demon might; that he's literally lost himself in his reading. To read and study in this manner was, potentially, not to be formed by rhythms of manliness, but to enter a less stable rhythm, one that meant both possessing and being possessed, being made and unmade.

I also need to pause once more over my own experiences. I mentioned that when I went to sixth-form college, being taught by Sean was a shift in what it meant to study books, a shift from extreme boredom to excitement and pleasure. But it was also part of a larger shift. The school at which I studied from the ages of eleven to sixteen was an unpleasant place in which to be conspicuously different. I kept my love of reading mostly to myself, knowing that to be conspicuously bookish meant becoming a target for mockery, or worse. And in ways that I couldn't have articulated then, and still can't fully now, I knew that this was connected to my being Jewish, which I also sought not exactly to conceal but to downplay, as the only Jewish child in my remarkably homogeneous year group. I may not have been beaten by my teachers as Milton was, but I know what it's like to spend years in a supposedly 'educational' environment where to be noticeably different was to attract derision and sometimes violence; where norms were narrow, and policed. Daniel

Boyarin refers to the 'widespread sensibility that being Jewish in our culture renders a boy effeminate', and while I didn't know this as a child – and certainly didn't know that it was the legacy of beliefs widespread in Milton's lifetime, and for centuries before and afterwards, that Jewish men menstruated, their bodies the antithesis of the regulated and self-contained Christian-classical ideal of a man – my own life as a reader is certainly bound up with my evolving awareness that to love reading, to care openly about things like poems, is entangled in complicated ways with what the society in which I live considers normal and what it tends to encourage as acceptable passions for boys and men.[47] I'll return to some of these points later; but I want to note that while my educational experiences might be vastly different from Milton's, his educational world at St Paul's – a school which, as late as the 1960s, had a quota for the entry of Jewish pupils – can nonetheless alert us to the assumptions about what is 'proper' or 'normal' (Christianity, say, or a certain version of maleness) that still pervade the ways in which children are taught to learn.[48]

If the manliness violently created in the classroom proved potentially unstable, the same was true of the split between the male, Latinate world of the school and the English-speaking household, realm of the mother tongue. Appalled though I am by the Gils' brutality, I still feel I've done them something of a disservice by only discussing their infamous thrashings, which were far from the only interesting (and sinister) thing about them. The elder Gil was a man of wide and eclectic interests – his surviving manuscripts cover topics from Christian Cabbala to medicine and cookery (recipes include gingerbread, almond butter, a 'fine pie', and treatments for haemorrhoids, syphilis, and 'pimples in the face'); fascinatingly, some of these are written on the backs of recycled sheets of medieval music, becoming a palimpsest of various pasts.[49]

But what stands out, for a man whose job required constant speaking and writing in Latin, is Gil's deep and serious engagement with the peculiarities of the English language itself, especially its poetry. In 1619, while Milton was a student at St Paul's, Gil published a book titled *Logonomia Anglica*, a fascinating and curious work that was entirely about English but written mostly in Latin, and which both professed reverence for his native tongue and sought to overhaul it, correcting its missteps and regularising its eccentricities – effectively treating it like one of his unruly schoolboys. Gil's account of English was ferociously nationalist, seeking to restore the purity of its Anglo-Saxon roots and imploring its readers: 'by that blood of your fathers which beats in your veins, retain, retain what still remains of your native speech and tread in the footsteps of your ancestors. Or will you make your own language a province of Rome?'[50] Gil continued a long tradition of worry about English as a mangled and mongrel tongue, a patchwork of borrowings from elsewhere, and the closeness of his phrasing to modern languages of national and racial purity is chilling. He took this tradition in unusual directions, however, and with more unpredictable results. Like the schoolroom itself, the *Logonomia* asked readers to attend to every tiny detail of English words – their etymology, syntax, and poetic rhythms – but Gil was particularly vexed by the language's irregularities of spelling and pronunciation, and proposed new rules, which would regularise them, as well as the reintroduction of Anglo-Saxon letters that had fallen out of use.[51] He exemplified fine English usage by extensively quoting from recent English poets, whom he saw as the equal of the great ancients, above all Edmund Spenser, whom Gil called 'our Homer'. Spenser, whom Milton would also grow to deeply admire, was best known for his sprawling and dauntingly complex epic poem *The Faerie Queene*, a tale of knights and monsters which also had moral, political, and metaphysical ambitions, all written in a deliberately archaic style. It's very likely that Milton was exposed to a range of English poetry by Gil at St Paul's, and encouraged to place and value it alongside ancient writings, in ways that helped shape his later inclination to mix and align these traditions. Furthermore, when we actually look at a page from *Logonomia Anglica*, it becomes clear just how weird Gil's project of poetic nationalism became in practice.

When Gil quotes several lines from Spenser, he does so to illustrate the rhetorical figure of 'synchysis', in which the order of words

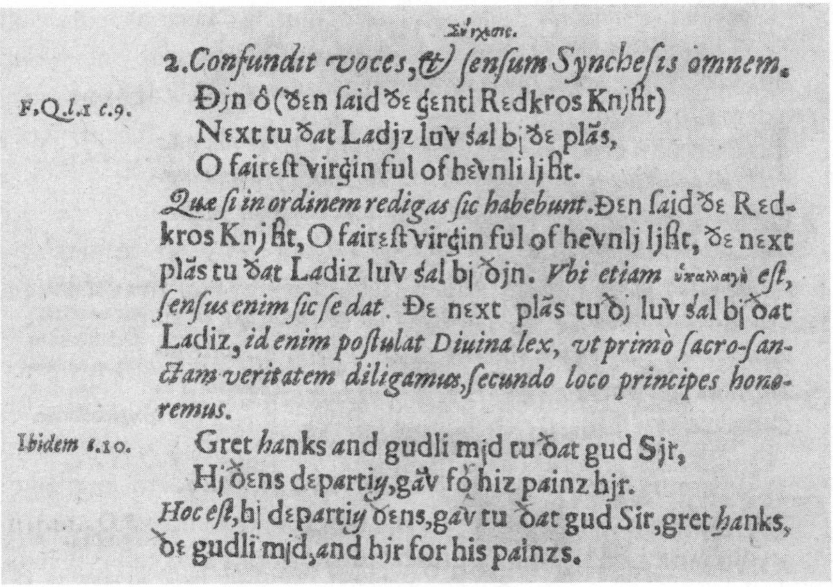

Σύγχυσις.

2. *Confundit voces, & sensum Synchesis omnem.*

F.Q.l.1 c.9. Ðjn ô (ðen said ðe gentl Redkros Knjht)
Next tu ðat Ladjz luv sal bj ðe plās,
O fairest virgin ful of hevnli ljht.

Quæ si in ordinem redigas sic habebunt. Ðen said ðe Redkros Knjht, O fairest virgin ful of hevnlj ljht, ðe next plās tu ðat Ladiz luv sal bj ðjn. *Vbi etiam* ὑπαλλαγὴ *est, sensus enim sic se dat.* Ðe next plās tu ðj luv sal bj ðat Ladiz, *id enim postulat Diuina lex, vt primò sacro-sanctam veritatem diligamus, secundo loco principes honoremus.*

Ibidem c.10. Gret hanks and gudli mjd tu ðat gud Sjr,
Hj ðens departiŋ, gāv fo hiz painz hjr.

Hoc est, hj departiŋ ðens, gāv tu ðat gud Sir, gret hanks, ðe gudli mjd, and hjr for his painzs.

FIGURE 5: Several lines from Edmund Spenser's *The Faerie Queene* as they appear in Alexander Gil's *Logonomia Anglica* (1619).

is disarranged for deliberate effect. He quotes them as they were originally written, then rewrites them as they would appear '*si in ordinem redigas*' – if they were arranged in proper order; this seems in keeping with the regularising, schoolmasterly drive of his mind. But in fact what he's quoted isn't Spenser at all, as any reader would have recognised it. Before he reorders the words, Gil has already rewritten them according to his proposed spelling reforms, with the lost letter 'eth' (Ð, ð) liberally substituting for *th*: so the first line, 'Ðin, ô (ðen said ðe gentl *Redkros* Kniht)', usually reads 'Thine, O then, said the gentle *Redcrosse* knight'.[52] What this page provides, at least to my eyes, is far from a clear distinction between eloquent Latin and purified English, which is what Gil seems to intend. It's more like a rather manic medley, a Greek word followed by a Latin translation followed by entirely alien, transmogrified English; one language framing another, but the latter so fully revamped that the native speaker is estranged from it, forced to experience it anew. The initial Latin explanation for synchysis states '*confundit voces*'

– 'it mingles voices' – and this is precisely what the page itself seems to do, mixing Gil's voice with Spenser's, English with Latin and Greek, Spenser's archaisms with the resurgence of an invented English past.

This mingling – this confounding – might better reflect the ways in which young minds were actually formed in his schoolroom than Gil's own vision of himself, perfecting English and Latin by sifting one from the other. The routine multilingualism of anyone who proceeded through the school and university system during Milton's lifetime is a fact that understandably tends to get downplayed by people who want these works to be read and valued in our present moment, because it makes writers who emerged from these systems appear difficult, excessively learned, elite and elitist. I understand these concerns – I've been trying in this chapter to understand the often peculiar ways in which the mind of this elite minority was formed – and yet I also think there's another way of looking at it which makes the matter more open, and potentially more exciting. I'll return repeatedly to Milton's multilingualism, and the way in which it formed his mind and writings throughout his life, but I can say at this point that the interest for me in the multilingual milieu in which Milton was taught is this: the schoolroom mechanisms for inculcating eloquence and manliness and virtue, I've suggested, constantly teetered on the brink of violence and theatrical performance and effeminacy in ways that threatened to reveal the fragile, artificial nature of the whole enterprise. In a similar way, a space in which the authority of Latin was reinforced by carefully partitioning it from English was also one in which a student could become estranged from *all* languages, caught in a space between them that could feel at once like the confusion of Babel and a rich arena in which language could be made anew. If Milton seems, to me, to be equally capable of reinforcing the stable edifice of 'English literature' and making it shift and waver, it's because this was the between-space of language in and from which he would go on to write throughout his life.

We can glimpse this possibility in his earliest writings. When Milton first collected his English poems for publication in 1645, the second poem was titled 'A Paraphrase on Psalm 114' and it bore the head-note: 'This and the following Psalm were done by the Author at fifteen years old.' This was a poem which Milton wanted his later readers to associate with his schooldays, to read as a classroom exercise, as I did when I imagined Gil instructing him in its trans-lation at the start of this chapter. It begins as follows:

> *When the blest seed of Terah's faithful Son,*
> *After long toil their liberty had won,*
> *And past from Pharian fields to Canaan Land,*
> *Led by the strength of the Almighty's hand,*
> *Jehovah's wonders were in Israel shown,*
> *His praise and glory was in Israel known.*

I'm not going to pretend that this is Milton's finest poem, and it's not one over which many readers have thought to pause for very long. By pinning it so clearly to his schooldays, Milton wanted both the poem and the young man who wrote it to be read as works in progress. But it is precisely for that reason that it leads me to ask what kind of process he wanted it to represent – how he *placed* this youthful exercise, and how he wanted us to place it – for there are more options than first meet the eye. Apart from anything else, Psalm 114 is the only text Milton translated not once but *twice*: a decade later he rendered it in Greek, and wrote a letter in Latin to his friend and former teacher, Alexander Gil the Younger, explaining that he undertook it 'before daybreak . . . with no set purpose certainly, but only on a vague impulse'.[53] This was clearly a psalm with a genuine and long-standing hold on his early im-agination, as it flitted between four languages.

It's tempting just to mine the early paraphrase for traces and anticipations of Milton's later preoccupations: the line 'After long toil their liberty had won' hints at a version of freedom as strenuous, arduously achieved, that became central to his mature world view. Likewise the phrase 'Terah's faithful Son' is Milton's invention, where the original Hebrew simply has '*beyt Ya'akov*', 'the house of Jacob': Jacob was indeed Terah's son, but it's notable that Milton, who had fathers and sons constantly on the brain (and whose lessons would have encouraged him to think in terms of literary paternity) chose these precise words. If he expands this particular phrase, however, what he leaves out is no less notable: he does not name the place from which the Israelites gained their liberty, Egypt, to which the original Hebrew referred with the wonderfully compressed words '*meyam lo'ez*' – which roughly means, as I suggested at the start of this chapter, 'from a strange-tongued people'. The verses describe Exodus as a separation not just of peoples but of languages. When Milton later translated '*lo'ez*' into Greek he chose a pleasingly polysyllabic word '*barborophonon*', which aims to sound as strange as the language it denounces, but in his English version he left it out altogether.

This kind of freedom isn't unusual – this is a paraphrase, after all, not a translation – but once alerted in this way to what isn't there, I find myself noticing other things. In particular, that these opening lines lack the division into two balanced halves that's the most salient characteristic of each verse in the Hebrew original. Indeed, there isn't a single punctuation mark in the middle of any of Milton's first half-dozen lines. But, if this suggests an aspiration towards uninterrupted smoothness, in other ways the lines are rhythmically jerky, three of the first four starting with a heavily stressed syllable (*When, After, Led*) and containing pairs of thuddingly stressed words (*blessed seed, long toil*). This mixture of ease and hard work feels like a fair reflection of the remarkably onerous and drawn-out process by which this paraphrase was probably produced, which is worth bearing in mind. In all likelihood, by the time he was studying Hebrew in the latter stages of his time at St Paul's, Milton would have been expected to memorise the English version from the recently published King James Bible, and a Latin version, either from the Roman Catholic Vulgate or a recent Protestant rendition; then he would have had to turn these into one another from memory, and try turning each of them into Greek; then into Hebrew; then the Greek and Hebrew into one another. After allowing himself an interlude of time for those exercises to fade from the forefront of his mind, he would start with the Hebrew text he had produced, and turn that back into

Greek, then Latin, and finally English; then he would compare each
of his versions with the authoritative originals in each language: all
these stages presided over by Alexander Gil senior, who was no mean
scholar of Hebrew and the other Semitic languages, and who wielded
the threat of the violence that he could inflict on boys who did it
badly.[54] The 'Almighty's hand' of the poem is also the hovering hand
of the schoolmaster, ready to descend with force.

If this sounds staggeringly complicated, it leads me to ask what
happens to a mind for which these twists, turns, repetitions became
a matter of habit. From the very beginnings of their contact with
Hebrew, which usually meant reading the Psalms, boys were
instructed in its ways of making poetry as well as its meanings, even
though its poetic features were poorly understood. Milton seems
to have believed that the poetry of the Bible was superior to 'all
the kinds of Lyrick poesy', but this also meant that it numbered
among them; it *was* a kind of poetry.[55] Scholars of his time were
particularly vexed by the apparent failure of biblical verse, given
its divine origins, to follow regular rules of poetic metre in the
manner of the Greeks and Romans. This led the great philologist
J. J. Scaliger to write that the Psalms were 'pure prose, albeit
animated by a poetic character', with only certain books of the
Bible seemingly 'bound by some requirement of *rhythmus*'. Scaliger
claimed that 'it is so far from being the case that a Hexameter or
Pentameter line may be found in the Holy Bible, that their lines
are composed not even of a constant *rhythmus*, but the *rhythmus* is
now lengthened or shortened to express the meaning'.[56] Scripture
is replete with rhythms, but they do not seem to obey laws: they
can neither be ignored nor categorised. Milton's poem seems to
record the simultaneous stress and ease of leaping between languages
to arrive at an overwrought final product, but it also strives to echo
the awkward but undeniable rhythms of Hebrew itself.[57]

The Psalms were everywhere in Milton's world – sung constantly
in church, repeatedly translated and ceaselessly published – and
they are everywhere in his later poems, all the way to *Paradise Lost*.
But translating the Psalms is both a logical and a strange choice
for a young poet like Milton, seeking to find his own voice, since

the texts themselves are obsessed with voices while making it resolutely unclear whose voice is whose. They are a miscellany of poetic
cries and utterances. Protestant readers, keen to stress the coherence
of the Bible, tended to attribute them all to the speaker who is
explicitly assigned to some of them, the biblical King David, and
make them all flow from one voice: but this altered rather than
changed the problem, since it was still God who spoke through
David, making it unclear whose the words ultimately were.[58] If
Petrarch, as I mentioned, was prone to lose sight of where his voice
ended and the voices of the ancients began, this was a troublingly
pagan model: in his famous *Defence of Poesie*, Philip Sidney denounced
the idea of the *vates* or inspired prophet-poet who receives 'heart-
ravishing knowledge' from the gods as 'a very vain and godless
superstition', but immediately acknowledged 'the reasonableness of
this word *vates*' when admitting that 'the holy David's Psalms are
a divine poem'.[59] To blend one's voice with the rhythms and many
languages of the Psalms, as the young Milton did, was to become
doubly a mouthpiece, speaking words that belonged straightforwardly neither to oneself nor to the biblical king from whom one
adopted them, but to God.

Milton might not have chosen this psalm at all – it might have
been thrust upon him by Gil or one of his other teachers. He or
they might have made their choice fairly randomly; he or they
might have read it as a statement of historical fact, David's description of the liberation of the Israelites from Egypt. But perhaps not.
It had been sung in St Paul's Cathedral, next door to the school,
in 1623, as part of the celebrations marking Prince Charles's return
from Spain without his Catholic bride, Israel's freedom from
bondage standing for England's dodging of the renewed papal
yoke.[60] Perhaps, then, Milton's burgeoning and enduring hatred of
all things Roman Catholic was fuelled and shaped by translating
this particular psalm in this particular moment.

But this particular psalm came with other associations as well,
ones less immediate and pressing – a set of not just theological and
political but literary resonances. In the second canto of his *Purgatorio*,
itself the second part of his *Commedia*, the great Italian poet Dante

Alighieri's poetic avatar stands by a sea over which a ship appears, fanning wondrously through the air: the Ship of Souls, bearing '*più di cento spirti*' – more than a hundred spirits, chanting together a glorious song. '"In exito Israel de Aegypto" / *cantavan tutti insieme ad una voce / con quanto di quel salmo è poscia scripto*' – '*In exito Israel de Aegypto* they sang altogether with one voice, with all that is written after of that psalm': the very same psalm that Milton paraphrased and translated.[61] Milton – whose immersion in Italian literature, including Dante, I'll explore further in the coming chapters – might or might not have known that in translating this psalm he was adding his own voice to the *cento spirti* who had sung it *ad una voce*. But there's more: in a famous letter in which he discussed the poetic strategies of the *Commedia*, Dante returned to this very psalm, using it as an example of the way in which his poem is '"polysemous", that is, having several meanings'. The psalm can be read literally, as the story of the Israelites' exodus; allegorically, as an account of the Christian's redemption through Christ; morally, as a description of the soul's movement from sin to a state of grace; or anagogically, as a way of understanding 'the passing of the sanctified soul from the bondage of the corruption of this world to the liberty of everlasting glory'.[62] All these possibilities, all these ways of meaning and of reading, crowd into, and coexist within, the same set of words.

While we can't know how much of this Milton knew as a schoolboy, he certainly knew by the time he published his two versions of this psalm, in 1645, that it was not just any extract from the Bible: it had been used by a great poet whom he deeply admired to exemplify the many ways in which, and levels on which, we can understand poetry. If I'm not sure how much to read into Milton's youthful poem, then, this difficulty in itself starts to seem deeply appropriate. This schoolroom exercise arrives to us as the product of a pirouetting and a thrashing about betwixt and between languages, forged in the crucible of English, Latin, Greek, and Hebrew, and perhaps Dante's Italian; and if it is, like the young Milton, poised between languages, it is also, like him, poised between the ways that poetry can mean or refer – to immediate political pressures, to the distant historical past, or to forms of theological truth that stand beyond time.

The ability of this psalm both to refer to a specific time and to stand outside time altogether has helped it resonate in different ways across the centuries. If the schoolboy Milton may or may not have known when he paraphrased it of Dante's musings on these psalms then one reader who did was James Joyce. Omnivorous reader that he was – of Milton and, it sometimes feels, of pretty much everything else – Joyce might have known that both Dante and Milton were attracted by this particular psalm. He certainly read the two poets in intertwined ways: in a lecture delivered in Trieste in 1912 Joyce commented that 'Il *Paradiso Perduto* di Milton è una trascrizione puritanica della *Divina Commedia*.'[63]

Joyce's massive novel *Ulysses*, studded with reminiscences of Milton, has as its penultimate section a story told through a series of catechistic questions and answers. The novel's central figures, Stephen Daedalus and Leopold Bloom, step out of the back door of Bloom's house together and into the garden. The narrator asks 'with what attendant ceremony was the exodus from the house of bondage to the wilderness of inhabitation effected', and 'With what intonation *secreto* of what commemorative psalm?', and answers: 'The 113th, *modus peregrinus: In exitu Israël de Egypto: domus Jacob de populo barbaro.*'[64] The very same psalm that Dante cited and unpicked, that Milton paraphrased. We're probably supposed to assume that it's Stephen who secretly intones these words, but it's also calculatedly unclear; the psalm seems deliberately to float above the two figures, lapsed Irish Catholic and lapsed Irish Jew; to hover between their voices, between the religious traditions they both represent and reject, just as the verses themselves are a central part of both the Easter Vespers and, spoken, as they were at family *seders* throughout my childhood, as part of the Passover *Haggadah*.[65] Between voices, countries, religions, languages: if this is more familiar as a description of the polyglot, shapeshifting Joyce, it's also, to me, the hazy zone of Milton's schoolroom, of his formative years.

4

24 December 1629: 'But Now Begins'

Where are we?
Unclear.

Vision is doubled, split, one possibility layered over and vibrating with another, but the two refusing to coalesce into a single scene. As if the two eyes are each seeing something different, peering in different directions like the revolving eyeballs of a chameleon, but into entirely different spaces, worlds.

When are we?

No clearer.

Time is what we're not supposed to notice; it's what allows our attention to take place, not something to which we attend. But that seems impossible, here. It too is divided; no, rather, it's overstuffed, full; there seems to be too much of it. Somehow the flow of time wants and manages to do impossibly different things all at once. It races eagerly ahead like a river swollen after rain; it curls around and back on itself like that river's eddies and whorls, its turbulent pockets and vortices; it seems to want to freeze into ice, hard enough to skate upon, and pause at the moment of its sudden crystalline stillness. None of these can happen, but none of these possibilities will surrender to the others.

One of the places, one of the times, seems easy to specify. Bread Street, again; the most comfortingly memorable of dates, Christmas Eve; the most poised and precise of times, dawn, the sun about to rise. The place is domestic familiarity; the time, the comforting regularity of the still ticking clock.[1] John Milton, home for the holidays from Cambridge, where he has studied and lived for large parts of the past five years, shuttling back and forth during the long vacations that separate the three terms into which each year is divided, and doing so with increased freedom now that he has elected to stay on for graduate study and his time is less rigidly organised by the university and its teachers. He is pivoting from one stage of life to another, changing but not changing, lingering in and between the same spaces as before but, perhaps, experiencing them in a new way. One eye flits over the familiar sights and textures of home, its comforts and furnishings; the room is largely the same, but he is not.

Something is about to happen, perhaps is already happening. Outside, the dark, and a clear, soft silence. Few sounds drift up from the streets, the cries of tavern-goers and stall-holders mercifully hushed. But it's not silence: there is something at the back of it, a resonance; something that, if we were to call it a sound, it would only be because no better word suggested itself. Hard to say if it is difficult to apprehend because it is distant, coming from somewhere as far off as the sun that's about to rise, or because it is so close, rustling at the very back of the mind.

The other eye scours a landscape: follows its paths and byways, measures its length and breadth, winds through its valleys and hills. It lights upon a place – a hut, perhaps, or a cave, some sort of opening in the scenery where it can find a purchase. But it cannot dwell there: what it finds is a point of light, which no sooner draws the eye in than it threatens to sear it, blind it. It slides away. But the other creatures who dwell hereabouts are somehow no easier to gaze upon. There is only the smallest amount of human chatter, a clue that there might be people in the vicinity; other beings are glimpsed in the distance, strange creatures with eerily shining, almost metallic faces. Perfected versions of people, floating above the landscape, imposing but blank, their superhuman calm having ironed out all rumples of expressiveness. They too are drawn to the point of light, but seem to have less trouble with it – perhaps because their gaze is single-minded, undistractable. The eye finds itself drawn to the shadowy outer reaches of the landscape. Things prowl there. Some other kind of being's unseeing eye flashes as it lolls in a floating socket; a haunch of white marble frothed with a sheen of sweat; a shadow of brass, blackened with a layer of soot, scored with the clawings of tiny hands. The ground creaks as if a huge finger pushes it up from beneath. Yet all is silent; the eye, strangely, can hear, yet all it hears is – nothing; a strange kind of nothing, though, that feels as full as the stretched seams of time itself.

FIGURE 6: Demons lurk beneath the manger in one
of William Blake's drawings for Milton's Nativity Ode.

Not quite silent. There is one thing that promises to pull the two eyes, their disparate places and times, back together into some kind of binocular focus: the sort of sound, if sound it can be called, barely there yet everywhere, that belongs to both. The sound – how is this possible? – has a shape; it is shape; it *takes* shape. It begins to gather, to pattern. There but not there. Then but not then. The sun breaks the horizon. The words begin to come.

◆

I've never been too sure what to do with facts when we're lucky enough to have them. Here's an apparent fact: on the morning of Christmas Eve 1629, a little over a fortnight after his twenty-first birthday, John Milton composed a poem on the birth of Christ that's usually known, and to which I'll refer, as the Nativity Ode. No, even that is not quite right. What I can say is this: in 1645, when Milton collected most of the poems he'd written up to that point in his life into a volume for publication, the poem with which he chose to begin the collection was titled 'On the Morning of Christ's Nativity. Compos'd 1629'. Readers who made their way further into the volume and read the Latin elegy addressed to Milton's schoolfriend Charles Diodati would find there a more specific pinning down of when the Nativity Ode was written. Milton described his poem 'about the infant cries of God' and explained: 'These are the gifts I have given for Christ's birthday: the first light of the dawn [*sub auroram lux*] brought them to me.'[2] This is the date on which he wanted us to first encounter him as a poet.

A date! Not just a date, but a fairly specific time of day! When Milton published his early poems, some of them are precisely dated in this fashion, but others are left to float in time: they do not adhere to a particular moment. And a great deal of scholarly ink has been spilt on solving these puzzles: spearing the poems to a precise moment. But even dating a poem as clearly as Milton does with his Nativity Ode is a stranger act than it seems. Any given date is a mixture of the repeatable and the unrepeatable; the absolutely singular, and that which will roll round reliably again. There will never be another Christmas Eve 1629, but there will (probably) be many more Christmas Eves. The year 1629 is not so much the poem's point of origin as its point of *departure*, its setting out towards an annually repeated future. The poem begins: 'This is the month, and this the happy morn . . .' But to what does the simple, everyday word 'this' refer? To which *when* does it point? The actual day on which Christ was born? Or the one on which Milton wrote his poem? Or the one on which we read it, if we choose to do so on another Christmas Eve morning? Or do these three possibilities somehow crowd into the same space, the same set of simple words?

When Milton wrote the Nativity Ode he felt that he was arriving at a profound turning point in his life, but it was not clear just what it would involve or mean; he wrote the poem because he wanted it to *be*, to crystallise, this sense of a turning point, but also to offer his readers their own pivotal experience. He had emerged from his undergraduate studies at Cambridge surer of the paths in life that he did not want to follow – taking Holy Orders, which had been his default plan; the law, which would be the lifelong pursuit of his younger brother, Christopher – than which path he would choose. What had begun to rumble within him during these years was a deep and durable conviction that he was destined to write, and to write works that would have an abiding public significance. But it was uncertain what form these works would take, and when he would be ready to write them. He was *full*: full of learning, full of ideas, full of potential, charged to a point of heightened alertness and awareness, and yet wavering between states of mind, and states of vision.

My aim in this chapter is to try and do justice to this fullness and this wavering: to explore the tools and the materials with which Milton had equipped himself for the writing of this poem in the years since he left St Paul's, and to account for the position, in-between times and spaces, that his first great poem occupies. It's significantly different from previous chapters in that, while these have each begun with a moment or scene from Milton's life and brought in his writing in more darting and episodic ways, now, for the first time, I will reverse this balance. Instead I will put the imagined world and the imaginative experience of a single poem at the centre, and let the facts and events of Milton's life orbit around it. I'll spend more time than previously on the detailed workings of this poem, whose hallucinogenic strangeness I've striven above to capture – to inhabit. I'll stay with the Nativity Ode for the first half of what follows, then seek to locate it in the course of Milton's life, especially his experiences at Cambridge. But while I might need to ask for my reader's patience in slowing down in this way with the Nativity Ode, my central interest lies in what this poem does to time, to its time and to our time, and moving slowly with and through it is a different way of weaving together the rhythms of Milton's life and of his writings.

For reading Milton's work makes me return again and again, as I've already suggested, to the simple fact that writing and reading a poem both *take time*, and that the quality of those two times are closely entangled with one another. A poem, at its most basic, is an offering up of time spent as an appeal to spend some time; it is an opportunity to have one's time occupied, shaped, and changed by someone else's way of inhabiting and being inhabited by time. I want to take seriously the idea that Milton experienced – and wanted us, his readers, to experience – a meaningful connection between the hesitations, pauses, changes of pace and direction of his unfolding life as he sought to make sense of it, and the minute shifts and bumps and changes of texture in poetic language as he shaped it.

Time is out of joint from the very start of the Nativity Ode, shifting and unsettled. 'It was the Winter wild,' the poem proper begins, 'While the Heav'n-born-child, / All meanly wrapped in the rude manger lies'.³ It *was* winter and yet the child *lies* in the manger: why not *lay*? Why mix present and past in this subtle way? A tiny change that is also a huge one, a double take or hesitation that ensures that the reading experience is strange, bumpy, from the outset. It is never quite clear, in reading this poem, exactly *when* we are supposed to be.

This uncertainty, this hovering between now and then, might be more apt than is initially obvious to a modern reader. What did it mean for Milton to choose the birth of Christ as a poetic subject, at this point in his life and in English history? The Nativity Ode is not just a Christian poem, but a poem about the literal birth of Christianity. Usually, the biggest problem for modern readers of Milton's work is that it relies upon knowledge of a reservoir of Christian stories, phrases, and ideas, known implicitly and offhandedly, that is no longer widely shared. At least on the surface, however, that's not a problem with this poem: everyone knows, roughly speaking, about Christmas. And a modern reader of the Nativity Ode would find in it at least some of the stock figures of a modern Christmas scene: the 'star-led wizards', the wise men or Magi, who 'haste . . . upon the eastern road' with gifts; the 'shepherds on the lawn' who 'Sat simply chatting in a rustic row'; the 'Bright-harnessed angels' who 'sit in order serviceable' around the baby Jesus at the poem's end; everything but the ox and the ass.[4]

The relative familiarity of the Nativity scene is a red herring. We're liable to go wrong if we assume that, because we know the story, we're ready for the poem. We need to stand back from our silent assumption that religions consist principally of *traditions*, *stories*, and *beliefs*. In the same way that I've tried to reorient our sense of what artworks do – shaping and transforming time for us – I'd suggest that we might in a similar way think of religions not only in terms of the beliefs that they mandate or imply, or the traditions that they transmit, but via the *kinds of time* that their adherents occupy. In fact, one of the principal functions shared by most religions seems to be refusing the plodding homogeneity, the unrelenting sameness, of time itself, but instead dividing and organising it, charging certain moments with heightened significance. When I encounter a religiously observant person, I find myself wondering, what do you believe? What is it like to believe what you believe? But I also find myself pondering other things, posing questions in my mind that would feel very odd actually to ask, because we are so unused to thinking in these ways. Questions like: what is time like for you? What, for you, is the shape of a minute, an hour, a day, a year, a life?

Approaching the matter in this way can help me understand why I find the Nativity Ode so powerful, even though I don't happen to be Christian; I can engage with Milton's religious poem as a powerful way of organising, navigating, and intensifying time, even if I don't share his beliefs. The division of historical time into the periods BC and AD, while it is rightly being replaced by the less explicitly Christological terms BCE and CE, is an everyday reminder that the Incarnation of Christ was understood above all as a division, a cut or caesura, in time. Christians no longer exist in the kind of time occupied by Jews who still await the Messiah (other than heterodox Jews like my ancestors, who thought that he had arrived in the form of Shabsai Tzvi); they exist *in* messianic time, waiting not for the Messiah's appearance but his return. Jews, we might say, exist in a *before*-time relative to the Messiah, whereas Christians exist in a *between*-time, in which the transformative event that is expected and awaited is the Second Coming and the Apocalypse, the end of the world that is at once its destruction and its purification. Time begins anew when Christ is born, but it effectively *begins to end* when he is crucified.[5] From this strange position of in-betweenness arises one of the basic dilemmas with which Christians in all ages have had to struggle: does human time become more valuable once it's been graced with divine presence by the Incarnation? Should every instant of the messianic between-times be treasured and turned to good? Or is human time rendered basically empty and worthless as a period of mere waiting, seeing out the clock before Christ returns and the long in-betweenness of the Christian era comes to a terrible and magnificent end?

I am very drawn to this problem of how to live in the between-time, which gives me a way to understand the central struggles of Milton's mind and writings. I ended the last chapter by suggesting that Milton's schooling led him to exist in a space between languages; a space full of possibility but far from comfortable. What distinguishes Milton for me is his set of powerfully incompatible responses to dwelling *in between*, and his ability to write in ways that capture and grow from these responses. He seems to want on the one hand to flee towards clarity, the clarity of clear divisions and distinctions, the clarity of Apocalypse that would bring the in-between time to an end; but he is also drawn to the in-between, led to dwell delight-edly in the realm of uncertainty, the *neither here nor there*, the *not yet*. We can find later writers who describe this space clearly, and it belongs to no single religion or philosophical school. Indeed, perhaps one way to understand religions and philosophies is as varying responses to the problems and attractions of in-betweenness itself. For the Jewish philosopher Martin Buber, the arrival of the Messiah 'becomes ever nearer, increasingly near to the sphere that lies *between beings*' – this is the sphere in which we must find a way to exist, together, until that divine arrival. The poet Rainer Maria Rilke refers in his *Duino Elegies* to a *Zwischenraum*, a space between, a wonderful word which is itself a play on the German term for an interim period, a *Zwischenzeit*, or *time between*: this is the space, and the time, in which Milton's Nativity Ode strains to reside.[6]

Remember that Milton wrote his poem, he told Diodati, as he glimpsed *sub auroram lux*, the light of dawn: suddenly it seems no accident that this is the time of day when the poem was begun. When else could a mind poised in this manner have begun to find expression but at the point when one state gives way to another, darkness to light, sleep to wakefulness – this finely balanced, wavering moment of the day; this time of in-between time?

The later sections of the Nativity Ode suggest that dwelling in *Zwischenzeit* and *Zwischenraum* was, as the twenty-one-year-old Milton bequeaths it to his readers, a delicate struggle, requiring acts of mental contortion. Milton's poetic voice allows itself to imagine the spectral sounds that fill the poem reversing the course of historical events themselves:

> *For if such holy Song*
> *Enwrap our fancy long,*
> *Time will run back, and fetch the age of gold . . .*

The longer final line, imagining the golden age restored, wants to stretch the music out a moment more, dilating time in the hope of reversing it. But no sooner is this possibility glimpsed than it is dismissed:

> *But wisest fate says no,*
> *This must not yet be so,*
> *The babe lies yet in smiling infancy,*
> *That on the bitter cross*
> *Must redeem our loss . . .*[7]

Suddenly the shorter lines seem chastening, curt: *not yet*. We remain rooted, or mired, in the between-times. Milton imagines perfection restored only to push it away into an imagined future. The language of time becomes particularly compressed and contorted at this crucial point: 'And then at last our bliss / Full and perfect is, / But now begins'. Milton imagines a perfected future, but says, oddly, that *then* it *is* – not that then it *will be*. When he says that it *now begins*, he must presumably mean the *now* of Christ's birth, the moment that he is describing, not the moment in which he is writing. It is no clearer when he, the poet, is than when we are supposed to be. But there's good reason for these difficulties, these loud grindings of the gears of time. The coming of Christ is the moment at which an eternal God saw fit to enter the time-bound realm of human existence, and thereby transform it. It is the moment where time and the timeless collide; where God's timelessness, which philosophers described as a *nunc stans* – a standing, perpetual now – enters the shifting flux of human time, its ticking sequence of disappearing nows.[8] *But now begins*: what this means, however, how to respond to this advent and live in the in-betweenness that it inaugurates, remains unclear.

The immediate effect of Christ's birth is the heavenly music that is distantly heard, that ripples across the world of the poem. From its opening the Nativity Ode is obsessed with sound and its absence, awash with music, the residue of Milton's musical childhood. The pure music of the planetary spheres that joins its 'ninefold harmony' to 'heaven's deep organ' in order to 'Make up full consort to th'Angelike symphony' is a purified, celestial version of Milton's father and his friends, playing together on Bread Street.[9] 'The air such pleasure loth to lose, / With thousand echoes still prolongs each heav'nly close': the twelve-syllable line tries desperately to perform what it describes, to make the description of this gorgeous sound last just a second longer, to stretch it out in vibrating time as the air itself would like to do.[10]

It is not the only spectral sound in the poem: the barely heard music contrasts with the fading after-echoes of dwindling, eerie sounds. Christ's coming was often understood as an ending as well as a beginning, the time at which the oracles of the pagan world fell suddenly silent, and Milton spins this idea into a grisly pageant of newly mute demons and false gods which reaches a crescendo at the end of the poem:

> *The oracles are dumb,*
> *No voice or hideous hum*
> *Runs through the arched roof in words deceiving.*
> *Apollo from his shrine*
> *Can no more divine,*
> *With hollow shriek the steep of Delphos leaving.*
> *No nightly trance, or breathed spell,*
> *Inspires the pale-eyed priest from the prophetic cell.*[11]

From the start of the poem we've been asked to think in terms of what's *not* heard – 'No war, or battle's sound / Was heard the world around' – as if the lack of war and battle is a kind of negative noise, and audible silence.[12] This is what is left when the oracles and the ancient gods fall silent. They leave with moans and clatters, the heavenly music wafting away the last remnants of their 'drear, and dying sound' – both a sound that is dying and also a sound of something as it dies – but the poem is still haunted by the demonic presences whose defeat it narrates. It suggests that we still hear something of what was once there in the particular silence that it leaves behind. As if there might, as Paul Goodman wonderfully suggests, be many kinds of silence:

> the dumb silence of slumber and apathy; the sober silence that goes with a solemn animal face; the fertile silence of awareness, pasturing the soul, whence emerge new thoughts . . . the noisy

silence of resentment and self-recrimination, loud with subvocal speech but sullen to say it; baffled silence; the silence of peaceful accord with other persons or communion with the cosmos.[13]

◆

The hope that 'Time will run back' to a lost golden age is given short shrift in the Nativity Ode, as we saw; the poem rushes ahead of itself even as it rushes back to the start of a new time; it cannot settle in the in-between time that Christ's arrival inaugurates. The poem's restless *when* is what allows it to shape and jolt my own time, my experiences as a non-Christian reader; but its precise dawn composition means that it also demands to be placed more locally within Milton's life, and it's to this that I now turn. I began by saying that Milton felt himself to be *full* at this point in his life – full of learning, full of undirected potential – and, as we saw, the word appears in his poem: 'our bliss / Full and perfect is'. In fact, the language of fullness was a well-established way of describing the effects of the Incarnation. As St Paul put it, 'when the fullness of time was come, God sent forth his son, made of a woman': it's as if time itself, rather than the Virgin Mary, is pregnant, swelling with divine presence, as the collision between the eternal and the time-bound fills time to bursting.[14] Just a few months before Milton wrote the Nativity Ode, a volume was published in London, a posthumous collection of sermons by Lancelot Andrewes, the learned bishop who had been the pre-eminent preacher in England until his death in 1626. It contained two sermons which ruminated extensively on this fullness of time. These sermons had both been delivered on Christmas Day before King James I, one in 1609 and the other in 1623, and both danced and weaved in Andrewes's characteristic style around the idea of time's fullness, picking apart every nuance of the biblical verses they took as their focus. Christmas, Andrewes insists, is 'a yeerly representation of the fulnesse of time', and our pious celebration of it should echo and repeat this fullness: 'The time, of [God's] Bounty-fulnesse' is recapitulated in 'the time, of our Thanke-fulness'.[15]

There's every reason to think that Milton was aware of these sermons, not just because he at times echoes them closely, but because while an undergraduate student at Cambridge he had written a Latin elegy to mark Andrewes's death.[16] Engaging with Andrewes through the unstable time of his Nativity poem also meant revisiting his own recent past, his student experiences and writings. But it's important to recognise that the 1629 publication of Andrewes's sermons was a far from innocent event. It had been undertaken and overseen by William Laud, then bishop of London, at a crucial point in his rise to a position of extraordinary dominance over the English Church, which was to last for the next decade. Laud pursued a fervently held vision of a national church rooted in what he believed to be its true and ancient traditions, under-written by powerful ecclesiastical and royal authority, expressed and reinforced by collective rituals carried out in ornate and magnificent church buildings.[17] To its many opponents, the Laudian programme was nothing less than a diabolic attempt to reinstate the popery that a series of English monarchs had painstakingly sought to eradicate in the preceding century.

Laud's aim in publishing Andrewes's sermons was to lay claim to a pious predecessor, and present himself as a perpetuator of the finest traditions. It was part of a wider programme on the part of Laud and his followers that would prove astonishingly effective in respect of the short-term dominance that they achieved, but that, in the longer term, would lead to great volatility and instability. When James I ascended the English throne, in 1603, he inherited a situation in which there was a dominant tone and style of religion, influenced above all by the austere theology of John Calvin, which argued for the divine predestination of all human souls, and the absolute inscrutability of God's eternal will to limited and time-bound human understandings. Yet there were also counter-currents, perpetuated by Andrewes and others, which placed greater emphasis on ceremonies and sacraments as crucial ways of honouring God, and which seemed to their opponents like a terrible relapse to the ways of the pre-Reformation Church. James, long ridiculed by historians as inept and capricious, proved deftly able to juggle and balance these competing positions and visions of the Church, ensuring that none could claim undue dominance.

When Milton sat down to write his Nativity Ode, however, he did so at the end of a decade during which this fragile edifice of religious compromise had finally collapsed, intertwined as it was with James's other great effort at compromise – his attempt in the final months of his life to retain a neutral position outside the religious wars that were ripping Europe apart. The wars that James's son Charles and his favourite, the Duke of Buckingham, were determined to wage in the 1620s required the grant of money by Parliament. When a series of parliaments were called, however, they proved less pliable than Charles had anticipated, and were resolved to scrutinise and dispute various aspects of royal power and prerogative, and to demand guarantees regarding the liberties of individual subjects in return for the money requested. In March 1625, mere weeks after Milton matriculated as a student at Christ's College, Cambridge, King James died, and Charles succeeded to the throne, soon thereafter marrying the teenaged French princess Henrietta Maria. This was quite an astute political decision since it promised an alliance with France against Spanish power, but it was disastrous for Charles's short-lived credentials as a Protestant hero, now that London was filled with the new queen's retinue of Roman Catholic priests and courtiers. Despite the marriage, Buckingham soon dragged England into an expensive and unwinnable war against France, and he continued to be attacked in Parliament as an incompetent who wielded excessive power over the new king, and as someone who was possibly a crypto-Catholic. In 1628, preparing for another naval expedition to France, Buckingham was stabbed to death in Portsmouth by a disaffected former sailor, and his death was greeted with an outpouring of jubilation that shocked and appalled Charles.

Another parliament was called in the early months of 1629, but it collapsed dramatically and acrimoniously in March when the MPs continued to criticise the controversial mechanisms by which Charles had extracted funds for war from the populace – most notoriously the 'forced loan' of 1626 – and the rise to dominance of Laud and

his faction, known as Arminians because their emphasis on ceremonial elaborateness and the potential redemption of the human
will was influenced by the Dutch theologian Jacobus Arminius.[18] In
a famous and dramatic scene when the Speaker of the House was
physically held down in his chair (his standing up would have brought
the session to an end), Sir John Eliot, one of the leaders of the
anti-court, Puritan-leaning group in Parliament, read and passed
resolutions which condemned 'innovations in religion' (on the part
of Laud and his followers) and the custom duties the king had
imposed. He and the other parliamentary ringleaders were imprisoned, and Parliament would not be reconvened for another eleven
years: Charles I's so-called 'Personal Rule' had begun.

I've felt the need to briefly rehearse these remarkable events because
they formed the backdrop against which Milton began seriously to
write, and to think of himself as a writer. The composition of the
Nativity Ode at dawn, its strained attempt to inhabit a distinctive
and unsettling kind of wavering in-betweenness, looks different
against this backdrop: English political and religious life in 1629
seemed itself to be poised at an in-between moment of uncertain
transformation, wavering between forms of government, authority,
and political and religious organisation.[19] The way in which time
itself was organised and understood, as the publication of Andrewes's
sermons on time's fullness that year makes clear, was not an abstract
question but a matter of intense dispute, on which different visions
of the organised Church and its relationship with the individual
believer might hang. But, having said all this, I also need to acknowledge that Milton's precise relationship to this religious and
political backdrop is remarkably difficult to specify. No period of
his life has been more contested by Milton's biographers than this
one: did he keep his head down, busy himself with intellectual and
poetic distractions, and conform, whether thinkingly or unthinkingly, to the dominant trends of thought and belief? Or was he
already becoming a radical, already beginning to think through the
positions that would ultimately set him at odds with every established form of religion and politics?

It's a difficult and ultimately impossible question to answer, not least because it relies on a distinction between intrinsically conventional and radical ideas which I find unhelpful. What interests me are the resources – not just the specific ideas but the habits of thought, the patterns of imagination – with which Milton equipped himself, which he later put to extraordinary use, and which I find myself drawn to explore and inhabit when I read him. But there are more specific reasons to be wary of deriving Milton's religious and political views from the poems, including the Nativity Ode, which were composed during the years of Laud's rise to power. The London in which Milton wrote his poem was a paranoid place – a place in which clergymen and ordinary people had specifically and repeatedly been warned against engaging with controversial religious questions, and in which Laud quietly but decisively clamped down on any nascent signs of radicalism. In March 1629 two anonymous papers were found in front of John Donne's house by St Paul's Cathedral which were effectively Puritan death threats aimed at Laud – who was warned to 'look to thyself; be assured thy life is sought' – and the Lord Treasurer, Richard Weston.[20] Another anonymous libel against the king, possibly by a female prophet, was posted on St Paul's Cross at about the same time.[21] This was Milton's neighbourhood, the backdrop of his childhood. He wrote the Nativity Ode in a febrile atmosphere of anonymous threats and the quietly authoritarian responses that they provoked, where friends and neighbours had reason both to scrutinise one another and to conceal their true beliefs. If Milton's radicalism seems to exist only in ambiguous hints, this could be because it did not yet exist – or because this was, at the time, the most prudent way to articulate subversive opinions.[22]

Certainly on the surface, nothing could seem more quietist, more conformist, than Milton's activities in these years. He went to Cambridge in 1625 to study, and encountered a course of learning that built upon and expanded both the content and the techniques of the education he'd received at St Paul's. He gradually began to master the rituals and the opportunities of the place, going on to deliver a series of public speeches in Latin on both serious and frivolous topics, flaunting his erudition and his ability to be puerile and rambunctious when the occasion called for it. He also began to seize opportunities to write Latin poetry for public consumption, writing pieces to mark the deaths not just of Lancelot Andrewes, as already mentioned, but also of the university's vice-chancellor, John Gostlin, and another bishop, Nicholas Felton. His earliest surviving original English poem, written in the winter of 1625/6, commemorated the loss of his infant niece to a cough, and so his earliest poetic forays were intertwined with and responsive to death in all its time-bound and untimely forms. He also wrote a series of Latin poems remembering the 1605 Gunpowder Plot, tying himself, like Andrewes in his sermons, to the royal calendar of remembrance and celebration. The longest and most ambitious, 'In Quintum Novembris', included his first sustained attempt to imagine Satan, who 'glides through the calm air on wings as black as pitch' ('*piceis liquido natat aere pennis*') across the Alps to Rome, where he injects into the brain of the sleeping Pope the foul plot that King James would escape.

Though he initially seemed to have enjoyed student life well enough, calling Cambridge 'the haunts of the Muses' in letters to friends, in the longer term he rarely had much of a good word to say about the place: neither the town itself, his fellow students, whom he described as 'almost completely unlearned in Philology and Philosophy alike', nor his teachers, whom he saw as mired in 'monkish and miserable sophistry'.[23] And it's certainly possible to construct a vision of life at Christ's College – an eccentric, sealed-off enclave in a damp backwater of a fenland town – which seems pretty grim. The college was run and its teaching undertaken by a master and thirteen fellows – all unmarried men who had taken Holy Orders – and each student was assigned one fellow as a tutor, in whose rooms he typically lived, sharing a bed with another student. The dubious charms of the place are captured by the fact that the temporary wooden building constructed around 1613 to deal with the problem of overcrowding was known, by the time Milton arrived at the college, as Rats' Hall.[24]

It's likely that arriving at Christ's would have felt like an extension of Milton's schooldays, but with his behaviour, his mind, and the ways that he spent and organised his time even more rigorously controlled. University picked up where school left off: the first year devoted to rhetoric, followed by two years of logic, and then moral philosophy and natural philosophy (physics, cosmology, and related subjects) in the fourth and final year, all taught via the finest classical authorities and their most learned and pious Christian expositors. Many of the works encountered at school recurred, many of the habits of mind inculcated there – repetition, memorisation, breaking texts down into parts to understand them and turn them into ready-packaged wisdom – returned, and were deepened and broadened. If this was how things worked year to year, it was underpinned by an extraordinary degree of day-to-day micromanagement, in both time and space: students were to speak Latin at all times within the college walls, and they were to leave these walls as seldom as possible, doing so only with a friend and with their tutor's permission – Christ's even employed a barber and a washerwoman to reduce the need to walk abroad. By 5 a.m. each day students were gathered for prayer in the chapel, and university lectures filled the morning, with breakfast and lunch eaten communally. The afternoons were freer, in theory, but Christ's required additional teaching by the fellows before service in chapel at 6 p.m., supper in hall, and the gates to be locked at 8 p.m., or an hour later in summer.[25]

These arrangements not only ensured orderliness in time and space but also reflected a rigidly hierarchical social order that was reinforced at every communal meal. Students were divided into categories: the richest and most socially elevated, the Fellow Commoners, had the (no doubt dubious) privilege of eating with the fellows; the poorest, the Sizars, would partly earn their keep by serving food at table to the Fellow Commoners and the middle group, the Pensioners, to which Milton belonged. It's easy to see how this intensely regulated set-up might produce a strange mixture of claustrophobia and loneliness, of always being with others and always feeling alone. When Desiderius Erasmus, architect of the curriculum and ethos at St Paul's School, moved to Cambridge in the early sixteenth century, he complained loudly to friends about the low quality of the fellows' intellect and the local beer, calling it 'a snail's life. We shrink and hide ourselves indoors, and are as busy as bees in study. There is a great solitude here, most people away for fear of plague; though when all are here it is still a solitude.'[26] Four centuries later William Empson, who wrote with piercing and eccentric brilliance about Milton's poetry while decrying his Christian theology, was thrown out of Magdalene College for the crime of being caught owning condoms as a young fellow, and wrote a wry poem which captured the feel of the college as a place of quiet but relentless surveillance: 'Remember what a porter's for; / He hears *ad portam*, at the door'; 'See where the chaste good dons in rows / (A squinting, lily-like repose) / Have heard more tattle than one knows'. Like Erasmus four centuries earlier, Cambridge for Empson was a 'strange cackling little town' where one is always lonely but never alone, always potentially seen, spied upon.[27]

Milton's relationship with this unobtrusive yet utterly rigid surveillance system would prove to be just as uneasy as Empson's three centuries later – or so, at least, some tantalising but inconclusive evidence suggests. John Aubrey, in notes gleaned from discussions with Milton's younger brother Christopher, wrote of the former's time at Cambridge that 'His 1st Tutor there was Mr Chapell, from whom receiving some unkindnesse, he was afterwards (though it seemed against the Rules of the College[)] transferred to the Tuition of one Mr Tovell.' Subsequently, above the words 'some unkindnesse', Aubrey added the words: 'whipp't him'.[28] The rhythms of learning and flogging still seemed to beat in parallel in Christ's – though, if this was the case, it would have been much less standard than a routine schoolroom beating, for students were whipped only on rare occasions, and not usually by their tutors. When Milton described himself in the opening lines of his elegy for Lancelot Andrewes as sitting sad, alone, and silent (*'Moestus eram, et tacitus nullo comitante sedebam'*), it seems reasonable to assume that he was referring not just to the grief for the dead bishop that he was busy professing but also to his own sense of beleaguered isolation.

Or is it entirely reasonable? I need to acknowledge that I'm not a neutral party here: I was a student in Cambridge (at Sidney Sussex, founded as a Puritan seminary at the end of the sixteenth century, and just a few hundred yards from Christ's), and I've spent my working life to date teaching in comparable colleges in Cambridge and Oxford. They certainly can be very strange places, refuges for wilful eccentricity and bad behaviour, for minor intrigue and petty resentments that can fester through the decades among people living and working in vague and constant proximity. But as institutions they tend to attract idealising and derisory exaggeration in equal measure. As my citation of Erasmus, alone with his thoughts and his watery beer, suggests, to disparage the climactic and intellectual dreariness of Cambridge was a long-standing mini genre in its own right. If Milton's world there can appear very closed and parochial, and his time ferociously managed, there is another side to the story. Milton was much less bound to Cambridge, physically or mentally, than the sketch I've just given might lead us to expect. His poems and letters from this period show how frequently he moved back and forth from London. He wrote a Latin poem to Charles Diodati claiming that he was enjoying himself with his books in London and was 'not anxious to visit the reedy Cam', and in 1625, 'at London among the petty distractions of the city', he wrote poems and letters in Latin to his former tutor Thomas Young, who had gifted him a Hebrew Bible in his youth. Young was now chaplain to the English Merchants in Hamburg, and was therefore perched in the midst of the unfolding Thirty Years War.

Most intriguingly, he kept in contact with Alexander Gil the Younger, continuing their 'almost constant conversations'.[29] Gil would become mired in controversy while Milton was maintaining their friendship, in a manner that confirms both the surveillance culture that prevailed in university colleges and the way in which national politics permeated their walls. In August 1628, days after the assassination of the Duke of Buckingham, Gil was drinking with friends in the cellar of Trinity College, Oxford, when he proposed a toast to Buckingham's killer, John Felton, and apparently mocked the king himself, saying that he had been 'led so long by the Duke': 'we have a fine wise king,' he unwisely continued, 'he has wit enough to be a shopkeeper to ask "what do you lack" and that is all.'[30] Gil's words, reducing Charles's thoughts to the cries of common stall-holders, were overheard by William Chillingworth, a fellow of the college who was, unfortunately for Gil, Archbishop Laud's godson (Chillingworth would go on to become an important theologian in his own right). He reported Gil, who was dragged from his school-room in September, imprisoned in the Tower, and sentenced to a huge fine and to have his ears cut off, one at Oxford, one in London.[31] It was only thanks to his father's desperate petitions that Gil escaped this grisly fate. Milton wrote nothing about these events, but his friend and former teacher's travails suggested the impact that loose words spoken within the confines of a college could have.

There are examples of these connections between college and national affairs closer to home, however, particularly in the person of a man who Milton must, at the very least, have known in passing, but whom we sadly have no evidence that he knew in person – the most eminent intellectual among the Christ's College fellows, Joseph Mede. Mede seems in some ways to embody the cloistered, cerebral habits of the quintessential college man: he came to Christ's as a student in 1603 and never left, devoting himself to the study of ancient languages and arcane scriptural questions, and studiously avoiding involvement in the theological disputes that were beginning to rip English society apart. But this picture is incomplete for two reasons. First, Mede put his scholarship to bold use, in ways that made it seem altogether less *recherché*. In 1627, while Milton was studying at Christ's, Mede published his magnum opus, *Clavis Apocalyptica*, in which he set out to interpret the notoriously elliptical descriptions of the end of the world from the Book of Revelations as an opaque but nonethe-less literal and decodable account of the Apocalypse, which he tentatively predicted would transpire in 1736.[32] The work, initially published in complicated Latin for a limited readership, was gradually translated into English and widely disseminated, and became a sensation. As the century went on, groups of radical Protestants tried to enlist its learning for their own apocalyptic predictions, and it paralleled Milton's own emerging views in various ways, not least in its denunciation of the Pope as Antichrist, and Mede's interest in the nature, habits, and even the nutrition of angels.[33]

Mede himself, however, resisted attempts to put his erudition to revolutionary use, insisting that 'I live in the university' where those who 'offer to meddle in ought that concerns the Publick . . . is taken notice of for Factious and a Busie-body'.[34] A wide range of English Protestants believed in the relative imminence of the end times, and so the belief in itself was not radical. Writing a short biography of Mede in 1662, Thomas Fuller was right when he wrote that 'the furious Factors for the fift[h] Monarchy' – among the most radical of the sects who emerged in the revolutionary years – 'hath driven that Nail which Master Mede did first enter, farther than he ever intended it, and doing it with such violence, that they split the truths round about it.'[35] Whether or not Mede helped tap the apocalyptic nail into Milton's mind as well, the crucial point is that Fuller's words abolish any absolute distinction between orthodox and radical, learned and popular, cloistered and worldly, when it comes to the movement and metamorphosis of ideas: the relationship is much more porous, the uses to which ideas can be put much less predictable.

Fuller makes clear in other ways that Mede's life was more varied than his careful self-image as a university scholar suggests: 'Of one who constantly kept his *Cell*, (so he called his *Chamber*),' Fuller notes, 'none Travailed oftener and farther over all Christendome.'[36] This is hyperbole, but certainly Mede travelled with great frequency between Cambridge and London and managed to be staggeringly well informed about domestic and international politics. Throughout the 1620s he wrote letters to his friend Sir Martin Stuteville – whose son he tutored at Christ's – crammed with carefully collated local and national gossip. In one of his letters he fills the front of the page with news of events in Parliament, of the arguments between the new king and his young French queen, who is 'very little of stature . . . but full of spirit & vigour', and at the bottom of the page he writes: 'This is such news as I have . . . will you heare what Cambridge affords on the other side of the leafe?'[37] At other times he proved he was well aware that what might seem like trivial college wranglings were in fact embedded in, and reflected, national politics – the local was not merely local. In November 1626 he wrote to Stuteville about the scuffles at Caius College following the death of the master, noting that the affair 'is like to produce some strange precedents to the utter overthrow of all elections of masters forever'.[38] Both the university as a whole and each of the individual colleges were complex ecosystems with competing religious factions, and this meant that, far from being a provincial refuge from the wider disputes that were breaking out in the country, Cambridge was a microcosm of them. Charles, the Duke of Buckingham, and Archbishop Laud all sought to impose their visions of the Church and of social order on the university, and met with both eager collaboration and fierce resistance.[39] The way in which colleges organised worship in their chapels, the level of ceremony that they observed, and the nature and position of the communion table were all ways of conspicuously endorsing – or thumbing a collective nose at – the Established Church as it took shape under Laud and Charles's control.

Mede's letters show the way in which, within the pressured atmosphere of the time that Milton was at Cambridge, events that might strike us now as either weird curiosities or scholarly minutiae were loaded with heightened religious and political significance. In the summer of 1626 a fish was gutted in the market at Cambridge and a half-digested religious book was found within its abdomen. Mede witnessed its emergence himself and identified the book in question, writing avidly to Stuteville: 'I send my Lady the Fish-book bound in the same order it was taken out of the Fishes belly.'[40] The debates about what this bizarre discovery meant, however, got mixed up with wider discussions of portents and omens – including an earthquake in March 1626 and a storm in London that washed corpses from their graves – that might have suggested God's anger at the state of England, with its king in thrall to his hated favourite Buckingham and his Catholic wife; how one interpreted the 'Fish-book' became a sign of one's political stance.[41]

The following year a Dutchman named Isaac Dorislaus arrived at Cambridge to take up a newly endowed professorship of history. Dorislaus chose to lecture on the Roman historian Tacitus – to modern eyes, not the most controversial of choices. But in fact it was explosive: Tacitus had discussed the basis of republican government, of civil liberty, and the grounds on which tyranny could be resisted, and had influenced the feared and admired political philosophy of Machiavelli. Dorislaus presented the Roman's thought in the boldest of terms, endorsing his claim that it is better 'to live with the inconveniences of liberty than to live as slaves subject to the offensive pride of kings'.[42] The lectures were a sensation and a scandal: Laud's allies in Cambridge complained to him, his foes defended Dorislaus, and finally the Dutchman was prevented from lecturing. He would eventually participate in the prosecution of Charles I, putting into practice the resistance to tyrants that he'd advocated at Cambridge, and was shortly afterwards stabbed to death in The Hague by English royalists while on a diplomatic mission.[43] The fact that mere lectures on Roman history could allow such dangerous opinions to be aired and debated can help us make sense of the later attempt by the philosopher Thomas Hobbes to blame the outbreak of the English Civil Wars on the universities, which, he insisted, were 'the core of rebellion' and 'have been to this nation, as the wooden horse was to the Trojans', since the teaching of 'arguments for liberty out of the works of Aristotle, Plato, Cicero, Seneca, and out of the histories of Rome and Greece' had been allowed to infect the minds of the gentry.[44] By no means was everyone with a classical education a radical – but such an education was far from intrinsically conservative, and could fuel the convictions of those who would resist a tyrannical monarch in the most violent ways.

When I taught in Cambridge I would take my students to the Wren Library, and, after we'd gawped at Milton's famous manuscript, I would show them a set of student notebooks from the 1640s that had lain hidden beneath floorboards until they were rediscovered during renovations in the 1970s. They contain a mixture of school and undergraduate notes on both religious and secular topics. It seems that they were passed on to newly arrived students, who were supposed to have internalised everything that they learned at school but could probably use a reminder. The notebooks were a comforting reminder that not everyone in the seventeenth century had Latin, or a memory, like Milton's: the notebooks have now been restored, and, while I'm glad they can now be more easily read, I admit that I pine for the wonderfully warped, water-damaged, and mouse-chewed state in which I first encountered them, a reminder of the waves of time that had washed over them while they lay quietly beneath the floorboards, and the warps and rumples that they left behind.

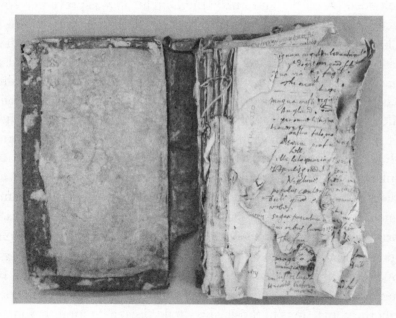

FIGURE 7: One of the student notebooks from the 1640s, before it was restored.

Milton was often happy to present himself as a run-of-the-mill student of the sort who used these notebooks: in a disputation attacking scholastic philosophy, he played to his audience, yawning at 'the pages of those vast and ponderous tomes of our professors of so-called exactitude' slaving away, like Mede, in their 'monkish cells'. In another, asking whether substance can be resolved into prime matter, he said that he preferred 'marvelous stories of ghosts and hobgoblins' to such monkish philosophy, whose arguments he was forced to rehearse: 'I cannot tell whether I have bored you, but I have certainly bored myself to extinction.'[45] His poems and speeches also show, however, that university learning exposed Milton for the first time to complex accounts of the human body and soul, of the heavens, and of time itself. The course of learning there was far less arid than he mockingly presents it, and left a deeper impact upon him than he's willing to acknowledge. A figure like the German Bartholomeus Keckermann, a prolific writer of textbooks, built on Aristotle's work to produce brilliant insights into the way in which the human soul is far from timeless and self-aware, but rather tangled up in the habits and desires of the body, endlessly distractable, playing out an internal drama of knowing and unknowing, and, when it is able to know itself, able as well to take great pleasure ('*voluptas*') in so doing.[46] It's impossible to pin Milton to one philosophical position at this early point in his life. Rather, his university writings show he was already mastering the art that he would go on to perfect in his later poems – not rejecting norms and conventions that he found stifling, but mastering them gleefully and energetically and turning them to his own purposes.[47] His mind darts in unexpected directions: his consideration of 'Whether Day or Night be the Most Excellent?' allows him both to delve into the eerily archaic myths to which he would return in *Paradise Lost* – 'Demogorgon, the ancestor of all the gods (whom I suppose to be identical with the Chaos of the ancients)' – and to glance at more recent phenomena that had come to light through European colonisation: 'to the Sun too, we are told, the American Indians even to this day make sacrifice with incense and with every kind of ritual.'[48]

And at times, amidst the intellectual carnival that Cambridge at least periodically became, we can catch glimpses of the later Milton, not just his interests but also his habits of mind and self-presentation. We encounter the same uncertain, poised alertness that I feel whenever I reread the Nativity Ode, the wandering sideways and backwards in time and space, a willingness to be destabilised rather than a will to control. He's there especially in the attack on Scholastic philosophy when Milton encourages his listeners to tear their minds from their learned books and

> let your eyes wander as it were over all the lands depicted on the map, and to behold the places trodden by the heroes of old, to range over the regions made famous by wars, by triumphs, and even by the tales of poets of renown, now to traverse the stormy Adriatic, now to climb unharmed the slopes of fiery Etna, then to spy out the customs of mankind and those states that are well-ordered . . . And do not shrink from taking your flight into the skies and gazing upon the manifold shapes of the clouds, the mighty piles of snow, and the source of the dew of morning; then inspect the coffers wherein the hail is stored and examine the arsenals of the thunderbolts. And do not let the intent of Jupiter or of Nature elude you, when a huge and fearful comet threatens to set the heavens aflame, nor let the smallest star escape you of all the myriads which are scattered and strewn between the poles: yes, even follow close upon the sun in all his journeys, and ask account of time itself and demand the reckoning of its eternal passage.[49]

A soaring, spiralling, looping flight, sideways across the surface of the earth and upward towards the heavens, a mind that dilates outward as far as it can take itself in every direction so that it can retract, back to where it started, but with a new sense of its own being: the mind that Milton both desires and wants his audience to desire. This expansive, exploratory flight is not without dangers: some of its topography resembles, as I mentioned earlier, the way made by Satan across the Alps in Milton's mini epic on the Gunpowder Plot written around the same time, and his very different Satan in *Paradise Lost* will be one of literature's great soarers and swoopers, and manage to implant a desire to do the same in Eve. But just because it's a dangerous and corruptible desire – to aspire to move mind, body, and imagination in this way – doesn't mean that it's the wrong one. Only through this kind of inspired, exuberant exercise of the mind, Milton tells his audience, is it possible to break out of the stasis, the paralysis, that is induced by too much of the wrong kind of learning: inundated with monkish philosophies, 'the student hesitates, as at a cross-roads, in doubt whether to turn or what direction to choose, and unable to make any decision'.[50]

When, at dawn on Christmas Eve in 1629, Milton began the Nativity Ode, I think he remembered this speech, delivered sometime in the preceding two years. In the poem too he sought to 'ask account of time itself and demand the reckoning of its eternal passage'. But, rather than doing this via the wild exercise of the learned imagination, as he had earlier urged his Cambridge audience to do, he wrote a poem that, in its shadowy cast of vanishing demons and idols, its flickering between time frames, its composition at dawn at a turning point in the ritual year, itself 'hesitates, as at a cross-roads, in doubt whether to turn or what direction to choose'. In doing this he managed, for the first time in his life, to make startling and haunting poetry out of this hesitation. The poem that hovers in the in-between of Christian time, a time that I will never occupy for myself, is the first of Milton's great poems, by which I really mean the first of his poems that truly matters to me; that I return to again and again; that has become part of my own rhythms, of my time.

It was not yet clear to Milton himself, however, whether writing this poem would end his hesitation – what kind of future, as a writer and as a person, it suggested for him. It would prove a turning point, but, as we'll see, it was a turning that would be slow and difficult, and have multiple stopping points along its creaking arc. The problem was, and would for some time remain, one of vocation, understood in its literal and etymological sense as a calling: what was Milton *called* to do and to be? The Nativity Ode clarified rather than solved the problem, because the most obvious answer – to do more of the same, to devote himself to devotional poetry, and continue marking the heaviest beats in the rhythm of Christian time – would quickly prove a dead end.

Before long – perhaps as soon as a few months afterwards – Milton tried writing a follow-up to the Nativity Ode, an Easter poem to mark Christ's death titled 'The Passion'. He used the same metre and rhyme scheme that he'd chosen for the introductory section of the earlier poem, and got fifty-six lines in before abandoning it. When Milton published his poems in 1645 he made the fascinating decision not to suppress his youthful misfire, but to include 'The Passion' with a note: 'This subject the author finding to be above the years he had when he wrote it, and nothing satisfied with what was begun, left it unfinished.'[51] Why would a poet putting his gathered efforts before the world as a claim to significance, even greatness, flaunt his failure in this fashion? It could be false modesty, a promise to do better at a later date: 'above the years he had when he wrote it' suggests it will eventually be within his grasp. But this is hard to accept, given that when Milton eventually wrote *Paradise Lost*, there too he turned swiftly away from the spectacle of the Crucifixion: when the Angel Michael shows Adam a panorama of subsequent human history he describes Christ 'nailed to the Cross / By his own Nation, slain for bringing life; / But to the cross he nails thy enemies'.[52] The literal nailing is barely glanced at, brushed aside: the Crucifixion is all triumph, no pain and gore. What this decision shows, I think, is Milton's emerging conviction that to engage with the central scenes and tenets of Christianity could not involve passive acceptance. The spectacles of Christ's birth and death were and should be difficult to apprehend. It should not be easy to approach them, or to position them in time and space. As we'll later see, he continued to wrestle with the question of Christ's place in time in his later writings, but the fragment on the Passion stands as proof that this wasn't a problem that could be solved with poetic effort in the absence of deeper inspiration. The magic of a Christmas dawn couldn't be forced.

PART II

5

10 August 1637: 'Yet Once More'

Yet once more.
Something is happening – and not just happening, but happening again, not for the first time. Not an event but a repetition. But of what?

Yet once more.

Three words. Short, simple, everyday words – a syllable apiece. While they're words I use often, I can't quite imagine beginning with them. 'Yet' is a strange place to start.

Yet once more.

Poetry takes shape in, and appeals to, strange kinds of obsession. It takes familiar words and makes them do peculiar work. It asks us to slow down and fixate where we would usually breeze past. But for how long? How much time does a single word, phrase, line of poetry want from us? When are we sure we're done with it? What would it mean to have done with it?

Yet once more.

Franz Kafka notes in his diary, on Christmas Eve 1911, how anxious he became as a child when his father used the word *ultimo*, a businessman's term meaning 'last month', whose significance 'remained a disquieting mystery' to him.[1] The word bounced unsettlingly round his childish head – he was captured not by its meaning but by its very sound, like an earworm, those snatches of noise and song that periodically infect our thoughts, stick to our brains. To be caught in repetitions of this sort can be disconcerting, deeply unpleasant, a sign of impaired functioning, but as Oliver Sacks, who considers what earworms tell us about the workings of the brain, puts it, '[t]here may be a continuum here between the pathological and the normal.'[2] Repeating something can be to kill it, or to be attacked by it; but, as readers of poems and hearers of songs and practisers of ritual all know, it can also make it reverberate newly through time, or rather enlist it for a new kind of time by wrenching it from its everyday context and making it momentarily strange.

Yet once more.

Samuel Beckett sometimes got snatches of Milton stuck in his head. In 1934 he wrote to his friend, the poet Thomas MacGreevy: 'I think what you find cold in Milton I find final, for himself at least, conflagrations of conviction cooled down to a finality of literary emission.'[3] Beckett can seem cold and distant in his work, but this seems like a clue as to how to read him too. Writing again to MacGreevy two decades later, Beckett remarked in passing: 'Can't get a verse of Milton out of my mind: "Insuperable height of loftiest shade."'[4] I've no idea why this particular line struck him, but I am drawn to this sense of Milton bouncing about his mind, one of Beckett's earworms, akin to the maddening and hypnotic repetitions through which he fashioned his plays.

Yet once more.

These simple words start to reverberate for me if I say them often enough. The vowels, I notice, seem to get longer in each word, or perhaps it's that my mouth has to move forwards in stages to make them: from the pinched grin, lips pulled back, that produces the *e* of *yet*, to the slackened descent of the jaw that makes the *uh* of *once*, to the protruding embouchure of the lips that drawls out the *aw* of *more*. If certain ordinary words get stranger the more we think about them, so too do our ways of making them, the fleshy twitches of our tongue, lips, and teeth.

Yet once more.

What does 'yet' even mean here? A scurry to the *Oxford English Dictionary* is my usual recourse. The oldest sense of the word, the one used in this phrase, marks or signals repetition: it has most obviously survived in the phrase 'yet again', which is roughly what the line seems to mean. Even this starts to seem strange to me, though. 'Once more' is a curious, paradoxical way of saying 'again': if something has happened once, and once only, how can it be repeated? How can there be more onces than one? Are all of our times a series of units, a set of succeeding one-offs? We start our stories *once upon a time*, not, as seems to happen here, *once again, upon yet another time*. I ask, once more, what sort of a way is this to start?

Yet once more.

◆

Here's something that happened at least once. One day in November 1637, John Milton sat down and began a poem with these three words. Or perhaps better to say: at some point during that month he wrote these words, and at some point he decided to make them the start of the poem he was writing. The Trinity Manuscript, his working notebook, suggests the struggle he underwent in deciding how to begin: the complete version of the poem, still with its own

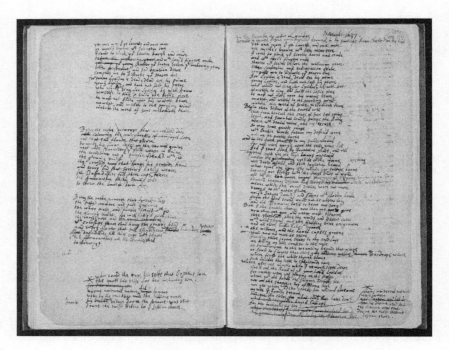

FIGURE 8: The opening of 'Lycidas' in Milton's handwriting in the Trinity Manuscript.

corrections and alterations, is preceded by a page of attempts crossed out and parts to be added, including a version of the opening lines, the residue of multiple attempts to get going.

But eventually the words were written, and would stand as the opening of the greatest and the strangest poem he had written up to that point in his life; the best short poem, in my and many others' opinion, that he would ever write; perhaps the greatest short poem in English, while certainly one of the weirdest. A poem to which I keep returning with undiminished wonder and disquiet, which I wish I could recite in its entirety but cannot. Instead I have snatches, phrases, some entire sections, rattling around my mind, often at the back of it, sometimes at the front. It begins as follows:

> *Yet once more, O ye laurels and once more*
> *Ye myrtles brown, with ivy never sere,*
> *I come to pluck your berries harsh and crude,*
> *And with forced fingers rude,*
> *Shatter your leaves before the mellowing year.*[5]

So this is where 'Yet once more' leads, but it hardly makes things clearer: the words are addressed not to a person or to the reader but to trees, to laurels and myrtles; and what's going to happen yet once more is their plucking and shattering (curious verbs: can leaves be shattered?). The opening words stand out: 'once more' is repeated within the first line, but, unlike the lines that follow, they are then left to hang by themselves – they do not rhyme with anything. The lines change restlessly in length and rhythm, not settling into a regular order or pattern; very different from the even sequence of stanzas that made up the Nativity Ode eight years earlier. With 'Lycidas' our rhythms are unsettled from the start: the rug starts to be pulled from under us before we have time to wonder what kind of rug we're standing on.[6]

Here's something that happened once, and only once. On 10 August 1637, at around half past seven in the morning, a boat set sail from near Chester. It made its way down the estuary of the River Dee, which traces part of the border between England and northern Wales, and navigated out towards the Irish Sea. Over the course of the day it traversed the Welsh coast and the northern side of the island of Anglesey; but in the late afternoon, before it could head westward towards Ireland, it struck one of the many large rocks that lie just below the sea's surface thereabouts, obscured by the powerful currents raking and churning debris from the seabed. It quickly sank, and all aboard were drowned: among them a man named Edward King, aged twenty-five, who had made the five-day journey to Chester from Cambridge, where for seven years he had been a fellow of Christ's College. He had been travelling back to the land of his birth to visit his family; his body was never recovered from the waters.

The following year a volume of poems was published in King's memory, titled *Justa Eduardo King*, and it was there that Milton's 'Lycidas' first appeared: it was the last poem in the volume, and the longest of its elegies, its poems of grief.

But in what sense does 'Lycidas' grieve Edward King? Was he Milton's to mourn?

Yet once more.

The voice that begins in this way does not want to begin at all. 'Bitter constraint, and sad occasion dear,' he tells us, 'Compels me . . . For Lycidas is dead, dead ere his prime.' The poem is untimely; King's death is early; the song is too soon, wrenched from the poet's mind before its proper moment. He calls for help, the first of many others that his voice will address: 'Begin then, sisters of the sacred well'.[7] The Muses will begin on his behalf: getting started is outsourced to others.

In the spring of 2017 my family and I were on our way back from a trip to Liverpool, which we'd chosen to take because my children were in the thick of one of the most entertaining of their transient obsessions, this time with the Beatles. Driving south, it occurred to me that we were as close as we were likely to be for some time to Chester – and that I'd never, so far as I remembered, seen the

Dee estuary – so we made a detour there. I'd read one scholar suggesting that King's boat would have departed from the north bank, near Great Neston, but the river has silted up to the point that this village is now some half a mile from the water.[8] We therefore opted for the south side, and found a spot called Greenfield Dock, which small boats were still using and where there were banks of daffodils in bloom and dogs being walked, providing distraction for the kids while I tried to decide exactly what I was doing there, staring out at the calm grey water. What I was trying to access, or understand.

I've already discussed the strangely thought-provoking kinds of disappointment that my Miltonic pilgrimages tend to provoke; several of them will feature in this chapter, and this one, on the banks of the Dee, took a particularly strange form. There's no reason to believe that Milton ever saw the waters I was staring at – the waters across which King travelled, which closed over his head, and whose rhythms roar and lap and trickle through 'Lycidas'. But in another, strange sense, I was therefore able to experience the very absence that the poem laments: I could cast my eyes across the waters at the sight of *no Edward King*, see for myself the absence of any bodily trace or physical monument.

Ruminating on the visit after we left, this chastening sense of absence threw me back in a new way on a gap of a different sort, one that's long troubled both Milton's biographers and readers of the poem: the absence beyond 'Lycidas' of any evidence that King really mattered to him; of any clue that they were friends, or even acquaintances; of any further mention of King in Milton's other writings.

I am less worried than some readers about the marginal role that Edward King seems to have played in Milton's life. Marcel Proust's biographer, Jean-Yves Tadié, intriguingly proposes 'a kind of law of literary biography: someone who plays a walk-on part in real life may become an important character in a book, because an image, which coincides with one's secret expectations, may resound in the imagination for a long time; in contrast, old friends, brothers, even lovers, may disappear without trace.'[9] The mere fact that there's no evidence of Milton's personal friendship with Edward King doesn't necessarily mean that 'Lycidas' is insincere in its claim to mourn him. To read it this way is to accept the comforting but ultimately illusory idea that our feelings and associations form a neat network and hierarchy, or that we care straightforwardly about those closest to us, and less the further we get away. But life isn't always that tidy. There are many people whom I've met fleetingly who have left lingering and consequential impressions in my mind, encounters to which I return with surprising frequency, just as someone who has played only a walk-on role in our lives might suddenly take a disconcertingly prominent role in a vivid dream, and make us wonder if they matter to us more than we realise, in ways that we little understand. Our memories and associations are an interwoven tapestry, interlaced like fine threads of varying hue with the lives that may intersect with ours fleetingly but that can still, as Tadié puts it, 'resound in the imagination for a long time'. This, I imagine, is what Edward King was to Milton.

If 'Lycidas' has seemed to some to be too full of its author to be a true mourning poem, it's also been felt to be, in a sense, too full of artifice – too fully a poem. In the place of the real Edward King we encounter endless literary allusions – especially to the traditions of pastoral, shepherds and their sheep in a picture-book landscape. Dr Johnson speaks for a great many modern readers when he writes of 'Lycidas' that 'it is not to be considered as the effusion of real passion; for passion runs not after remote allusions and obscure opinions. Passion plucks no berries from the myrtle and ivy . . . Where there is leisure for fiction there is little grief . . . Its form is that of a pastoral, easy, vulgar, and therefore disgusting: whatever images it can supply are long ago exhausted.'[10] Strong words: the poem is too learned to be passionate; the very act of writing it proves that the grief cannot be real; writing it in dreary, tired conventions makes it hard to stomach.

Dr Johnson was as troubled by the strange rhythms of 'Lycidas' as he was by its artificial qualities: 'the diction is harsh, the rhymes uncertain, and the numbers [i.e. the rhythms] unpleasing.'[11] Here, at least, I fully agree with him. But to me the poem's awkward, unpleasing, and uncertain rhythms and rhymes are quite deliberate; after all, Johnson's pejorative term, 'harsh', is borrowed from the poem's third line. 'Lycidas' has a lot to tell us about how Milton's sense of himself and his ambitions was changing in the course of the 1630s; but it also has a lot to tell us about the harsh, uncertain rhythms of grief and hope, of friendships formed and dissolved; rhythms poised, yet once more, between languages, between nations, between land and sea and sky.

Yet once more.

Suddenly, after nearly forty lines, the poem swivels to address Lycidas directly, to cry into the void that it bewails:

> *Thee Shepherd, thee the Woods, and desert Caves,*
> *With wild thyme and the gadding Vine o'ergrown,*
> *And all their echoes mourn.*

A tangled sentence; it finishes with another short line, cut off abruptly like King's life. It feels very un-English, standard word order abandoned: the object, the shepherd Lycidas, comes first; then the cluster of subjects, desolate places and unkempt plants; only at the very end the main verb, telling us what they are doing, the activity that binds them together: mourning. Is Milton indulging here in a groan-worthy pun? Are we to hear 'wild thyme' as 'wild time', time itself run amok, grief itself sprouting stalks and tendrils?

'Lycidas' refuses to stay in its own time; it sends its wild shoots out into later literature. In the second chapter of James Joyce's *Ulysses* its author's alter ego, Stephen Daedalus, teaches a room full of schoolboys, and demands that one of them, Talbot, read aloud from the book that they are studying:

> A swarthy boy opened a book and propped it nimbly under the breastwork of his satchel. He recited jerks of verse with odd glances at the text:

– Weep no more, woful shepherd, weep no more
For Lycidas, your sorrow, is not dead,
Sunk though he be beneath the watery floor . . .[12]

A chapter later Stephen, on the beach, thinks of a man drowned nine days before off Maiden's Rock, his body still not recovered. Stephen's inner thoughts mingle the dead man's watery fate and the poem that he has just been teaching with the loss of his own mother: 'A drowning man. His human eyes scream to me out of horror of his death. I . . . With him together down . . . I could not save her. Waters: bitter death: lost.'[13] Edward King, the anonymous drowned man, Stephen's mother, all drowning together, sucked into the amorphous watery embrace of the sea, of forgetting; but also the embrace of Joyce's massive and incessantly watery novel, in which they meet and coalesce.

It's fitting that Stephen Daedalus is teaching 'Lycidas'. The American poet John Berryman wrote a short story, 'Wash Far Away', about teaching the poem to a classroom who wrestle with the question of whether the poem is ultimately about Edward King or about Milton, and decide that it is both.[14] Something about this poem brings out the teacher in poets, and the poet in teachers. 'Lycidas' feels like it needs to teach us something powerful, without having quite made up its mind just what that is.

Rivers trickle and snake through this poem. It calls to the nymphs who failed to intervene 'when the remorseless deep / Closed o'er the head of your loved Lycidas', and could not be found 'playing on the steep, / Where your old bards, the famous Druids, lie . . . Nor yet where Deva [i.e. the Dee] spreads her wizard stream'.[15]

'Wizard' stands out for me here. The *Oxford English Dictionary* cites this line as the first instance of the adjective used to mean 'magic, enchanted, bewitched'. It doesn't cite another use of the word in this sense for a hundred and fifty years. The wizard stream flows towards the place of 'old bards, the famous Druids': even if Milton never set foot near the Dee, my mini pilgrimage there felt worthwhile because the specific landscape mattered to him, mattered as a place rippling with ancient enchantment. Anglesey, where Edward King's vessel was wrecked, was traditionally identified as the ancient seat of the Druids, figures who blended poetry and magical incantation; who could change the world with their poems and songs in a manner that Milton feared might be beyond him. This ancient Britain is lost; there are no more wizard streams, only murderous ones.

Yet once more.

As the poem builds to its first moment of true crisis the forlorn cry to the nymphs and the once 'wizard stream' of the Dee gives way to these extraordinary lines:

> *Alas! What boots it with uncessant care*
> *To tend the homely slighted shepherds trade,*
> *And strictly meditate the thankless muse*
> *. . .*
> *Fame is the spur that the clear spirit doth raise*
> *(That last infirmity of noble mind)*
> *To scorn delights, and live laborious days;*
> *But the fair guerdon when we hope to find,*
> *And think to burst out into sudden blaze,*
> *Comes the blind Fury with th' abhorred shears,*
> *And slits the thin-spun life.*[16]

There is, to put it mildly, a lot going on here. What, Milton is asking, is the point of having lofty poetic aspirations – why 'strictly meditate the thankless muse', why pursue the gnawing and relentless seriousness that accompanies 'uncessant care' – when a life as full of promise as Edward King's can be ended so suddenly and pointlessly? His answer seems until now to have been the pursuit of fame, renown, the 'spur' that drove him '[t]o scorn delights, and live laborious days', but this discipline and self-sacrifice seems like a sick joke in the face of sudden and meaningless death.

The last of the lines that I've quoted are among my favourite in the poem. There's an amazing sense of enormous potential about to be made manifest, a life poised on the brink of decisive action,

about 'to burst out into sudden blaze' – when the 'blind Fury' enters
and ends it all. This is a bizarre pair of words since the blind
Atropos, whom the Greeks believed measured and managed the
thread of mortal lives, was a Fate, not a Fury: Milton deliberately
chooses the wrong word, his own outraged ire at the injustice of
it all seeming to leap to furious life. The 'shears' with which the
pastoral shepherds tend their flocks are suddenly wielded by this
faceless, nightmarish apparition. And is there a more gruesomely
satisfying set of five words to say aloud in all of English poetry
than 'slits the thin-spun life'? The sense of horror and doom evoked
by the slippery, lisping sequence of s, l, and th sounds; the vowels
gradually growing longer and more open, culminating with the
whining vowel of the lost *life*. And the slowly dawning strangeness
of that very word: we expect 'slits the thin-spun thread', but it's life
itself that's slit. The verb itself is shiveringly strange. It's not threads
that are usually slit, it's vulnerable body parts: throats.

When the blind Fury slits the thread, however, things don't end
as decisively as we might expect. In fact things immediately continue,
but in a remarkable way: with a new kind of intervention. Here
are the lines again, as they continue:

> *Comes the blind Fury with th' abhorred shears,*
> *And slits the thin-spun life. But not the praise,*
> *Phoebus replied, and touched my trembling ears;*
> *Fame is no plant that grows on mortal soil,*
> *. . .*
> *But lives and spreads aloft by those pure eyes,*
> *And perfect witness of all judging Jove . . .*[17]

Reading these lines for the first time, it's easy to skip over just what
has happened in them. Until this moment, for the entire seventy-
five lines of the poem that we've read, there's no indication that
the words of the speaking shepherd are addressed to anyone but
the barren and depleted landscape he inhabits. But suddenly the
words are answered – and by no less a figure than Phoebus Apollo,
Greek god of the sun. There are no quotation marks here: we only

gradually and retrospectively realise that the single line 'And slits the thin-spun life. But not the praise' is in fact divided between two voices, mortal and immortal, the one to which we've been growing used and a new voice thundering from above as the god swoops from nowhere to flick the poet's earlobe like a chastising schoolmaster. He offers punishment, however, instead of reassurance: even if life is fleeting and uncertain, the pursuit of renown is still worthwhile for it will be recognised where it matters most, not by other people but by God. When I read this poem aloud, with my students, I like to pause for several long silent seconds in the middle of this line, to stretch out the moment in which the poet's mind hits rock bottom with nowhere else to go, as if the poem might end on this despairing note, as indeed it seems to want to; to make Phoebus's suddenly emerging voice sound as a genuine and unprecedented interruption of all that has gone before.

We may be in the realm of gods and Furies, but more pressingly recent events hover in the background. In June 1637, just two months before Edward King's death, three Puritans – the physician John Bastwick, the clergyman Henry Burton, and the lawyer William Prynne – were publicly mutilated in London for the crime of writing pamphlets against the prelacy overseen by Archbishop Laud, who, since the beginning of Charles I's personal rule, had come to wield ever more control over the nature and governance of the English Church. The vicious punishment of three citizens of high social status was shocking, and created widespread resentment against the unfettered exercise of royal and ecclesiastical power. The specifics of the mutilation were widely reported and lamented: the men had their ears cut from their heads. Prynne, who had lost part of his ears to punishment three years earlier, had the remaining stumps hacked and sawed, and the letters *SL* for 'seditious libeller' branded on his cheeks. Trembling ears, furious slitting; their horrible punishment reverberates through Apollo's entrance in 'Lycidas', transposed into the realm of Milton's mythic and poetic fears.[18]

If the punishment of these three men suggested the brutal direction in which those with power in the realm were tending, the fate of Edward King spoke more specifically to Milton's anxious and burgeoning sense of his own poetic vocation, and how easily and abruptly it might be brought to nothing. I now need to interrupt myself, Phoebus-like, and say a little more about the stages this personal crisis went through between the writing of the Nativity Ode in 1629 and 'Lycidas' in 1637, and how Milton spent these years. In the weeks following the writing of the former poem, as I noted in the last chapter, Milton penned a Latin elegy to Charles Diodati, and in it he ruminated not only on the kinds of poems he planned to write but also on the kind of life he needed to live, the kind of person he needed to be, in order to write them: banqueting and carousing was all well and good for frivolous writers, but 'the poet whose subject is, one minute, the holy counsels of the gods above, and the next, those deep-buried kingdoms where a savage dog barks – let this poet live frugally . . . let herbs provide his harmless diet . . . In addition his youth must be chaste and free from crime, his morals strict and his hand unstained [*rigidi mores, et sine labe manus*].'[19] As Milton moved from undergraduate to graduate studies at the outset of the 1630s, three things happened in conjunction: he decisively abandoned his belief that he was destined for a life in the Church; he developed a percolating conviction that he was destined instead to pursue greatness as a poet; and he decided that, this being the case, he would need to pursue a life of virtue and moderation – perhaps even commit himself to total sexual abstinence (refraining even, as the 'hand unstained' suggests, from masturbation), at least until marriage.[20]

The writings that survive from Milton's years of graduate study suggest that he bided his time and continued honing his skills in several languages, arming himself with tools for pursuing whatever his poetic vocation would end up looking like. He continued to seek out opportunities to write poems lamenting the deaths of public and local figures – one on the Marchioness of Winchester, two on the university carrier, Thomas Hobson, whose business ferried people and goods between Cambridge and the capital. As his studies grew more advanced, Milton continued to undertake the public Latin exercises required of students who wanted to graduate, but he did so in increasingly ambitious, playful, and searching ways. The longest and most complex of these exercises shows Milton once again leaping deftly between modes and languages, but doing so not as part of a serious academic occasion, but during a time for approved foolery – a slice of learned silliness. This was a 'Salting', a rite of passage that was particularly popular when Milton was at Cambridge, in which first-year students delivered a speech (usually in Latin). If it met with approval, they were rewarded with beer; if not, they would have to down heavily salted beer (the Latin for salt, *sales*, was often used to mean wit). A master of ceremonies was chosen from among the older students to manage the occasion, playing the role of surrogate father to his gathered sons: it was this for which Milton was chosen, probably in 1631. He undertook the role with gusto, finding his feet as a sort of student stand-up comedian, aware both that the role didn't come naturally to him and that he was surprisingly good at it: 'I will not shrink from singing the praises of jests and merriment to the best of my powers,' he proclaims, 'even though I must admit I have very slight aptitude for them.'[21] He suggests at the start that he'd previously been less than popular with his peers (perhaps unsurprisingly, if Milton was as strident as he could be about his beliefs that drinking, fornicating, and masturbating were all obstacles to greatness), and refers to 'those who had previously shown me only hostility and dislike because of disagreements concerning our studies'.[22] He also says that he's aware of the nickname he's been given – 'Some of late called me "the Lady"'; as his widow reported to John Aubrey decades later, Milton 'was so faire, that they called him the Lady of Christs College'.[23] By the end of the speech he's basking in his new-found popularity, and mixing praise for the learned comedy of Cicero and Erasmus with the same taste for fart jokes that he would later display in *Paradise Lost*, where the fiery winds of Hell 'leave a singed bottom all involved / With stench and smoak': in his Salting speech he observes that 'I should not like the cheerful sounds of laughter to be drowned by groans from the posteriors in this assembly.'[24]

The vision of Cambridge life this speech provides isn't all that appealing, to say the least. Clever students mixing Latin witticisms, wine, and fart jokes is just a little too close to the worst kind of smug, sealed-off privilege which is still all too commonly associated with Cambridge and Oxford, even though, at least in my experience, it survives only in small pockets. But, as Milton's acknowledgement of his Lady moniker suggests, the fact that this display was an elite ritual doesn't mean he didn't also use it to reflect on questions that mattered to him. This becomes clear when he announces that he will 'overleap the University statutes . . . and run off from Latin into English' and launches into a poem beginning 'Hail native language', in which he doesn't just praise his mother tongue but describes in remarkably physical terms the way in which speaking it shaped his mouth as a child: 'Hail native language, that by sinews weak / Didst move my first endeavouring words to speak / And mad'st imperfect words with childish trips, / Half unpronounced, slide through my infant lips'. Milton starts with the faltering beginnings of language but eventually imagines the heights to which it might ultimately take him, elevated to 'where the deep transported mind may soar / Above the wheeling poles, and at heaven's door / Look in'.[25] Mere words, first sliding through the infant's lips, allow the adult poet to soar to Heaven.

At the outset of the Latin speech, Milton claims that 'the alternation of toil and pleasure usually has the effect of annihilating the boredom brought about by satiety and of making us the more eager to resume our interrupted tasks.'[26] His thought at this stage of his life seems conflicted, drawn towards rhythms that lurch back and forth between extremes, a swinging between states like the pendulum of a clock, rather than to a lingering in-betweenness of the sort towards which he strove in the Nativity Ode: it's a case of Latin then English, work then play. The same tendency was brought to a beautiful peak in these years when Milton wrote a pair of poems, titled 'L'Allegro' and 'Il Penseroso', in which he inhabited and embodied two alternative ways of being in the world: one dominated by 'Jest and youthful jollity / Quips and cranks, and wanton wiles', living in pursuit of 'unreproved pleasures free'; the other, committed to 'divinest Melancholy', withdrawing from the superficial world and aspiring 'to walk the studious cloisters pale'. Because Il Penseroso longs to hear a divine music that will 'Dissolve me into ecstasies / And bring all Heaven before my eyes', he resembles Milton as we instinctively imagine him, sombre and serious. Because it comes second in the sequence, readers have tended to assume that the poems represent something like Milton growing up, acknowledging youthful pleasures and then setting them aside for something weightier.[27] I think there probably was part of Milton that believed or wanted to believe this, but it's not the whole truth, and we should recognise it as a comforting and oversimplified story. Milton will never stop thirsting after 'unreproved pleasures free', though he will worry a great deal about what these pleasures can be, how they can be recognised and justified. What the pair of poems suggests to me isn't the confident superseding of one way of life by another. Rather, it's the pendulum continuing to swing back and forth between positions that he cannot yet reconcile or work out how to navigate between. It would not be until he wrote 'Lycidas' six years later that Milton would once again find a way of lingering hauntingly in in-betweenness, the *Zwischenraum* between states: a poem dwelling between England, Wales, and Ireland; between land, sea, and river; between lament and triumph, despair and consolation, violence and recovery; and, above all, between the voices that crowded in upon him when he set out to write.

Yet once more.

Another voice thunders into the poem from above. He is named, but not transparently, the 'pilot of the Galilean lake'. St Peter? Or Christ himself?

The pilot jangles the 'massy keys' that he holds, shakes his 'mitred locks', and begins to speak, lamenting the loss of a worthy youth when so many of the worthless could have been more happily sacrificed. 'Blind mouths!' – this is what he contemptuously calls the dispensable ones.[28] A startling pair of words. Unseeing maw, untasting eyes; body parts as mixed and mangled as Lycidas's lost corpse. John Ruskin was the first to spot the buried puns: a bishop is, etymologically, one who sees; the pastor one who feeds; these unholy wastes of space do neither.

It's a pivotal moment in the poem, and in Milton's writing life. For the first time he turns his words unmistakably against the sorry state of the Church that he saw around him. If the lines could be taken to refer to Roman Catholics, they also clearly gesture towards the violence with which Archbishop Laud and Charles I were forcing their vision of a ceremonial and hierarchical church on the nation. The Laudian clergy are flimsy and phoney, caring only for their own power and not for the souls of their charges:

> *And when they list, their lean and flashy songs*
> *Grate on their scrannel pipes of wretched straw,*
> *The hungry sheep look up, and are not fed,*
> *But swoll'n with wind, and the rank mist they draw,*
> *Rot inwardly, and foul contagion spread:*
> *Besides what the grim wolf with privy paw*
> *Daily devours apace, and nothing said . . .*[29]

What a superb torrent of adjectives. 'Flashy', to mean showy but inane, was a very rare word when Milton chose it – and a fine, offhand way to dismiss the entire Laudian programme of cere-monial beauty. Contempt rolls in the *r* sounds of *scrrrannel* (meagre and shrivelled, a word that Milton invents here) and *wrrretched*, and again in *'rrrank'* and *'rrrot'*. The grim realities of shepherd life, of the gases that inflate and ruin the bellies of ill-tended sheep, suddenly waft their stench into the pastoral world, as the pilot spits in fury at those who fail so miserably in tending to their flocks.

But who is the wolf here? Might Milton have been attracted to this well-worn, clichéd choice because it spoke to him on a deeper level – because there is, in a different sense, something wolf-like about the poet himself? Wolves were commonly believed to disinter recently buried corpses. The playwright John Webster, in lines that T. S. Eliot remembered and rewrote in *The Waste Land*, had a character cry: 'But keep the wolf far hence, that's foe to men / For with his nails he'll dig them up again'.[30] What was Milton seeking to do in this poem but dredge up a fresh corpse, like a kind of sea-wolf?

As 'Lycidas' unfolds, however, the poem itself becomes something less like a single wolf's howl than like a pack of wolves.[31] Elias Canetti writes wonderfully of the wolf pack in motion and the place of each wolf within it: 'In the changing constellation of the pack, in its dances and expeditions, he will again and again find himself at its edge. He may be in the centre and then, immediately afterwards, at the edge again; at the edge and then back in the centre.'[32] The wolf pack is an animal version of what Canetti calls, among humans, 'the *rhythmic* or *throbbing* crowd'.[33] This is how the voices in 'Lycidas' work: their uneven rhythms bursting into dominance for a moment, fleetingly leading the pack while they say what they have to say, then absorbed back within its fluid throng, no single one allowed to dominate or to lead for long.

Milton finally finished his formal studies after roughly six years of intensive back and forth between Cambridge and London, with a decent track record as a poet and a public orator but still largely unknown to the wider world, and shorn of his secure sense of vocation. At around the same time, probably in 1632, his father, aging and increasingly disinclined to involve himself in the doings of the Scriveners' Company, decided to leave Bread Street behind and move the family to Hammersmith – today a part of the sprawl of London but then a village several miles west along the Thames. Now the Thames became Milton's way of making his way back to London, to see friends and purchase books. The river became part of his daily life.

Yet once more.

Edward King makes his way from the river out to the sea and is lost. The vast waters swallow Lycidas, creating the aching spectacle of his utter absence:

Ay me! Whilst thee the shores and sounding seas
Wash far away, where ere thy bones are hurled,
Whether beyond the stormy Hebrides,
Where thou perhaps under the whelming tide
Visit'st the bottom of the monstrous world;
Or whether thou to our moist vows denied,
Sleep'st by the fable of Bellerus old . . .[34]

No certainty here but a series of empty possibilities: perhaps this, perhaps that. The sheer loss of the hurled bones begins to spawn reassuring fantasies – that there is some supernatural, submarine realm in which Lycidas might have found refuge. As Milton spins these yarns his mind ranges across the entirety of the British Isles, from the Hebrides in the distant north to Bellerium, the Roman name for Land's End, in the south.

The geography matters here, for once again political disputes hover in the background of the poem's mythological texture. The question of who, if anyone, owned the seas around the British Isles had been a matter of intense debate. The great Dutch jurist Hugo Grotius had argued in 1609 that the seas lay beyond the limits of human possession and could be navigated freely. He had been refuted by the English lawyer and Hebraist John Selden, who claimed in his books *Mare Clausum* – 'the Closed Sea' – that the kings of Great Britain had continuously and from time immemorial 'occupied' the seas surrounding their dominion. Charles was delighted, and required Selden's book to be placed in various official settings and granted royal approval.[35] One reader of the poems written after Edward King's death linked them to this dispute directly, writing in the manuscript that the waters in which he drowned were 'The King's Seas, J. Selden's *Mare Clausum*'.[36]

Edward King died, it seems, in disputed and intensely politicised waters. Throughout the 1630s, even as Charles kept his distance from the savage wars on the Continent, he aimed to augment the nation's standing and his own honour by increasing the size and magnificence of the Royal Navy. October 1637, between Edward

King's death and the publication of 'Lycidas', saw the launch of Charles's massive and lavishly expensive flagship, the *Sovereign of the Seas*, intended, as the name suggests, to assert and defend his royal right of maritime ownership. Badly overloaded, the ceremonial launch of the *Sovereign* was an embarrassing public failure: after some technical tweaks she was eventually relaunched at night, entirely without pomp.[37] With Charles's continued refusal to summon a parliament, these vanity projects had to be funded by other means, especially the hated 'Ship Money' levy which English towns were forced to pay, and for the refusal of which some prominent figures were imprisoned: the cracks in royal authority, the disputes as to the limits of royal power that would divide the nation in the 1640s, were beginning to show. The 'whelming tide' that had swallowed Edward King was also the arena in which politics was being played out.

It was in Hammersmith that Milton continued to wrestle with the question of how to be a poet – what such a choice would mean, and how to justify it. He wrote an impassioned Latin poem, 'Ad Patrem', to his father, which expressed some of the same hopes about what poetry might achieve as his Cambridge poem to his native tongue: 'poetry still retains some trace of the Promethean fire. The gods love poetry . . . My fiery spirit which whirls round the hurtling spheres is already singing, as it flies among the starry choirs, a deathly melody, an indescribable song [*inenarrabile carmen*].'[38] Oddly, this poem addresses his father as an implacable hater of all things poetic: 'Do not despise divine poetry, the poet's creation,' he implores him, but there's nothing to suggest that Milton's father ever did.[39] It's hard to tell whether the poem is sincere – aimed at winning over a father who, even if he didn't dislike poetry, sincerely disliked his son's lack of a better plan for his future – or another learned game, an attempt to win him over by teasingly suggesting that if he doesn't approve, it can only be because he hates poetry altogether.

The deeper problem was that it wasn't entirely clear what it would mean, for someone in Milton's position, to devote himself to poetry in the manner that he implored his father to allow him to do. It wasn't clear what kind of activity, what kind of work, the writing of poetry was: what a life devoted to it should look like. It was neither respectable nor plausible to announce oneself as a poet-prophet, especially when one was an unknown university student. As the poet-critic John Hollander puts it: 'A poet's work can appear to be very strange. It can look, for example, like a manual labourer's utter respite from work (sitting in a rocking chair, thinking, remembering, muttering, humming).'[40] None of these activities were likely to impress the ambitious, financially savvy, and upwardly mobile father who had paid for Milton's education as a decent return on his investment.

One option was to write for the commercial theatre, which Milton had certainly experienced, and with which he had various connections. In an earlier poem to Diodati he had described his delight in watching 'raging Tragedy' (*furiosa Tragoedia*) unfold on the London stage – 'It makes me sad to watch, yet watch I do, and find a pleasure in the sadness.'[41] His father was a trustee of the Blackfriars playhouse, and probably helped secure the commission for Milton's first published poem, 'On Shakespeare', which I discussed in the introduction to this book. In 'L'Allegro', Milton praised 'the well-trod stage' and especially 'sweetest Shakespeare, fancy's child'. The thrilling recent discovery of Milton's annotated copy of Shakespeare shows how carefully he read the playwright's works, adding comments in the margins and correcting printing errors.[42] But despite these serious forms of engagement, nothing suggests that grubbing around in the commercial world of the theatre would satisfy his poetic ambitions.

The chief alternative would be to attach himself to the aristocratic world, writing works on commission and hoping for favour and patronage from the wealthy. And it was this option that Milton initially tried. He received a commission to write a short theatrical entertainment, titled 'Arcades', to be performed in honour of Alice, dowager Countess of Derby, at Harefield, around ten miles from Hammersmith. How this commission came about – and when exactly the work was written and performed – is unclear, but Milton

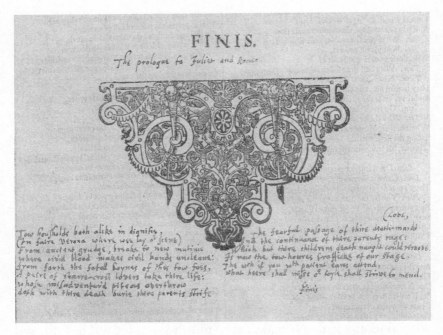

FIGURE 9: Milton's writing in his copy of Shakespeare's plays. Here he has copied the prologue to *Romeo and Juliet* on the final page of the preceding play, *Titus Andronicus*, since the prologue was omitted from the Folio edition of the plays. We see Milton not just accepting the works as printed but creating his own complete Shakespeare.

would go on to collaborate fruitfully with Henry Lawes, the well-known musician, who had been acting as music tutor to three of the countess's young grandchildren for several years, and so it's likely it was his father's strong network of musical connections that first brought the young Milton to Lawes's attention. 'Arcades' itself is not that interesting or significant a piece of writing, other than its introduction of a figure named 'The Genius of the Wood' who speaks the majority of its lines, and guides the nymphs and shepherds to their destination; the figure of the 'Genius', the spirit of a place, would stick in Milton's mind.

Yet once more.

'Lycidas' begins to end with another startling shift: not the entrance of the latest thundering voice, a new wolf leading the pack, but an abrupt and unexplained turn from despair to consolation:

> *Weep no more, woeful shepherds weep no more,*
> *For Lycidas your sorrow is not dead,*
> *Sunk though he be beneath the watery floor,*
> *So sinks the day-star in the ocean bed,*
> *And yet anon repairs his drooping head,*
> *And tricks his beams, and with new-spangled ore,*
> *Flames in the forehead of the morning sky . . .*[43]

'Yet once more' gives way to 'weep no more'; the poem's repetitions seem to be drawing to an end. The man for whom the various voices have been mourning is not dead at all, but has ascended, like a newly rising star, 'Through the dear might of him that walks the waves'. His arrival in Heaven is a strange one: 'With Nectar pure his oozy locks he laves, / And hears the unexpressive nuptial Song, / In the blest Kingdoms meek of joy and love.'[44] The detail that Lycidas needs to wash his slimy hair is odd – the mire and muck of the deep still cling to him as he arrives on high. And the consolation only gets stranger: no sooner are we told of his heavenly ascent than another alternative is introduced: 'Now Lycidas the Shepherds weep no more; / Henceforth thou art the Genius of the shore.'[45] So he is not, it seems, securely ensconced in Heaven, but destined, like the Genius of the Wood in 'Arcades', forever to haunt and to inhabit the very shores by which he died. The piling up of alternatives makes the very attempt at consolation seem suspect – as if the poet is trying too hard. But the final glimpse of Lycidas haunting the shorelines seems right: to return him to the realm where the poem has unfolded, the shore, the shifting arena where land meets water, where the strange treasures thrown back by the seas belong to anyone lucky enough to find them.

I have said that 'Lycidas' sends out its shoots and tendrils to later writers; given how widely and deeply Milton was read in nineteenth-century America, it seems not unlikely to me that the poem's gorgeously resurgent 'day-star', its 'new-spangled' beams flaming across the morning sky, left its mark in the mind of the amateur poet Francis Scott Key when he first scribbled down the lyrics to 'The Star-Spangled Banner'.

Mostly Milton resisted the pull towards the public world that the commission to write 'Arcades' offered; not for him the life of Henry Lawes, singing for his supper in an aristocratic household, giving their progeny the benefit of his talent. He began at this time to fill the notebook that we now know as the Trinity Manuscript – cramming it not just with drafts and redrafts of his poems but with ideas for the great works that he was ultimately determined to produce. The most remarkable of these pages contain his scattered ideas for dramas, the form in which he then seems to have believed that his ambitions could best be fulfilled. He considered stories from British, classical, and biblical history as his subject matter – and suddenly, in the midst of his sketch for a drama based on the fall of humankind (which a later page will show that he considers calling 'Adam's Punishment' or 'Adam Unparadiz'd'), we can glimpse for the first time the sparks of the work that would allow him, three decades later, to make good on his ambitions: he has lightly scrawled two words, *Paradise Lost*.

The problem, once again, was time: Milton had as yet few achievements with which to justify these lofty intentions – just the twin conviction that he would produce such a work, and that the time to do so would not, and could not, be now. The pressure of time passing; the best way to inhabit it; whether to take charge of or surrender oneself to its rhythms: these were the questions that animated and preoccupied him. It was at this point that he wrote the poem 'On Time', to be set on a clock, which I discussed in the first chapter. And in December 1631, as he turned twenty-three, he took stock of the problem in direct terms, in the first English sonnet he had written in some years:

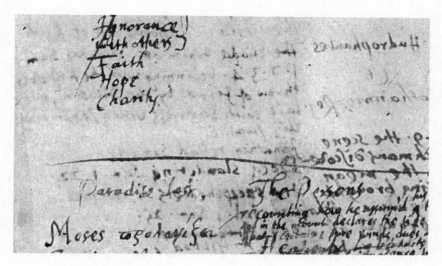

FIGURE 10: Milton's ideas for dramas from the Trinity Manuscript, including the words 'Paradise Lost'.

How soon hath Time the subtle thief of youth,
Stolen on his wing my three and twentieth year!
My hasting days fly on with full career,
But my late spring no bud or blossom sheweth.[46]

Already twenty-three and with little to show for it; an education but no meaningful use to which he can put it; living with his parents again, dragged out of London by their decisions. He observes forlornly that 'inward ripeness doth much less appear' – maybe he has already achieved, inwardly and invisibly, more than meets the eye – but the best he can do is resign himself, and keep faith that God will let him know when the time is right: 'Yet be it less or more, or soon or slow, / It shall be still in strictest measure even / To that same lot, however mean, or high, / Toward which Time leads me, and the will of Heaven.'[47]

This sonnet was originally lodged within a longer piece of writing: a letter, in English, to an anonymous friend, who was clearly worried that Milton was beginning to slink away from the world and lose himself in his private studies. Milton thanks the friend for acting 'as a good watch man to admonish that the howres of the night passe on (for so I call my life as yet obscure, & unserviceable to mankind)'. He recognises the risks of relinquishing his hold on the world altogether, 'whereby a man cutts himselfe off from all action'; but he insists that this is not the case with him, using as his justification the 'due and tymely obedience' taught by Jesus's parables of the talents, in which a servant is chastised for failing to invest his master's money wisely, and of the vineyard, in which the labourers who join the harvest day late receive the same pay as those who have toiled all day, which encourages 'not taking thought of beeing late so it give advantage to be more fit'. But he recognises in the letter that these are attempts at self-consolation: 'I am something suspicious of myself,' he adds, '& doe take notice of a certain belatednesse in me.'[48] It was important to wait, but not for too long; miss one's moment, and the Blind Fury might strike.

In 1634, after around two years of mostly reading and occasionally writing at home in Hammersmith, it became clear that the Countess of Derby's family had been sufficiently pleased with 'Arcades' to offer Milton another commission, this one much longer, more ambitious, and presumably better paid. In 1631 the countess's son-in-law John Egerton, the Earl of Bridgewater, had been appointed by Charles I to the important post of President of the Council in the Marches of Wales, and lord lieutenant of the regions on either side of the border between England and Wales. He, his wife, and the three youngest of his seven children were to make a prolonged ceremonial progress through the lands for which he was now responsible, ending at their new home, Ludlow Castle. Milton was to write the script and Henry Lawes the music for a masque, a spectacular performance starring Lawes himself and the Egertons' three children, to mark their arrival.

Court masques had become an increasingly important part of the monarch's repertoire of spectacle under James I, and continued so under his son. As mentioned in the second chapter, they mixed poetry (most famously and frequently written by Ben Jonson, whom Milton praised as 'learned' in 'L'Allegro'), ingenious theatrical spectacle, and music, some of it provided by men in John Milton senior's immediate circle. Masques were among the most spectacular ways for the court to represent itself to itself, talk to itself, draw and redraw the magic circle dividing it from the world at large. They were written for specific public occasions, and performed only once, unless the monarch specifically requested a repeat. Vastly expensive, and followed by lavish banquets, they were episodes of conspicuous consumption, demonstrating the power, the largesse, and the elegance of the court. The king sat at the physical centre of the audience, where all could see him, spectator and spectacle all at once. He was the focal point of the masque, giving it shape and coherence, just as he was of the court, which in turn sat at the centre of the nation, and gave it shape. Or so, at least, was the intended message.

Milton's commission was significantly different. The Earl of Bridgewater's new role was an important one, but it also required him to leave the centre behind and situate himself at the periphery, in a complicated kind of in-between zone. English views of Wales were contradictory in this period. The country was seen, on the one hand, as the place where Britishness had begun: the nation's mythical founder, the Trojan prince Brutus, was said to have arrived in Wales, and both King Arthur and Merlin were also held to have come from there. When Henry VII arrived to claim the throne in the late fifteenth century, he made much of these myths, relying on his Welsh birth and ancestry to justify his king-ship.[49] But if Wales was associated with the roots of the Britons and the Tudor monarchs of the previous century, and therefore intertwined with Englishness, it was simultaneously viewed as absolutely and threateningly other. Since the Middle Ages the region had been associated with monsters, and because its alien language and wild terrain made it resistant to royal authority and religious orthodoxy alike, it remained one of the 'dark corners of the realm', in need of vigilant supervision.[50] This is what the Earl of Bridgewater was supposed to provide: but he faced considerable challenges. He had legal training, but the Welsh Marches were notoriously characterised by constant clashes of jurisdiction, disputes as to which laws applied and who should oversee them, reflecting tensions between local and national authority.[51] Even the question of what the Marches were, where they began and ended, was slippery – a question requiring careful attention to language. As Francis Bacon wrote earlier in the century, it hinges on 'a true construction of a monosyllable, the word *marches*', which 'signifieth no more but limits, or confines, or borders'.[52] Precisely where these borders lay, and who had the right to define them, meant that a great deal hinged on the way in which this single word was understood.

On the surface, the masque Milton wrote endorses and assists the earl's mission to bring civilised control to a wild and unruly region. Its main characters are lightly veiled versions of the children who were to play the roles: the Lady, played by the fifteen-year-old Alice Egerton, and her brothers, played by John and Thomas, aged eleven and nine. The brothers become separated from their elder sister in the forests around Ludlow; she is found by the enchanter Comus, carousing with his crew of monstrous hybrids, and he tries and fails to persuade her to abandon her commitment to chastity. The boys are found and assisted by a spirit who descends from Heaven – played by Lawes, their music teacher – who helps them drive Comus off and rescue her. But she remains frozen to his enchanted throne until finally liberated by the ministrations of another supernatural being, the nymph Sabrina, once a virgin princess who drowned herself in the Severn to escape the wrath of her stepmother, 'And underwent a quick immortal change / Made goddess of the river'.[53]

In my experience of teaching *Comus* over the years, what strikes modern readers the most is its intense creepiness: the way in which it revolves around the virginity of a teenage girl, which is a matter of concerted public interest, both to her family and to the wider world. Her younger brothers discuss her sexuality in lofty philo-sophical terms: 'O that hapless virgin our lost sister,' worries the younger brother, 'Where may she wander now?' The elder one reassures him that their sister 'has a hidden strength / Which ye remember not . . . 'Tis chastity, my brother, chastity / She that has that, is clad in complete steel'. The Lady herself refuses to explain to Comus, after he tempts her, 'the sage / And serious doctrine of virginity', since he is unworthy to hear it – but had she done so, 'the brute Earth would lend her nerves, and shake'. And at the close, saved by a virgin, the Spirit presents the children, the daughter's virginity intact, to her parents, having endured 'hard assays'.[54]

As this summary suggests, *Comus* isn't an easy work for modern sensibilities to enjoy, but I'm not persuaded by those who would argue that this is beside the point, an inappropriate imposition of our views on gender and sexuality onto the past. It's certainly possible, and valuable, to read *Comus* as a historical reminder of the ways in which women's sexuality and procreative capacity have been made a matter of collective scrutiny and concern – the whole future of the Egerton family and of the Welsh Marches seems to hinge on Alice Egerton remaining steadfast and virginal. And there were particular reasons why the Egertons might have been eager to project this image of familial virtue, and of sexual virtue in particular. Three years previously their close relative, Mervyn Touchet, Earl of Castlehaven, had been publicly executed in one of the most notorious, complex, and lurid scandals of the early seventeenth century. He was convicted of rape and sodomy, the first peer of the realm to suffer capital punishment in more than a century. In the course of the trial a picture emerged of life in the Castlehaven household at Fonthill Gifford in Wiltshire which sounds like the plot of a baroque revenge tragedy or a seedy historical novel. The earl was said to have sodomised his male servants and favourites, and held his wife down while one of these favourites raped her. What led to his conviction, however, was not just a sense of his personal wickedness or depravity in committing these acts, but the fact that he was already a dubious figure – with Irish roots and Roman Catholic leanings – and that he had failed to uphold his duties as an aristocratic man. He had neglected to control not just his unruly desires but his servants, to whom he gave excessive money and power. Fonthill Gifford was a kind of world turned upside down, in which were played out the gruesome effects of allowing the hierarchies that divided and organised men and women, husbands and wives, masters and servants, parents and children, all to collapse.[55] It would be understandable if the Bridgewaters needed to emphasise that their own household was in much better order – that their children understood and were being trained in virtue, and were able to perform it for the approval of their parents and the wider community. One of the Earl of Bridgewater's earliest acts as president was to investigate the rape near Ludlow of a fourteen-year-old girl, in which, though a conviction was not achieved, he showed significant diligence and serious concern.[56] No one could accuse him of condoning the kinds of crime committed by his disgraced relative.

So we can certainly read *Comus* as a work intended to reassure its original audience that sexuality, and especially the sexuality of children and adolescent girls, can and should be controlled and restrained, and that the household and the whole of society relies on this restraint. But even if these are its aims, it's riven with tensions and uncertainties in the way that it pursues them. And these tensions seem to arise in part because if Milton wrote *Comus* for a performance which he would never witness, it seems in other respects an intensely personal work, a chance to ruminate on the problems of vocation, and the balance between engaging with and retreating from the world, with which he was intensely preoccupied. Thanks to his student nickname, the Lady of Christ's, many have been tempted to see the Lady in Comus as a figure for Milton himself, protecting her own virginity just as Milton was wondering whether a vow of chastity would be necessary to fulfil his poetic ambitions. But while there's certainly truth in this, I think it's a partial one. *Comus* reads more like Milton shining the white light of his character into a glass prism and watching its parts be split into a spectrum of different personas. Aspects of him are scattered across the masque's characters: not just Lawes's guiding spirit, desiring to teach and to instruct, and the chaste Lady, but, more troublingly, there's something of Milton in the enchanter and tempter Comus himself, who creates an alluring scene in the same way that Milton offers one to his audience, and who gives an astonishingly beautiful account of the rich treasures and pleasures of existence, pleasures that it would be foolish and miserable to spurn:

> *Wherefore did Nature pour her bounties forth,*
> *With such a full and unwithdrawing hand,*
> *Covering the earth with odours, fruits, and flocks,*
> *Thronging the seas with spawn innumerable,*
> *But all to please, and sate the curious taste?*
> *And set to work millions of spinning worms,*
> *That in their green shops weave the smooth-haired silk*
> *To deck her sons . . .*[57]

Milton would never stop craving a version of the abundance that Comus depicts, never stop wondering if, rather than turning his back on it altogether, there was a version of it that could be enjoyed without sliding into unacceptable excess. The vision of God's creation of the Earth that Milton would eventually offer in *Paradise Lost* closely resembles Comus's: it too teems with innumerable life forms, like the 'parsimonious emmet', the lowly ant, 'provident / Of future, in small room large heart enclosed', just as the enchanter attends to the 'millions of spinning Worms' whom he fleetingly spins into imagined life.[58]

The sense that Milton's imaginative loyalties might be more divided than the plot of *Comus* suggests is confirmed by the problems with which he fills its ending. The brothers fail to learn their lesson: the Spirit clearly tells them that they must break Comus's wand, and bind him, in order to end his magic when they rescue their sister; but they conspicuously fail to do so. It's this failure that leaves their sister glued to the enchanter's 'marble venomed seat / Smeared with gums of glutinous heat', a disconcerting mix of the stonily rigid and the stickily sexual.[59] Their failure is useful for the narrative, for it necessitates the shimmering apparition of 'Sabrina fair', summoned from her home 'Under the glassy, cool, translucent wave', who frees the Lady with a sprinkling of drops from her 'chaste palms moist and cold'. Water here does not engulf for good, as it would Edward King: Sabrina overcomes her drowning and saves the day, washing away the glutinous residue of temptation.

But the Lady never speaks again in the masque. There is no return to the thundering words with which she defended herself to Comus. She joins the dance, but has nothing more to say. Is this a sign that she has achieved what she needed to, and is now demurely silent, an accessory to her father's power as she will one day be to her husband's? Perhaps. But it could make her more like the figures at the end of Shakespeare's plays – and *Comus* is full of the traces of Milton's Shakespearean reading at this time – who fall silent in ways that suggest that we will never fully understand them: Iago, Shylock. Hers might be a silence as full as that which accompanied the arrival of Christ in the Nativity Ode – a silence conspicuously crammed with possibility. Comus escapes to fight another day, the Lady withdraws from language: Milton's vocational struggle, his indecision between engagement and disengagement, appears profoundly unresolved.

Like the banks of the Dee, Milton almost certainly never laid eyes on Ludlow either; but since he was writing for something that was going to happen there, he had reasons to care about the specifics of the place. While my visit to the Dee had been impromptu, I decided to make a more carefully planned visit to Ludlow with Sean, my friend and former teacher. At least there was a clear destination, a sense of something definite to do: stand in the ruined hall of Ludlow Castle where the first and only performance of *Comus* took place, on 29 September 1634.

Where the Dee had provided me with a blank spectacle of absence, in Ludlow, a quaint and picturesque town full of handcrafted goods and high-end delicatessens, it was easy to fall under the Comus-like spell of the place and drift between the traces of the seventeenth-century world that could still be glimpsed there. Very pleasant they were too: the tomb of Ambrosia Sidney, sister to the poet Philip, whose father Henry was one of Bridgewater's predecessors as president. The chance to follow the River Teme as it curved around the town, and hear the water babbling closest to where Sabrina first rose from her own 'rushy-fringed bank'. The hills beyond, from which, a decade after *Comus* was performed, Parliamentary soldiers battered the castle with cannons. And the ruins of the castle itself – shattered doors still hanging from their hinges; the shell of the great hall, smaller than I'd expected; the remnants of the nearby kitchens, from which servants would have carried over the heaped dishes to be served following the masque. Sean and I sat and read together through Geoffrey Hill's collection of poems, *Scenes from Comus*, trying to work out whether the specifics of this place had affected the modern poet who responded most electrifyingly to Milton, and to his Ludlow masque in particular. Hill was attuned to, and stunningly retuned, the landscape in which we found ourselves:

> *The river the forest, the river is the forest,*
> *the forest the river, swamps of loosestrife*
> *choking fecundity. Sabrina, she also, chaste*
> *genius of teeming and dying,*
> *I fancy her*
> *trailing labiles, placentas, uncomely swags.*
> *My own lines double here as her lianas.*[60]

The memory that sticks in my mind from this mini pilgrimage, however, was none of these – not a fragment of the seventeenth-century past that allowed me to feel connected with the true origins of *Comus* nor a piece of responsive literary greatness. It was rather another strange piece of happenstance. When we ascended the tallest tower in the castle, we found the top crowded with a group of schoolchildren on a trip, all in uniform, who seemed to be waiting for something to happen. It became clear that they were gathered round one of their number, a boy who couldn't have been more than ten or eleven years old. He took a cello from a case that he had somehow schlepped to the top of the tower, sat on a chair, and began to play a piece of Bach from memory with remarkable skill. We all stood, rapt, by what the Spirit in *Comus* calls the 'soft and solemn breathing sound' that 'Rose like a steam of rich distill'd Perfumes, / And stole upon the Air'.[61]

I couldn't believe my luck. Less than a hundred yards from where Milton's masque was first performed, here was a scene that seemed its modern equivalent: teachers and students, children performing before adults, beautiful music rippling through the Ludlow afternoon. But then the boy finished, we all applauded, and it suddenly became more prosaic, distasteful. One of the teachers had been filming the performance on her telephone; I heard her colleague mutter in her ear that he would arrange for it to be put on the school's website. They led the crowd of children back down the stairs. The boy who had played the cello was momentarily forgotten, left behind to struggle with the bulky instrument, and Sean and I helped him to return it to its case and begin to navigate the spiral of stone stairs back towards the ground.

This boy is one of those individuals whose place in my memory is disproportionate to the brevity with which his path crossed mine, perhaps like Edward King for Milton. The more I thought about him the more I realised that, though it felt at first like disappointment or disenchantment as the spell of the music was broken, in fact it was the whole strange scene that really did resonate for me with *Comus*. Milton's masque is, for me, both spellbindingly beautiful and profoundly uncomfortable – a document not just of Milton's own hopes and fears, and of the bizarre fascinations of a culture with a young woman's virginity and sexuality, but of the ways in which children are asked, in their upbringing and their education, to perform versions of themselves for the benefit of adults, to reassure us with their normality and impress us with their virtuosity. *Comus* is all of these things in a fascinating, troubling, inextricable combination; just as I can remember both the sound of Bach wafting from the top of a ruined castle, and the sight of a small boy, having done what was required of him, staggering forgotten down its winding steps.

Yet once more.

In the final moments of 'Lycidas' the rug is pulled out from under our feet. We have assumed from its beginning that we have been listening to the poet, or to a version of him: the voices that enter have shaken our sense of who is speaking, but nothing has prepared us for how it ends.

> *Thus sang the uncouth swain to the oaks and rills,*
> *While the still morn went out with Sandals grey,*
> *He touched the tender stops of various Quills,*
> *With eager thought warbling his Dorick lay:*
> *And now the Sun had stretched out all the hills,*
> *And now was dropped into the Western bay;*
> *At last he rose, and twitched his Mantle blew:*
> *To morrow to fresh Woods, and Pastures new.*[62]

Who is this 'uncouth swain'? Why Milton's abrupt decision to distance himself at the close, to say suddenly at the poem's end that all this was spoken by another? Perhaps to keep alive and uncertain our sense of where the poem is coming from, of the self from which it emerges; to turn its poetic voice into just one among the cast of characters whom we have heard in the poem, yet one more of the howls and growls that we have heard from its wolf pack; a way of answering the poem's fears that a life and its potential can be lost, by keeping its own possibilities, its own futures, as open as those of Lycidas himself, in two places at once, rising upwards to Heaven and flitting sideways across the shore.

In 1636, a few years after moving to Hammersmith, Milton's parents decided to relocate again. This time they chose the village of Horton, which today is tucked amidst the reservoirs that cluster just to the west of Heathrow Airport. Milton, the money earned from his aristocratic commissions still not enough to support himself, moved with them. It was here, in this small and unspectacular village, that he would write 'Lycidas' the following year. But the beginning of 1637 was marked by another loss, much closer to home – on 3 April Milton's mother, Sara, died. We know lamentably little of her character or her interests, her loves and her hates, the habits of thought and speech that she might have passed on to her son.

Milton was so silent about her death that it is tempting to suggest that some of the grief that poured out of him for Edward King, so in excess of what their relationship seems to have been, was displaced from his mother's recent death, a chance to continue mourning by disguised means.

I think this must be true in part, though I remain sceptical: it still feels like an attempt to impose a reassuring hierarchy and order to the feelings that a person must have for the people who populate their lives. But Sara Milton's death, and the presence of her tombstone in the parish church at Horton, did give me an excuse for another Milton excursion in Sean's company, our appetite having been whetted by the Ludlow visit a few months before. I'll say more about this trip, and about what else Milton did in Horton in the late 1630s, in the next chapter; I want to end this one with our arrival there, and with my sense of what it meant to travel to this unprepossessing place in search of, not a person, but a poem. It was a day of strange coincidences and hastily improvised schemes: I hadn't had the time to plan very well, and the church was locked when we arrived; fortunately the vicar's phone number was on display in the porch, and he agreed to come and let us in. We duly saw Sara Milton's tombstone, and the Victorian stained-glass window bearing Milton's image.

While we waited for the vicar to arrive, however, we wandered the few hundred yards down the road to the site of the house in which Milton lived while in Horton, and where 'Lycidas' was presumably written. The house itself is long gone, replaced in the nineteenth century by a large building named Berkyn Manor; but it was clear that this too was in the process of being replaced, heavy-duty vehicles roaring down the muddy track next to the house, some kind of property development in process, corrugated iron fences topped with barbed wire suggesting that visitors were not welcome. A chat with the woman living in the converted gatehouse confirmed that the owner, a farmer who was also mayor of the village, wouldn't permit entry; she also let slip that this was because the house had sat derelict since the 1980s, its contents locked inside and slowly decaying, and it had become a popular destination for adventurers who love to trespass in derelict places.

We had to leave without seeing the inside of Berkyn Manor, and it will probably be demolished or redeveloped before I ever get the chance to do so, but a foray on the internet confirmed what the woman had told me. The interior of the house, as documented by a daring and anonymous trespasser with a high-quality camera and the skills to use it, is one of the more extraordinary things that I've seen. Books slowly decay on shelves as ceilings and floors collapse around them; desk drawers and kitchen shelves are still replete with their deteriorating contents; a piano's keys slowly buckle and collapse. It looks at once as if it has just been vacated – as if the occupants have left in a terrible hurry, like the absent crew on a ghost ship – but also as if it has sat this way not for decades but for centuries, eons, the piles of dust and debris growing incrementally higher, the furniture sinking into oblivion with glacial slowness.

The inside of Berkyn Manor has nothing to do with the house that Milton lived in – it just happens to stand on the same site. And yet it's another of those chance encounters which nonetheless feels meaningfully connected to my experience of reading and returning to his poems. The house that holds its form, that seems from the outside to be solid, if decrepit, but that turns out to be collapsing from within; the photos that seem at once to freeze time and to testify to the disparate speeds at which it passes; these seem to speak, more powerfully than my time on the banks of the Dee or at the tombstone of Milton's mother, to the fate of Edward King, and to the poem that commemorates him.

'The dead body', observes Thomas Laqueur,

lives on many time scales: the hours, days, weeks or months it takes for the person to whom it belonged to leave this world and for her material remains to be put where they belong; the indeterminate time, from years to centuries, it takes for the body, flesh and bones to become dust; the years, decades, and, for the lucky few, even longer in which a person might stay in memory with her body as its locus . . . the millennia and longer in which basic forms of the care of the dead have existed since Neolithic times, if not earlier.[63]

In 'Lycidas' Milton strives to return to Edward King's lost corpse the gift of this continued existence, across and between times; to allow him, like Berkyn Manor and its contents, both to persist and to dissolve in time. But he can do so because, as this poem insists in its startling cast of voices and its flickering between worlds and time frames, to mourn is to be deranged and disordered in time, to seek to join the dead body in its many-timedness.

Our most reassuring stories about grief want it to follow a smooth progression that allows the mourner to leave it behind, to emerge unscathed and restored: whether these are the five discrete stages of grief as described by the psychiatrist Elizabeth Kübler-Ross – denial, anger, bargaining, depression, acceptance – or Freud's earlier distinction between mourning, which follows a clear course and comes to a successful end, and melancholia, which is interminable, and hence pathological. The poet Denise Riley, whose son died with appallingly unexpected suddenness in his twenties, refutes these linear models entirely; she writes in crystalline and harrowing terms of her experience, following his death, of 'living in suddenly arrested time': 'a sudden death,' she writes, 'for the one left behind, does such violence to the experienced "flow" of time that it stops, and suddenly wells up into a large pool.'[64] Grief, Riley insists, does not leave the griever unchanged: 'Time "is" the person. You're soaked through with it . . . It's not the same "I" who lives in her altered sense of no-time, but a reshaped person. And I don't know how she'll turn out.' Her notes from the depth of suspended time can, she explains, 'walk around only the rim of this experience. At times they loop back on themselves, for one effect of living inside such a temporal suspension is that your reflections will crop up all over again but as if, on each occasion, they're newly thought.'[65]

The frozen, collapsing time of mourning, with its slow

transformations and its strange and insistent recursions, resonate for me with the crumbling time capsule of Berkyn Manor, and with the crumbling time capsule of 'Lycidas', written on the same site hundreds of years before. Milton's poem is a startling crystallisation of the experience that Riley describes: time looping back on itself, endlessly repeating itself, but insisting in the process that Milton will emerge from writing it, and that we might emerge from reading it, as a different person.

But I cannot quite end there. I have skipped, in my own recursions to 'Lycidas', over one of its most famous and mysterious moments. The speech of the 'pilot of the Galilean Lake', with its grim wolves, ends with these ominous words:

> But that two-handed engine at the door
> Stands ready to smite once, and smite no more.[66]

What is the two-handed engine? Probably no line in Milton has provoked more scholarly guesswork. Did Milton mean the two testaments of the Bible? Is it the sword wielded by the Angel Michael at the Last Judgement, or his scales, or both? Or a sheep hook? Or a cross? Or something else altogether?

I was teaching this poem a few years ago and explaining to my students how many theories it had provoked, when one of them replied: 'Oh . . . well it has two hands and it's about to strike, so I assumed it was a clock.' I was struck silent: the idea had never occurred to me. When I read around a bit, I discovered that the idea had previously been floated, but that, because so few clocks had minute hands when the poem was written, the alternative suggestion is that Milton had in mind a turret-clock automaton: a human figure who would strike (or 'smite', an alternative term) the hours on a church clock.

I don't think this solves the mystery of these lines: any single explanation is likely to feel inadequate to the calculated vagueness that makes them so richly sinister. But it does seem right to add this to the list of possibilities – to imagine a timepiece, tolling the end of all things, at the centre of a poem that shapes its own time and ours with such hallucinogenic variety. One of the online photos reveals that somewhere in the depths of Berkyn Manor, in the midst of its crumbling floors and decaying bookshelves, is an object that might stand for the very kernel of Milton's poem: a small pendulum clock, surrounded by cracked and peeling paint, frozen at 3:47. No flow of time; no ticks, no tocks; the earworm of 'yet once more' giving way to the pregnant silence of 'smite no more'.

6

19 May 1638: 'Your Thoughts Close, and your Countenance Loose'

Dinner in Paris. Milton has made it. Upon arriving in the city, thanks to letters of introduction carefully arranged before he left England, he has been 'warmly received' in the household of the English ambassador, John Scudamore, Viscount Sligo.[1] But, since arriving, nothing has gone to plan. The city is as loud and dirty as London, as ungainly in its huge sprawl. Scudamore himself seems distracted and irritable. Milton has the feeling that the ambassador could not turn him away, but hardly welcomes his arrival. The only point at which the viscount seems briefly to light up is when he shows Milton his private chapel. At first it seems merely a courtesy, though the man is horribly proud of it. Milton catches his breath as he enters the gloomy chamber, his eyes roving over the altar, covered with rich damask cloth and topped with lit candles, as well as glinting silver vessels for the celebration of the Eucharist. The ambassador, he thinks, must have accepted this den of popish idolatry as part of his lodgings; but no, to his astonishment, the man begins to explain proudly that he has fitted it out himself at great expense. Know you, Scudamore asks, of the late and lamented Bishop Andrewes of Ely? Milton murmurs that in fact he wrote a poem to the good bishop's memory in his student days. Scudamore's face lights up: the room in which they stand, he explains, was built on the very plan of Andrewes's private chapel! The viscount takes communion there every month – every month! Such pious frequency! – and he knows that, although some French papists spitefully refer to the services there as 'the English Mass', his friend the archbishop would approve. The archbishop: the name of

Scudamore's powerful friend, William Laud, is dropped into the conversation every few sentences. Thanks to their shared admiration for Andrewes, the viscount assumes that Milton is a fellow lover of ceremony, and he shows his visitor his proudest achievement in Paris: Laud's speech, delivered at the trial of the Puritans Burton, Bastwick, and Prynne, that the viscount has translated into French. You must take a copy, he urges, as Milton tries to smile gratefully; tries to suppress the image of the three men's sliced and mangled ears, his imaginings of their singed and branded flesh.[2] You must also send me your poem on Bishop Andrewes, the viscount continues. Milton nods, neglecting to mention that since his Cambridge days he has seen a great deal more of the kinds of men whom Andrewes inspired – men like Laud, who mutilate those seeking the truth, and his lesser acolytes, happy to leave their congregants' souls to rot while they fill their churches with trinkets and diversions. Such men sicken him; the more he has read, since he wrote those early poems, about how the Church had been in its infancy, the harder he finds them to stomach. He had known that his travels would ram even worse errors down his throat, and he welcomed the provocation; but he had not expected to meet them embodied by the first Englishman to show him hospitality. He strives to show no flicker of disapproval. The advice he was given revolves in his head: keep your thoughts close, and your countenance loose; closed thoughts, open face.

That night's dinner is scarcely more comfortable. The mood in the room is tense and confusing. There is much muttering about the Earl of Leicester, who, Milton gleans from the comments that he half hears, is also in Paris, acting as a second ambassador and treading deliberately on Scudamore's toes at every turn. Milton would rather hear from the learned men around the table, for this is exactly the kind of gathering in which he hoped to be involved upon leaving England. One thing Scudamore has managed to do in Paris is insinuate himself into the circles of learned and witty men, who like nothing better than to eat and talk. Milton still strives to keep the expression on his face frank and open – a hint of a smile that he hopes looks slightly knowing, as if he has enjoyed many such gatherings before, without becoming sardonic. It doesn't help that much of the conversation is in French: he's studied the language by himself but has little affection for it, its rhythms failing to sing to him like those of Italian, and he's forced to listen out for snatches of familiar English and Latin to help him keep up. They seem mostly to be talking of other men, men who are not present, names he cannot place – he has heard the name 'Hobbes' mentioned before, but doesn't know who the man is – and one that he can, the Dutch philosopher Grotius, whom he knows that Scudamore counts as a friend, and whom he is eager to meet while in Paris.

It doesn't help that, while he's trying to keep up with the chatter, he keeps glancing out of the corner of his eye at the man sitting immediately to his left. Although he's immensely tall, he sits crumpled in his seat, as if weighed down by moroseness. His features are handsome but his hair is unkempt, thinning at the front, long and straggly behind – or not so much unkempt, Milton suspects, as artfully arranged to look that way. He's probably only a few years Milton's elder, but his mood and garb give him a more venerable look. Once or twice he has turned his head and tossed a scrap from the table to his dog – a squat, muscular mastiff, its eyes as light and watery as its master's – who sits patiently a few yards off, tethered to the base of his chair. The man, dressed entirely in black, has said little bar a couple of sentences in what sounds like perfect French to the man on his other side, a pompous mathematician, and so Milton assumes he's a local. The latest dish has arrived, and Milton stares at it nervously: a green globe covered with an armour of leaves, giving it a look that is part vegetable, part reptile – as if, he thinks idly to himself, the apple and the serpent of Eden had produced offspring. It stands in a pool of melted butter, a heady stench of mint and garlic wafting from it. Milton stares at it for a few seconds, utterly unsure of how to eat it, and sure that he's about to humiliate himself; he starts to assail it with his knife, when, suddenly, the man in black's hand darts out and skewers it with his fork. It is eaten thusly, he tells Milton, murmuring in a deep voice that could boom through the room if he chose, and with an accent that suggests origins that are not at all Parisian, but lie not far from

London. Pinning the green sphere on the plate, he discreetly shows Milton how to peel back the scaly leaves, slice out the disconcertingly hairy layer of fibres beneath, find the edible flesh, and swirl its pieces in the minted butter before lifting it to his mouth.

To Milton's surprise, the man then continues to speak with him. We have such weeds in England, he explains, and we call them hartichokes: they say King Henry was the first to grow them, and they remain a rich man's food – a pound for a few dozen! They came hither to France from Italy, a hundred years ago, when Queen Catherine arrived from Florence with her army of cooks and taught men hereabouts how to eat. Before then the French ate like beasts, cramming their spiced hashes into their gullets by hand. But this way of cooking them is truly Italian, and truly modern – *tartufato*, they call it, 'truffling'.[3] Everything is done in Italy more finely, I would say – and here his sombre eyes smile for the first time: I hear that you soon will venture there yourself?

For all that he had sat in near silence for the first hour of the dinner, the man in black loves to talk. He seems to know everyone and everything. The dinner goes on for some hours, plate after steaming plate, and so too does their conversation. His name, the man in black explains, is Digby; he's kinsman to the Earl of Bristol, of whom Milton has of course heard. He likes to ask Milton a question, listen to the answer with a smile playing at the corner of his mouth, and then rumble out a meandering response in which he will drop several names, tell a story that sounds both impossible and has the ring of truth about it, and make suggestions that Milton tucks away carefully in the chests and cabinets of his memory palace. He explains each dish as it emerges – what it's called, how it's to be eaten, the origins of every ingredient that it contains, the name of a noblewoman with whom he's eaten it. He explains that he wears his solemn garb for his dead wife – Milton is about to mention that he has also suffered a recent loss, his mother, when the man in black mentions that her death was five years since. He asks Milton how he passed his time before his travels; mostly reading, Milton admits, touchy about his lack of a more respectable pastime or profession – a great deal of reading. And whom have you read?

Milton mentions the Italians whose writings he loves – Dante, Ariosto – and the man in black nods but waits quietly for him to continue; so Milton names some of the Fathers of the Church through whose dense volumes he has patiently worked his way in the preceding years, chewy names that his parents and friends greet with stares of blankness or here-we-go-again rolls of their eyes: Cyprian, Tertullian, Ignatius of Antioch, Clement of Alexandria. To his surprise, the man in black smiles and nods. Ah, the Fathers. Just last week, he tells Milton, I sat with my kinsman George, the Earl of Bristol's son, in a side chapel at the Church of Saint Germain, and we talked of them at length. We debated which, of the several religions that at present have course in the world, a prudent man should rationally venture his soul upon. And I warned him that he must not read the Fathers with a forelaid design, looking to shake their authority; that their disagreements can be reconciled; that their authority still buttresses that of the Church.[4] Only then did Milton realise that, when the man in black spoke of *the* Church, he did not mean that of their shared homeland – he referred to the Church of Rome. The man was a self-confessed papist Englishman, the first to whom Milton had knowingly spoken. The words of advice echoed in his mind again: *I pensieri stretti, ed il viso sciolto*, closed thoughts and an open face; he strove to remain impassive. As if the man in black could read his mind, could hear the Italian that Milton was chanting to himself, he tactfully changed the subject: but enough of their dusty wisdom. Let us talk of Italy. You must tell me of your intentions. I presume that you will go via Leghorn, and see Florence. I will tell you where the finest of times can be had there by a man of your learned sensibilities: the dinners and the conversation of the academies will certainly outshine this mediocre evening; there you will find both poetry and diversion. In my youth I had the pleasure of speaking in one myself, to some applause. And if it is books that you care to see, let me tell you of the finest volume of Petrarca that ever I bought, once owned by a man who became Pope. The librarians can help you – the finest of them is in Rome, a German named Holst, though he visited England and speaks our language well. I shall tell you where to find him, and you must use my name. And of course, there is today's wisdom to be sought, as well as yesterday's. And here he fixed Milton with his pale-eyed gaze: I presume that you have read the great Galileo?

✦

We left Milton in the last chapter in Horton: a small and sleepy village which was in many ways a retreat from the lively intellectual worlds amidst which he had grown up. And yet somehow, within a year of publishing 'Lycidas', he had left England for the first and only time in his life, and found himself in another great European metropolis, Paris, en route to Italy where he would experience a wide array of political and cultural centres in dizzying succession. This chapter will suggest some of the ways in which this leap was made possible. Milton's lifelong conviction that difference had to be actively courted and transformatively encountered – even, and perhaps especially, difference of a sort that felt threatening and alien – first crystallised during his European travels. But this sense of difference and contrast is less simple than it seems. It was also a development of tendencies in Milton's reading, in his learning, in his thinking, and in his personal relationships, that had been percolating for years before his departure. Leaving for Europe was a way of making reading flow naturally into action, and his travels challenge any sharp distinction between life in the world and the life of the mind.

It's for this reason that, rather than lingering at this imagined dinner in Paris to which I'll eventually return, I will begin making sense of this most dramatic and abrupt of transpositions in Milton's life by returning to Horton, where he lived with his parents until his mother's death. The day that I visited with Sean was a grey and dismal caricature of English weather, and after seeing the church and the exterior of Berkyn Manor, it was not clear what we should do next. We had lunch in a nearby pub, and it was only then that I remembered the other part of this trip which I'd intended, but ultimately failed, to organise.

I've already alluded to the activity that took up most of Milton's time in Horton, when he was not writing poems of his own: reading – avidly, voraciously, exhaustively, and exhaustingly. Emerging from Cambridge with his potential vocations in tatters, he prevailed upon his parents' patience and their relative wealth, living with them while he continued his studies, but in an idiosyncratic and self-directed way. Years later he wrote, looking back at this time:

> On my father's estate, whither he had retired in old age, I spent my whole time at leisure [*otium*] in turning over the Greek and Latin authors; although I occasionally exchanged the country for the city, either for the sake of purchasing books, or for learning something new in mathematics or in music, in which I at that time delighted.[5]

This is an idealised account, produced at a moment in his life when Milton, by then a prominent advocate of regicide, was defending his reputation to a European audience. But even if he did not spend his 'whole time at leisure' (he continued to be involved in his father's financial affairs, not to mention the writing of *Comus*), reading certainly dominated his time and took most of his energies. His surviving commonplace book records only the tip of this iceberg of effort, and even that is staggering: snippets culled from countless pages and tomes, wide and various in scope, but dominated in particular by theology, especially the writings of the Church Fathers, and by ancient, medieval, and more recent history. These complex and forbidding works were seasoned and leavened by Italian literature, especially the poetry of Dante and Ariosto. But before we get into any more of these details, a practical question arises: now that he'd relocated to a quiet village from a home on the doorstep of the bibliophile's paradise that was St Paul's Churchyard, where was he getting hold of these books? The most obvious answer is that he was buying them on trips back to the city, 'for the sake of purchasing books', mentioned above – but the kind of tomes he was reading would have been expensive to buy and cumbersome to carry. So it's likely that he had access to a library, the closest major collections being the Bodleian Library at Oxford, still only a few decades old and a long but not impossible journey away, and the library at Eton, about which I'll have more to say shortly. In 2002, however, the Milton scholar Edward Jones resurrected an intriguing additional possibility by pointing out that many of the theological works Milton read at this time were located a short horse ride from Horton in one of the most curious private collections in England, the so-called Kedermister Library. This collection of more than three hundred weighty volumes is attached to the church of St Mary the Virgin in nearby Langley, bequeathed by John Kedermister just a few years before Milton's family moved to the area.[6]

Unfortunately, as with the church in Horton itself, I had entirely failed to plan for this part of our trip, but once again I was rescued by the generosity of the local clergy: an online search gave me the phone number of the vicar of St Mary the Virgin, who agreed to give us access to the library once the lunchtime playgroup with which he was occupied came to an end. And so we drove the twenty minutes to Langley, where neither the library nor its surroundings were at all what I expected. While Horton still had the feel of an isolated village, protected from the sprawl of nearby towns by the reservoirs that ring it, Langley is effectively part of Slough – a town firmly associated in the British psyche with the quintessence of suburban dullness, as both the target of John Betjeman's poem which begins 'Come, friendly bombs, and fall on Slough' and as the setting for the 2001 mockumentary sitcom *The Office*. Milton in Slough, it's fair to say, is not the pilgrimage I'd envisaged; but in another way, as with my London walk with Sean, the very incongruity had its own useful effects – a reminder that reading can happen almost anywhere; that histories are not always legible at a glance.

Robin, the vicar, was still busy with a raucous group of children when we arrived, and so Sean and I wandered around the church spotting various interesting and Miltonically flavoured bits and pieces: some medieval wall paintings showing through the reformers' fading whitewash; a huge and amazingly well-preserved coat of arms of Charles I (of all people), so large and detailed that its makers had decided to give the lion and the unicorn on it resplendently erect penises. Our eyes were caught by a curious structure on one side of the church, in the south transept, unlike anything I'd seen in a parish church before: a set of wooden walls painted to look like marble, its windows obscured by wooden lattices, and the whole structure covered with intricate decorations and Latin phrases, including a painted eye bearing the ominous legend *Deus videt* – 'God sees'. But we couldn't see the library, or work out where it might be.

When the vicar finished and found us, he agreed to let us into the library, which, it turned out, was accessed through this same painted area. The wooden walls themselves, he told us, had been built by the Kedermister family, who were minor local nobility, to contain their private pew; they could access it by a side door, which meant that they would at no point have to share the same holy space as the poor and lowly parishioners. It was a monument, I thought as I stood inside it, to the claustrophobia to which snobbishness and disdain leads. These were people who preferred lurking in their ornate box over praying communally, visible to the painted eyes of God but not to the poor. At one end of the private pew, down a few steps, was a door painted in the same fashion, and this swung open to reveal the library within. It was a remarkable space, and entering it was an extraordinary moment. Its panelled walls were painted with even greater intricacy than the inside of the pew: landscapes, small figures, and abstract patterns. The walls themselves swung open on hinges and turned out to be panels covering the crammed bookshelves. We were able to leaf through books that Milton certainly knew well, like Augustine's *Confessions*. Could it have been this very copy? There is no firm evidence that Milton ever came here; no smoking-gun marginalia. In the library, we were in the realm of the *might have*, the *could have*, not even allowing ourselves the *must have*. But just as the unhistorical layering of Berkyn Manor over Milton's Horton home seemed to augment rather than erase its significance, so the very uncertainty and incongruity of this extraordinary library, its tenuous link to Milton and its ornate seclusion from its suburban surroundings, seemed apt. It made the Kedermister Library a fitting place for Milton, not because I could locate him there with certainty but precisely because it seemed to represent, within one intricately painted and secluded pocket of Slough, the collision of worlds and the revelation of startling possibilities that reading him and following in his footsteps had by then come to involve.

FIGURE 11: The Kedermister Library.

Milton reading for countless hours in the Kedermister Library is an intriguing but lonely scene. His only companion would have been the attendant stipulated in John Kedermister's bequest, whose duty it was to 'take special care that no Books be lent or purloined', and also to keep the painted room 'Sweet and Cleanly from Cobweb dust or any other foul or offensive thing'.[7] But Milton was not entirely cut off from his friendships during these years. In 1637, at the same time that he was writing 'Lycidas', he sent multiple letters to his old schoolfriend, Charles Diodati, one of which ended by asking, 'if you conveniently can, please send me Giustiniani,

Historian of the Veneti'.[8] Diodati, a year or so younger than Milton, was the son of an eminent physician, Theodor Diodati, whose family had – like many Italian Protestants – migrated from Tuscany to London. As Milton's mind began to be set upon travelling, and to swivel with particular intensity towards Italy, he was happy to call on an old friend with knowledge of the country to send him a fifteenth-century historical work for useful background reading.

But Charles Diodati was a great deal more to Milton than a source of books. He's entered my account once or twice already, but it's time to bring him into the foreground, for the two men had continued to exchange letters and poems in the more than a dozen years since they both left St Paul's. In their friendship were entangled and entwined not just Milton's feelings for this individual but also everything which Diodati represented for him, and with which Milton was deeply concerned at this point in his life. Italy, and foreignness. English, Italian, and the nature of language itself. The problem of vocation, and the extent to which one should involve oneself in, or withdraw from, the world. The nature of intimate human relationships – real, imagined, and the inescapable mixture of the two. Perhaps the best way to summarise their relationship – at once the simplest and the most complicated way of putting it – is to say that Diodati was the love of Milton's life.[9] But it's the precise nature of this love that both cries out and tantalisingly refuses to be fully understood.

I've already touched in the previous chapters on Milton's engagement with Italian language and literature, and suggested that it might have been provoked both by his father's musical circle, which included anglicised Italians and Italianated Englishmen, and by his schooling. On one level this Italophilia was not unusual, if something of an anachronism: the century before Milton's birth had seen multiple vogues for Italian fashions, fictions, and turns of phrase, which were alternately embraced, satirised, and actively denounced as vulnerable to the seductive lures of foreignness and popery. But Milton's interest was much deeper and more extensive than most of those who indulged in these fashionable pursuits. Years before he ever considered travelling to Italy he immersed himself in the Italian language until he achieved an astonishing level of fluency, probably with the help of one of the many Italian immigrants living in London who earned money by offering private tuition.[10] He must have supplemented these studies with his own personal efforts, since some of his earliest writings were a series of accomplished sonnets in Italian. These are mostly experiments in love poetry, which have the mannered feel of a young person trying out powerful emotions that he hasn't yet experienced. What distinguishes them is Milton's self-conscious sense of his own foreignness to the language he's using, a foreignness that both perturbs and stimulates. In one sonnet he imagines being jostled by a crowd of young lovers, who ask him: 'Why, O why do you write your love poems in an alien and unknown language?' ('*perché scrivi, / Perché tu scrivi in lingua ignota e strana . . . ?*'). In another he describes the way in which 'on my nimble tongue love raises up the new flower of a foreign language' ('*il fior novo di strania favella*'), comparing it to a young shepherdess watering 'an exotic little plant' ('*l'erbetta strana e bella*') on a barren mountaintop. This is a striking image, one which I find far less light and airy than the general tone of the poem. Milton's description of the Italian language as a flower taking root on and in his '*lingua snella*' – his nimble, flickering, dextrous tongue – carries with it a strange sense of his body actually being transformed, made into something new, by the practising of this new language, and not in an entirely comfortable way, as it drives its roots down into the fleshy soil of the tongue.

We tend to think of the learning of a language as a challenge for the mind, and especially for the memory; but, as we already saw with his schoolroom experiences of Latin, for Milton it would have been much more bound up with the changing rhythms, the practice and the pain, of the body, and we need to keep this in mind when making sense of his delighted dabbling in Italian. The most remarkable account that I know of this way of relating to Italian as a bodily as well as a cerebral experience was captured centuries after Milton by the Russian poet Osip Mandelstam, who, rather than understanding learning as a matter solely of the mind, advocated a form of 'rhythmic education', a 'miracle' that 'transforms the abstract system into the people's flesh'.[11] Mandelstam had achieved this himself through his intense and transformative reading of Dante. For him, 'Dante's rhythms . . . glorify the human gait, the measure and rhythm of walking, the footstep and its form'. But Mandelstam was only able to grasp this physical basis of rhythm, this sense of Dante's poetry being bound to this way of marching beyond oneself and into the world, via the bodily experience of learning the language itself:

> When I began to study Italian and had barely familiarised myself with its phonetics and prosody, I suddenly understood that the centre of gravity of my speech efforts had been moved closer to my lips, to the outer parts of my mouth. The tip of the tongue suddenly turned out to have the seat of honour. The sound rushed toward the locking of the teeth.[12]

We'll never know quite what it was like for Milton to learn Italian, but I feel it must have involved something of this sense of physical transformation, of a change penetrating the very core of his bodily being, which is recalled in the discomforting image of a plant propelling its spindly roots into the delicate flesh of his nimble tongue. If to walk out into the world, to strike out for Italy, was to follow in the footsteps of Dante's lines, then this journey with and away from himself had already begun when Milton reshaped his reading, his writing, and perhaps his very body, by making his own the rhythms of Italian, and losing himself in them.

It was not just his own body that was implicated in this fashion when he wrote in Italian. Milton very deliberately drew his closest friend into this poetic world, where novelties of language and desire promised or threatened to transform his very physical self, addressing him in a sonnet which begins '*Diodati, e te 'l dirò con maraviglia*' – 'Diodati, I'll tell you something which amazes me'. The revelation turns out to be the news that he, Milton, who has long scorned love, has become captivated by a *Pellegrina bellezza*, a foreign or roving beauty. There are several ways in which it's tempting to read this poem. This beautiful woman might, as some of Milton's earlier biographers liked to speculate, be a real person – perhaps a member of London's Italian community; alternatively, she might be read more symbolically as a representation of the allure of Italian, or of foreignness more broadly – the call to Italy that Milton would soon answer when he undertook his travels. But I also feel sure that this poem is in some sense not only addressed to but is actually about Diodati himself, Milton's Anglo-Italian friend, who had, since leaving St Paul's, studied at Oxford; travelled to Geneva and lived with his uncle, the eminent Calvinist theologian Jean Diodati; and practised medicine under his father's tutelage, moving back and forth between Chester and London. A set of activities that, in marked contrast to Milton's moving around the clock face of London in accord with his parents' plans, can certainly be described as *pellegrino*. Fittingly, their exchanges across these years floated between languages – in addition to the Italian poem, they included two letters that Diodati wrote to Milton in Greek, and two poetic elegies and two letters by Milton, all in Latin. It can feel at times like these are nothing more than the exchanges of two extremely clever and well-read schoolfriends, smart alecs who are merely playing – playing at love, at learning, at philosophising, and perhaps, most disconcertingly, playing at friendship itself, continuing the deft and eloquent putting on and off of personae and languages in which they had been rigorously trained at St Paul's. But, on the other hand, there's the persistent feeling that something else shines through their exchanges, a pair of identifiable personalities which are not just shaped and moulded by the very conventions that they deploy but which shape and transform them in turn. And the accompanying sense that these are two people who do intensely feel and care for one another, making use of the readiest-to-hand and most socially acceptable language in which that feeling can be expressed.

My feeling that the Italian sonnet is in some sense 'about' Diodati himself as a wandering beauty is reinforced by one of the Latin poems Milton addressed to his friend, in which he describes glimpsing on a London street 'a whole host of girls, with faces just like goddesses', who 'go to and fro along the walks, resplendently beautiful', until 'by chance, I caught sight of one girl who was far more beautiful than all the rest [*Unam forte aliis supereminuisse notabam*]: that radiance was the beginning of my downfall'. He fell passionately in love, he tells Diodati, but the girl disappeared, never to be seen again. This moment is strikingly reminiscent of one of the most famous first encounters in all of literature – the moment in Marcel Proust's *À la Recherche du Temps Perdu* when the narrator first glimpses Albertine, the woman with whom he will become enamoured and all-consumingly obsessed. She is first sighted as part of 'a strange mass of moving colours' which gradually resolves into a group of girls, who crystallise further until one of them can be more clearly seen 'walking along pushing her bicycle'. Like the girl in Milton's poem who emerges as an individual, only slowly and incompletely does this girl, Albertine, step forth from the group: 'I glimpsed her oblique, laughing glance, looking out from the inhumane world that circumscribed the life of their little tribe, an inaccessible *terra incognita* . . . what must I have seemed like to her? What sort of world was the one from which she was looking at me?'[13]

I'm not suggesting that Proust knew Milton's early Latin poem (though the title of his novel, ending *Temps Perdu*, does intriguingly recall *Paradis Perdu*), but the resemblance is still striking, not least because it's become commonplace to see Albertine as a fictionalisation of Proust's chauffeur, Alfred Agostinelli, with whom she shares many similarities, and to see their relationship in the novel as a thin veil for Proust's homosexuality. The poet Anne Carson calls this 'the transposition theory', according to which all the figures in Proust's novel must be mentally replaced by the real-life individuals who inspired and explain them. She writes that while this theory 'is a graceless, intrusive, and saddening hermeneutic mechanism, in the case of Proust it is also irresistible'.[14] We might say the same, in a broader way, about reading Milton: it's frequently irresistible to say that certain figures in his writing – the Lady in *Comus*, Adam, Samson – just *are* him, even as it feels horribly reductive to make these transpositions. There's a similar temptation to read the lady of the Italian sonnet as a figure for Diodati. But it's a temptation of a very different sort, based on the inclination many readers have shared in speculating that Milton's relationship with Diodati had an erotic or sexual dimension. Might the Italian lady in his early poem *be* Diodati in the way that Proust's Albertine *was* Alfred Agostinelli, and for the same reasons?

This raises the thorny problem of whether we can decide, on the basis of a few highly artful and evasive writings, what really went on in these two men's minds and bodies. Some have been happy to psychologise Milton, to dissect his character on the basis of these letters and assign him 'a latent homosexuality which on occasion might emerge and a homoerotic personality'.[15] But the problems with such a diagnosis are many, most obviously its begging the question of whether such a thing as an intrinsically 'homoerotic personality' exists. Once again, the question that interests me is not so much what Milton was or what he did as what we want from Milton – who or what we want him to be or not be, and why. The interpretative challenges here fascinate me because they throw such a bright light on the difficulties involved in categorising and defining a whole range of emotional and sexual relationships, in Milton's time and in ours.

One obvious riposte to this account of Milton's 'latent homo-sexuality' is that the category of homosexuality is a much later invention – not that people of the same biological sex in the seventeenth century did not love or have sex with one another, but that the idea of an intrinsically homosexual *person* is not formu-lated until the late nineteenth century. Another is that the intense, passionate friendship between Milton and Diodati was entirely in keeping with the norms and practices of seventeenth-century friendship, which often involved men embracing, kissing, sharing beds, professing their love for one another as a kind of spiritual marriage. The Anglican priest Jeremy Taylor wrote that 'the love of friends [must] sometimes be refreshed with material and low caresses; lest by striving to be too divine it become less humane.'[16] Friendship between learned men, one of the crucial ways in which social and political relationships were publicly managed, was always unstable and ambiguous, and it was by virtuoso navigation of this instability that men proved their sophistication.[17] But I find myself dissatisfied by both of these responses, which feel in different ways like evasions, ways not just of respecting historical difference but of hiding behind it.

It seems more important to me to acknowledge the ways Milton and Diodati themselves played with the nature of their shared love in a manner that was both daring and veiled behind learned allusion, making its tone difficult to decode – which may have been part of the point. This is what Diodati is doing when, in one of his letters to Milton, he tries to tempt his friend away from his relentless reading: 'Live, laugh, enjoy your youth and the hours,' Diodati urges, 'and stop reading the serious, the light, and the indolent works of ancient wise men, wearing yourself out all the while.' He counsels his friend instead to 'be merry, but not in the manner of Sardanapalus in Soli'.[18] The encouragement to abandon learning is itself highly learned; the historical reference abstruse – but also highly suggestive. Sardanapalus was a semi-mythical Assyrian king, notorious not just for his sexual licentiousness but specifically for his effeminacy and his disruption of social hierarchies and gender differences: dressing in women's clothes and having indiscriminate sex with men and women.[19] Certainly not a happy or an entirely comfortable comparison for the man nicknamed the Lady of Christ's. But potentially not for Diodati either, given that the English fear and loathing of Italy was often expressed by depicting it as a den of sodomy. Indeed, Edward Coke, the foremost lawyer in the land, claimed that Italians first brought homosexuality to England, and reminded his readers that 'buggerare is to bugger, so buggery cometh of the Italian word'.[20] There is more at stake in this allusion than meets the eye. One way of interpreting this would be to see Diodati alluding to Sardanapalus as a negative example precisely as a way of inoculating their friendship from a dangerous comparison by making it on his terms. Such sins are further east, displaced from the Italy of his forebears and into Asia, and back into the distant past – insulating their friendship from any similar suspicion, and allowing the sexual possibilities of male friendship to remain legible, and to be enjoyed, as an open secret.[21]

But if this is true of the letters and poems that they exchanged directly, it also allows me one last glance backwards at 'Lycidas'. I discussed in the last chapter my strange sense that the grief unfurled in that poem seems uncomfortably excessive for a man whom Milton barely knew, and suggested one explanation – displaced grief for his mother. But another possibility is that this poem is awash with powerful emotion siphoned off from his friendship with Diodati, with whom Milton actually had many of the formative, youthful experiences that he somewhat spuriously claimed to have shared with Edward King. This opens up new meanings for the moment in the poem when the nymphs, helpless before the Fury's indiscriminate slayings and slittings of life's thread, are compared to the mythical figure of Orpheus, 'Whom Universal nature did lament, / When by the rout that made the hideous roar, / His goary visage down the stream was sent'.[22] Milton is referring here to a famous myth, and one that preoccupied him throughout his writings as he struggled with his own status as a poet. Orpheus was a classical figure who suggested the power of poetry to shape the world, but also its limits and its dangers. He was said to be able to charm the very trees and rocks with his poems and songs, but when he descended to the underworld to rescue his beloved Eurydice, he failed, even though the ghosts of the dead themselves wept at the beauty of his creations. In 'Lycidas', however, Orpheus appears in a more disturbing guise: Milton focuses on the terrible end to the myth, when Orpheus, returned from the underworld, rejects the love of all women and is horrifically torn to shreds by them in a bacchanalian frenzy – 'the rout that made the hideous roar' – his head floating down the river, his watery dismemberment even more terrible than Edward King's. Yet there's one detail in the most famous account of the myth, by the Roman poet Ovid, that is often suppressed in retellings of the story to which Milton chose to allude. Orpheus doesn't just turn away from women because he misses Eurydice: Ovid writes that he 'taught the folk of Thrace / The love for tender boys, to pluck the buds, / The brief springtime, with manhood still to come'.[23] The great poet dies in part for his love of boys. This is part of a network of covert and glancing references to love between men and boys that is woven through the densely mythological text of 'Lycidas'; and as Milton would have known from reading one of his favourite poets, Spenser, poets often used pastoral names to disguise a 'very speciall and most familiar freend', retaining 'some savour of disorderly love, which the learned call pæderastice'.[24] I suggested in relation to both Milton's school and university years that his exposure to classical learning was inter-woven in complicated ways with the rhythms of violence and the possibilities of pain and covert pleasure. Both of these are present in the retelling of Orpheus, behind which might also beat the rhythms of his love for Diodati, told in a learned language conveni-ently and self-protectively open to many interpretations.

I've tried to show here that Milton and Diodati's love for one another was no more straightforward for them to speak about than it is for me to speak about: that it was navigated through learned games and evasive hints. Part of me wants to respond with deliberate directness, to accept a story in which homosexual love and sex are everywhere possible. Recent scholars have thankfully become much less inclined to identify intrinsically homosexual personalities through history, and have tended to think instead in terms of *queer possibilities* – the ways in which an individual or their writings might not fit into, might actively disrupt, the prevailing norms of their culture. I see the merits of this approach, but I also recognise the value of the pioneering queer theorist Eve Sedgwick bluntly asking, 'If a gay Marlowe, what about a gay Spenser or Milton?'[25] The very notion of a gay literary canon, throwing historical caution to the winds, is a valuable counterweight to the alternative, which is to assume that the conventions of friendship are enough to explain away such an idea altogether, to prevent us from even considering it. This leaves heterosexuality as the norm that must be assumed and does not need to be argued for; a lazy, limited, and limiting way to think. Saying that Milton and Diodati were 'just friends', insisting that their exchanges took place entirely within the conven-tions of learned and playful humanist friendship they had learnt at school, is to dodge the problem, not remove it: after all, I've already suggested that their school curriculum tended to destabilise the very forms of manhood that it sought to create. Above all, it assumes that we know what it is to be 'just friends'. To assume that Milton's friendship with Diodati either must or must not have had a sexual element because it was uniquely intense is to assume, falsely, that we know what sexuality and friendship are when we encounter them, and that we can always distinguish between them. Another way to put this would be that the course of an intense, formative friendship belongs within, but also has the power to alter and transform, the intense knot of rhythms that makes up a life. The psychoanalyst Theodor Reik, pondering the fact that *Takt*, a social virtue, also refers in German to musical time or rhythm, suggested that 'happy love is largely dependent upon the temporal concordance of the individual rhythm of two human beings'.[26] Milton and Diodati, I would say, seem in their friendship, and in the letters and poems they exchanged, to have achieved this temporal concordance, the meshing of their respective rhythmic knots. Perhaps this is just a complicated way of saying, again, that Diodati was the love of Milton's life. But in saying this, I want to keep the nature of this love *actively open*: neither to decide that it must or must not have been sexual, nor to throw up my hands and say we can't know, and move on, leaving our assumptions unchanged; but rather to make our continued not-knowing into the reason to read their exchanges of letters and poems, and to care about their shared love after nearly four hundred years. The reason these early writings matter to me is because they hold out the promise of other ways of relating, other forms of relationship, from those that I already know how to categorise and can therefore anticipate; new rhythms of love.

Writing 'Lycidas' pushed Milton's mind to the fringes of the British Isles, the threshold between England, Wales, and Ireland; between land, river, and sea; between life and death, loss and recuperation; and, perhaps, between friendship and desire. It's also a poem steeped, in terms of both form and content, in Milton's growing knowledge of Italian poetry and poetics, and in this sense too it seems to resonate with the continued rhythms of his friendship with Diodati,

who was in many related ways a threshold figure; this may have
been the shared characteristic that brought them together.[27] The
cumulative effect of Milton's mind being pushed to the frontiers
in all these ways was a transition, by the spring of 1638, from
imagined to actual travel. He began to turn in earnest to the prac-
ticalities of the plan that he had been formulating: a trip to the
Continent, through France and into Italy, then possibly further east
to Greece. As I've suggested, this wasn't so much a turn from
bookish concerns and imagined worlds back to the real world, but
a way of making the two connect. To travel to lands already known
in part by reading their histories and their great poems in order
to bring them to life. Leaving the country, however, was no easy
prospect: a passport had to be obtained, which granted permission
not to enter other lands but to leave the shores of England. Here
Milton made use of the connections he'd thus far forged, turning
to Henry Lawes, who had composed music for, and performed in,
Comus. Lawes managed to secure him 'A sufficient warrant, to Justify
yo[u]r goinge out of the Kings Dominions'.[28] But Milton would
also need help, in the form of letters of introduction, to ensure a
warm and safe welcome upon arriving in Italy, and for this a good
option lay close to home. If Diodati was the Anglicised Italian
through whose friendship Milton's ambitions to travel were grown
and honed, he also, in the relative isolation of Horton, had a
prominent Italianate Englishman close to hand: Sir Henry Wotton,
the provost of Eton.

Given that the young Milton's immersion in Italian, and in the
works of Shakespeare and Spenser, were throwbacks to the
Elizabethan age, he must have been thrilled to encounter Wotton,
who was himself a living throwback to the same era. Wotton had
been a close personal friend of John Donne, and the two men had
exchanged verse epistles, in one of which Donne famously claimed
that 'more than kisses, letters mingle souls'; another friendship shot
through, as all of Donne's closest relationships with human beings
and with God tended to be, with intense and uncategorisable jolts
of desire.[29] Urbane and cosmopolitan, but also learned and erudite,
Wotton had travelled widely in his youth. He lived for a year with

the great classical and biblical scholar Isaac Casaubon in Geneva, developing deep theological interests, but also sailed with Donne to the Azores. He learned Italian so well that he managed to conduct a spy mission disguised as a merchant named Ottavio Baldi, in order to thwart a plot to poison James I. His experiences and his canniness made him the ideal choice as ambassador to Venice, a post which he assumed on three occasions during a period of high religious and political tension (as we'll hear in a later chapter), which he navigated deftly while also finding time to write a treatise titled *The Elements of Architecture*, bringing the built splendours of his travels to an English audience. Wotton was a seasoned bordercrosser, able deftly to bridge the worlds of art, literature, and high politics, and though Milton knew him for a relatively short time (Wotton had assumed the position at Eton in his retirement, and died during Milton's travels), I suspect that he was a powerful example for the aspects of himself that Milton was still struggling to reconcile. Wotton knew the advantages and the dangers both of leaving home and of returning; the need to take on conspicuous elements of foreign sophistication while remaining, with equally conspicuous resoluteness, oneself.[30]

More immediately, Eton was another spot at which Milton might have continued his programme of independent study, since it had an outstanding library. Wotton had brought home with him a stunning set of manuscripts of both classical and Italian works – intricately hand-illuminated texts by Seneca and Cicero, Vitruvius on architecture, Homer in Greek with ample commentary, the *Commedia* with figures of Dante and Virgil painstakingly painted, to name a few. If these provided a taste of what the libraries of Italy might offer an omnivorous young bibliophile, the country's attractions were also made present in the form of the 'familiar domestic things' that Wotton had also brought back from Venice – glassware, musical instruments, and perhaps even long-lasting nibbles, including parmesan cheese and olives, for which he'd developed a taste.[31]

Whichever of these flavours of Italy they shared, Milton and Wotton struck up a quick rapport, and the older man agreed to help and advise the younger with regard to his travels. To show his gratitude, Milton sent Wotton a copy of *Comus*, proud enough of his most substantial work to date to send it as a gift. Wotton was delighted with this 'dainty peece of entertainment . . . whereunto I must plainly confess to have seen nothing yet parallel in our language', and which left its reader *'con la bocca dolce'* ('with a sweet mouth').[32] He then launched into advice for Milton's travels, suggesting both an itinerary and a set of strategies, which the younger man seems to have valued enough to follow quite closely. While it was 'above all, Italy' that Milton wanted to see, Wotton observed that 'I suppose you will not blanch Paris in your way', and he provided a letter of introduction to Michael Braithwaite, a former diplomatic colleague from Venice now attending the English ambassador in the French capital. This experienced man would be able to offer 'good directions for the shaping of your farther journey into Italy'. But Wotton also provided his own advice for how Milton should carry himself when he reached the latter country. He recalled a dinner in Siena at the house of a man named Alberto Scipioni, who had hard-won knowledge of the perils and intricacies of Rome which Wotton was then about to experience, and so he decided 'to beg his advice, how I might carry my self securely there, without offence of others, or of my own conscience. *Signior Arrigo mio* (sayes he) *I pensieri stretti, & il viso sciolto* will go safely over the whole world.'[33] These were the words that rang in Milton's ears as, for the first and only time in his life, he left the shores of England behind: *I pensieri stretti, & il viso sciolto* – closed thoughts, and an open face, or, as Wotton himself (who was fond of quoting the words) elsewhere translated them, 'Your thoughts close, and your countenance loose, will go safely over the whole world.'[34]

What was it like for Milton to cross the Channel in the late spring of 1638? He was surely used to travelling by water, down the Thames from Hammersmith into London, but this was his first time on the seas. Did Edward King linger in his mind? A strange time to make a first crossing, the year after writing a poem of shipwreck and death by water, of drowned locks dripping briny ooze and bones swirled across the seabed. Perhaps he was distracted by the feeling, for the first time, of being truly *somewhere else*, a place where one's everyday qualities – language, accent, style, and manner – would suddenly be markers of difference and distinction. Travel for leisure and self-cultivation was even more the privilege of the very few in his lifetime than it is today, but it was also, in a deeper sense than is easy to appreciate today, a true risk. I don't mean just the routine perils of drowning or robbery or illness, but an existential risk in and of itself. Various theories, lingering in adapted forms from classical writings, still understood people as temperamentally bound to the land and the climate into which they were born: for an English person to exchange the cold and damp of northern Europe for the dry heat of the Mediterranean could be severely perilous. The aim of travel was to return a different person from when you left; but there was always the risk that this transformation could be excessive, unsettling, monstrous. Henry Wotton himself was well aware of these risks: he recognised that 'Travel is reputed a proper meanes to create wise men . . . because it forces circumspectness on those abroad, who at home are nurs'd in security'; freedom from the comforts and conventions of home is part of the point. Yet he ultimately concluded that the English traveller 'least discredits his travels, who returns the same man he went'.[35] The transformative shock of the foreign was to be both embraced and disavowed. Joseph Hall, the most trenchant opponent of educational travel, put the matter pithily when he insisted that 'few young travellers have brought home, sound and strong and (in a word) English bodies'.[36] Milton, I've suggested, was already in various ways uncertainly or unstably English by the time he left the country; there was no guarantee that he would not return transformed to his very core.

And so we return to that dinner in Paris. At this point I need to put my cards firmly on the table. What evidence is there that this dinner, or one like it, ever took place? None at all. What evidence is there that he ever met Sir Kenelm Digby, the man next to whom I seated him? Again, none. So why have I troubled you with it? On one level I must own up to some self-indulgence, though of a sort I am happy to defend. Digby is another figure from Milton's era in whom I have invested many years of thought, whose writings I have read and in whose footsteps I have sometimes travelled. I've often been thinking about the two of them at the same time, and so of course they are braided together in my mind: in this sense, bringing in Digby reflects my own interconnected preoccupations, akin to my earlier mentions of Hopkins or Joyce.

But there's also a significant difference, and an alternate basis on which I've imagined this scene. Unlike these later writers, Milton very much *could have* met Digby. I don't just mean this in the vague sense in which he could have met any of his contemporaries: he could have met Digby in the time, place, and manner that I described. This possibility is in itself significant, not just for understanding the context in which Milton found himself upon leaving England, but for what it says about the seventeenth-century world more broadly. Digby was a close friend of John Scudamore, and part of the learned circle the viscount gathered around him in Paris during the time when Milton stayed with him. Their shared connection with Scudamore is what got me thinking about their incongruity as a pair, for in many ways Milton and Digby represent the polar extremes of seventeenth-century life. Digby seemingly embodied everything that Milton despised and devoted his life to denouncing: he was a Roman Catholic; he was firmly royalist in his politics, and would soon return to England, where he would spearhead Queen Henrietta Maria's attempts to raise money from recusant English Catholics for Charles's Scottish wars, earning himself a spell of prolonged imprisonment by Parliament. He was also a glamorous, debonair, attention-seeking *bon viveur*: the seeming embodiment of the loose-living Cavalier, as Milton might seem the quintessential stern and moralising Roundhead.

For this reason alone, finding them moving in the same circles when England was on the eve of revolutionary civil war was intriguing. But once I started to place them more systematically side by side in my mind, I was struck as much by parallels and overlaps in their experiences and interests as I was by the glaring differences between them. For a start, despite the cliché of the period as one of clear and visible polarities, religious differences were not necessarily an obstacle to personal friendships and shared interests. Milton's lifelong fear and suspicion of Roman Catholics didn't prevent him from forging meaningful and enduring connections in Italy, as we will see later, while Digby's close Puritan friends included the émigré governor of Massachusetts, John Winthrop junior. Suddenly the map of connections and allegiances starts to feel more muddled. I alluded above to Milton and Digby's shared theological interests – both spent the exact same period, the mid 1630s, steeped in Patristic writings. Digby was beginning to develop a deeply idiosyncratic philosophy of body and soul, as Milton himself would go on to do, and this reminds me that contact with Scudamore was also Milton's first time intersecting with a serious and independent group of thinkers. Thomas Hobbes was back in England at the time, so he and Milton could not have met then, but just a few months previously Digby had sent Hobbes a copy of René Descartes's *Discours de la Méthode* (1637), praising it as 'a production of a most vigorous and strong braine', and thereby forging a consequential connection between two of the foremost philosophical minds of the age.[37] Aubrey would later claim, based on conversations with Milton's widow, 'that Mr Thomas Hobbs was not one of his acquaintance: that her husband did not like him at all: but he would acknowledge him to be a man of great parts, and a learned man. Their interests and Tenets were diametrically opposed.'[38] The last claim is both true and untrue: Milton and Hobbes were profoundly different in religious and political outlook, but they developed shared commitments to a materialist conception of the world and to the need to account for the basis of human political life, even if the answers they found were very different. Milton's mixture of disdain and admiration for Hobbes makes sense on this basis: *Paradise Lost* is often in silent dialogue with Hobbes's philosophy, and it seems more fitting that they could have been at home in the same Parisian circles, albeit a few months apart.[39]

Digby, too, had spent a period of his youth in Tuscany and

Rome, so this was a context in which travel between these urbane centres, of the sort Milton was undertaking, made eminent sense. Furthermore – to anticipate my next chapter – Digby had become a member of a learned academy in Siena, and delivered a set of orations before its members, as Milton would soon do in Florence; while numerous Englishmen visited these academies, it was highly unusual to become a participating member in this way. Milton would go on to meet and correspond with the Vatican librarian, Lukas Holste or Holstenius, as would Digby (it's not clear whether he knew him at this stage), and this was just one of the meaningful connections that both men would make in the cultured worlds dominated by the Barberini, the Pope's family, in Rome. And finally, there was the question of food. Digby was a renowned gourmand, an inventive cook and invet- erate collector of recipes; Milton, while known to be far more abstemious, would develop an understanding of himself and of the human predicament – from the causes of his own blindness to the causes of the Fall – that revolved around the temptations and the pleasures of eating.

This remains, I admit, highly circumstantial: both men shared each of these individual interests and activities with a number of their contemporaries, but I still find the full array of parallels quite remarkable. My reason for putting Milton and Digby together at dinner is not – or not only – an indulgence of my own preoccupa- tions, but another way of breaking down the assumption that the context or the company in which Milton belongs is obvious. He is, as I've shown in various ways, both close and foreign to me, and following him into the worlds through which he passed suggests ways in which he was subtly foreign to himself. These worlds in turn were never stable and self-identical, never uniform or easy to categorise in a way that our desire to get a firm grip on the past tempts us to do. Digby was a strange kind of Englishman, who spoke and wrote in several languages, lived much of his life abroad, wavering and disparate in his allegiances and his interests: but I'm not too sure whether this would have represented a nightmare for Milton at this stage in his life, or a kind of ideal; an embracing of, a wild extrapolation from, tendencies and patterns to be found within his own personality and inclinations.

Digby's presence in Scudamore's Parisian circle is also a reminder that, paradoxically, it was only when he left England behind that Milton encountered at the highest levels the volatile and conflicting elements that were beginning to rip through the religious and political life of the British Isles. Since 1636, Scudamore's position in France had been undermined and made increasingly untenable by the appointment of Robert Sidney, second Earl of Leicester and nephew of the poet Philip Sidney, as extraordinary ambassador, leading to a series of embarrassing public clashes about matters of precedence and authority. Scudamore was a close friend and follower of Archbishop Laud, and had the trust and support of King Charles, but not of the queen, Henrietta Maria. It says something about the tangled nature of courtly politics and international diplomacy at this point that a Roman Catholic queen chose the staunchly Protestant, puritanically inclined Leicester as her agent, because he shared her antipathy both to Spain and to Cardinal Richelieu, and could be trusted to contest the interests of both. Leicester and Scudamore undermined one another at every turn, and their differences were most apparent in the manner in which they chose to worship: Scudamore in his ornate private chapel, built on Laudian principles and Lancelot Andrewes's template; Leicester at a French Reformed church at Charenton, emphasising his affiliation with the Huguenots and the embattled international community of Protestants. This was a move sure to please the puritanically inclined in England who lamented Charles's continued refusal to join the struggles of the godly that were convulsing Europe as the Thirty Years War dragged devastatingly into its final decade. In the year before Milton's departure, the deeply opposed views of the nature of the English Church and its forms of worship which had divided the country ever since Henry VIII's split from Rome, and that had taken on more openly opposed forms since the late 1620s, burst back to the surface, having been denied their usual arena for negotiation by Charles's continued refusal to call a Parliament. Localised criticism of the sort offered by Prynne, Burton, and Bastwick grew into a much larger clash when Charles and Laud decided to impose their English prayer book and its norms for worship on Scotland, a piece of overreach which drove resistance out into the open. In autumn 1637, as Milton was preparing to leave England, there were street riots in Scotland, assaults on bishops and privy councillors, denunciations of the king. Local riots became incipient rebellion, and armed conflict of some sort seemed in the offing, though no one could yet have predicted the bitter revolutionary war whose touchpaper had been lit. Paris, in any case, was no refuge from these violently opposed views of English religion. Rather, through the mini civil war already underway between England's two ambassadors, it offered a chance to encounter them up close.

Paris does seem to have granted Milton his first confirmed encounter with a figure from the forefront of European religious and political debate in the form of the Dutchman Hugo Grotius, who was then in exile from his homeland, having narrowly escaped a life of incarceration when he was smuggled out of prison in a laundry basket. He was in Paris acting as ambassador for the Queen of Sweden. Grotius was a close friend of Scudamore's, and the pair had a series of half-hearted discussions about the possibility of unifying the English and Scandinavian churches. I briefly mentioned Grotius in the previous chapter, in the context of debates around the ownership of the seas, and this is just one area in which he made a profound impact on later debates in international law, and on the philosophies of religion and politics. Grotius's writings were among the most complex, original, and influential responses to the broader crisis created by the religious reformations and ensuing wars of the sixteenth century, which had forced a widespread rethinking of the very principles that held human societies and forms of political organisation together, or, more to the point, were failing to do so. Drawing upon Aristotle's account of the human being as *zoon politikon*, a naturally political animal, Christian thinkers had developed a theory of a divinely ordained social hierarchy, topped by monarchs at its apex, as the representatives of God on Earth. But the sixteenth century revealed the shakiness of this theory, and the need to understand the basis on which individuals owed their allegiance to these structures, or could justifiably seek to alter or resist them. Grotius confronted these problems head on and came to see civil society as something not derived from divinely guided human nature, but rather constructed by individuals as possessors of rights. He cast doubt on the validity of religious power and authority as a separate sphere, and sought instead to describe with quasi-mathematical simplicity a minimal, basic form of natural law and sociability, necessary for any society to function, which protected people from undue harm and the violation of their basic property rights. Beyond this, as he notoriously put it, 'a People may chuse what Form of Government they please'. These ideas would go on to be adapted, debated, and developed in different directions by Hobbes, by the great Hebraist and jurist John Selden, whom Milton admired, and by Milton himself.[40]

Again, we can't know what exactly Milton and Grotius spoke of when they met. The meeting doubtless had much more of an impact on the former than it did on the latter, since Milton wrote years later that Scudamore 'on his own initiative introduced me, in company with several of his suite, to Hugo Grotius, a most learned man . . . whom I ardently desired to meet', whereas Grotius never mentioned the meeting at all.[41] One way of seeing this encounter is as Milton's first contact with the political ideas and disputes that would preoccupy him for the two decades following his return from his travels. But I give these details of Grotius's thought because his example also provides a different way of understanding the shifts that Milton will go on to make, one that is less obvious to modern eyes. As I've suggested, Grotius's writings placed unprecedented emphasis on the state and on human political forms as things that are *made*, that are created, *by people*. He was influenced by his deep reading in classical rhetoric: the writings of Cicero, no less central to Milton's early education and that of every other Latinate schoolboy, emphasised language itself as something that could create and maintain communal bonds, albeit in volatile and mutable ways.[42] This meant seeing the political state as something made, in part, by acts of and utterances in language – and therefore as not altogether different in kind from a poem. During Milton's lifetime poets, especially Italian poets, became much bolder in asserting the connections between God's creative acts and their own. Torquato Tasso, whom we'll encounter in the next chapter, claimed that 'an excellent poet . . . is called divine for no other reason except that by working like the supreme artificer he comes to share in his divinity'.[43] But this conventional, lofty idea became far more dangerous when the very foundations of human political life also came to be seen as a matter of artifice, of creating something with words. Milton had worried throughout the 1630s about his own vocation as a poet – a word derived, as Philip Sidney famously pointed out, from the Greek word *poiein*, meaning 'to make'.[44] His travels would be both a new departure and the next stage in a lifelong attempt to understand what it meant to create with words: poems, political forms, one's own self. His encounter with Grotius may have provided his first glimpse of the deep and surprising connections between these kinds of making; what it certainly did do, as we'll shortly see, was give him an appetite for meeting European figures who were learned, renowned, and notorious.

7

20 July 1638: 'The Tuscan Artist'

On a clear day, a mile and a half outside Florence, the sun spills its rays across the whitewashed walls of a villa perched amidst the hills. Two figures walking in its main courtyard are sheltered from the worst of the heat. They make their way, with inching slowness, around the perimeter path, passing beneath the scented leaves of the lemon trees and skirting the bed of artichokes, their livid violet flowers bursting from the scaly bulbs, as they talk quietly to one another, their words wilting to sighs in the warm, heavy air. Strain though I might, I cannot make out their words: what can they be saying to one another?

They're an odd pair. Their slow pace is dictated by the elder of the two: his boxer's nose and default frown suggest a willingness to fight his corner when needed. But his body, racked with pain from a hernia, has grown frailer as his lustrous beard has made the shift from grey to white, and his eyes, eyes that were the first to glimpse startling secrets of the cosmos, have fallen sightless, their rims still reddened from a meagre hour of sleep each night. This is the mathematician, philosopher, and astronomer, Galileo Galilei. The other man is a few months from thirty, his eyes darting sideways to his venerable companion, determined to absorb every word but compelled to sweep in fleeting panic to the courtyard's shady corners to check that he is not being watched, scrutinised, noticed. Traveller, aspiring but largely unheralded poet, sometime bookworm and malingerer, university graduate without a trade or a plan – John Milton. So careful is he to protect and cherish this encounter, which he will long remember, that I cannot hear what he has to say.

Milton and Galileo, Galileo and Milton: it's almost too good to be true. The poet of paradise and the searcher of the stars, side by side. The patriotic Protestant and foe of tyrants sharing a sunny afternoon with the man who scandalised the Catholic Church, then bit his tongue and swallowed his truth in order to appease it. Not just a poet and a scientist, but two men who've often been taken to embody greatness in poetry and science, strolling arm in arm. Ever since I've first learned of it, this meeting has stood at the centre of my imaginings of Milton – precisely because it seems at once so apt and so incongruous. And I'm not alone. A journalist writing on Milton's four-hundredth birthday wonderfully suggested that 'it's like those comic-book specials in which Superman meets Batman – there's something strange about imagining these two figures inhabiting the same age'.[1] The plot of Dan Brown's thriller *Angels and Demons* hangs on the discovery of a papyrus in the Vatican Archives, written by Galileo and with lines added in the margin, sensationally proving that '*John Milton was an Illuminatus*'.[2] Something about these men meeting seems to belong in the world of comic books and secret societies; as if there must have been something conspiratorial about their conversation; as if pleasantries exchanged by geniuses must be rich with clandestine significance.

Perhaps because it's so perfect, and so tempting an encounter to embellish, some have doubted that it took place at all. But Milton certainly insisted that it did, and an outright lie would be a needless risk. Seven years later, in his treatise *Areopagitica*, Milton recalled that while visiting Italy he had 'found and visited the famous Galileo, grown old, a prisoner to the Inquisition, for thinking in Astronomy otherwise than the Franciscan and Dominican licensers thought'.[3] Galileo certainly had visitors during the house arrest in which he lived out his final years, and, as we'll see, Milton had extensive contacts in Galileo's immediate circle. Of all the conversations the pair might have had together, it's by far the most tempting to imagine them discussing Galileo's most famous device, and the heavenly discoveries he had made with it a quarter of a century before; to imagine their conversation extending late into the summer evening, as darkness eventually fell and the stars overhead became visible. Let's picture the older man summoning his assistant and disciple Vincenzo Viviani, who has been waiting all this time in the shadows and noting down his master's every word, and telling him to pass the young English visitor the object that Viviani holds in his hands – a narrow three-foot tube, its wooden frame cloaked in brown and red leather and marked with faded tracings of gold paint. Let's imagine that Milton pointed the cylinder at the heavens, clamped his open eye to the narrow aperture, and pivoted it slowly until he found the glowing disc of the Moon, expanded to a massive size, and gawped at the crinkles and gullies revealed in its surface. Let's hear the blind Galileo, now robbed of such sights and able to enjoy them only via the wondering gasps of his visitors, as he leans towards the young Englishman's ears and murmurs the word: '*Ecco!*'

◆

Why is it so particularly tempting to those who are captivated by this encounter (and I include myself in their number) to imagine Milton staring through Galileo's telescope? For the simple reason that, when *Paradise Lost* was published three decades later, it was studded with allusions to the Tuscan astronomer, imprisoned for 'thinking in Astronomy otherwise'. In book 5 of that poem, when the Angel Raphael is dispatched from Eden to warn the first human beings of Satan's threat and the golden gates of Heaven swing open, he is able to take in the cosmos at a glance, 'As when by night the Glass / Of Galileo, less assured, observes / Imagined lands and regions in the Moon'.[4] This is the only time in an epic poem bristling with proper names that Milton mentions one of his contemporaries. Twice more in the poem Galileo is alluded to but not named: Satan's vast shield, we are told, 'Hung on his shoulders like the Moon, whose orb / Through optic glass the Tuscan artist views / At evening from the top of Fesole' – a hilltop town near Florence from which Galileo had gazed at the heavens.[5] And, when Satan stops off on the Sun en route to Earth for a quick moment of contemplation, he becomes 'a spot like which perhaps /

Astronomer in the Sun's lucent orb / Through his glazed optic tube yet never saw'.[6]

Tuscan artist, astronomer: both are surely Galileo, further suggesting that their encounter continued to thrum in Milton's mind over the ensuing decades, and returned to its forefront when he sought to make the entire created cosmos his poetic purview. But it's also clear from these mentions that his feelings were, in longer retrospect, far from unmixed. Galileo's view of the heavens is *less assured* than the angel's (though it's not clear that this phrase is as snarky as it first sounds – after all, the sight of all fallen mortals is less assured than that of an angel), while the lands in the Moon are merely *imagined*. Most obviously, it is *Satan's* massy shield and bulk that are compared to the moon-marks and sun spots glimpsed from Tuscany: hardly flattering. As we'll see, this is a pattern that repeats itself in *Paradise Lost*, and which is difficult to decode. Milton's 1638–9 travels were, as I began to suggest in the last chapter, pivotal in his emerging sense of himself. It was during his travels that he first wrote, boldly and openly, of his ambition to produce a great epic poem, and so it's perhaps not surprising that we should find traces and echoes of his trip when he eventually did so. But it was an ambition that took some decades to realise, not the smooth trajectory towards greatness that he might have hoped. And this fact, as well as the curiously mixed quality of his experiences in Italy – from the enthralling and mind-expanding to the dangerously seductive and simply dangerous – help to explain the sprinkling of these reminiscences between Hell and Heaven, their transposing to the realm of the 'imagined', the artfully created in-betweenness of 'as' and 'perhaps'.

It's Milton's very ambivalence towards his travels in Italy – his tendency to see those experiences as both formative and fraught, to be treasured in memory and held at bay – that particularly draws me to this period in his life. There's an appealing parallel between Milton's wrestling with Italy – foreign and familiar, appealing and off-putting – and my own shifting relationship with him. His uncertainty provides a foothold for my own. I also have a slightly different relationship to this part of his life from a practical perspective.

Whereas in the previous chapters my retracing of Milton's life and imagination was a matter of hastily organised days out and spur-of-the-moment diversions, following in his footsteps to Italy took more planning. I was fortunate to be able to do so when the opportunity arose to travel to Florence and its environs in order to make a documentary about *Paradise Lost* for BBC Radio. My experiences on this brief but illuminating trip were, by turns, informative, thrilling, baffling, tiring, embarrassing, disappointing, surprising, moving, and amusing – pretty much a microcosm of my experiences with Milton over the years. What the trip also brought home to me, however, as this and the following chapter will make clear, is that I'd been wrong to think of 'Milton in Italy' as a single, integrated experience in his life, with the encounter with Galileo standing as its centre of gravity. By travelling to the Italian peninsula, Milton was entering not one new environment but a cluster of them; there was not a single new culture for him to encounter, but a whole map of overlapping and interlocking people, places, and experiences. By the same token, the encounter with Galileo itself was not one clear thing – Batman meets Superman or genius of science meets genius of poetry. As with the encounter with Kenelm Digby that I imagined in the last chapter, the meeting between these two men has come to seem less like a meeting of complementary opposites than like an encounter between two minds bristling with similarities that cut across the differences of age, nation, and religion. And tempting though the scene with the telescope remains, it became harder for me to retain, not least because there were so many things that they might have discussed.

Let's return, then, to the Villa Il Gioiello, and strain our ears anew to catch their conversation. Perhaps they were reminiscing, exchanging tales of their younger years. Galileo might have mentioned to Milton the schooling he received, from the age of eleven, at a monastery high in the hills, some twenty-five miles to the east of Florence. The monks there at the time were a learned bunch, especially the abbot, 'a man of rare and acute mind', well versed in theology, mathematics, astrology, and cosmology. Galileo had enjoyed the peace and spectacular views so much that he wondered about a monastic calling for himself. Even after his plans changed, he returned to the monastery in his twenties, while struggling to make a living as a teacher of mathematics, and tutored the brothers there in the art of perspective.[7] More recently, however – a sad sign of the times – some had come to see the monks as mere figures of fun: one mischievous Florentine poet loved devising practical jokes to play on them, like stealing their hoods from the clothes line, putting them on the heads of donkeys, and riding back and forth below the monastery windows.[8] But they remained an erudite and hospitable bunch, and perhaps Milton should visit while he was in Tuscany. The name of their order, and the monastery itself, was Vallombrosa, 'shady valley'. A fine name, Milton thought, as he rolled it silently around his mouth: *Vallombrosa*; *Vallombrrrrrosa* . . .

Or perhaps they weren't just talking to one another. Let's lean in a little closer: is that one of them humming or whistling a tune, perhaps Milton describing one of the singing virtuosi whom he had heard since arriving? Certainly another of their shared passions was for music – and, in fact, both were sons of musical fathers, and had retained musical interests even as their ambitions moved, to their fathers' perplexity, in other directions. There was, granted, a significant difference here: Milton's father was a talented amateur, making music with friends in the gaps of his busy scrivening; Galileo's father Vincenzo was among the most significant musical figures of his day, important as a composer but even more so as a theorist. His *Dialogo della Musica Antica et della Moderna* (1581) had sought to return music to its pure, ancient roots, arguing that the Greeks gave great emotional power to their music by matching it carefully with words. Galileo, as I had cause to mention in an earlier chapter, sought to measure gravity by singing a folk song as a reliable measure of time, so music was part of his homespun experimental repertoire. Perhaps, then, this is what the men spoke of, hummed, and whistled – Galileo giving his English visitor some inside knowledge on the most promising places to hear and buy Italian music of the most elegant and affecting kind.

This possibility already moves us away from any clear split between the great artist and the great scientist. Galileo was steeped in all of what we would now call the arts, and he and Milton would have had as much to say to one another about the forms of the beautiful as their shared passion for the stars. Before his blindness, Galileo had been a highly talented draughtsman: the speed with which his account of the Moon's rough and uneven surface came to be accepted was due in part to the deftness with which he could draw and paint it, and the incorporation of the Moon's pockmarked surface into works by his painter friends like Lodovico Cigoli did a great deal to increase the popularity of the Galilean view of the cosmos before it was finally denounced by the Church.[9] Galileo, friends with artists across the peninsula, would have been the ideal guide, even in his blindness, to the different styles and the great works that should be on his visitor's radar for each stage of his journey: the distinctive masterworks of Rome, Naples, and Venice. Here I have less to go on, since Milton was frustratingly uninclined to mention the paintings and sculptures that he saw in Italy – though this doesn't mean, as I'll go on to suggest, that there's nothing to be gained by working out what some of them might have been. If they did speak of painting, then, they must have murmured softly, for I can scarcely catch their conversation at all.

But by far the most plausible possibility – the subject that, if I had to wager money on it, I'd venture formed the bulk of their conversation – is poetry itself. These men might have found it easiest to converge not around the narrow aperture of a telescope but over the pages of a book of verse. Galileo was a lifelong, passionate, meticulous, and highly opinionated reader of poetry, and this too was by no means entirely separate from his scientific pursuits. As well as penning a few sonnets of his own, earlier in his life Galileo had delivered lectures before the Accademia Fiorentina, founded by the Medici rulers of the city to promote its language and its great poets, on the greatest of them all, Dante Alighieri. He applied his sharp mathematical mind to Dante's vision of Hell, which he described as a conical void beneath Jerusalem, its dimensions derived from precise estimations of the poet's own height (three *braccia*, around six feet) and the average height of a giant.[10] But he was no less steeped in more recent Italian poems, and the debates they'd occasioned. The most sustained and significant of these was the dispute over the relative merits of Ludovico Ariosto's sprawling, playful, ironic poem *Orlando Furioso*, written in the earliest decades of the sixteenth century, and its much more serious and anxious successor, Torquato Tasso's *Gerusalemme Liberata*, which sought to make the poetry of chivalry and adventure into a vessel for the theological precepts of the Counter-Reformation. For decades scholars had argued over whether Ariosto's poem violated the rules for poetry laid down by Aristotle; whether, if he did, it mattered; whether this poetry, with its digressions and its self-conscious wit, was a perpetuation of ancient epic by other means or a distinct form altogether, known as *romanzo*. Tasso himself had waded into these debates, explaining and justifying his poetic choices with a clarity and forcefulness greater than any practising poet before him. But Galileo was trenchant and unapologetic in his own preferences: he told another visitor to his villa that reading Tasso after Ariosto was like eating sour little citrons after sumptuous melons (a comparison perhaps called to mind by his garden there, of which he was extremely proud). He likened opening a volume of Tasso to entering 'the *studietto* of some curious little man', stuffed with oddities from antiquity hoarded for their own sake, such as 'a petrified crab, a dried chameleon, a fly and a spider encased in a piece of amber' ('*un granchio pietrificato, un camaleonte secco, una mosca e un ragno in gelatina in un pezzo d'ambra*'). Ariosto's poem, by contrast, was 'like a regal gallery, ornamented with a hundred ancient statues by the most celebrated sculptors . . . full of rare, precious and marvellous things, and all of supreme excellence'.[11]

Even when Galileo was not discussing these and other poets directly, their words and their imaginative habits were woven into his own patterns of thought and phrase, and, even more than his skill as a draughtsman, his sensational scientific success until his trial and disgrace owed a great deal to his status as one of the greatest writers of Italian prose. His mastery of literary forms ranging from polemical treatise to dialogue, his ability to create both hilarious caricatures and fully realised characters as scape-goats and mouthpieces; these skills contributed to the emphasis on '[q]uickness and nimbleness of thought, economy of argument, and also imaginative examples', that, for the great Italian writer Italo Calvino, was the defining feature not just of Galileo's writing but of his scientific world view.[12]

Regarding all of these poetic interests, Galileo would have found in his young English visitor a receptive and startlingly well-informed mind, especially for one who had only been in Italy a few months. I've already discussed Milton's transformative immersion in the rhythms of Italian, including the work of Dante, and he also care-fully read the *Vita di Dante* by another great Italian writer, Giovanni Boccaccio. His surviving annotations show that he was alert to parallels with his own personal circumstances, and drawn to the depiction of a great poet struggling heroically with his surround-ings.[13] Milton was no less engaged with Ariosto and Tasso, not least because the dispute over their work raised the questions with which he was beginning to wrestle, and with which he would wrangle until the end of his life: was it possible to write an epic poem in the modern age? And if so, what should it be like? While Milton might seem most obviously to resemble the self-consciously serious and difficult Tasso, he also turned to Ariosto at key moments. Most strikingly, when he later announced his intention at the opening of *Paradise Lost* to perform 'Things unattempted yet in prose or rhyme', he paradoxically made his boldest claim to originality by translating Ariosto's own, similar aspiration to perform '*cosa non detta in prosa mai né in rima*' ('what has never before been recounted in prose or rhyme').[14] The same poets who engaged Galileo, and moved him to feats of intellectual dexterity and grandiloquent pronouncements, were already present in, and would become even more intricately woven into, Milton's thoughts and fluctuating poetic ambitions.

Of all the conversations that I can allow myself to imagine them having on that summer day in the Villa Il Gioiello, this one, a discussion of poetry, seems the likeliest, by which I really mean the richest in possibility; the most conducive to my sense of what Milton brought to and took from his Italian travels, the year which I will see in this and the next chapter as pivotal in his life. But not a pivot in a straightforward sense, from one way of being or writing to another. Life, no matter what Milton sometimes wanted himself or us to believe, is rarely that neat or linear. We can see *Paradise Lost* beginning to take shape on his Italian travels, but only in furtive glimpses and unrealised hopes, which is perhaps why these travels leave the most ambiguous of traces in the poem's hellish landscape. Now, as *Making Darkness Light* pivots with Milton towards the second half of his life, *Paradise Lost* will continue to hover over his actions, emerging as a rumbling and decreasingly distant possibility: it doesn't belong to one clear and definable period in Milton's writing life any more than it belongs to one period or part of my own reading life, but rather resonates throughout it.

First, then, let's step back and find out how Milton came to Florence in the first place. In May 1638 he left Paris and travelled south through France to Nice, where he again swapped land for sea and proceeded to Italy, stopping briefly at Genoa and then continuing to the Tuscan port of Livorno, known to the English as Leghorn. Genoa was an independent republic, the first time Milton set foot in the kind of political realm for which he would later work and advocate. Livorno, part of the grand duke's Tuscan territories, was a cosmopolitan port, with a growing community of merchants from England and across the globe, as well as a large and prominent Jewish community. When I visited the city in 2013 interesting remnants of its earlier history were still visible on its rather shabby exterior. I was only able to see the English cemetery – which contains the grave of the eighteenth-century novelist Tobias Smollett, a reminder of the long continuity of English presence in the town – through locked gates. A more uncanny experience was created by the Piazza Grande, whose curious familiarity, I later discovered, was explained by the fact that it provided the architect Inigo Jones with the inspiration for the Italianate redesign of Covent Garden, already in process during the 1630s, so Milton may even have seen this pocket of Tuscan architecture being recreated in the heart of London. Most striking was the monument to Duke Ferdinando I de' Medici, constructed in 1595, but altered in the mid 1620s when four bronze North African slaves were added, chained and cowering at the duke's feet as he stared out at the waves. Another English traveller, John Evelyn, saw the monument in 1644 and praised 'those incomparable statues . . . one of the best pieces of modern worke that was ever done'.[15] Now divided from the sea by a busy and grimy road and the buildings of the modern industrial port, it's a curious, unsettling reminder that in Milton's day Livorno was a place both of multicultural openness and co-existence, and one of cruelty and enslavement. The sea welcomed strangers but was also an arena for religious war, mutual enslavement, and cynical exploitation in the pursuit of profit.

Milton probably didn't linger too long because he was impatient to arrive at one of his principal destinations. As he later recollected:

> I reached Genoa, then Leghorn and Pisa, and after that Florence. In that city, which I have always admired above all others because of the elegance, not just of its tongue, but also of its wit, I lingered for about two months. There I at once became the friend of many gentlemen eminent in rank and learning, whose private academies I frequented – a Florentine institution which deserves great praise not only for promoting humane studies but also for encouraging friendly intercourse. Time will never destroy my recollection – ever welcome and delightful – of you, Jacopo Gaddi, Carlo Dati, Frescobaldi, Coltellini, Buonmattei, Chimentelli, Francini, and many others.[16]

The speed with which, and extent to which, Milton was able to gain access to these academies is striking: some combination of letters of introduction from Henry Wotton and Viscount Scudamore probably helped. Milton's desire to see Florence, and his reasons for wanting to see it, were fairly standard. English travellers to Italy always made it a priority to see the city, with its 'streets very long, streight, large, and faire . . . beautified with many stately Pallaces', 'graced with many large *Piazzes*, and in them many statues', and, looming above the whole, 'the most magnificent and admirable Fabrick of the *Duomo*'.[17] Wotton himself, during his diplomatic days in Italy, had praised Florence, 'whither many are drawn of our English gentlemen, by the beauty and security of the place, and purity of the language'.[18] Milton's feelings for the language and the writings of Florence in particular – especially its three greatest writers, Dante, Petrarch, and Boccaccio – went far beyond these conventional interests, and the fact that he managed to enter the learned academies and befriend their members was highly unusual: few others, as I mentioned in the last chapter, managed it. Milton's emphasis on the 'elegance' of Florentine dialect and 'genius', and his contact with 'persons eminent for their rank and learning', also had a defensive edge, however, designed to insulate him from the more dubious motives for travel to Italy. Wotton would have been well placed to warn him of these dangers: after praising the beauty and purity of Florence, he immediately noted the presence there of a 'certain knot of bastard Catholics, partly banished and partly voluntary residents there', exiles from England looking to lure more of their countrymen towards popery.[19]

Given these risks, it's all the more striking that Milton was happy to advertise his Italian friendships. He would continue to do so over the coming years, publishing the praise he received from members of these academies as part of the preface to the 1645 collection of his poems, and continuing to correspond with these friends over the course of a decade. I'll have more to say about his relationship with Catholicism, which is more complicated and ambivalent than first meets the eye, in the next chapter. But what may have made these connections possible was the curious nature of the academies themselves, where discussion of serious theological questions was strictly prohibited. Many of these organisations had sprung up across Tuscany in the course of the sixteenth century, in conscious emulation of the famous, semi-mythical gatherings of cultured minds from the ancient and more recent past: Plato's academy in Athens, and the Florentine academy of the fifteenth century clustered around Lorenzo the Magnificent, led by Marsilio Ficino and devoted to interpreting Plato's wisdom. These academies had written constitutions, a complicated hierarchy of elected offi-cials, and meetings at which members delivered learned orations or read poetry. Over time they became more frivolous, devoted to playing with knowledge rather than pursuing it; they were gentle-men's clubs as much as scholarly societies. The two academies with which Milton became connected were called the Svogliati – the Listless – and the Apatisti – the Apathetic. As these light-hearted names suggest, such academies delighted in learned jokes and witti-cisms, and particularly enjoyed wordplay of all sorts. The *dubbi* or 'doubtful questions' that they debated included such topics as 'Whether black or blue eyes are more to be esteemed in a beautiful face' and 'Whether the fire of love is aroused more by seeing the beloved's smile or tears'. They also hosted lavish banquets with food-themed *dubbi* known as *cicalate*, 'chats', focused on culinary topics such as 'Which came first, the chicken or the egg?', 'In praise of Salad', and 'On the similarity of watermelon and pork'.[20]

What we've seen of Milton's life thus far makes his presence at frothy gatherings of this sort less incongruous than it might other-wise seem. The best preparation would have been his student orations at Cambridge, with their deft dance between learned and scatological humour. But I don't want to overplay the frivolity of the academies. The men whom Milton remembered meeting included some who shared his deep commitments to questions of poetry and language – particularly the nature of Italian, of which the Tuscan form was solidifying as the dominant literary dialect; its nature, and its value relative to the authoritativeness of Latin, were topics of frequent discussion. This was a long-standing issue – Dante had addressed it in his *De vulgari eloquentia*, a work, in Latin, defending the Italian in which he wrote his great *Commedia* – but it had grown to increased prominence among the academies, and had taken on a new urgency in the seventeenth century as part of the complex process by which vernacular languages came to be associated with distinct nation states. Claims for the purity and dignity of Tuscan Italian argued for both parity with Latin and distinction from it, as well as its superiority from other, supposedly less sophisticated regional varieties of the language. There was therefore much at stake in understanding the ways in which languages were both interconnected and distinct.[21]

Pre-eminent among the names Milton listed as friends were Carlo Dati, a polymath in his late teens who had already published poems and was well versed in history, painting, and science. Dati would later heap praise on Milton, which the latter would include in the 1645 collection of his poems, describing him as one 'who in his travels has made himself acquainted with many nations and in his studies, with all; that like another Ulysses, he might learn all that all could teach him; skilful in many tongues [*polyglotto*], on whose lips languages now mute so live again, that the idioms of all are insufficient to his praise'.[22] The quality that strikes Dati is that which still strikes me: Milton's molten movement between languages.

An equally significant name on Milton's list of Italian friends, when it came to questions of language and identity, is that of Benedetto Buonmattei, an eminent priest who was in the final stages of completing his monumental work *Della Lingua Toscana*, a systematic grammar of Tuscan Italian.[23] While in Florence, Milton wrote a Latin letter to Buonmattei, summing up his reverence for literary Tuscan Italian by describing himself as 'glad to go for a feast to Dante and Petrarch'.[24] While the language of banqueting reflects the indulgent academic context in which he and Buonmattei met, it was actually rather easy for Milton to revere these particular Tuscan authors since there was a long tradition of Protestants claiming them for their cause because both had resisted papal authority and suffered the consequences.[25] Milton implored Buonmattei to include in his book a guide to pronunciation and a who's who of the finest Tuscan authors, for the benefit of foreign readers. Yet what strikes me most in this letter is Milton's praise for Buonmattei as akin to a ruler who defends his subjects from war and civil strife; Buonmattei seeks similarly to protect the people's language 'and in a sense to enclose it within a wall'. Just as a ruler needs 'a noble ferocity and intrepid strategy against an enemy invading the boundaries', so Buonmattei 'undertakes to overcome and drive out Barbarism, that filthy civil enemy of character which attacks the spirit of men'.[26]

I'm inclined to see Dati's response to Milton, and Milton's to Buonmattei, as capturing the two sides of Milton's mind present in his travels and thereafter. On the one hand an impulse towards literal and imaginative movement, between languages and nations, described as a Ulyssean wandering, suggesting an identity as porous and protean as that of Odysseus. On the other hand a desire to erect rigid borders, to recognise the threat of the alien barbarian and hold it at bay with 'noble ferocity'. Only by recognising both sides of this dynamic as genuine aspects of Milton's character can I seek to understand him; only by recognising the deep tension between these impulses can I make sense of how he himself has come to be seen as both a great national poet and, as we'll see again later, as exactly the kind of barbarian whom he denounces here, allowing the language to be invaded and corrupted by an excess of otherness. I read his response to Buonmattei as anxious, defensive: in a characteristically ambivalent double movement, at the moment when he was most literally surrounded by foreignness, and felt the divisions between languages and identities becoming most porous, he sought to erect them with the utmost ferocity and rigidity.

Looking back on his experiences in Florence three years later, Milton wrote that 'in the private academies of Italy, whither I was favoured to resort, perceiving some trifles which I had in memory, composed at under twenty or thereabout (for the manner is that everyone must give some proof of his wit and reading there), met with acceptance above what was looked for . . . which the Italian is not forward to bestow on men from this side of the Alps'.[27] If nothing else, this comment shows that Milton had mastered the quintessentially Italian art of *sprezzatura*, or nonchalance: the carefully cultivated appearance of not trying too hard. The poems that he wrote were supposedly youthful frivolities, dashed off from memory. One more recently written possibility would be the poem to his father defending his choice of a poetic vocation, 'Ad Patrem'. His claim to 'acceptance' is far from hollow, since the minutes of the Svogliati show that whatever Milton read was praised as *poesia*

Latina di versi esametri molto erudita, Latin poetry in very erudite hexameter verses.[28]

The first person named on Milton's list of his Italian friends, Jacopo Gaddi, made the gathering at which Milton spoke possible, and presided over it. Though a poet in his own right, his main impact on Florentine cultural life was as founder of the Svogliati, whose meetings he hosted at his *palazzo* on Via del Giglio. When I went to Florence for my radio programme on Milton, I visited this building, now converted into the flashy Hotel Astoria, with the producer of the programme, Melissa. She managed to persuade the receptionist to let us wander around inside. It was fun to imagine Milton gathering with the other academicians amidst the splendour of the *palazzo*, whose high and ornately painted ceilings and soaring staircase were far grander than any residence he'd probably experienced in London or Cambridge, never mind in Hammersmith or Horton. The roof terrace afforded a splendid panorama of Florence, and the floating sound of church bells ringing nearby and farther off was a gentle reminder of the way that Florentines in the seventeenth century would have located themselves in both time and space. The owners of the hotel seemed somewhat invested in encouraging visitors to imagine what Milton had made of all this. A plaque on the outside wall noted that John Milton had visited, '*trovando a Firenze l'Italia dei classici*', finding in Florence the Italy of the classics. More intriguing was the claim on the hotel's website that one of its courtyards might have inspired Milton's depiction of the Garden of Eden. If exploring the rest of the hotel allowed us an enjoyable, evocative kind of literary tourism, however, when we entered the courtyard in question I was right back to the kind of bathos and disappointment I'd experienced on Bread Street. Unlike the still splendid interior of the *palazzo*, this was a dingy, airless, entirely unimpressive space, dotted with tired and light-starved pot plants. We burst out laughing at the outrageous idea that this was the space that inspired *Paradise Lost*.

But why? Yes, there's something cheeky and cynical about the hotel's suggestion (which now seems to have disappeared from their website), but weren't they simply catering to the very desire that had brought me – and, in a sense, had brought Milton three hundred and eighty years previously – to Italy? The desire to locate great works of art within the specific places and spaces that had inspired them. To *locate* Milton's imagination. I didn't think this was what I wanted, but the courtyard in the Hotel Astoria felt almost like a deliberate mockery of my belief that I was above such sentimental desires. What this latest pilgrimage of disappointment helped me understand was that I wanted to visit these places not to explain the final form of Milton's poetry but to experience something of their point of departure. It helped me see that I was interested in such places precisely because I felt that they did have some kind of relationship with his poems, but one that posed rather than answered the problem of the connection between them.

This isn't to say that I don't think we can connect Milton's experiences in the Florentine academies with his later poetry in any meaningful way; but their residual presence is, as we've seen, scattered, various, and ambiguous. In the middle books of *Paradise Lost*, the Angel Raphael visits Adam and Eve in Eden to warn them against Satan's threat. He makes the striking decision to stay for a meal – a cornucopia of delights that Eve prepares, none of it needing in its paradisal state to be cooked: 'No fear lest dinner cool', the narrator tells us, in a moment of comically precise attention to detail. Adam and Raphael sit in long discussion, and it is through the angel's voice that the first human and the poem's reader hear the backstory that has been unspoken until this point: the manner of God's creation of the universe, of Satan's rebellion, and of the War in Heaven that ensued. Adam asks for more and more detail about the nature of the cosmos, of angelic life, and even of angelic love and sex, which, in another strikingly naturalistic moment, makes Raphael blush: 'the Angel with a smile that glowed / Celestial rosy red, love's proper hue, / Answered':

> *Whatever pure thou in the body enjoy'st*
> *(And pure thou wert created) we enjoy*
> *In eminence, and obstacle find none*

Of membrane, joint, or limb, exclusive bars:
Easier then air with air, if spirits embrace,
Total they mix, union of pure with pure
Desiring; nor restrained conveyance need
As flesh to mix with flesh, or soul with soul.[29]

This is a striking moment – not least because we only meet male angels in the poem, and they're described here as interpenetrating one another's bodies. It worried C. S. Lewis enough that he harumphingly warned his readers that 'since these exalted creatures are all spoken of by masculine pronouns, we tend, half consciously, to think that Milton is attributing to them a life of homosexual promiscuity'; but, he quickly insisted, 'the real meaning is certainly not filthy'; angels have no sex, and are referred to as male only because 'the masculine is certainly the superior gender'.[30] Lewis seems to be working hilariously hard here to explain away an issue that Milton by no means had to raise in his reader's mind, and it's tempting to see this as another version of Milton's elusive homo-eroticism, an after-echo of Diodati that again hovers between the spiritual and physical. But even this isn't clear, because Raphael is responding to a challenge by Adam, who questions the angel's dismissal of human sex as inferior and human bodies as 'exclusive bars', fleshly prisons; what he experiences in his physical intimacy with Eve isn't just 'procreation common to all kinds', but, in a phrase of beautiful simplicity, 'Those thousand decencies that daily flow / From all her words and actions'.[31]

The essential point here is that the action of these middle books, the lavish banquet followed by a languorous discussion of the mysteries of the universe and of human and spiritual relationships, seems closely analogous to the activities of the Florentine academies, where the nature of love was a matter of frequent discussion; the homosexual possibilities that are boldly hinted at resonate with English views of Italians rather than angels.[32] Raphael's admonition to Adam not to push his questions too far – 'Think only what concerns thee and thy being' – is a demand for pious moderation, but also an attempt to avoid controversial topics in the manner of the academies.[33] Here too there's a playfulness that accounts of Milton's work often miss, and that again speaks to the tone of Florentine debate. Near the beginning of their discussion in book 5, as he starts his account of the origin of all things, Raphael says:

> *High matter thou enjoinst me, O prime of men,*
> *Sad task and hard, for how shall I relate*
> *To human sense the invisible exploits*
> *Of warring spirits*
> . . .
>   *how last unfold*
> *The secrets of another world, perhaps*
> *Not lawful to reveal? Yet for thy good*
> *This is dispensed, and what surmounts the reach*
> *Of human sense, I shall delineate so,*
> *By likening spiritual to corporal forms,*
> *As may express them best, though what if earth*
> *Be but the shadow of heav'n, and things therein*
> *Each to other like, more then on earth is thought?*[34]

This is a crucial and immensely slippery passage in which Raphael seems to say several things at once, risks contradicting himself, and leaves Adam and us in a state of profound uncertainty as to the status of the astonishingly detailed narrative of things heavenly and hellish that we are about to receive. Raphael begins with a clear and absolute division between 'human sense' and the world of 'warring spirits', such that whatever he tells Adam will be a necessarily imperfect account of what really happened, a form of accommodation to the inferior sensory and mental capacities of even an unfallen human being. But Raphael himself, for all that he does know, cannot gauge the magnitude of the problem: *perhaps* such secrets are not lawful to reveal. He'll use spiritual descriptions for 'corporal forms' that '*may* express them best', but he can't be sure. And then, astoundingly, he partially retracts the division that he's set up: 'what if Earth / Be but the shadow of Heaven' after all, and happenings in the two realms can be described in the same language? But it's only another possibility – a what if? – with which we're left to wrestle. Raphael's problem is, of course, also Milton's, magnified all the more by the fact that the latter's audience is fallen, and hence even more limited in mind and sense. The whole of *Paradise Lost* arrives to us under two guises at once: on the one hand the claim that all this is true, deposited into the brain of an inspired poet each night by a divine muse. On the other hand the concession that all this is merely the closest to truth that's possible under the circumstances, given that we cannot measure the gap that matters, the gap between the human and the divine, with our limited human minds. This is a problem usually considered in a theological vein, but I'd suggest that the playful set of possibilities and counter-possibilities via which Raphael presents it to us – we're once again in the in-between realm of 'perhaps', 'may', 'what if?' – owes something to the style of easy, witty intellectual exercise with which Milton familiarised himself in Florence.

But just as I settle into this thought, just as I feel able to point at a straightforwardly positive impact of Milton's Italian experience not just on the content of his poems but on the way he navigates his poem's unstable status, an alternative swings into view. By the time we reach Raphael's ambiguous disclaimer in book 5 and his ensuing colloquy with Adam, we've already encountered a very different take on the academic debate in book 2, among the fallen angels who convene in Hell. Time is never straightforwardly linear in *Paradise Lost*. Milton does not start, as the Book of Genesis does, in the beginning, but somewhere in the middle, giving us first Satan and his cronies, then Heaven, and Eden with Raphael's return to the origins of creation only after that. The devils stage a debate on how best to proceed, which is a tour de force of alternative rhetorical styles, a corruption of language's expressive powers encapsulated by Belial, whose 'tongue / Dropped manna, and could make the worse appear / The better reason'.[35] When the foregone conclusion of Satan's departure for Eden comes to pass, the devils left behind devote themselves to exploring Hell, and to sporting contests. Others sing, and, in a moment of sublime stillness, 'the harmony / (What could it less when spirits immortal sing?) / Suspended hell'. Meanwhile 'Others apart sat on a hill retired, / In thoughts more elevate, and reasoned high / Of providence, foreknowledge, will and fate'.[36] I find this vignette of the devils making music and trying to philosophise in Hell strangely moving. Read a certain way, it could work as testament to the capacity of the mind and its creativity to flourish even in the most devastating and deprived conditions. Milton seems to want us to mock their phoney pretensions – or does he? Is not Hell also suspended for us in this flickering moment? In any case, while he seems to have the vanity of godless attempts to achieve wisdom in his sights, the combination in book 2 of rhetorically elaborate and ultimately inconsequential debate with the meanderings of elevated thought and reason also seems to recollect, in a very different key, the Florentine academies. Milton's Italian memories were something to treasure; but, as with the recollections of Galileo, they seemed also to lead his mind into an infernal realm.

It was with Galileo in mind that Melissa and I undertook the next stage of our own Italian sojourn in Milton's footsteps, but before travelling to the Villa Il Gioiello itself we stopped at the Museo Galileo, which stands on the north bank of the Arno, a short walk from the crowds and jewellery shops of the Ponte Vecchio. I'd looked at pictures of Galileo's telescope, and seen some similar early devices in English museums, but this was my first chance to see the real thing, the humble optical tube that had changed the world. We were given an informative guided tour of the collection and then invited to meet the museum's director, who had in his office a working replica of the telescope, which he allowed us to peer through. While the museum's collection was full of Galilean relics, including his finger bone, this was the experience that stayed with me. I'd never really thought to wonder before how Galileo actually saw the moons and stars above him – the precise form in which his telescope brought them before his eyes. What struck me, in a basic but crucial way, was just how tiny the visual field of the telescope was. Its narrow aperture brought near that which lay distant, but only a tiny section at a time. Aiming the telescope out of the window at a terracotta roof some way off, I could see its individual tiles with remarkable clarity, but only a few at once. I had to *read* the roof, almost as if each cluster of tiles were a word made up of distinct letters, only gradually adding up in my scrabbling mind to the larger object of which they were a part. I had thought of telescopes as *opening up* the heavens in a new way, of making their vastness apprehensible and inviting. But this seemed like a much more fragmented, piecemeal experience. I thought less of those moments in *Paradise Lost* when Milton opens up the massiveness of space – what he wonderfully calls 'the vast profundity obscure' – and more of the moment where the austere divinity first appears and views Satan himself.[37] God 'bent down his eye' from Heaven and 'surveyed / Hell and the gulf between, and Satan there / Coasting the wall of Heaven'.[38] We spend the first two books of the poem in overwhelming, uncomfortable, engaging proximity with Satan, both emotional and physical; suddenly he is a dust mote floating in the distance, a far-off inconvenience to be peered at indifferently – like an object brought into focus at the end of a Galilean telescope.

The next leg of the journey was the winding drive into the hills outside Florence that took us to the Villa Il Gioiello: the shady inner rooms in which Galileo and Milton might have met; the sunbleached, tree-lined courtyard. I have said enough about this encounter already, so I'll add just one more reflection here on its potential impact. Milton's experience in the Florentine academies very likely led to their connection: his 1647 letter to Carlo Dati ended by sending good wishes to Galileo's illegitimate son Vincenzo, who most likely facilitated Milton's visit. Galileo, as I mentioned, was heavily involved in these academies himself, delivering his lectures on Dante before the Accademia Fiorentina, and the wit and elegance with which he spoke and wrote suited such gatherings well. This is another backdrop against which some of the later peculiarities of *Paradise Lost* came into new focus for me. Given Milton's naming of, and allusions to, Galileo in the poem, scholars have long debated whether through his cosmic vision Milton endorses the emerging Galilean view of the heavens as immeasurable, changeable, and with the Earth orbiting the Sun as just one of countless mutable bodies moving within its vastness; or whether he was still wedded to the antiquated Ptolemaic world view which placed the Earth at the centre, surrounded by a Matryoshka doll of unchanging, harmoniously revolving heavenly spheres. The fact that Milton's connections with the emerging experimental science of his day are so tangential and evasive, and that his reverence for the ancients, including their geography and cosmology, was so overt, has made the latter seem more likely. And yet it's notable that the most explicit mention of the heavenly spheres in *Paradise Lost*, while it doesn't mention Galileo, is couched in multiple layers of biting irony and dizzying complication that are indebted to the astronomer and his literary preoccupations. It occurs when Milton describes Satan, on his way towards Earth, pausing on the 'firm opacous globe / Of this round world', a paradoxical 'windy sea of land' where he 'Walked up and down alone bent on his prey, / Alone, for other Creature in this place / Living or lifeless to be found was none'. Or rather, Milton immediately continues, 'None yet', for he anticipates the future time when 'all things vain' will float into this region like vapours from the Earth, and it will be inhabited by those who err and overreach the most heinously. He lists some of them: the builders of the Tower of Babel, the most foolish of the Greek philosophers, and, above all, 'eremits [hermits] and friars / White, black and grey, with all their trumpery', who will fly hopefully towards Heaven only for a wind to blast them back into this region:

> then might ye see
> Cowls, hoods and habits with their wearers tossed
> And fluttered into rags, then relics, beads
> Indulgences, dispenses, pardons, bulls
> The sport of winds: all these upwhirled aloft
> Fly o'er the backside of the world far off
> Into a limbo large and broad, since called
> The Paradise of Fools, to few unknown
> Long after, now unpeopled, and untrod . . .[39]

It's a deeply strange moment: suddenly we're thrown forward from the origins of free will and evil to Milton's time and to his personal preoccupations, as the standard paraphernalia of anti-Catholic polemic abruptly clatters across the poem's cosmos. There's a whiff of scatology about it too: the close proximity of 'sport of winds' and 'backside of the world' shows that Milton was still fond of the fart jokes he'd employed in his student orations. Time bends and twists here: we are asked to picture both the elemental emptiness of this realm at the moment when Satan passed through, and the crowds of fools whom it will, but does not yet, contain. The mixture of tones is jarring, distracting, at a crucial point in the poem's action. And yet it makes better sense once we recognise that Milton is concocting here a heady brew of cosmology, theology, and poetry. The reference to 'limbo', which was the first circle of Dante's Hell, suggests that he has his old fascination with the *Commedia* in mind; but he also states that monstrous errors 'wander here, / Not in the neighbouring Moon, as some have dreamed'.[40] This is a reference to one of the most entertaining episodes in Ariosto's *Orlando Furioso*, in which the knight Astolfo, searching for the lost wits of the eponymous Orlando, flies to the Moon where he finds John the Baptist, who acts as lunar custodian to all deranged minds. So Milton is consciously alluding to, and seeking to correct and surpass, two of the Italian poets whom he admired the most – but also the two whom Galileo admired the most, and who were repeatedly debated and defended in the Florentine academies. This is also the point in the poem at which the system of 'crystalline spheres' that makes up the Ptolemaic cosmos is openly described: but it's been taken both as Milton's dogged adherence to this outdated view, and as an obvious satire of it, a symptom of his fidelity to Galileo.[41] I find it hard to decide: the region is described as *real*, however satirically – visited by Satan in its eerily empty state, awaiting its future influx of idiocy. I find it more convincing to see it as his final homage to the great Florentine astronomer: nodding cheekily towards Galileo's favourite poets in the act of correcting them and undermining the old cosmology in the kind of impish, ambiguous ways of which Galileo was himself the master; a way of making learned jokes, full of suggestion but avoiding absolute claims to truth, that both of them had encountered in the academic world of Florence.

The mockery of monks, their 'Cowls, hoods and habits', was, however, troubling for another reason. If Milton met any monks in person, this too was likely to have happened in Italy. I alluded above to the fact that Galileo was educated by a monastic order at Vallombrosa, some twenty-five miles east of Florence, and there has been a long-standing question as to whether Milton himself might have visited the monastery. Here too the evidence is slender, ambiguous – not least because, like so many of his other Italian associations, he placed it near the start of *Paradise Lost*, in Hell. When Satan pulls himself from the lake of fire on which we first meet him, he surveys the fate of his followers who have survived the terrifying plunge from Heaven and now 'lay entranced / Thick as autumnal leaves that strow the brooks / In Vallombrosa, where th'Etrurian shades / High overarched embower'.[42] There's been much debate about whether Milton ever actually travelled to the place he names. The comparison to fallen leaves is found in Homer, Virgil, and Dante, so might just be Milton's way of signalling the epic tradition to which he belongs; perhaps he just liked the name Vallombrosa (it is a wonderful name), and used it as a way of putting his own stamp on a hoary comparison. But the precision of the description has made many believe, or want to believe, that he visited; and so off we went, driving east of Florence for more than an hour, imagining how onerous and dangerous the trip would have been in 1638.

Whereas I wouldn't necessarily urge you to go out of your way to visit Bread Street, Horton, or the Hotel Astoria, I would whole-heartedly recommend Vallombrosa if you ever have the opportunity to go. Part of the excitement even before we arrived was the sense of joining a long list of literary pilgrims who'd made the journey with Milton in mind in earlier centuries. They included some of his most famous admirers. William Wordsworth wrote a pretty poor poem, 'At Vallombrosa', which noted of Milton's visit that 'The Monks still repeat the tradition with pride, / And its truth who shall doubt?'[43] Mary Shelley, who would later make the reworking of *Paradise Lost*'s exploration of creation and separateness central to her novel *Frankenstein*, arrived at the monastery soaked by sleet, and the monks plied her with coffee and *rosolio*, the rose petal liqueur that they distilled.[44] She had better luck than the poet Elizabeth Barrett Browning, who hoped to spend three months there but was turned back by the monks, who wouldn't allow a female to be resident – a reminder that, as with Virginia Woolf's experience with the Trinity Manuscript, following Milton's footsteps has often been a very different experience for women and men.[45] But I'd also been intrigued to discover figures less readily associated with Milton who knew of his connection with the place – like the philosopher Friedrich Nietzsche, who in November 1885 wrote to his mother from Florence of his plan to 'retreat into the wood-, mountain-, and cloister-solitude of Vallombrosa ... the place is famous: Dante and Milton have glorified it, the latter in his description of paradise.'[46]

FIGURE 12: The Monastery at Vallombrosa.

As we wound our way up towards the monastery, the view back down over the Tuscan countryside became ever more spectacular, drenched in the setting of the sun that had beaten down on us at Villa Il Gioiello. By the time we arrived at our hotel it was too late to scope out the monastery and so, after enduring the worst meal I have ever eaten in Italy but after a good night's sleep, we headed there the following morning. Fittingly, given Milton's description of 'th'Etrurian shades' (Etruria, an ancient name for Tuscany, combined with a word that can mean literal shadows, but also carries ominous, ghostly suggestions), it was a much gloomier day and the monastery was shrouded in cloud. The young monk who had been deputed to show us around gave us a brisk tour of the monastery's kitchens, some of its grander rooms, and the monks' cells, relatively few now inhabited by permanent residents: all delivered in rapid-fire Italian, which I did my best to follow and summarise on the spot into Melissa's microphone. This was also the site of the greatest faux pas that I committed on my Miltonic travels, the point at which I wished a gust of wind would hoist me aloft and blast me up to the Paradise of Fools where I belonged. The young monk had spoken to us only in Italian, and was showing us the collection of relics left by the monastery's patron saint; he spoke of this patron at length, as is, of course, completely his right. While I was intrigued by the idea that Milton had seen these objects – that they could have leapt back into his mind when he wrote of the 'relics, beads', and other Roman Catholic 'trumpery . . . upwhirled aloft' in *Paradise Lost* – the protracted details of the saint's life were less relevant to us. My Italian comprehension already pushed to its limits, I muttered to Melissa that it would be simplest to let the guy keep talking and edit it out later. It was rude, and ungrateful, and I should have known better. Not long after, we had walked with this same young monk to the top of the tall hill inside the monastery grounds, passing a series of caves with tiny ledges in which anchorites had once lived. At the top was the monastery's guest house, and on the side, another modern plaque claiming Milton for the place: *Giovanni Milton*, it read, *studioso dei nostri classici; devoto alla nostra civiltà; innamorato di questa foresta e di questo cielo* – student of our classics, devoted to our civilisation, enamoured of this forest and this sky. Milton claimed back by the place he claimed in passing in his epic poem, rooted between these trees and this sky. Only at this point did the young monk reveal that he spoke perfect English, and the depth of my earlier blunder sank in. He was too polite to show any offence, but I still feel a flush of shame when I think of it. I should have remembered Henry Wotton's advice myself: *I pensieri stretti, ed il viso sciolto.* It was a sobering reminder of my own foreignness in this place, the ease with which it's possible to become complacent when trespassing in a space that is not one's own; a caution against arrogance that I took with me as we said our farewell to the monk and tramped about beneath the trees of the Vallombrosan forest, summer foliage rather than autumn leaves beneath our feet, staring up at the trees overhead and wondering whether Milton had ever seen them.

8

14 February 1639: 'Majestic Show of Luxury'

Another musical evening – a grand one. Milton spent the previous day – a prospect that would have seemed shocking and impossible just a year before – in the Vatican library, the book-lined belly of the Beast. He and his new friend Lukas Holste, one of the senior librarians, had drifted amiably in their quiet chatter between Italian, English, and Latin, and Holste showed Milton some of his most treasured manuscripts: a history of the world in ancient Greek that he had acquired on a recent trip to Malta; the writings of the philosopher Michael Psellos, who wrote with capti-vating power on the bodies of angels.[1] Milton had talked to Holste about the academies of Florence that he had so enjoyed, and the librarian had insisted that his English guest join him that evening at one of the grandest Roman equivalents, the Umoristi. Co-founded decades before by Pope Urban himself, the pontiff and his nephew the cardinal, Holste's patron and the most powerful man in Rome, still attended on occasion. Holste implored Milton to accompany him to the next night's gathering.

The Umoristi meet at the house of one of its other founders, Paolo Mancini, on the Corso. Holste guides Milton deftly through the entrance, and they take their place at the side of the spacious hall where the academy's proceedings unfold. Milton scans the room, taking in the wall hangings, all of which contain clever plays on the Latin word *humidum*, from which *umoristi* derives: those gathered are humourists, the witty ones, but also the wet or the soggy ones.[2] Holste points out a few faces in the crowd: the great collector Cassiano dal Pozzo, whose house is said to be a Noah's Ark of riches, with two of every wonder that the world holds; as usual he is with two of his French protégés – Holste knows one, the painter Poussin, whose reputation is on the rise and whose farmyard name makes Milton smile; he thinks that the other is a recently arrived viola virtuoso. Then he explains what the evening will hold: a speech by the designated Lord of the academy, followed by *discorsi* from other notable members. These will be witty enough, Holste promises, but the main event will be a musical performance by a singer named Leonora, said to have the finest voice that Rome has ever heard. It is so exquisite, and the lady so talented, that it is rumoured the academy will make her its first and only woman member. Then Holste gives a clue as to the motive behind his invitation: he has agreed to contribute to a book of poems in praise of the Lady, and hopes that Milton, whose verses were so admired in Florence, might do the same.

The evening as it unfolds is pleasant but unspectacular; the speeches are no wittier than those Milton has heard at Gaddi's *palazzo* in Florence, and there is an off-putting sense of the participants trying too hard, straining to outdo one another in their virtuosity, and in their praise for the ill and absent pope: one musician, Mazzocchi, even sings his own *a cappella* setting of one of Urban's poems.[3] By the time that Leonora finally arrives to sing, Milton's mind has started to wander. Her voice is fine enough, and he will certainly crank out some poems in her honour to keep Holste happy. Perhaps he'll call her an angel, say that she holds the audiences of Rome spellbound, that should do the trick.

Then suddenly, in the midst of her song, something about her voice hits him. It's as if the rest of the room has frozen in darkness, and only he and the sound are present. As if he had first to get used to her voice without focusing upon it so that it could seep into him unnoticed. He's pinned to the wall against which he leans, rapt. The notes seem to come from elsewhere. It's astounding, but teetering on the brink of the obscene, the inhuman. The voice doesn't seem to issue from her body – it's like some superhuman creature, angel or demon, creeping from her throat into the room, stalking across to where he stands and slithering into his ear. She's no longer singing; he's no longer listening; both of them are *sung*.

The last note ends. The voice vanishes. Everything returns to normal, almost as if it hadn't happened. It stays with him strangely not as a sound but more like a scent, its after-echoes an ambrosial fragrance wafting across the heavens.[4]

◆

It was upon leaving Florence after a two-month stay that Milton made the first of his two visits to Rome. He passed over this first sojourn quickly in his retrospective account of his trip – 'having been detained about two months in this city by its antiquities and ancient renown . . . I proceeded to Naples'. And so, although I've begun in Rome, I'll do the same, following him first on his Neapolitan visit and then returning as he did to the papal city. The contrast between Florence and Rome on the one hand, and Naples on the other, would have been particularly extreme for Milton, as it is for me, though for different reasons. While I have visited the former two cities on numerous occasions, I have never visited Naples, and my plan to do so in time to write about it was torpedoed by the global pandemic in the midst of which I am writing, and so it remains thus far a place that I know only through books, pictures, films, and my imagination. For Milton, it meant entering for the first time the vast empire of the Spanish Habsburgs. Spain had ruled over Naples and the surrounding provinces, which formed part of the so-called Kingdom of Sicily, since the fifteenth century. It was governed by a series of Spanish viceroys – at the time of Milton's trip this was Ramiro de Guzmán, Duque de Medina de las Torres – who had worked hard to impose obedience on the local nobility, creating in the process a series of tensions that were productive and explosive by turns: between courtly Spanish and the local dialect of Italian; between Spanish and Italian styles of post-Tridentine Catholicism, and the art that expressed and responded to its pious forms; between the heavily taxed countryside and the wealthier but ever more crowded and divided city. Naples had, when Milton visited, the largest population of any city in southern Europe – more than three hundred thousand people, four times the size of Rome, and smaller only than London and Paris across the entire Continent. As a great port city it seemed both to repel the invading world – massive stone fortifications advertising Spanish imperial might – and to welcome it in. English visitors were invariably struck by what George Sandys in 1610 called 'the concourse of sundry nations to this haven' which 'doth adde an over-abundance to their native plenty'.[5] People and languages from across the known globe converged here. As one local dignitary put it, 'Naples is the whole world.' But if this meant grandeur and magnificence, it also meant squalor. Locals and travellers alike testified to the desperate beggars, the most wretched known as *lazzari*, who thronged the streets by day and slept in any available corner by night. 'The dregs of humanity', wrote the same dignitary, constantly making 'a murmuring . . . as if it were the buzzing of bees'. Squalid though their lives were, starvation was even more likely in the provinces, so they continued to flock to the overcrowded city. Buildings began to be built to five or six storeys, twice as high as anywhere else in Europe. Between the languorous, lavish world of the Spanish court, the teetering, precarious domiciles, and the awful poverty on constant display, it was a place of particularly visible and violent extremes.[6]

Milton secured a prominent and well-connected guide through the Neapolitan labyrinth in the person of Giambattista Manso, Marquis of Villa. He later made the bizarre claim that he was introduced to the marquis 'by a certain hermit with whom I had travelled from Rome'. I go back in my mind as I read this to the anchorites' tiny ledges at Vallombrosa: there's a comedy road movie to be made about this; how had Milton fallen in with such a man? Manso's connections were wide and varied, and notably included Galileo, whom the marquis had praised as a 'new Columbus' for his discovery of new heavens [*scovrimento de' nuovi cieli*].[7] What mattered most to Milton, however, was Manso's close association with the poet Torquato Tasso, whom Galileo so disliked. Tasso had stayed in Manso's villa near Naples on several occasions, and, as Milton noted, the poet 'addressed his book on friendship' to the marquis. Manso in turn wrote an influential biography of Tasso that was published in 1621, a quarter of a century after Tasso's death.[8] While still in Naples Milton wrote a lengthy Latin poem to Manso, later to be included in his 1645 collection, in which he praised the marquis because 'Great Tasso and you were once joined by a happy friendship [*Te pridem magno felix concordia Tasso / Iunxit* – the verb meaning 'joined' is wittily disjoined from the rest of the sentiment by a line break] which has written your name on the pages of eternity', and heaped praise on him as the epitome of wise old age.[9]

There were various reasons for Milton to gravitate at this point towards a man with close connections to Tasso. Though he too wrote sonnets and pastoral dramas, Tasso had done more than any other poet to try to explore the basis on which a modern epic poem could be written, seeking, against Ariosto's easy-going sprawl, to reconcile his own writing with the tenets both of Aristotle's *Poetics* and of the Counter-Reformation Church. In the process he explored questions, and laid down precepts, that would deeply influence Milton in the writing of *Paradise Lost*, and that were already pushing to the forefront of his mind in Naples. As I mentioned earlier, Tasso compared the creative activities of the pious poet to those of God, and he also insisted that the writer of a virtuous epic 'needs the highest virtues'. Milton, as we'll see, would go on to identify the virtue of poet and poem in similar fashion. Tasso also explored both the differences and the connections between languages, insisting that 'the sublime and the exotic in diction derive from foreign words', while warning that 'Judiciousness is needed, however, in combining foreign words with native ones so that they result in an entirely clear and entirely sublime composition.'[10] Perhaps most intriguingly, he made a concerted argument for the value of what he called *asprezza* – roughness, or a specific kind of difficulty – in epic. For him, this was essential in order to achieve the most important quality of all, 'magnificence'. *Asprezza* could be created in various ways and on various levels: by stretching the sense of the poetry out over several lines, creating 'the prolonged suspension of meaning'. The use of complex, Latinate words; the harsh combination or running together of sounds; making words 'keenly felt' through alliteration and by 'intensifying the rhythm at the end of the verse' – all contributed to the effect. In terms that anticipate Mandelstam's claim, which I quoted earlier – 'Dante's rhythms . . . glorify the human gait, the measure and rhythm of walking' – Tasso insisted that when Dante employs such techniques 'it resembles someone who stumbles as he walks a rough path. But this roughness suggests somehow the great and magnificent.'[11]

These aspects of Tasso's theory were all adopted and developed by Milton in various ways when he wrote *Paradise Lost*, and they offer a useful alternative response to the feeling that often confronts me and many other readers when they read it – that it is strenuous, overcomplicated, *difficult*. One response to this difficulty, at the root of much scholarship, is that we simply need to *know more* – to equip ourselves with the knowledge that Milton possessed, so that what seemed difficult will begin to dissolve into informed ease. This can be useful, but it might not be the best or only response. Tasso's example suggests reasons why poets might deliberately strive for difficulty – to unsettle their readers, to make them trip and stumble on a path that winds and bumps, to contort the norms of sound and sense, to push language to its limits and see what we meet when we get there. *Asprezza* helps me remember that difficulty might not be something to be scared of or to be solved, but rather to be wrestled with so we can marvel all the more at what happens to us in the process.[12]

While Milton was in Naples, Tasso also seems to have influenced him in a more immediate way. Milton by this point had chosen the subject matter for the epic that he was now explicitly hoping to write. Tasso had urged modern poets to turn away from classical plots: 'the subject of an epic must be drawn from Christian and Hebrew history, not from Gentile history . . . The epic poet, thus, must take his theme from the history of a religion held true by us.' Only a basis in pious truth could free the poet to invent within appropriate limits. 'History of distant eras', Tasso suggested, 'affords the poet greatest leeway for invention', and he specifically suggested:

'Such are the times of Charlemagne and Arthur and those which either preceded or succeeded them a little.'[13] At the end of his poem to Manso, Milton wrote openly for the first time of his epic ambitions: 'if only the inspiration would come [*O modo spiritus ad sit*]', he might 'call back into poetry the kings of my native land and Arthur, who set wars raging even under the earth, or tell of the great-hearted heroes of the round table, which their fellowship made invincible.'[14] These lines reflect Milton's deep reading in British history and myth before his Italian travels, and present one of the most intriguing roads not travelled in the history of literature: what if, instead of *Paradise Lost*, we had Milton's *Arthuriad*? What these lines suggest to me is the tension that was beginning to build within Milton's sense of himself at this point, as we saw in the letter to Buonmattei, and as we'll see in future chapters. He desires to present himself as a national poet, restorer of the hoariest British foundation myths to poetic dignity; but he articulates these nationalistic ambitions in the international language of Latin, to an Italian papist, lodged in a chaotic, cosmopolitan, conspicuously Catholic city perched on the edge of the Mediterranean.

Manso was a generous guide to Milton in this potentially overwhelming environment: 'he conducted me all over the city and the Vice-regent's court, and more than once came to visit me at my lodgings'. Milton was careful, later, to emphasise the religious gulf between them over which their friendship built a precarious bridge: Manso apologised that he could not show his guest around more extensively, 'because', Milton claimed, 'I had not thought proper to be more guarded on the point of religion', suggesting an unwillingness to conceal his Protestantism even in the heart of Habsburg Naples. Later Milton reprinted Manso's epigram praising his mind, manners, and soul, and punningly lamenting that in every respect other than piety Milton is no 'Angle' but rather an angel.[15] These defensive gestures are a reminder that being friends with the marquis and emulating Tasso were risky enterprises that obliged Milton to emphasise his impeccable piety. Nor was Naples an altogether respectable place to suggest that one had become an epic poet. Tasso became a powerful model for Milton because he presented himself both as Aristotelian rationaliser and, ambiguously, as a prophetic vessel for divinely inspired utterance; 'when the poet speaks in his own person, he is allowed to think and speak *as though* with a different mind and a different tongue and much beyond ordinary usage, because *we believe him* inspired and rapt with divine *furor*'.[16] Tasso doesn't quite commit himself to the reality of such divine inspiration, but his words read rather differently in relation to the growing fascination with his protracted struggles with madness, which Manso did a great deal to popularise. Tasso's intense melancholy and vivid delusions were much analysed and diagnosed by his contemporaries, and later made him a hero for proponents of artistic idiosyncrasy like Lord Byron, who had himself locked in the cell known as Tasso's Dungeon in Ferrara to see if he could experience the poet's visions. Milton was well aware of this tradition, writing in one of his Roman poems that Tasso became besotted with a woman 'and his mad love [*insano amore*] for her drove him out of his mind'.[17] Tasso was open to divine inspiration, but his wits were unstable for more worldly reasons.

This, however, was not the only example that Naples offered of extreme, volatile forms of what it meant to make art. While it is harder to verify the impact of the wider scene on Milton, this is still worth exploring for its resonance with his enduring artistic preoccupations. In the poem to Manso, Milton mentioned another of the marquis's poetic protégés, '*dulciloquum . . . Marinum*', the 'sweet-voiced' Giambattista Marino. This Naples-born poet was renowned for ingenuity, virtuosic wordplay, and ornate artificiality, as well as notorious for multiple spells in prison and his aura of uncontrolled sexuality; not at all the kind of writer whom Milton wanted to become.[18] But there is another artistic figure whom Milton does not name, even more infamous than his friend Marino, whom Manso also befriended and supported in Naples: Michelangelo Merisi, known to posterity by the name of his birthplace, Caravaggio. The great and infamous painter had fled to Naples from Rome in 1606 after stabbing to death a man named

Ranuccio Tomassoni in a brawl following a ball game. By then he had developed a reputation for daringly integrating into his sacred paintings the humdrum and sometimes loathsome texture of reality, scandalously using common people as models for figures of great holiness and retaining their imperfections; their wrinkles and pockmarks, their filthy feet and fingernails. He had a volcanic temper – once hurling a tray of artichokes at a waiter who couldn't tell him whether they were cooked in oil or butter – and a voracious sexual appetite. He brought with him to Naples his apprentice Francesco Boneri, known as Cecco del Caravaggio, who was rumoured to be his catamite. His glamorous, decadent reputation and pyrotechnic talents made him much in demand when he arrived

FIGURE 13: Caravaggio, *The Seven Acts of Mercy.*

in the city, and his most prestigious commission was to paint a grand picture for the altar of the recently constructed Chiesa del Pio Monte della Misericordia in central Naples, illustrating the Seven Acts of Mercy. The church had been built by a lay confraternity founded by seven young noblemen hoping to alleviate the conspicuous suffering of the city's poor; one of the seven was Manso, and the astounding painting that he helped commission still hangs on the same spot today.[19]

Milton, as I've mentioned, was frustratingly silent about the paintings that he saw in Italy; but he surely *must* have seen this one. If Manso showed him around the city, how could the marquis not have shown him the looming masterpiece he had helped to bring into being? *The Seven Acts of Mercy* is a teeming, crowded, initially baffling painting. It was very unusual to depict all of the seven acts in one combined image, and they are not clearly distributed between the figures; the painting demands to be read, decoded, in time, even as one is drawn up short by the fleshy immediacy of the bodies on display, the ridged back of the figure in the foreground and the grubby soles of the corpse being slid out of sight. The painting is a temporal vortex, several time frames seeming to collapse into one another. Figures from the Old and New Testaments, the classical world, the medieval world, and Caravaggio's own time exist side by side; and, at the top of the painting, the timelessness of the sacred bursts startlingly into this confection of human times, as the Madonna and Child seem to ride on the back of two spiralling, embracing angels, one of whose arms dangles plaintively down into a human realm it cannot reach.[20] Early viewers were both astounded and shocked by what Caravaggio produced. They noted the luminous, mysterious light flooding into the scene from the top left; the man who 'drinks with open mouth, disgustingly letting the wine run into it' (actually, drinking water from an ass's jawbone); the 'bizarre manner' of the whole. Would Milton have been repulsed by this intense, murky, thronging scene? Or would he have seen in it a way of combining the human, the angelic, and the divine, the fleshly and the ideal, the time-bound and the timeless, into a single, daringly realised space? Would he have pondered this way of making many times present at once in a way that demanded both an expenditure of time and a transformation of individual time on the part of the viewer? Might he have wondered whether such a feat was possible in words?

More than any artist in history, Caravaggio seemed able to channel and give form to his manifestly unstable personality in acts of creativity that pulsed with the violence of which he was capable. Somehow in the midst of their violence, his paintings managed to open up new possibilities of human interconnectedness, both in the kinds of relationship they depicted and in the way that they asked viewers to relate to them. Caravaggio was able to convey a deep sense of the bodily acts that had gone into making his paintings, and to make the viewer aware of his or her own body as they stood before them. It's also certainly possible that Milton could have heard of Caravaggio's sexual relationships with boys. A few years later another English traveller, describing the seductive painting of Cupid for which the painter's twelve-year-old apprentice had served as model, scrawled in his notebook: 'Checco del Caravaggio, 'tis called among the painters, 'twas his boy . . . 'Twas the body & face of his own boy or servant that laid with him.'[21] But, as with Milton's own sexuality, I am less concerned with Caravaggio's own possible homosexuality – or, as a recent biographer puts it, his 'omnisexuality' – than in the expanded repertoire of human relationships which his work provides, and that his art, and Italy in general, might have provided Milton. His ability through his painting to make human individuals and their bodies both intensely present and profoundly enigmatic to one another.[22] It is this combination that resonates for me with the explorations of human interconnectedness and separateness that, as we'll see, Milton would go on to undertake in his later work.

Furthermore, at the precise moment Milton visited Naples, there was every reason to think that Caravaggio's paintings remained a vital presence in the city, whether or not Manso showed them to him. During his brief and troubled sojourns there, Caravaggio had a transformative impact on Neapolitan painting. Cecco had become a superb painter in his own right in the 1620s, and others had jostled to assume the mantle of Caravaggio's stylistic innovations and personal unscrupulousness. Chief among them in the 1630s was Jusepe de Ribera, a Spaniard trained in Rome whose work emulated Caravaggio's virtuosic contrasts of light and dark, and his ability to root the viewer to the spot before a painting through the intensity of the figures depicted.[23] Ribera was also the leader of a cabal of painters who sought to protect their pre-eminence by nefarious means: when the Roman painter Domenichino was commissioned to paint the Cappella del Tesoro at the start of the 1630s, Ribera and his followers terrorised and sabotaged him, threatening violence and often sneaking into the chapel to scrub out his previous day's work.[24] Milton arrived at the end of what has been called 'the most volcanic and contradictory decade' in the city's artistic history.[25] Great artists passed through, learning from Caravaggio and other past greats and leaving their own stylistic mark: from Diego Velázquez, who visited in 1630-1, to the greatest female painter of the age, Artemisia Gentileschi. She and Milton passed like ships in the night, since she left for England to join her father Orazio at the court of Charles I in London at the end of 1639, the exact moment when Milton arrived in Naples.[26] While the impact of Naples's artistic world on Milton is impossible to verify, the more I peer into it the more the web of connections that this group of painters represents, seems to resonate with the writer and the person he was in the process of becoming. A world in which artists drifted between countries and language with ease; in which the kind of person that one was and the kind of art that one produced seemed inescapably connected; in which violence and creativity seemed troublingly woven together.

The description of his actions upon leaving Naples is the least coherent part of Milton's retrospective account of his travels. 'As I was preparing to pass over also into Sicily and Greece,' he claimed, 'I was restrained by the melancholy tidings from England of the civil war; for I thought it base that I should be travelling at my ease, even for the improvement of my mind abroad, while my fellow citizens were fighting for their liberty at home.' These sentiments were neatly invented in retrospect. In fact, while Charles I was at war with the Scots, civil war was still two years away, and given that Milton continued to travel for several more months, he was apparently in no rush to join the fight for 'liberty at home'. Instead he returned from Naples to Rome. Just as he proudly proclaimed his unguardedness in matters of religion in Naples, Milton likewise insisted that 'in the city even of the sovereign pontiff himself' he spoke up for his faith, at great personal risk. But he may have needed to make this claim precisely because he had thrown himself into the life of the papal city so wholeheartedly. In his last major poem, *Paradise Regained*, Milton would depict Satan showing Jesus (by means that intriguingly resemble the use of 'glass / Of telescope') an alluring view of 'great and glorious Rome, queen of the earth', crammed with gorgeous gardens and buildings, 'pillars and roofs / Carved work, the hand of famed artificers / In cedar, marble, ivory or gold'.[27] Jesus is 'unmoved' by 'this grandeur and majestic show / Of luxury', but it's less clear that Milton was.[28] In October 1638, before his trip to Naples, he entered the belly of the Beast, dining at the English College, the seminary that for half a century had trained Jesuits and sent them to England in the hope of reconverting the nation. His dining companions included the fourteen-year-old Patrick, Lord Cary, son of the prominent Catholic convert Lady Elizabeth Cary.[29] Also present was Henry Holden, a secular priest who a decade later became involved in a scheme known as Blacklo's Cabal, seeking to win toleration from Oliver Cromwell and asking him to grant English Catholics the same status as any other religious sect if they distanced themselves from the Pope and pledged their primary allegiance to England.[30] While in Rome Milton would also win the admiration of a Benedictine monk, who praised his poems as the equal of Homer's and Virgil's: his name was Matteo Selvaggio. Or at least that was one version – he was known more prosaically as Matthew Savage, but his true name was David Codner, an Englishman whose Italian was so flawless that he could pass as a local.[31] Milton mixed freely with Englishmen who had enthusiastically embraced the language, religion, and culture of Rome to the point of transforming themselves entirely, taking the tectonic shifts of identity and vocation that he was undergoing to an unapologetic extreme. It was as if he was suddenly running with the grim wolf pack who had devoured the innocent sheep of 'Lycidas'.

No wonder Milton later felt the need to insist that he was so vocal in his Protestantism while in Rome that, during his Neapolitan visit, he heard from merchants there 'of plots laid against me by the English Jesuits, should I return to Rome, because of the freedom with which I had spoken about religion. For I had determined within myself that in those parts I would not indeed begin a conversation about religion, but if questioned about my faith would hide nothing, whatever the consequences.' Undeterred by these rumoured plots, he returned to Rome where 'if anyone attacked the orthodox religion, I openly, as before, defended it'.[32] If anyone in England were to question his dining companions in Rome, he could safely insist that he was only defending the faith, at great personal risk. A similar retrospective distancing from the pleasures of Rome can be glimpsed near the opening of *Paradise Lost*, alongside the infernal recollections of Florence. Using 'wondrous art', the fallen angels refashion the materials of Hell to construct a palace whose 'fabric huge / Rose like an exhalation' from the earth. Named 'Pandaemonium', Milton's coinage, the structure is

> *Built like a temple, where pilasters round*
> *Were set, and Doric pillars overlaid*
> *With golden architrave; nor did there want*
> *Cornice or frieze, with bossy sculptures graven,*
> *The roof was fretted gold.*[33]

This sounds strikingly similar to the splendour of St Peter's: when John Evelyn visited the cathedral in 1644 he eulogised its 'stupendious Canopy of Corinthian brasse', its columns 'all over gilted with rich gold', the whole building 'a thing of that Art, vastnesse & magnificence, as is beyond all that ever mans industry has produced of this kind'.[34] But even as Milton echoes this vastness and magnificence, he belittlingly shrinks the devils who enter

255

Pandaemonium: 'Behold a wonder! They but now who seemed / In bigness to surpass Earth's Giant Sons / Now less then smallest Dwarfs'. Their diminution is completed with a scoffingly bad pun: 'Thus incorporeal spirits to smallest forms / Reduced their shapes immense, and were at large.'[35] The gigantism of the devils, and of the Roman architecture behind it, have been reduced to tiny individual pieces – almost as if glimpsed through the narrow aperture of a Galilean telescope.

But it's possible to read these retrospective dismissals and shrinkages another way: not as demonstrating Milton's confidence and contempt in the face of Roman Catholicism, but as expressions of the need to violently differentiate himself from something with which he had a more ambivalent underlying relationship, as we can see by glancing ahead at his later works. Granted, he denounced Catholicism furiously and consistently. His principal objection, as we'll see, was that its errors eradicated true human freedom, but he was equally disgusted by the physical practices and paraphernalia of Catholicism, as we saw in the last chapter in relation to the Paradise of Fools. In his major and unpublished theological work, *De Doctrina Christiana*, Milton aimed his fire at the central Catholic sacrament, and the one which had been most angrily debated during the Reformation: the Eucharist. In line with much Protestant polemic, he insisted that God's flesh is 'not what anyone's teeth can feed on, but what faith alone can', dismissing the physical significance of the bread and wine, and the possibility that they truly became the divine body and blood. As he colourfully put it, 'if we eat his flesh, it will not remain in us, but (to be utterly frank [*ut dicam quod honestissimum est*]) after being digested in the stomach will finally be voided'.[36] Catholics, Milton bluntly insisted – continuing a long tradition of scatological satire – are committed to believing that they are shitting out God.

There doesn't seem to be much in the way of ambivalence here. Against these strong denunciations, however, we must weigh Milton's striking decision to redeploy the language of the Eucharist in *Paradise Lost*. The narrator, describing Raphael settling down with Adam for the Edenic feast that I discussed in the last chapter, insists that the angel did not just eat 'seemingly . . . but with keen dispatch / Of real hunger, and concoctive heat / To *transubstantiate*'.[37] He chooses the immensely loaded word, with which Catholics described the reality of God's presence in the transformed bread and wine, to insist on the reality of angelic digestion. Why, we might reasonably ask? It becomes clear that his aim is not merely satirical when Adam and Raphael finish their meal and have a lengthy discussion, which begins with the first man asking the angel whether earthly food can bear comparison with heavenly repast. Strikingly, Milton chooses this apparently strange topic as an opportunity for Raphael to articulate a vision of the entire world, and the processes that hold it together. 'O Adam,' he explains,

> one almighty is, from whom
> All things proceed, and up to him return,
> If not depraved from good, created all
> Such to perfection, one first matter all
> Indued with various forms, various degrees
> Of substance, and in things that live, of life;
> But more refined, more spiritous, and pure,
> As nearer to him placed or nearer tending
> Each in their several active spheres assigned,
> Till body up to spirit work . . .

One first matter all: this striking claim sees Milton's angel, at a stroke, unify all of creation. Heaven, Earth, Hell: all are forged from the same material. All these regions and the objects that they contain are 'Differing but in degree, of kind the same', and the same is true of body and spirit. This is a universe that has a hierarchical order, but that order is fluid, molten, in ceaseless process. Everything is material, but a thing becomes more and less 'spiritous' and 'refined' depending on its closeness to or distance from God. This is a world that thrums with potential, a world of constant becoming. Just as leaves and flowers spring from roots, Raphael explains, so too do reason and imagination blossom from the body with which they are continuous: everything is 'by gradual scale sublimed', suggesting both the alchemical process of purification and the sense that it is made sublime, magnificent. And it is on the basis of this interconnectedness, Raphael explains, that he can eat with Adam, since 'time may come when men / With angels may participate'. If he and Eve remain obedient, 'Your bodies may at last turn all to spirit, / Improved by tract of time, and winged ascend / Ethereal, as we, or may at choice / Here or in heavenly paradises dwell' – the same possibility, as we saw in the last chapter, that might allow bodily human love to develop into the total interpenetration of spirits.[38] It's an astonishing vision of prelapsarian life as provisional rather than static perfection: if all goes to plan, the very divisions that structure the universe – between the human and the angelic, between Earth and Heaven – will shrink to irrelevance. The suggestion that, for an angel, to eat is to 'transubstantiate', the suggestion that gives rise to this line of thought, now appears in a different light. Milton uses the word because the process of *mere matter becoming divine* which he mocks in the Roman Catholic doctrine of the Eucharist is not banished in Eden but generalised, made into the rule rather than the miraculous exception: it is the principle by which the universe operates before the Fall, an incessant ennobling of the material and human world as it shifts and changes in its trajectory towards God. The whole of Eden, the entire world of *Paradise Lost* until the Fall, is always and everywhere transubstantiating.[39]

Everything does not, of course, go to plan. Milton is giving us both a dazzling vision of such a world and the melancholic sense that it has been irretrievably lost, that we can only glimpse it with our limited, fallen minds and words. But this also suggests a crucial place for the kinds of Roman Catholic errors that he strove to reject. All of his experiences in Italy, and particularly in Rome, would have confronted Milton with the full extent to which Catholics sought to locate God in material objects, practices, gestures, and experiences of the body. But whereas many Protestants simply rejected this entire way of thinking and strove to focus solely on the Spirit and the Word, Raphael's words show how fully committed Milton would remain to an ideal of human life in which the mental blossoms from the physical, the spiritual from the bodily, and all remain interconnected manifestations of one first matter. Milton had probably not yet developed this world view when he was in Italy; but, given how deeply idiosyncratic his theological vision would become, it's worth remembering that Italy was associated in the English mind with atheism as much as with the lures of Catholicism; the peninsula bristled with unorthodox religious beliefs, from learned heterodoxies to sophisticated folk cosmologies developed by artisans and peasants.[40] I wouldn't say that Milton was dissimulating when he later denounced Catholicism, but he was making his relationship with it seem much simpler than it really was. He too wanted to envisage a world in which God both made matter and was, perhaps, made matter.

When Milton's devils enter Pandaemonium he compares their 'hiss of rustling wings' to 'bees / In spring time' who 'Pour forth their populous youth about the hive / In clusters'.[41] This simile allows a breath of vernal air that makes the hot claustrophobia of the poem's infernal opening all the more stifling by contrast. The beehive was a standard image for political gatherings at least since Virgil, but this moment also brings Milton's Hell back to Rome. Evelyn noted that the columns in St Peter's were festooned with 'little Puti, Birds, & Bees', the last especially significant because they were 'the Armes of the Barberini', the family of Pope Urban VIII, born Maffeo Barberini, who had condemned Galileo and who had reshaped the entire culture of Rome.[42] Urban was a brilliant intellectual, but his position from the outset of his papacy in 1623 was unstable. He had been elected unexpectedly, in controversial fashion, and at a tense moment in European religious politics. The Barberini family was Tuscan, not particularly distinguished, and had close ties with the France of Richelieu, which risked alienating the Spanish monarchy. The Pope became a grand patron of the arts and sciences, which both reflected his own interests and ambitions – he was an accomplished poet, and fascinated by astrology – and was a way of burnishing his family's reputation for benevolence and sophistication as they filled their pockets. New palaces were constructed, painters such as Nicolas Poussin were cultivated, scholars were encouraged and funded, lavish and carefully choreographed banquets thrown.[43] By the time Milton arrived in Rome, Urban's reputation for open-mindedness had been damaged by his turning against and imprisoning his once close friend Galileo; he had fallen ill and retreated from public life, with one rumour claiming that, when he appeared at a window, it was in fact his corpse, made to move by the ingenuity of Bernini.[44]

Urban's place at the centre of Roman cultural life had been taken by his nephew, Francesco, the senior cardinal who had long been loaded with prestigious offices and rich benefices by his uncle, and who was his chief surrogate. He was effectively head of the Church's diplomatic activities, and sat at the centre of a web of communications stretching across Europe. Francesco was a serious intellectual and scholar in his own right, patron to Rome's foremost polymaths – men like Athanasius Kircher, who pored over Egyptian hieroglyphs and Chinese characters and tried to resurrect crayfish from their ashes, and Cassiano dal Pozzo, who compiled drawings of antiquities, flora, and fauna from across Italy into his massive 'Paper Museum'. These were the circles towards which Milton gravitated, apparently with none of the anxiety that characterised his dealings with Jesuits and English Catholics; it was much more continuous with the easy-going, cultured milieu of the Florentine academies. The two areas of interest to Milton that were particularly prominent in the Barberini programme were scholarship and music, and his connections with the one seem to have led him naturally to the other. He was introduced, probably by a scholar whom he had befriended named Antonio Cherubini, to one of the Vatican librarians, the German Lukas Holste, known as Holstenius. As Milton knew, Holstenius had spent time in England in his youth – 'you gave three years' work to Scholarship at Oxford', he recorded in a letter – but later converted to Catholicism and was given the task of building the Barberini a world-class collection of books and manuscripts. The very year that Milton arrived in Rome, Holstenius helped set up a Latin and Greek printing press in Cardinal Francesco Barberini's official residence, the Palazzo della Cancelleria.[45] He also enlisted Milton in his search for manuscripts. When the latter made a brief second visit to Florence, Holstenius asked him to visit the famous Laurentian library – already a tourist attraction due to its intricately carved ceiling 'of cedar very curiously wrought with knots and flowers' and its collection of more than nine thousand rare volumes – and copy one of the Medici codices for him.[46] Unfortunately Milton's efforts proved fruitless: 'In that library', he explained to Holstenius, 'nothing can be copied except by previous permission, nor may one even bring a pen to the tables.'[47]

While this particular attempt was frustrated, Milton was still a world away from the solitary study he'd been undertaking in Horton a year previously, operating instead within a pan-European network of scholars that spilled across national, linguistic, and religious boundaries. His friendship with Holstenius also opened other doors for him, since the librarian did Milton the favour of 'mentioning me to Cardinal Francesco Barberini' himself. In February 1639 Milton was invited to attend a musical entertainment at the new theatre added to the Palazzo della Cancelleria; and, if gadding about Italy in search of manuscripts was a far cry from his parents' humble village, this extravaganza of music and pageantry would have been an equally huge leap from the musical evenings on Bread Street or the songs of *Comus*. When the cardinal gave 'that public musical entertainment', Milton reported to Holstenius, 'with truly Roman magnificence, he himself, waiting at the door, singled me out in so great a throng, and, almost seizing me by the hand, welcomed me in an exceedingly honourable manner'; he even managed to secure a brief private audience with the cardinal the following day.[48] Musical pageants were among the most important of the public spectacles funded by the Barberini: this one was a landmark for it was the first ever comic opera, titled *Chi soffre, speri* (*May He Who Suffers, Hope*).[49] It lasted a full five hours of lavish, ingenious, and conspicuously expensive performance before an audience of three and a half thousand people.[50] The performance was less about plot, which was clunky – a poor man killing his favourite falcon for love, and unearthing buried treasure, among other events – and more an occasion for the virtuosic singing of the *castrati* and the wonders of the set, designed by Bernini. This was art that sought to over-whelm ear and eye in a crescendo of sensory overload. Never again in his life would Milton experience a piece of combined political and religious theatre on this scale.

And so we loop back, again, to where we began this chapter. In Rome – whether, as I suggested, with Holstenius's help, or by other means – Milton also had the chance to hear the voice of Leonora Baroni, one of the most celebrated sopranos of the day, and wrote a series of short Latin poems in her honour. Baroni was part of Cardinal Barberini's circle, and was learned as well as talented: proficient in numerous languages, a poet as well as a singer.[51] Milton's poems to her are pretty standard fare, written for the volume of lavish praise to which Holstenius also contributed, but there's one moment from them that is, for me, different. It's a sort of equivalent to what Roland Barthes described in photographs as the *punctum*, which can mean 'sting, speck, cut, little hole – and also a cast of the dice'.[52] The punctum is the jarring detail that disconcerts and attracts, and makes one sharply aware of the gulf of time dividing you from that which you perceive: 'This new *punctum* . . . is Time.'[53] I want to believe that this moment, which stands out for me and stood out for Milton too, represents the sting in time or the little hole poked through time by an experience of beauty that stopped him in his tracks, and showed him that there was some deeper part of himself more fully at stake in what could have been an exercise in flattery. The moment as *punctum* that I imagined for him at the meeting of the Umoristi reads as follows:

> *Nam tua praesentem vox sonat ipsa Deum.*
> *Aut Deus, aut vacui certe mens tertia coeli*
> *Per tua secreto guttura serpit agens;*
> *Serpit agens, facilisque docet mortalia corda*
> *Sensim immortali assuescere posse sono.*

The sound of your voice makes it clear that God is present, or, if not God, at any rate a third mind which has left heaven and creeps warbling along, hidden within your throat. Warbling he creeps and graciously teaches mortal hearts how to grow accustomed, little by little, to immortal sound.[54]

Something happens here; conventional praise morphs into something very strange. Who sings when Leonora Baroni sings? Her voice is so fine that it no longer belongs to her, ceases to emanate from her, cannot be reconciled with the body from which it issues. Maybe God is heard, but the compliment is also a theft, a dispossessing. Milton immediately backs away from the potential sacrilege: maybe not God after all but a mysterious '*mens tertia*', a third mind, which scholars have variously interpreted as a cherub, the Holy Spirit, and the World Soul.[55] But this heavenly visitor, this guest from on high, is a strange, awkward creature. It does not soar or reverberate through her body; rather, it creeps [*serpit*] through her throat [*guttura*], like a sinister foreign body, almost a parasite. The creeping is repeated across a line break: '*serpit agens / Serpit agens*'. It's difficult reading these repeated words not to think of the *serpent* to which the Latin verb lent its name; the words seem to slither from one line to the next, each pair of them beginning and ending with a hissingly sibilant *s* sound. This inevitably calls to mind *Paradise Lost*, where Satan will select as his vessel 'The *serpent subtlest beast* of all the field', and is last seen in the poem transformed back into a giant snake and surrounded by the 'dismal universal hiss' of his followers (remember Tasso's claim that magnificent *asprezza* could be achieved via 'words that are keenly felt through vigorous accentuation or alliteration').[56] The praise of Leonora Baroni has something of this hiss about it: there are no fewer than six more sibilants in the last line that I quoted – '*Sensim immortali assuescere posse sono*'. Things still sound sinister even as the meaning of the lines shifts towards immortality.

Milton's earliest English sonnet was addressed to the 'Nightingale, that on yon bloomy spray / Warblst at eve', sending its 'liquid notes' into the world.[57] This bird's imitative song made a conventional poetic choice – it was a particular favourite of Shakespeare's – but I wonder if Milton also had in the back of his mind Plutarch's haunting anecdote, from his *Moralia*: 'A man plucked a nightingale, and, finding but little to eat, said "You are just a voice and nothing more."'[58] Voice and body refuse to fit together into a whole; the relationship between them remains a disconcerting mystery; a mystery that Leonora Baroni encapsulated.

It's very likely that the singers whom Milton heard in Rome performing in *Chi soffre, speri* had attained a degree of technical virtuosity, an extraordinarily complicated and refined set of physical and mental skills, far in excess of anything Milton had heard in England: the hyper-precise coordinating of breath, the minute modulating of the flesh and gristle of the mouth and vocal tract, that we associate today with the trained opera singer. Philosophers in Milton's day were intrigued and perturbed by the human voice: was it matter or spirit? Aristotle stated that only a creature with a soul had a voice, but it seemed rooted in and inseparable from the body out of which it emanated.[59] It's hard to reconstruct in our minds, amidst the wide modern availability of performed and recorded music, just what a new and striking kind of experience hearing these virtuosic voices must have been. Going to the opera is now the most genteel and self-consciously sophisticated of pursuits, and those who go know exactly what to expect; performing one's knowingness, pretending to find nothing fundamentally strange or extravagant or unsettling in the basic conventions of the form, is part of what it means to be a sophisticated opera-goer. But Milton's poem can help us hold the defensive temptations of sophistication at bay.

To make sense of the strange and scintillating way in which he described Leonora Baroni's voice, it's worth glancing briefly back at the founding scenes of opera. Just a few years before Milton's visit to Florence, a man whom he met there, Giovanni Battista Doni, wrote to Pietro de' Bardi to ask questions about the latter's father, who had been instrumental in opera's origins.[60] Bardi explained that his father 'formed a certain sort of delightful and continual academy' in Florence, known as the Camerata, which focused on music; its chief figure is familiar to us, 'Vincenzo Galileo, the father of the present famous astronomer', who was seeking to restore the ideal unity of word and musical sound that he believed characterised ancient Greek practice. Vincenzo's experiments were taken up by other musicians and collectively they developed the *stile rappresentativo* – recitative, hovering between speech and song, which became the signature of opera, though it was 'then considered almost ridiculous'. A singer like Giulio Caccini, building on these experiments and debates, could sing 'in a manner that astonished his hearers'. Bardi recalled that he was present as a child at the first ever performance of the first ever opera: *Dafne*, with music by Jacopo Peri, which was 'recited and sung privately in a small room. I was left speechless with amazement.'[61]

The sense that a great singer's voice does and does not belong in and to their body is, I think, the intuition that Milton had when he made Leonora Baroni's voice creep, strange and warbling, through her throat. She would certainly have been the first woman whom he heard sing with this level of virtuosity, but his poem is also a reminder that the impossible relationship between body and voice that operatic singing pushes to the fore is even more troublesome when the body from which the voice emerges is female. Women were barred from singing in public fora, the high parts taken by *castrati*, since the musical woman, as I mentioned in relation to John Milton senior's milieu, was seen as dangerously seductive. At the same time Milton was in Rome the French viola virtuoso André Maugars – who had visited London in Milton's youth and knew his father's friend Antonio Ferrabosco – also heard Leonora Baroni sing. He praised her intellect and understanding as well as the 'high compass' of her voice, which 'so ravished my senses that I forgot my mortal state, and thought myself among the angels'; but he also felt the need to stress that 'Her [vocal] leaps and her sighs are not at all lascivious, her glances have nothing of lewdness and her gestures have the correctness of a proper young lady.'[62] These were risks against which she had to be defended; her singing drew a dangerous degree of attention to her body as its source. Milton's poem feels like a prophecy of what opera would become later in its history once its most famous singers were women:

'on the opera stage', Catherine Clément writes, 'women perpetually sing their eternal undoing'; or, as Stanley Cavell puts it, opera summarises the 'countless forms in which men want and want not to know woman's voice; to know and not to know what and that she desires'.[63]

We've seen that Milton was raised in an educational world in which women's voices were both excluded in advance and made persistently present in ventriloquised, reimagined, male-scripted forms; and we've seen that this seems to have produced a distinctively ambiguous identity in him, the Lady of Christ's College, who staged parts of himself as the Lady of *Comus*, and who might well have seen part of himself reflected again in the musical, poetic, multilingual Leonora Baroni, possessing and possessed by her remarkable voice. Describing his own lifelong love of opera, Wayne Koestenbaum writes: 'Listening, your heart is in your throat; *your* throat, not the diva's.'[64] I'm tempted to say that this is what Milton experienced when he heard Leonora Baroni – her voice and his heart, all at once, in his throat; an experience that survives in the formulaic praise of her that he offered when he found himself imagining her wondrous voice as a separate entity creeping through her *guttura*, that harsh-sounding Latin word that he would have felt like a lump in his own throat as he articulated it. Another form of overwhelming Italian art by which his whole being, his porous body, was invaded; a model for the kind of utterance he might achieve as a poet but one that threatened to undo him – as English, as a Protestant, as a man. An undoing that he feared and craved. A woman's voice *captured*, in the sense of being both described and contained, safely in his words, but nonetheless escaping, creeping through the little hole of the *punctum* poked in time as I read it, its osmosis breaking down the boundaries between female singer and male listener, between the voice in which Milton meant to write and the warbling voice that we fleetingly hear.

Milton finally extracted himself from Rome, with its richly troubling combination of artistic allures and religious threats. After the return to Florence, on which he failed to copy the Medicean codex for

Holstenius and resumed his friendships with his fellow academicians, he travelled through the Apennines, stopping briefly at Bologna and Ferrara before arriving at the last of the Italian locations in which he would spend a substantial period of time: Venice. To enter the territories of the Most Serene Republic, as it called itself, was to experience a profoundly different form of cultural and political organisation, as I'll shortly discuss. But in one respect at least, Milton's time in Venice was continuous with his Roman experience: he maintained his search for new kinds of music. We've already seen that he bought musical books in London during his Horton period, and he had continued to buy books enthusiastically throughout his travels, probably including Continental volumes on English religion and Galileo's banned *Dialogue on the Two World Systems*. In Venice he added the works of Dante and Tasso as well as 'a Chest or two of choice Musick-books of the best Masters flourishing about that Time in Italy'. These were part-books, perhaps intended to be sung with his father's circle of musical friends upon Milton's return, and included sophisticated scores by Luca Marenzio, Orazio Vecchi, Antonio Cifra, Carlo Gesualdo (the notorious prince of Venosa, an artist capable of truly Caravaggian spasms of violence who had murdered his wife and her lover) – and the greatest composer of the day, Claudio Monteverdi, who was still alive and residing in Venice when Milton arrived.[65]

By the time Milton arrived in Venice in the spring of 1639, Monteverdi had lived there for more than twenty-five years, having been appointed as *maestro di cappella* at St Mark's Cathedral, where he could achieve much greater wealth and cultural prestige than the role of court musician allowed. He made his reputation as a composer of religious music and dazzlingly intricate madrigals, often setting works by the same poets whom Milton's friend Manso had patronised – Marino and Tasso – to music. In the process he engaged in novel ways with the relationship between music and words, and between the rhythms of music, poetry, and the natural world. Monteverdi's eighth book of *madrigali* was published the year before Milton's arrival, and is therefore a likely candidate for him to have bought if he was on the lookout for the latest musical fashions. It contained a setting of lengthy chunks from Tasso's *Gerusalemme Liberata*, in which Monteverdi produced his own musical equivalent of Tasso's *asprezza* or magnificent roughness – the *stile concitato*, or 'agitated style', involving notes repeated with head-spinningly virtuosic speed. These nimble, restless rhythms brought to life in new ways the effects that Tasso's poem of crusade and conquest described: the hoof-beats of the heroic Tancred's horse as he rode into battle, the clashing of sword on armour once he arrived; violence made musical, musical rhythms pushed to the point of violence.[66]

Venice had first arisen as a settlement following the fall of the Roman Empire, and had flourished. By the late Middle Ages the dominance of the Republic in the waters of the Mediterranean had allowed it to build up a huge, scattered empire, belying its diminutive size as a territory. As a result of its maritime conquests Venice became a great cosmopolitan centre, synonymous with trade and commerce; it was also a great nexus for the exchange of information, news, and reports from across the Mediterranean and Europe flowing there along with cloth, books, and foodstuffs.[67] The very fabric of its buildings, influenced by centuries of mercantile contacts with the Ottoman Turks, made it a visual collision of the Eastern and Western worlds.[68] Its large and visible Jewish community, confined by night to the *ghetto*, was subjected to incessant antisemitism and demands to convert, but forms of more productive cultural overlap were also possible. Milton arrived in the city shortly before the death of Sarra Copia Sulam, a Jewish woman who in her younger years ran a literary salon at her house attended by Jews and Christians, and who committed to writing her unorthodox views on the possible mortality of the soul.[69]

By the time Milton visited, however, Venice's maritime dominance was a thing of the past, with efforts more focused on expanding the Republic's Italian territories; the increased range and power of the Ottoman navy, and the relentless activities of North African and Dalmatian pirates, had shrunk their power. But the myth of Venice endured, among both Venetians and outside observers. Its form of aristocratic republicanism, presided over by the elected Doge and his Great Council, was seen as a model of stability, justice, and fairness, especially when compared to the wars, intrigues, and betrayal that ripped apart so many of the Italian city-states. Regardless of how true this account actually was, over the centuries Venice would be looked to as a model by any group seeking to found a durable republic: the Dutch in the sixteenth and seventeenth centuries, the French and American revolutionaries at the end of the eighteenth. It retained an aura of specialness and mystery for centuries. Proust's narrator would spend much of his novel fanta-sising about Venice based on his reading; the prospect of actually visiting it so overwhelming that for years, in a brilliantly bleak comic detail, just thinking about it made him too ill to actually consider travelling there. He finally manages to visit, experiencing a characteristic mixture of wonder and deep disappointment, his gondola guiding him around the canals 'like the mysterious hand of a genie leading me through the maze of this oriental city', which nonetheless struggled to live up to his 'inner Venice'.[70]

Milton, as I previously suggested, would have had the chance to develop his own 'inner Venice' from the histories he'd read, as well as from the artworks and the stories of Henry Wotton. During Wotton's time as ambassador, Anglo-Venetian relations had been both strengthened and complicated by the most serious of clashes between Venice and Rome, which unfolded soon after his arrival in the city in 1604. At the end of the sixteenth century a group of young patricians decided to re-establish Venice's political and economic grandeur, which meant asserting the Republic's independ-ence from the papacy just as the Counter-Reformation Church was trying to centralise and augment its own authority. The inevitable clash between Venice and Rome led to the interdict of 1605–7 and the Pope's excommunication of the Doge.[71] Wotton saw this, wrongly, as an opportunity to cement an Anglo-Venetian alliance that would see the Republic embrace Protestantism. He was particu-larly drawn to Paolo Sarpi, the Servite friar who emerged as the leading light of Venetian intellectual life during the interdict, and the most erudite and vocal critic of papal overreach and abuse of power.[72] Wotton mistook Sarpi for more of a kindred spirit than he actually was – he sent his portrait back to England so that King James could 'behold a sound Protestant, as yet in the habit of a Friar'.[73] In fact Sarpi was much harder to categorise. His interests were wide-ranging, encompassing history, law, and experimental science: he was a close friend of Galileo's until the latter's decision to choose Florence over Venice as the venue for his telescopic experiments ended their friendship. His theological views, while hidden from the world behind a veneer of conformity, seem to have been startlingly idiosyncratic, to the point of doubting God's exist-ence altogether.[74] Even after the Venetian interdict ended and the Pope and the Doge reconciled – to Wotton's disappointment – he continued as ambassador to cultivate Sarpi. In 1617, on his second embassy to Venice, he smuggled back to England in diplomatic bags Sarpi's greatest controversial work, the *History of the Council of Trent*, which was published in London in 1619; Sarpi's other major work, the *History of the Inquisition*, was translated into English the very year that Milton visited Venice.[75]

There can be little doubt that Milton heard of Sarpi from Wotton; he would go on to read Sarpi with immense care after his return from Italy, and would cite him in his commonplace book more often than any other recent European writer. Sarpi had written trenchantly on many of the questions that would preoccupy Milton for the next decade of his life: Milton lifted excerpts from Sarpi on marriage and divorce, showing that Roman Catholics forbid clerical marriage for 'cunning reasons' (*rationes astutas*), and exer-cised control over rare cases of divorce only to pursue 'profit and copious power' (*lucrum . . . authoritatemque*). More strikingly, he would cite Sarpi in the section of his commonplace book titled '*De bello civili*' – 'Of civil war' – to the effect that 'Tyrants pretend that they wage war not for reason of religion but against whomsoever [they choose] as rebels, and under that pretext.' It was crucial to understand and maintain the distinction between religion and political power, or the supposed defence of the one would permit the abuse of the other.[76]

Milton also later turned to Sarpi to understand the origins of censorship, in the section of his commonplace book headed 'Prohibition of books when first used'. Sarpi had claimed that 'in the church of martyrs there was no ecclesiastical prohibition'.[77] While more open to censorship than Milton would soon become – his main concern was to limit Church censorship to theological matters alone – Sarpi still provided a powerful example of independent thought and the force of ideas, as they might be practised in an aristocratic republic.[78] Books were potent to Sarpi, dangerously so: 'The matter of books seemes to be a thing of small moment, because it treats of words, but through these words comes opinions into the world, which cause partialities, seditions, and finally warres. They are words, it is true, but such as in consequence draw after them Hosts of armed men.'[79] Milton may not have read Sarpi closely by the time he was in Venice, but he certainly shared a growing sense of the real worldly effect that words might have; the words he had read were what, in a sense, propelled him to Italy, and words – read, spoken, and sung – had continued to surround him during his travels there. As he left Venice and began his homeward journey, the huge and consequential questions raised by Sarpi's writings in defence of the Republic awaited him.

I will say one more word about the questions raised for Milton by visiting Venice. I suggested earlier that his meeting in Paris with Grotius, the first major theorist of republicanism whom he encountered in person, resonated with the broader question of what it meant to think of a political state as a *created thing*, not altogether unlike an artwork or a poem. Venice, I'd suggest, embodied this same point in a vivid way; but, more specifically, it provided a vivid model of the political state as something *created in, and existing in and through, human time*. The clash with Rome at the time of the interdict accentuated the gulf between two ways of locating politics in time. The papacy was the representative on Earth of the eternal realm of the divine; in a similar manner, divinely anointed monarchs connected the time-bound to the timeless. But republics were founded by humans, according to the specific circumstances of time and place. What made the longevity of Venice so remarkable was that it had survived its fragile origins in human time. Like every republic, it was at root an innovation, a human creation, which began and unfolded amidst the flux of human temporality. This was a feature of republics, and of Venice in particular, that fascinated Renaissance historians and political philosophers. The most infamous of these was Niccolò Machiavelli, whose masterwork *The Prince* is most famous now for its disenchanted, cynical view of politics as an art of manipulation; but in that work he was trying to make sense of how political action must look when it was responding to the shifting contingencies of a humanly created system, not to a set of abstract and eternal values.[80] In Venice, these problems had apparently been solved because the mechanisms of government had evolved over the centuries to such a sophisticated stage that they had become both highly complex and a matter of routine, practically automatic: the process of electing the *Maggior Consiglio* (Great Council), for example, combined randomness and choice so as to make the character and preferences of each individual elector matter as little as possible.[81] For related reasons, Venetians took pride in their lack of knowledge about their founders, because it showed that they had constructed the state for the benefit of all and not, as one historian put it, for 'their owne private glorie or commoditie'. This was reflected by the fact that 'there are in Venice to bee found none, or very few monuments of our ancestors . . . There are no stately tombes erected, no military statues remaining.'[82] These absences were a strange kind of testimony to the seamless functioning of the Republic: there was no need to hearken back to great times of the past because this was a society that had been founded so ingeniously in human time that it could persist through it without the need for exceptional individuals. But this sense of being custodians of a political system artfully constructed in time also gave ordinary Venetians a sense of time as something that they could and should master effectively and efficiently. Meticulously achieved commercial success reflected the unique longevity of the Republic and its self-perpetuating systems. At the height of its power, as one historian puts it, this sense of organisation was embodied in 'the voyages of the Venetian galleys. With a rhythm worthy of comparison with a superb piece of clock-work, these voyages time the economic life of the West, to the very great advantage of the Venetians. Their sequence and interconnection constituted, indeed, a kind of masterpiece.'[83]

How much of this Milton would have experienced or intuited during his month in Venice, I am not sure. My interest lies rather in suggesting other ways in which to understand the connections between poetry and politics – connections that would preoccupy Milton for the rest of his life – than those that we usually use. It's most straightforward to think of art as being political in terms of its *message*. But throughout *Making Darkness Light* I've been suggesting that we view artworks, with Milton's help, differently: as ways of organising and disorganising, shaping and reshaping, human time; of allowing us to experience it differently and anew. Political systems, republics and monarchies, are also ways of organising human time, shaping and limiting how it must be lived. They are unspoken arguments about human time, its nature and its value. When Milton returned to England he would turn the focus of his energies away from poetry and begin to engage in the political realm, but the account of Venice that I've been developing suggests some ways in which such a transition might have been possible: both poetry and politics in the seventeenth century were deeply concerned with what it meant to create; with what it meant to make power, in time.

Leaving Venice and heading north, Milton travelled across the Alps to Geneva. This was to leap from one end of the theological spectrum to the other: having exposed himself to the intense sensuality of the Counter-Reformation in Rome and Naples, he now found himself in what had been the city of the doctrinally and liturgically severe John Calvin, and which still adhered to his stringent style of discipline. He was met there by Jean Diodati, staunchly Calvinist theologian and uncle of his friend Charles. And in Geneva (if, as seems likely, it had not already reached him as he flitted about Italy) he received devastating news: months before, while he was in Florence, Charles, his oldest friend, the love of his life with whom he could share his words and his passions, had died.

Some time thereafter Milton managed to write a poem in Diodati's memory, titled 'Epitaphium Damonis'. As with 'Lycidas', he turned to the conventions of pastoral as a framework for his grief. He chose now, however – in keeping with the ancient languages in which they had corresponded – to write in Latin. Like 'Lycidas', this poem oddly mixes intense grief with personal memories and abstract reflection, though it never ascends to that earlier poem's haunting array of voices; grief more fully felt seemed to require a higher degree of formality if it were to be expressed at all. Milton recalled the differences of character that lay at the base of their intimacy, recalling Diodati's 'flashes of Attic wit and your cultured jokes', and he curses himself for allowing his desire to travel to separate himself from his friend: 'Alas, what wanderlust [*vagus error*] drove me to foreign shores, across the skyey summits of the snow-clad Alps? Was it so very important to me to see buried Rome?'[84] The rest of the poem, however, answers this anguished question with a firm yes: he uses it to celebrate and revisit his Italian experiences, naming and praising Dati, to whom he later sent a copy, and Manso.[85] As with 'Lycidas', the ending of the poem makes it stranger and more interesting. Milton imagines futures for himself and the dead Diodati that are very different. His friend, like Edward King, he sees ascend to Heaven; but whereas Lycidas washed his oozy hair and was welcomed serenely, Diodati's celestial welcome is something else. Because his friend 'never tasted the delight of the marriage bed', apparently remaining a virgin, he can experience pleasures of a startlingly intense kind: 'you will take part forever in the immortal marriage rite, where singing is heard and the lyre rages in the midst of the ecstatic dances, and where the festal orgies rave in Bacchic frenzy [*Festa Sionaeo bacchantur et orgia thyrso*]'.[86] Sexual abstinence and sexual excess are strangely united here, as they might in some perhaps unacknowledgeable way have been in their friendship. The frenzied Bacchantes who, in Ovid and in 'Lycidas', tore Orpheus to shreds for loving boys more than them, are now reinvented as Diodati's dancing partners in the mad whirl of a markedly un-Christian Heaven. This is where Milton chooses to leave his friend. His own future is different. He hopes that his shepherd pipe, 'transformed by my native muses, will rasp out a British tune'.[87] This wish would be realised, but not with anything like the speed he hoped; the state of the England in which he arrived would mean that *Paradise Lost* would have to wait.

Milton could have written 'Epitaphium Damonis' in Geneva or soon after his return to England; certainly its Janus-faced gaze, fixed on both the country he had just visited and the one to which he was returning, fit a place of composition somewhere between the two. There's no doubt in any case that, while in Geneva, Milton was reflecting on what he had so far achieved, and how to present to the world the effect that his travels had had upon him. In June 1639, before leaving the city, he signed the *album amicorum* or friendship album of a man named Camillo Cerdogni, a Protestant of Neapolitan origin. Milton wrote two snippets of poetry. First he quoted himself, inscribing the final lines of *Comus*, the work with which he had impressed Henry Wotton before departing: 'if Vertue feeble were / Heaven itself would stoop to her'. A pious sentiment, though an incongruous one in a Calvinist city, where God kept an austere distance from even virtuous human affairs. Next he copied a line from the epistles of the Roman poet Horace: '*Caelum non animum muto dum trans mare curro*'; 'I change the sky but not my mind when I cross the seas'.[88] The claim that he had been unaffected by the pleasures and temptations of Italy was a useful one to make to his Genevan hosts, who might have been suspicious of a man who'd spent a whole year in Italian travel, and mixed with Roman Catholics of every stripe. It might also be a useful claim when he returned home to similar suspicion. But as a one-line summary of all that he had undergone and experienced in Italy, as an attempt to inoculate himself against all that was new and had the capacity to expand and reconfigure his mind: who was he really trying to convince?

PART III

9

10 August 1642: 'Knowing Good by Evil'

A young woman paces agitatedly in the narrow hallway outside a closed door, listening to the violent thuds and yelps of agony that escape from within. The man whom she has recently married is once again beating and haranguing one of his nephews for some error the small boy has made in his studies. She tries to make the rhythm of her footsteps match the thudding of birch on tender young flesh, so her husband won't hear her walking back and forth, and perhaps also to merge her suffering with the boy's, in a quiet act of solidarity.

Two months ago Mary Powell had never even met John Milton, the man who is now her husband. He arrived one day in the village of Forest Hill in Oxfordshire, seemingly out of the blue, to see her father. She knew that it had something to do with money. Overheard conversations suggested that her father's debts had been mounting up. He never spoke of them to her directly, batted away her nervous questions with brusque reminders that it was none of her concern. When Milton arrived there was a feeling of forced fun about the place; they all had to play along, pretend that they always ate and danced and caroused this lavishly, this cheerily, that the repayment of a debt as trivial as twenty-four pounds each year (she heard her mother whisper the amount) was nothing to a family as content and industrious as theirs.

Milton was hard to place. She couldn't even tell what colour his eyes were – they seemed to change depending on the light. At times he would spring into life, join the festivities in a sudden fit of abandon, but only, it seemed to her, when he managed briefly to forget himself. She overheard him telling tales of his recent travels to a rapt audience of her relatives, and then too his face lit up, as he told them of a narrow escape or a thrilling encounter. But at other times he would glower into the middle distance, as if at some malevolent spirit, and she heard him several times berating the servants for minor slips and faults.

She and Milton had exchanged only a few words by the time he and her father disappeared together into a chamber to discuss business. When the two men re-emerged her father gathered the family together, and, speaking as if she were not present, told them that the gentleman was going to take Mary as his wife. Even in the midst of her shock, the thought crossed Mary's mind as her mother embraced her that a deal had been struck. She had been auctioned off, and her dowry would be mixed up somehow with the money that her father owed. There was no chance that her husband-to-be would want to suffer the shame of throwing his father-in-law into debtors' prison. They were married quickly, and without fanfare; not in the village church, St Nicolas's, but a mile north, in the church of St John the Baptist at Stanton St John, the village in which Milton's father had been born. They travelled to London with her mother and some close cousins, to celebrate there with his family. But it became clear that here in London Milton would not allow himself even the fleeting festivities that he had enjoyed in Oxfordshire. As soon as he could, he retired to his study, and to his books. She barely saw him, and they barely spoke; mealtimes were silent; their night-time fumblings, which seemed to confuse them both, scarcely less so. Her relatives soon returned to Forest Hill, and she was alone.

She could have coped. She could have dealt with the silence, left him to his books, started building a world of her own; she could have done it all if it weren't for the sound of the beatings. On most days his nine- and ten-year-old nephews – now *her* nephews too, she had to remind herself – would arrive for their lessons. Sometimes Mary would overhear snatches of their learning in languages she could not understand. On good days they would laugh together – even, when they had finished their arithmetic or their geography, sing together. She would hear Milton's voice, soaring as he became animated, and she would think that he must be a fine teacher, able to find the right words for any lesson. But sometimes the boys were tired, or distracted, or occasionally insolent. They would make mistakes with their grammar, forget the previous day's lesson, stare into space. His patience was short, and the thrashings would begin. She quickly learnt to recognise the rising tone of his voice, his frustration with the stupidity before him, a sign that violence was in the offing. She would hear the smack of his hand or the lash of the birch switch. She would hear them whimper and sob, and she would brace herself for the inevitable noise of the next stroke, the pounding rhythm producing an awful song of agony. She heard the sound when she closed her eyes at night and it reverberated in her dreams. Within a few weeks, Mary knew she had to get away: from the sound, from London, from him.

She told him that she missed her mother and needed to return for a short time to Oxfordshire. Milton seemed more annoyed by the distraction than bothered by the request, and, without giving the matter much thought, nodded his assent. She and her serving maid packed a few belongings and left the house on Aldersgate Street, making the short walk south towards Newgate, where the coach had dropped them off just a few weeks previously. She remembered the massive inn, heaving with people arriving in and departing from the capital; it had seemed as huge and shabby and sinister as the city itself. From either side of the gateway into the vast coachyard a terrifying visage stared down at her, the twisted features of a heathen, with a third carved face mounted on the front of the inn itself and providing its name, the Saracen's Head. They had timed it well; the next coach to Oxford would soon depart, and they secured space aboard.[1] Before long the city melted into fields. Its incessant hum, and the silences and cries of her new home, started to fade from her mind.

It would be three years before Mary saw John Milton again.

◆

I find myself, with the above sequence of events, suddenly distanced from Milton – trying, for the first time, to see him through the gaze of another rather than striving to imagine the world through his eyes. And this is, I confess, in part because I have reached the transition in his life and in his mind that I find hardest to inhabit sympathetically, to reconcile myself with. I've suggested in the preceding chapters that Milton's travels in Europe involved his most concerted and consequential exposure to challengingly new forms of experience. He responded to these encounters with deep ambivalence – as he did to most things – but Milton's travels none-theless capture him in a state of startling receptivity to the foreign and the new. I realise that I want his life and his activities, upon his return to England, to reflect this new-found openness and sense of adventure. But, at first glance, they don't. It's only by taking a broader view of the second half of Milton's life, and the writings that he produced, that we'll ultimately find these features returning in his poetry, in astonishing forms. But the years immediately following his return seem to represent something more like a snail-like retreat into a shell; a tendency on Milton's part to defend himself against the perplexing and the novel, in domineering and aggressive ways. And nowhere is this truer than in the infamous case of his abrupt marriage, three years after his return from Europe.

The remaining decades of Milton's life would feature a series of intensely complicated entanglements of the personal and the polit-ical, the intellectually abstract and the intensely felt. It therefore seems entirely fitting that Milton undertook the journey to Oxfordshire during which he married Mary Powell – who was fifteen years old, making her less than half his age – at a moment of extreme national turbulence. He left London shortly after Charles I had himself departed the capital, following a series of clashes with Parliament, and returned with his new wife shortly before the king raised his standard at Nottingham on 22 August 1642, marking the formal beginning of the English Civil Wars. It seems even more appropriate in retrospect that Milton's nuptials would coincide with these events so closely, because this was a marriage that, it's tempting to say, quickly became a civil war in its own right. Mary Powell returned to Oxfordshire within weeks, and soon the pair were separated by the chief battle lines drawn between Royalists and

Parliamentarians. This is at least part of the reason why their separation dragged on for years; and Milton, as we'll see, wrote a series of works in which his anger and frustration at his marriage and subsequent separation expressed themselves in uncomfortable, often outright nasty ways.

In choosing to begin this chapter with Mary Powell – imagining her reasons for leaving Milton after a few weeks of marriage, and her mood when she left – I'm conscious of joining a long tradition of attempts to try and recapture her voice and personality, her motives. Milton's first biographers ventured various possible reasons for their speedy separation; especially that, as John Aubrey puts it, she was 'brought up and lived where there was a great deal of company and merriment, dancing etc.', and that arriving at Milton's London residence 'she found it very solitary'.[2] Biographers ever since have been happy to fill the gaps with further speculation: that the still virginal Milton was shocked by the challenge of an actual flesh and blood woman; that she either withheld sex from him coquettishly or that he was traumatised by the reality of sex, by the need to relate to his messily unpredictable body rather than his mighty mind; that he was, in A. D. Nuttall's memorable phrase, dead from the waist down.[3] No episode from Milton's life has done more to cement his reputation as a joyless, prudish misogynist: the quintessential Puritan. Writers of fiction have tried to get into her head and come to similar conclusions: from the Victorian novelist Anne Manning, who provided Mary with a fictional diary, to Robert Graves's novel *Wife to Mr Milton*, depicting the poet as a sour killjoy. Their union also provided inspiration for the most famous literary marriage of a vivacious young woman to a desiccated, cerebral older man – that between Dorothea Brooke and Mr Casaubon in George Eliot's *Middlemarch*.[4]

Perhaps, in continuing this small tradition of trying to imagine the moment of her departure from Mary's perspective rather than from his, I am simply evading aspects of Milton that I find less attractive, seeking to hang on to my own ideal version of him in the face of the facts. I hope that this will ultimately not be the case; that I will have managed to be frank about the whole of my responses to Milton, including the ways in which I find him difficult, alien, sometimes unpleasant. It feels important not just to turn to Mary Powell at this moment but to reflect on my motives for doing so, which feel somewhat divided. On the one hand I feel moved to restore her, even briefly, to the centre of my narrative, to refuse to see her only as refracted through Milton's bitterness and resentment. I've already acknowledged the difficulty of recapturing his mother, and the same is true of the two women he later married, a reminder of the ways in which women in the seventeenth century leave fewer traces, and this spurs me to try to say more of Mary, of whom we know at least a little. It's for this reason that, when I read the meagre hints that remain of the kind of person she might have been and her possible reasons for leaving Milton so quickly, what stuck in my mind was not the possibility of sexual difficulties, or the lack of merriment and dancing that seem to suggest naivety and frivolity; it was rather the detail recorded by John Aubrey: that Mary 'oftentimes heard his Nephews, beaten, and cry. This life was irksome to her.'[5] This seems to me like something worth holding on to, worth trying to recapture. A glimpse of the fact that not everyone accepted as normal the kind of routine violence that Milton experienced as a schoolboy and as a student, that he now inflicted on his own nephews, and that is such a recognisable strand of his character in the 1640s. That the horror she felt as she heard these beatings might offer a way of capturing something both about her, and about him.

On the other hand I'm keenly aware that, in striving to cross this particular threshold and occupy the viewpoint of a younger woman, distant from me in age, gender, and circumstance, I'm at risk of merely repeating Milton's own habits, when he found or placed versions of himself in the minds and voices of the Lady in *Comus*, Leonora Baroni, and, as we'll further see, Eve and his female muse in *Paradise Lost*. What makes these various instances curious and compelling is the difficulty of deciding whether Milton is simply creating these women as vessels for his own preoccupations, or whether, at the same time, he is striving to be inhabited and transformed by them in ways less predictable and easy to control. This makes me feel that the risk of imagining my way briefly into Mary Powell's mind is one worth running, especially at this point in Milton's own life. As we'll see in this chapter, the value of seeking to encounter, and of being transformed by, the genuinely different was an insistent feature of his works in the 1640s – most notably in the greatest of his prose writings, *Areopagitica*. And it's in this aspect of his writings that we can see how his travels abroad continued to shape his ways of thinking. We'll encounter in new forms Milton's deep sense of his own specialness colliding with a desire to speak to all people as potential equals. We'll also witness his inclination to retreat from the world into the confines of his own mind vying with a countervailing impulse to expose himself even, or especially, to ideas and experiences that threatened every-thing he held dear. We saw these tensions at work on his travels, in his letter to Buonmattei warning against barbarian invasions and his defensive insistence in Geneva that his mind remained unchanged. We began to see it too when I looked ahead to *Paradise Lost*, where Milton envisaged a clear hierarchy of creation which was at the same time fluid, molten, in process. The startling shifts and collisions that tore up the English political and social worlds of the 1640s were echoed by no less volatile shifts in Milton's life in this decade: false starts, surprises, bold and incongruous decisions. Never could he have anticipated at the start of the decade where he, or the British Isles, would end it.

The most obvious sign that something had shifted during Milton's travels came when, soon after his return, he finally ended his extended reliance on his father and moved from Horton back into London. He initially lodged with a tailor named Russell in St Bride's Churchyard, to the west of St Paul's, before finding himself 'a pretty Garden-House . . . in Aldersgate Street, at the end of an Entry'. He chose it 'by the reason of the Privacy, besides there are few Streets in London more free from Noise than that'.[6] Today, unsur-prisingly, this is no longer true; Aldersgate Street is the site of Barbican tube station, and offers a barrage of sounds. But, if no trace of the quiet garden house remains, it proved another worthwhile part of London for Sean and me to wander around with Milton in mind, not least because it was a stone's throw from the church of St Giles Cripplegate where Milton's father would be interred in 1646, and where he himself would eventually be laid to rest. Hereabouts the layers of London's lost, recovered, and super-imposed histories are particularly visible. It was only when German bombers levelled this part of London in 1940 that the substantial sections of the ancient city wall about which one can now wander were revealed. We paused to watch two women playing guitar and violin, perched incongruously on a section of wall jutting out into a narrow canal that was covered in waterlilies.

Milton's poems to Manso and in memory of Diodati showed that his poetic ambitions had continued to grow during his travels. He seems upon his return, for reasons that aren't entirely clear, to have shifted his focus from epic to drama, and it was at this point that he filled the pages of the Trinity Manuscript with ideas for plots, including one for a play set in the Garden of Eden. His travels might have influenced him: Grotius had written a Latin play, *Christus Patiens*, and, on one of the same days that he read his poems in Florence, Milton would have heard a scene from a tragedy being recited.[7] He toyed with dozens of other ideas for plots drawn from the Old Testament and from British history: if things had gone another way, we might now remember Milton only as the man who wrote some scintillating early poems, then took a wrong turn with his long-forgotten tragedy *Ethelbert of the East Angles slain by Offa the Mercian*.[8] Even at this stage, however, *Paradise Lost*, one of the possible titles he noted down, was the idea that he took the furthest: he wrote down half a dozen lines of verse, 'Satan's Exclamation to the Sun . . . which verses were intended for the beginning of a Tragœdie which he had designed, but was diverted from it by other business'.[9] These lines survived in the fourth book of his epic; already he was planning (perhaps on the model of Shakespeare, who dared to begin *Richard III* with a soliloquy by its demonically seductive protagonist) to confront his audience with Satan from the very beginning. This is the time at which his great poem of beginnings properly began.

The problem was that ideas for sacred or historical drama would not pay the bills or help maintain a household. 'National poet' was not a job for which one could apply, and while he continued to make money via property deals and moneylending, this still could not answer his sense of a calling. And so Milton began to accept private pupils on Aldersgate Street, transforming his residence into an informal schoolhouse. His first and principal students were his nephews, John and Edward Phillips, who lodged with him, and soon he was teaching the children of various prominent aristocrats, including, most intriguingly, the son of Lady Katherine Ranelagh, sister to the great chemist and experimental philosopher Robert Boyle, who had advanced interests of her own in practical chemistry.[10]

To move from travelling about Italy, meeting Galileo and dodging wicked Jesuits, to running a small private school might seem like something of a comedown, and indeed it has seemed so to many of Milton's biographers. Samuel Johnson wrote:

> Let not our veneration for Milton forbid us to look with some degree of merriment on great promises and small performance, on the man who hastens home, because his countrymen are contending for their liberty, and, when he reaches the scene of action, vapours away his patriotism in a private boarding-school. This is the period of his life from which all his biographers seem inclined to shrink. They are unwilling that Milton should be degraded to schoolmaster.[11]

Johnson was touchy on this subject – he himself was a failed teacher, having lasted only a few months at a grammar school – and was keen to defend Milton's choice of 'honest and useful employment' as 'an act which no wise man will consider as in itself disgraceful'.[12] There is, I think, a simpler way of making sense of this transition in Milton's life. I've already made clear how deeply I think Milton was formed by his school and university experiences, and the peculiar way in which students were expected both to subject themselves to rigid rules and aspire to forms of supple versatility. From the earliest, his writings seemed determined to teach and doubtful that successful teaching was possible all at once; most obviously *Comus*, written for three children and their tutor, crammed with didactic lessons but ending with the enchanter's escape and the Lady's inscrutable silence.[13] His time as a schoolmaster should be seen as the crystallisation of a lifetime spent wrestling with what it meant to teach and to learn: as a student, as an individual, as a larger human collective.

There coexisted in Milton's mind two ideas of what it means to learn, both widespread in his culture but given an extreme and complicatedly connected form. On the one hand learning as the incorporation of *stuff*: facts, rules, information. On the other hand learning as something that changes someone in the deepest patterns of their thought and feeling – that reknots the rhythms of their soul. I'm not simply opposing these ways of learning or saying that one is bad and the other good: there are great and distinct pleasures to be had in absorbing new information and in coming to think differently, and many problems in modern education arise from an artificial separation of the two. The thrill and the challenge of reading Milton is that he demands both, insists that the two are interconnected, and demands both that we know more and that we seek to change ourselves. There's a sense both of the pleasure of these demands and of their potential brutality in the way that he taught his nephews: within a year they could sight-read Latin 'and within three years they went through the best of Latin and Greec [*sic*] poets'. 'As he was severe on one hand,' John Aubrey claims, 'so he was most familiar and free in his conversation to those to whome [he was] most severe in his way of education' – a familiarity best captured when he and his students sang together, perhaps replicating those early musical evenings on Bread Street, and making use of the part-books that Milton had shipped back from Venice.[14] If the rhythms of music were part of their learning, then the severity included, as I've already suggested, replicating the rhythms of violence by which Milton himself had been formed when he beat his weeping nephews. A strange knot of care, familiarity, severity, and violence is in this scene of teaching.

In 1644 – by which time, as we'll see, he had a voice in the public sphere – Milton was asked by the polymathic Samuel Hartlib to compose a treatise on 'the reforming of Education'. Hartlib, born in what is now Poland, had in 1628 taken refuge in England from the religious wars on the Continent. He had developed a wide and varied network of correspondents, through which he pursued the concern with education which was foundational to the utopian pursuit of encyclopaedic knowledge, and which he believed would lead to the establishment of universal peace.[15] Through Hartlib Milton maintained his connection with pan-European intellectual life, albeit a connection now flavoured with Protestant millenarianism. The reformed curriculum that Milton envisaged is extraordinarily taxing, and, given his and Hartlib's forward-looking and transformative aims, strikingly rooted in the writings of the ancients: ancient Greek and Roman biology, astronomy, cartography, history, as well as poetry, all read in massive amounts and digested at remarkable speed. Sunday was for Bible study, in Greek and Hebrew, as well as an introduction to Aramaic. The only noticeably modern part of this course of study was the prominent place Milton gave in it to Italian.[16] The language itself was to be learned. Taking for granted that every student would share his remarkable linguistic skills, Milton suggested that 'they may have easily learnt at any odd hour the Italian tongue'. Even more unusually, he insisted that when they spoke Latin 'their speech is to be fashion'd to a distinct and clear pronuntiation, as near as may be to the Italian, especially in the Vowels. For we Englishmen being far Northerly, do not open our mouths in the cold air, wide enough to grace a Southern Tongue.'[17] Milton had made a subtle change to his handwriting when he returned from his travels, changing the way he wrote the letter *e* from an epsilon (ε) to an italic *e*; almost as if he wanted to incorporate a subtle Italianness into his linguistic identity, as he encouraged his students to do.[18] Poetry also took on an Italian tone in his ideal vision. Logic was still to be taught, but it was subordinate to 'a gracefull and ornate Rhetorick', which would allow students to produce poetry that is 'less suttle and fine, but more simple, sensuous, and passionate'. One route to this was reading not just Aristotle and Horace but 'the Italian commentaries of Castelvetro, Tasso, Mazzoni, and others', who teach 'what the laws are of a true Epic Poem, what of a Dramatic, what of a Lyric'.[19]

All this carefully timetabled reading was to be balanced with bracing practical activity: sword-fighting skills, horsemanship, and 'all the locks and Gripes of wrestling'. Milton's ambitions were lofty, infused with Hartlib's hopes that education could be not just transformative but redemptive: 'The end then of Learning', he boldly stated at the outset, 'is to repair the ruines of our first Parents', to reverse the effects of the Fall.[20] He looked back both to the Garden of Eden and to his own educational past, salvaging the best of the humanist pedagogical system with its reverence for the ancients and its attempts to weld bookish knowledge to practical, real-world effects while dismissing the universities that are 'not yet well recover'd from the Scholastick grossness of barbarous ages'.[21] If these grand, transformative aims call to mind classrooms of austere Miltonic supermen, serenely exchanging Greek and Hebrew wisdom between bouts of swordplay and wrestling, he also retained the humanist belief that learning must originate in pleasure and play. Endless and excruciating Latin and Greek classes, demanding that students compose verses and orations that they cannot understand, were a waste of time: 'These are not matters to be wrung from poor striplings.'[22] They must not have knowledge forced upon them but rather be 'enflam'd with the study of Learning'. When it came to arithmetic and geometry, for example, these could be taught 'even playing, as the old manner was'.[23] When he came to fill the section headed '*De liberis educandis*' in his commonplace book, Milton wrote that 'The nature of each person must first of all be observed and not bent in another direction', and he quoted his beloved Dante to that effect. Absorbing knowledge was never, for Milton, separable from the desires, the pleasures, the games of learning; games that the readers of his poems were also invited to play.

While I certainly agree with Johnson that it's wrong to say that Milton was 'degraded to schoolmaster', it was not a permanent vocation. Rather, it was a way of buying time productively while he made sense of the very different national situation into which he had returned. As we've seen, his later claim that he rushed home from Italy when civil war broke out was false, but the situation into which he returned was highly complex and unstable. The protests that broke out in 1637 over Charles I's and Laud's wild overreach in seeking to impose a new prayer book in Scotland had grown by 1639 into a National Covenant, asserting the Scots' commitment to their own, more austere and bishop-free forms of worship and church governance. Still reluctant to call a parliament after the chaotic debacles of the late 1620s, Charles was finally forced to do so in April 1640, naively assuming that the MPs would do his bidding and vote to fund his war through further taxes. It soon became clear, however, that the king had unleashed the resentment regarding his personal rule that had rumbled throughout the British Isles for the past decade, and rather than voting for subsidies, the MPs demanded clarity regarding 'the liberties of the House and kingdom' and the right to debate perceived abuses within the royal administration. Charles, frustrated and outraged, dissolved the assembly, thereafter known as the 'Short Parliament', after a mere three weeks. In August, however, the Scots army entered England, and Charles was forced in November to convene another parliament. Its fate was very different from its predecessor; the Long Parliament would not be formally dissolved for thirteen years, by which time the king had been executed.

During this period those who had been forced to suppress their loathing of the Laudian style of religion that had enjoyed a decade of dominance over the Church began to mobilise. The Covenanters' open opposition to episcopacy changed the sense of what was possible in England, energising both those who despised the Laudian bishops in particular and those who hated the institution as a whole. In response, prominent churchmen began seeking to redefine and justify the episcopacy, notably the learned and relatively conciliatory Joseph Hall, Bishop of Exeter. Matters came to a head in January 1641 when Hall published his latest defence of prelacy, *An Humble Remonstrance to the High Court of Parliament*. The opposition to Hall was led by a group of Puritans writing under the acronym Smectymnuus. The *t* and *y* in this strange sequence of letters was Milton's childhood tutor Thomas Young, who had once gifted him a Hebrew Bible and with whom he had exchanged affectionate letters in the 1620s. Young had returned from Hamburg to England in 1628, and it was likely via this friendship that Milton entered the fray. He wrote an anonymous postscript to one of the Smectymnuans' works, and then, between early summer 1641 and the spring of 1642, he churned out in rapid succession no fewer than five prose works, denouncing what he saw as the sickening excesses of the Laudian bishops and of the institution itself: *Of Reformation touching Church-Discipline*; *Of Prelatical Episcopacy*; *Animadversions upon the Remonstrants Defence against Smecytymnuus*; *The Reason of Church Government*; and *An Apology against a Pamphlet*.

Reading these anti-episcopal works is a curious, exhilarating, and frustrating experience. They are impassioned, vivid, at times obscure and at others darkly funny. Milton reveals in these writings a deep vein of talent that had not been on display in his earlier poems, and which could perhaps be glimpsed only in his satirical Cambridge oration and the denunciation of the grim wolves of 'Lycidas': an aptitude for satire and insult, for an almost demonic glee with which he rains down both learned and scurrilously demotic invective upon his opponents. Once again he's cheerfully scatological: 'Wipe your fat corpulencies out of our light,' he tells his opponent in *Animadversions*.[24] In *An Apology* he compares his foe's mangling of language to the mangling of bodies, in terms that recall the thread-slitting Fury of 'Lycidas': 'certainly this tormentor of semi-colons is as good at dismembring and slitting sentences, as his grave Fathers the prelates have been at stigmatizing and slitting noses.' He then spins out a convoluted and deeply unpleasant riff, comparing a bishop's hoarding of multiple benefices to a group of gouty toes which are hidden in a single sock that sends 'a fouler stench to heaven'. All of this foulness is granted the highest stamp of approval: 'Christ himselfe,' Milton insists, 'speaking of unsavoury traditions, scruples not to name the dunghill and the jakes.'[25] Throughout several of the tracts these stinking, deformed bodies are contrasted with the true Commonwealth, which 'ought to be but as one Christian personage, one mighty growth, and stature of an honest man, as big, and compact in virtue as in body'.[26]

Milton discovered a genuine flair for this kind of polemic, for righteous indignation verging on violent fury which has ample precedent, from the jeremiads of Old Testament prophets to the anti-Catholic writings of Martin Luther. I'm also tempted to see his lashing of his episcopal opponents with his tongue as of a piece with his lashing of his nephews with birch rods in the schoolroom. But I still can't help but read them with a degree of frustration, as a misuse of the talents and ambitions that he brought back from his travels. The learning he'd spent years acquiring is on rampant display – he batters his enemies with the whole range of his classical and theological reading. His reading in up-to-date political theory is no less on display, including figures whose relevance had been sharpened for him on his travels: he praises Sarpi, 'Padre Paolo', as 'the great Venetian antagonist of the Pope'.[27] But these tracts have taken the place of the great poem into which he had planned to pour his erudition, his fervour, and his unleashed intellectual energy. My frustration may, I admit, be a symptom of my desire to see the complex and poetic Milton as the *true* Milton, even as I recognise his conflicting dimensions. But I think it's also because, for all their wit and learning, their entertaining cruelty and triumphant vitality, the arguments of the tracts are chiefly negative. Their principal and unrelenting message is this: bishops are bad, a disgrace, and a blight. Milton's main aim, as he puts it, is 'characterizing the Depravities of the Church'.[28] What does not emerge, however, is a strong positive alternative. Whether or not the Smectymnuan group was deliberately engaged in resurrecting Presbyterianism – the governance of the Church by a combination of clergy and laymen through a system of committees – Milton himself soon lost faith with the Presbyterians, and the tracts offer little in terms of a precise vision for the future of the Church.

Instead of a positive programme, we find in these tracts the displaced energies of the poem that he had not yet written. Milton turns again and again to his favourite poets in denouncing the idolatrous and avaricious figures whom he deplores: Dante, Petrarch, and the medieval English poets whom Protestants often claimed as their precursors, Chaucer and Gower, are all cited. Even when not naming poets explicitly, he redeployed their imaginative energies and mingled them with his own.[29] One soaring paragraph in *Of Reformation* moves from recalling the 'many darke Ages, wherein the huge overshadowing train of Error had almost swept all the Starres out of the firmament of the Church', to breathing in 'the sweet Odour of the returning Gospell', which allows him hope for success in 'Shaking the Powers of Darknesse, and scorning the fiery rage of the old red Dragon'. This vivid passage rewrites in miniature the opening book of Spenser's *Faerie Queene* – a poem to which Milton was probably introduced, as I mentioned in the third chapter, by his schoolmaster Alexander Gil. That poem's first book begins with a memorable monster named Error who wraps the hero in her 'huge train [tail]' and vomits toads and books over him before he beheads her, and it ends with the hero defeating 'a Dragon horrible and stearne'.[30] Milton compresses this sprawling poem into a paragraph; it is Spenser viewed through the distancing, particularising lens of a Galilean telescope.

Moments like this show the extent to which Milton in this cluster of tracts is concerned not just with unmaking but with making and remaking. In this sense, too, Milton was responding in subtle ways not just to his poetic preoccupations but to the wider scene in England. The Long Parliament in the early 1640s issued an 'Order for the Suppression of Innovations' in worship, seeking forcefully to reverse the Laudian liturgical reforms, and specifying 'That all Crucifixes, scandalous Pictures of any One or more Persons of the Trinity, and all Images of the Virgin Mary, shall be taken away and abolished'.[31] A wave of iconoclasm swept through the country, especially in East Anglia and in London. It was then that the Cheapside Cross – past which Milton had walked each day as he returned home from school, and which was scarred by several generations of attacks and transformations – was finally destroyed. While the violent fervour of Milton's writings seems to echo the actions of the iconoclasts, his techniques were less akin to those who sought to eradicate error altogether, leaving behind only an empty plinth or a whitewashed wall; he was closer to the earlier variety of English iconoclast in the sixteenth century, who tended to leave the mangled and metamorphosed object in place as a warning and a reminder, who realised that violence was a way not just of destroying but of making something new.[32]

The connection between this kind of iconoclastic violence and poetic making comes to the fore in *Reason of Church Government*, the only one of Milton's five tracts to have his name on the title page and make his authorship explicit. Milton's attacks on Hall had provoked a response, *A Modest Confutation of a Slandrous and Scurrilous Libel*, which speculated about the kind of man who might have written so biliously: it was condescending, dismissive, and alarmingly accurate, speculating that the author must be an unmarried recent university graduate of modest means. This attack on his character was both an affront to Milton and a gift, for it allowed him to put into print the clearest articulation yet of his character and ambitions, describing the poet that he both hoped to be and, in a limited sense, already was. He was aware that doing so broke with the conventions of satirical polemic, which usually involved insults and derision slung from behind the veil of anonymity: 'although a Poet soaring in the high region of his fancies with his garland and singing robes about him might without apology speak more of himself than I mean to do,' Milton wrote, 'yet for me sitting here below in the cool element of prose . . . to venture and divulge unusual things of my selfe, I shall petition to the gentler sort, it may not be [i.e. cause] envy to me.' He went on to detail the impeccable education provided by his father and the warm reception he received 'in the privat Academies of Italy', all of which had given him 'that resolution which Ariosto follow'd' (Galileo's favourite poet invoked again) 'to fix all the industry and art I could unite to the adorning of my native tongue'. It's a telling moment: his travels have resolved him to do for the English language what the great poets of Italy did for theirs. He offers his boldest account yet of the good that an inspired poet can do for the minds and souls of his nation. Listing the great poetic achievements of the past, from the Bible to Sophocles' tragedies to Tasso, he concludes: 'These abilities, wheresoever they be found, are the inspired gifts of God rarely bestow'd, but yet to some (though most abuse) in every Nation: and are of power beside the office of a pulpit, to imbreed and cherish in a great people the seeds of vertu, and public civility.'[33] It's a moment of astonishing passion, sincerity, bravado, and hubris, placing himself in this grand prophetic tradition and claiming so much for his potential significance to the nation.

What we sense in these tracts is not just that Milton's iconoclastic destruction of his opponent and the creation of his own poetic self are two sides of the same coin. We also witness the continuation of his conviction, first displayed in the Nativity Ode and 'Lycidas', that creating a poem was a way of recreating himself; that the poet is a maker in this double sense, a maker of the world without and the self within. He stated this with wonderful clarity in *An Apology*, writing – in words that closely echo Tasso, as we saw in the last chapter – that 'he who would not be frustrate of his hope to write well hereafter in laudable things, ought him selfe to bee a true Poem, that is, a composition, and patterne of the best and honourablest things'.[34] Poet and poem, life and work, mirror and shape one another; the making of one is the making of the other. What is beginning to come newly to the fore is a conviction that this kind of making of poems and of oneself is inseparable from the making and remaking of the political world; from the creating of a commonwealth.

The backdrop against which Milton wrestled with these questions of Church governance and his own poetic ambitions was volatile in the extreme. The year 1641 saw a Catholic uprising in Ireland, and the very real atrocities committed against the Protestant population were used and exaggerated in England to inflame anti-Catholic hysteria. Returning to London from his disastrous Scottish campaign, the king clashed with Parliament over who should control the army sent to suppress the Irish rebellion. In January 1642 Charles led several dozen armed guards to the House of Commons to arrest five prominent MPs on charges of treason, for supposedly encouraging the Scots invasion and accusing the queen of Catholic plotting. The five Members, warned of the king's plans, were in hiding, and the Speaker of the House, William Lenthall, sensationally declared his allegiance to Parliament over the monarch. Charles left the House of Commons, and soon after left London, which was abuzz with rumours that the king's army would soon attack and retake the city. War was now an inevitability.

It was while these events were unfolding that Milton made the two abrupt and surprising decisions that I've already described. The first was to leave London for Oxfordshire in order to collect the latest instalment of a long-standing debt. Perhaps the heightened tensions of the city, and the exertions of pouring his energies into his anti-episcopal writings so intensely and so quickly, made this an attractive moment at which to escape to the quiet of the country. But even more startlingly, he returned from Oxfordshire married to Mary, the fifteen-year-old daughter of his debtor, Richard Powell.

When Mary returned to her family after a few short weeks of married life, the subsequent hardening of the civil war battle lines between London and Oxfordshire made reconciliation a practical impossibility, and entwined the course of their marriage with national events. Following the first major confrontation of the war, the gory but inconclusive Battle of Edgehill on the outskirts of Oxfordshire, the king had occupied Oxford and made it his base. The Powells were deep in Royalist territory; so too were Milton's father and brother, who had moved from Horton to Reading, and were under siege there. His father joined Milton in London in 1643, but his brother Christopher remained loyal to and active in the king's cause: this was the moment when they were wrenched apart by their divided loyalties. Milton doesn't seem to have involved himself directly in the buzz of activity as London prepared for possible invasion by the king: he didn't, it seems, work on his horsemanship or sword skills like the students in his imagined academy, and his poetic activities were limited to one very strange sonnet in which he implored the anticipated invaders – 'Captain or colonel, or knight in arms' – to leave his house unscathed since its occupant, as a poet, 'can spread thy name o'er land and seas'.[35]

The bulk of his energies were again directed towards prose writings, and these would combine his deep learning and personal preoccupations in a manner far more shocking than the anti-episcopal tracts. In August 1643 he published *The Doctrine and Discipline of Divorce*; this was followed in early 1644 by a heavily revised and expanded version, and in the ensuing eighteen months by three further works on the topic of divorce: *The Judgement of Martin Bucer*, *Tetrachordon*, and *Colasterion*.

The most striking feature of these works to a modern reader is that they use strange means and often deeply unpleasant language to propose what has come to seem like an uncontroversial idea, especially to the Protestants whom Milton was addressing: that two people should be allowed to divorce simply because they did not like one another, and had decided that they were incompatible. This was, however, by far the most controversial argument that Milton would make until he defended the killing of a king, and the first time that he had publicly identified himself with a position that was so idiosyncratic and with which so few of his contemporaries would agree. The fact that Milton felt able to do so was a response to the exciting and turbulent conditions in which he wrote. In July 1643, a month before his first divorce tract appeared, Parliament had convened the Westminster Assembly, a combination of MPs and English and Scottish divines who would debate and determine a new doctrinal and liturgical direction for the Church. It was a moment of extraordinary possibility, with changes and proposals that would have been unthinkable three years before suddenly being aired and discussed. The enforced Laudian conformity of the 1630s had imploded, and now the conflicting principles and inclinations that had never been more than awkwardly soldered together were newly visible, and the subject of open debate.

It was this lack of a clear and certain future that made possible Milton's series of radical interventions on the topic of divorce. The deep personal wounds that he experienced through marriage to and separation from Mary Powell are thinly veiled, as if part of a story that he's telling about someone else. In *Doctrine and Discipline* he writes that even 'The soberest and best govern'd men' can be tricked into a bad marriage: 'who knows not that the bashfull mutenes of a virgin may oft-times hide all the unloveliness and naturall sloth which is really unfit for conversation'. Furthermore, the more virtuous the man, the more vulnerable he is to such deceptions: 'it is not strange that many who have spent their youth chastely, are in some things not so quick-sighted.'[36] In this treatise Milton also suggests that some marriages end not because of deception but simply through mutual incompatibility, thanks to 'nature's unalterable working'.[37] But by the time he wrote *Tetrachordon* his bitterness had festered to the point that it is always the fault of the woman, who was 'purposely made for man', and 'whose wilfulness or inability to be a wife frustrates the occasional end of her creation' as well as depriving him of 'his natural birthright, and that indeleble character of priority which God crown'd him with'.[38] In a marriage that fails because the woman refuses to fulfil her divinely allotted role, sex is reduced to grim and joyless labour: it is 'to grind in the mill of an undelighted and servil copulation'.[39] If a couple are trapped in such a marriage then 'instead of beeing one flesh, they will be rather two carkasses chain'd unnaturally together; or as it may happ'n, a living soule bound to a dead corpse'.[40] There's no doubt, when it came to his own marriage, which he saw as which.

What do we want from Milton's writings on divorce, and what do we get from them? It's easy to dismiss them as the bitter score-settling of a sexually inexperienced man, faced with a woman less perfect and pliable than the ones he'd met in books or heard sing in Rome. Or to see them as the laying bare of the misogynist viciousness that lies at the heart of his thought, and of patriarchal thought more generally. There is certainly truth to both of these judgements. In no way do I want to downplay the petulance and intermittent brutality of these tracts, and it's easy to see why Samuel Johnson claimed that 'there appears in his books something like a Turkish contempt of females, as subordinate and inferior beings . . . He thought women made only for obedience, and man only for rebellion.'[41] This is the source of what Sandra Gilbert and Susan Gubar, following Virginia Woolf, called 'Milton's Bogey': his ability to stand for female writers as 'the misogynistic essence of what Gertrude Stein called "patriarchal poetry"'.[42] And it's a tendency that's by no means absent from his later poems. We meet it again in *Paradise Lost* when Satan encounters Sin, his daughter and incestuous lover, as he departs from Hell: she 'seemed woman to the waist, and fair, / But ended foul in many a scaly fold / Voluminous and vast, a Serpent armed / With mortal sting', and she perpetually gives birth to slavering hounds who 'creep . . . into her womb, / And kennel there, yet there still barked and howled / Within unseen'.[43] A disgust at the female body, emblem of all that is monstrous and corrupting, that is all the more depressing for its predictability.

I'm not interested in trying to exonerate Milton, and any of the ready-to-hand defences seem trite, prone to slide into parodic simplifications of the past and exonerations of the present: that he was writing in and expressed the convictions of a thoroughly patriarchal society (which easily becomes 'everyone was sexist in the olden days'), that he identified with female voices and chose a female muse ('some of my best friends are imaginary women'), or that as a great poet he must have been subtly critiquing, rather than reproducing, the views of his time ('no genius could be that much of a bad guy'). I certainly don't believe these excuses, but I start from the position that misogyny, like other forms of hatred, involves the soldering together of a strange bundle of incoherent beliefs and assumptions while treating them as a logical and natural whole. Compelling artworks neither elude these forms of incoherence nor serenely stand apart from them; but what they can do, via their forms and their techniques and not necessarily with the conscious awareness of the artist responsible for them, is lay bare the cracks in the construction of these ways of thinking and the energy with which they are soldered together, making manifest the history of their often invisible workings.

I realise also that, by looking ahead to the depiction of Sin, I've drifted from Milton's divorce writings, which are fascinating documents but not great works of art, to *Paradise Lost*, which certainly is; in that poem Milton will depict a man confronting and eventually forgiving the woman who betrayed him. After they have both eaten the apple, Eve throws herself down before Adam and begs his forgiveness: 'Between us two let there be peace,' she implores him, insisting that her sin is worse than his, and that she is 'sole cause to thee of all this woe'.[44] Only then, seeing her excessive self-abasement, is Adam able to distance himself from his own wild feelings, and they are reconciled. Many readers have followed Milton's nephew Edward Phillips in seeing this moment as a recapitulation of Milton's eventual reconciliation with Mary Powell, which, Phillips claims, was effected at the house of one of Milton's relations when their friends had managed to smuggle Mary back from Oxfordshire. Milton 'making his usual visit, the Wife was ready in another Room, and on a sudden he was surprised to see one whom he thought to never have seen more, making Submission and begging Pardon on her Knees before him'.[45]

While these scenes of supplication resonate with one another, however, I think it's too much of a simplification to see these parts of *Paradise Lost* – or indeed, the divorce tracts themselves – as raw autobiography. In the case of the poem, the stakes are changed once the story is moved to the Garden of Eden, because here Milton is not just describing the differences between men and women but showing the origins of this difference, which has multiple possible effects. Most obviously it naturalises gender difference by depicting Adam as always possessing the 'priority which God crown'd him with'. As the narrator bluntly puts it, when he describes the first appearance of Adam and Eve, 'He for God only, she for God in him'.[46] There would seem to be little more to say on the matter.

But the basic fact that, according to Genesis, Adam is created before Eve also puts the emergence of human beings into time, makes it into narrative, and something that is shown coming into being cannot possess the same stability as something that is absolutely original, or whose origins are lost to the mists of time.[47] It's worth remembering here that the creation of men and women in Genesis is one of its more confusing aspects, since it seems to happen twice. First we are told that 'God created man in his own image, in the image of God created he him; male and female created he them.'[48] This seems to suggest God creating male and female together, at the same moment. A few verses later, however, we get the more familiar account of Adam's creation from dust, and Eve from his rib, on the basis that 'It is not good that the man should be alone'.[49] Modern scholars would explain this inconsistency through the different scribes and authorial voices responsible for Genesis, and the historical process by which it was amalgamated, but a Protestant like Milton was committed to believing each fragment of the text to be the literal word of God. These are the tensions upon which Milton elaborated when he took it upon himself to expand the meagre, suggestive verses of Genesis, pregnant with implication and filled with unexplained gaps and leaps of logic, into a detailed and continuous poem.

In his divorce tracts Milton gave extensive attention to the loneliness against which Eve's creation was intended to guard, arguing that 'by loneliness is not only meant the want of copulation'; he was arguing, against the Roman Catholic position that its principal purpose was procreation, that 'in God's intention a meet and happy conversation is the chiefest and noblest end of marriage'.[50] *Paradise Lost* pushes this thought much further, exploring both what such conversation and what loneliness itself might have looked like before the Fall. Eve and Adam – it's strongly implied, if not quite explicitly stated – have sex in Eden, something many Christian exegetes denied: the closest that we get to certainty is the claim that the pair 'Straight side by side were laid, nor turned I ween / Adam from his fair spouse, nor Eve the rites / Mysterious of connubial love refused'.[51] Their sex, however, is only one part of the integrated whole that their actions make up before the Fall – the 'thousand decencies' that, as we have already seen, Adam defended against Raphael's strange vision of angelic love, homoerotically pure but disembodied. Adam and Eve's bodies and souls, their thoughts and emotions, their interior and exterior worlds, all flow freely in and out of one another, support and reinforce one another. If their relationship is as bluntly hierarchical as 'He for God only, she for God in him' suggests, it's also the kind of molten, temporary hierarchy that we saw described in the last chapter, where all difference might be overcome in the spiritual process by which the 'one first matter all' strives to perfect itself.

Of course this does not happen; what happens instead is the Fall, which locks these hierarchies in place. But expanding upon Genesis demands that a source be found for the catastrophe that occurs, and for this purpose Milton focuses on the fact that Adam is not mentioned in Genesis when Eve is tempted: the serpent speaks only, inexplicably, to the woman. Milton therefore attributed to Eve a desire for the very solitude, the separateness, that she was created to alleviate in Adam. When they are working together in the garden she observes that its fecundity is so rampant that they must separate to work effectively: 'what we by day / Lop overgrown, or prune, or prop, or bind, / One night or two with wanton growth derides / Tending to wild'.[52] Milton is so committed to process and change that he could not envisage a static paradise, but its wild energies become a problem. Their work is oddly necessary – paradise left untended would run rampant. Their routine intimacies become a problem as well. 'For while so near each other thus all day / Our task we choose', Eve worries, 'what wonder if so near / Looks intervene and smiles, or object new / Casual discourse draw on, which intermits / Our day's work brought to little.'[53] They distract one another, and risk falling behind. Adam's response is borderline passive-aggressive: 'if much converse perhaps / Thee satiate, to short absence I could yield'.[54] I guess we can take a break, if you're sick of me. And indeed they part, and Eve meets Satan disguised as the serpent, and is tempted.

What's striking about this moment of parting, however, is that their separation is presented as a perfectly reasonable, logical response on Eve's part to the practical challenges of their situation, to a breakdown in the mutually reinforcing delights of Eden: affection and conversation get in the way of necessary labour instead of flowing together. It's hard to shake the feeling, moreover, that Eve also simply wants to get away from Adam, that his constant desire to converse, kiss, hold hands is becoming an irritation as she seeks to focus on her work. That he's a bit cloying, a bit needy. This might seem like reading too much into the poem, but it's worth remembering that, while Milton complained about enforced solitude in the divorce tracts, in many other ways he desired above all to be single, and singular, like Eve herself. In one of the poem's most striking moments, when Adam asks for a companion because he can take no pleasure alone, God responds:

> *What thinkst thou then of me, and this my state,*
> *Seem I to thee sufficiently possessed*
> *Of happiness, or not? who am alone*
> *From all eternity, for none I know*
> *Second to me or like, equal much less.*[55]

God quickly insists that this was just a test, but for a flickering moment we are allowed to glimpse divine being not as serene superiority but as aching loneliness – the lack of a companion and an equal. Perhaps it's better to say that the impulses to be unique and solitudinous on the one hand, and to be companionable and responsive on the other, were at war with one another in Milton's mind. This makes it all the more striking, however, that it's Eve, not Adam, who shares this desire for solitude within the poem – and not just when she departs before the Fall, but from the very moment of her creation. When she describes her first moments of consciousness, Eve recalls being led by the sound of moving water towards a pool and seeing another creature, whom she did not recognise as her reflection, gazing at her 'with answering looks / Of sympathy and love'.[56] She might have lingered there for ever, she recalls, had God's voice not intervened and led her to Adam. When she first saw Adam, however, she found him 'less fair, / Less winning soft, less amiably mild, / Than that smooth watery image' and she turned to flee until Adam's 'gentle hand / Seized mine, I yielded, and from that time see / How beauty is excelled by manly grace / And wisdom, which alone is truly fair'.[57] This episode, entirely Milton's invention, is a deeply strange and equivocal one. It's certainly possible to read it as displaying, and justifying, the same violent patriarchal energies that animate and deform the divorce tracts. Eve at the pool is a clear rewriting of Ovid's Narcissus; her natural state is self-regard, and she needs a man's firm grip to lead her onto the straight and narrow. But it's the very fact that

Eve's discovery of her subservience is just that – a *discovery* – that opens up the possibility of reading it otherwise. What we see here is that even in its unfallen state, women's supposedly natural position is not natural at all: it needs to be created, to be brought about by the force of Adam's words and his grip. This is not to say that the gendered hierarchies of the poem are subverted, still less overturned. Rather, it shows how patriarchal stories become dangers to the very order they seek to justify by the compulsion to tell them. They reveal that order's origins, both in force and in time. Milton may here have been replaying the firm and decisive grip that he wished he'd exerted on Mary Powell to keep her in, or return her to, London. But the more he turns the inevitability of his superiority into a story, the more he distends its rhythms, the less inevitable it starts to seem.

Like *Paradise Lost*, the divorce tracts both pulse with the redirected personal energies of Milton's marriage and its psychological impact on him, and yet are never reducible to them. Although Milton's experiences prompted him to argue for marriage based on true companionship and divorce as justified by its absence, he pushed his argument far beyond his experiences. These tracts are filled with the fruits of his learning, and are particularly reliant on his reading in Hebraic and rabbinical discussions of marriage, which had been given new currency via the learned studies of John Selden, the greatest Hebraist in England, who was a member of the Westminster Assembly.[58] In a broader sense, however, to see Milton's tracts as merely an expression of his personal resentments is to miss the point. He was not bringing the grievances of his personal relationship into the public realm: the personal *was* the political at this moment.[59] The Assembly gave extensive attention to the question of marriage because, as we've previously seen, the individual household was understood as both the basis and a microcosm of the entire political system. The bonds of mutual obligation that connected the members of a household were the same that held together a king and his subjects. It becomes clear in the light of this point exactly why Milton's argument for divorce was so potent and terrifying to his contemporaries. When the Assembly debated marriage they asked whether it was a civil or religious procedure – what kind of contract or bond it constituted. If this bond was weakened, if it could be unmade, what other kinds of bonds might be undone? Milton made these connections darkly clear: 'He who marries', he wrote, 'intends as little to conspire his own ruine, as he that swears Allegiance: and as a whole people is in proportion to an ill Government, so is one man to an ill marriage.'[60] A people, it seems, might divorce themselves from a tyrant.

The dangers of Milton's view were quickly noted, and, it was claimed, they had a tangible impact on the views of ordinary people. In 1646 the Puritan clergyman Thomas Edwards published a book titled *Gangraena*, which was a compendium of the alarming views held by the sects that had proliferated during these revolutionary years. Edwards included in it a summary of the view articulated in *The Doctrine and Discipline of Divorce* 'That 'tis lawfull for a man to put away his wife upon indisposition, unfitnesse or contrariety of minde', and grouped Milton with sects who supposedly practised polygamy and rampant sexual excess. Edwards then claimed that a woman called Mrs Attaway, after deciding to 'look more into . . . Master Milton's Doctrine of Divorce', decided that 'she had an unsanctified husband', and 'accordingly she hath practised it in running away with another womans husband'.[61] This may have been mere scaremongering, but it must have been plausible to Edwards's readers in order to work. Mrs Attaway was a Baptist preacher, a former lace maker, who felt the Holy Spirit move within her and preached to crowds of more than a thousand people that the Kingdom of God was at hand and all would be saved.[62] Milton may well have been personally appalled by this woman taking inspiration from his divorce tracts, but that's beside the point. It's a reminder that he wrote at a time when increasing numbers of women had access to books, and the opportunity to mull upon them and act upon the ideas in them. It's a reminder too that he was writing at a moment of wildly proliferating forms of expression, of theological and linguistic inventiveness, as the established order collapsed around his and Mrs Attaway's ears, and the bonds that held wives to husbands and subjects to kings started to loosen.

Milton's insistence upon the right to divorce was the fruit of his growing conviction, which aligned him most strongly with the Independents in the Westminster Assembly, that the state had no right to interfere in matters of individual choice. The causes of divorce, as his intensive reading of his Parisian acquaintance Hugo Grotius had further convinced him, 'reside so deeply in the radical and innocent affections of nature, as is not within the diocese of Law to tamper with'.[63] In 1644, in the midst of writing the divorce tracts, he paused to address to Parliament his most remarkable prose treatise, *Areopagitica*, in which he would place even greater emphasis on the sanctity of individual decision. The provocation for this work was the June 1643 licensing act, which had responded to the upsurge of new voices by seeking increased state control over what could be published.[64] Milton's opposition to these restrictions on what could be said and thought inspired the most electrifying and famous prose that he ever produced. Censorship, he insisted, was wrong, misguided, and ineffective. His lifelong commitment to reading as a trans-formative activity, one that makes a life rather than merely adorning it, shines through when he writes (in terms echoing Sarpi's account of their worldly impact) that 'Books are not absolutely dead things, but doe contain a potencie of life in them to be as active as that soule was whose progeny they are; nay they do preserve as in a violl the purest efficacie and extraction of that living intellect that bred them.' The rhythms of an individual's life pulse in the book that he or she produces; for that reason one might 'as good almost kill a Man as kill a good Book; who kills a Man kills a reasonable creature, Gods Image; but hee who destroyes a good Booke, kills reason it selfe . . . a good Booke is the pretious life-blood of a master spirit, imbalm'd and treasur'd up on purpose to a life beyond life.'[65] These thrilling paeans to the power of reading 'a good Booke' broaden into a justification for exposing oneself to books and ideas of all kinds, even those that one reviles, in a soaring passage that I must quote at length:

Good and evill we know in the field of this World grow up together almost inseparably; and the knowledge of good is so involv'd and interwoven with the knowledge of evill, and in so many cunning resemblances hardly to be discern'd . . . It was from out the rinde of one apple tasted, that the knowledge of good and evill as two twins cleaving together leapt forth into the World. And perhaps this is that doom which Adam fell into of knowing good and evill, that is to say of knowing good by evill. As therefore the state of man now is; what wisdome can there be to choose, what continence to forbeare without the knowledge of evill? He that can apprehend and consider vice with all her baits and seeming pleasures, and yet abstain, and yet distinguish, and yet prefer that which is truly better, he is the true wayfaring Christian. I cannot praise a fugitive and cloister'd vertue, unexercis'd & unbreath'd, that never sallies out and sees her adversary, but slinks out of the race, where that immortall garland is to be run for, not without dust and heat. Assuredly we bring not innocence into the world, we bring impurity much rather: that which purifies us is triall, and triall is by what is contrary. That vertue therefore which is but a youngling in the contemplation of evill, and knows not the utmost that vice promises to her followers, and rejects it, is but a blank vertue, not a pure.[66]

This is a dense and superb passage, many of its boldest claims made in passing as if uncontroversial. Milton wants to insist that evil must be known, encountered – it cannot be conquered if it is avoided. He turns instinctively to the story of the Fall to make this point, offhandedly suggesting that the routine phrase 'knowledge of good and evil' actually makes the two mutually dependent, each only knowable in relation to its opposite: 'that is to say of knowing good *by* evill'. This insistence on the value of encountering evil develops into something like a Miltonic ethics of confrontation, of exposure to that which is foreign and challenging: we must exercise our virtue, we must seek out that which is contrary to what we think of as our deeply held convictions, if we are to purify ourselves, rather than remaining spotless and untested blanks.

I love and admire this passage – it's one of the pieces of Milton's writing to which I return, in my reading and in my mind, the most frequently. Its power can certainly help us to understand the extraordinary influence that this particular treatise of Milton's has had. Though he wrote in response to a particular and shifting set of circumstances, this treatise has become one of the central, classic texts of Western liberal views on free speech and independent liberty to choose. *Areopagitica* was adapted and applied by radicals and revolutionaries in France and America in the 1780s, as they undertook their own republican experiments. In 1788 the Comte de Mirabeau published a much altered and compressed version of *Areopagitica*, translated into French as *Sur la Liberté de la Presse*, replacing Milton's claim that virtue could only be achieved through transformative encounters with the insistence that the envisaged Republic would progress towards perfect knowledge.[67] In America, Milton's words and ideas were woven into the minds and writings of many of the revolutionary leaders, notably Thomas Jefferson, who saw Milton as a model to be emulated and ultimately surpassed. The insistence on individual freedom that lies at the heart of the above passage from *Areopagitica* – the claim that each person must enter the race for truth for themselves, purify themselves by their own trials and exposures to that which is contrary – helped inspire the most famous piece of writing for which Jefferson was at least partly responsible, the Declaration of Independence. It was another of Milton's prose treatises from the 1640s, however, *The Tenure of Kings and Magistrates*, that this document echoed most closely. The first draft of its second sentence – 'We hold these truths to be sacred and undeniable; that all men are created equal and independent' – was even closer than the famous final version to a thought that Milton had put in characteristically spikier terms: 'No man who knows aught', he insisted, 'can be so stupid to deny that all men naturally were born free, being the image and resemblance of God himself.'[68]

While Milton's thundering defence of the need for transformative individual encounters with truth and error still resonates – and remains a key point of reference for modern writers writing against totalitarian censorship, such as J. M. Coetzee – its place within the logic of *Areopagitica* as a whole is a curious one.[69] I partly value this treatise because it allows me to see the ways in which Milton's European travels continued to shape his mind – and indeed this is the tract in which he mentions the meeting with Galileo, and cites and builds upon Sarpi's writings against papal censorship as the antidote to what the astronomer suffered. Milton's trip to Italy was when he most obviously sallied out in the manner that the treatise describes, testing and purifying himself by trial with what he found contrary, changing himself in the process and relinquishing his cloistered blankness. But in other ways, for all its boldness and openness, the tract is narrow, tentative. It allows for censorship after publication: books can be burned or suppressed as long as they are published. It both calls for open-mindedness and closes itself off. It is better, Milton claims, 'that many be tolerated, rather than all compell'd', but quickly he assures his audience that 'I mean not tolerated popery', since it 'extirpats all religions and civill supremacies'.[70] His kinship with great Europeans like Sarpi and Galileo sits uneasily with a narrow nationalistic frenzy according to which 'Methinks I see in my mind a noble and puissant Nation rousing herself like a strong man after sleep, and shaking her invincible locks.'[71]

The reasons for this tension lie partly in the context in which Milton wrote: Parliament remained a volatile arena of conflicting forces, and Milton aimed to appeal to the full spectrum of opinion. Hatred of Catholicism and a sense of England's sacred destiny were among the few things on which these groups agreed, and to which he could safely appeal. But I also think that these are expressions of the deep and productive conflict within Milton's imagination, between inclusivity and exclusivity, hierarchy and equality, openness and closure. If *Areopagitica* has become a classic text of Western views on free speech, its very popularity means that its most magnificent moments are frequently taken out of context, as straightforward axioms when in fact Milton's mind was much more ambivalent. In the past few years I've seen its words quoted by narrow-minded English nationalists and self-proclaimed defenders of free speech who would place it in the service of racism and xenophobia. It's worth remembering that if Milton could partly inspire the insistence that all men were born free, a few decades earlier in America his words had been used to justify exterminating the Native Americans who were 'devils in the flesh', no better than the usurping angels of *Paradise Lost*; and more obviously that Jefferson, who reshaped Milton's language of basic human liberty in such resonant and inspiring terms, could be a particularly notorious and exploitative owner of slaves.[72] Milton's hatred of Catholics, distasteful though it might be, is a useful reminder that the arena of free speech is never as open as its self-appointed defenders often claim. I prefer to read Milton's call for 'triall . . . by what is contrary' as a reminder that if we're lucky enough to believe that we can speak freely, one of the responsibilities of this freedom is that we must seek to understand and to eliminate the restrictions and exclusions that structure the arenas in which we speak. Only then – I would say, and Milton would seem both to strive towards and to resist the thought – are we truly exercising our virtue.

This series of prose writings had made Milton a prominent and controversial public figure. He was clearly concerned about his reputation and determined to cling on to his primary identity as a poet, since in 1645 he oversaw publication of most of his poems to date, in English, Latin, Greek, and Italian. I've referred to this volume numerous times in the preceding chapters, but we can now see what a striking and bold move this was at this time. When Milton was beginning to be publicly recognised as radical, a man whose works could make women leave their husbands and threatened the bonds between monarchs and subjects, he presented himself as a learned, urbane, and respectable poet. But in other ways the volume was as mixed and multifaceted as Milton himself: most obviously in its unusual array of languages but also in the range of allegiances that it advertised. 'Lycidas' was given a new headnote claiming that it foretold the fall of the Laudian clergy, but elsewhere the volume was larded with praise by his Italian Catholic friends, and it was published by a man, Humphrey Moseley, who was most associated with prestigious Royalist publications. This strange mixture might itself, like the broad address of *Areopagitica*, be Milton's way of presenting himself as capacious and open-minded in contrast to the violently divided allegiances of the moment. But, as so often in his life, I think Milton made a practical and tactical decision, driven by the urgencies of the present while also speaking to his deeper personal concerns. The volume was a compendium of rhythms and of times: the varying learned metres in which the poems were written, but also the multiple time frames and competing voices of the Nativity Ode, 'Lycidas', the poem to Leonora Baroni, and the other works we've encountered in the preceding chapters. This was a volume that could be read as a national prophet-poet finding his voice, and as a gorgeous cacophony of linguistic and imaginative parts acting as a connected but disparate whole.

Despite publishing these earlier poems, Milton had little time for new verse in these years. In 1646 he continued to experiment with the personal and political possibilities of the sonnet, in ways that show the divided directions of his mind. Just as he was emerging as a polemical firebrand, Milton wrote a sonnet to his old friend Henry Lawes, who wrote the music for, and performed in, *Comus*, as well as helping Milton when he set off on his travels. Milton praised the Royalist Lawes for making music that augmented rather than obscured the beauty of words, and ended by referring to Dante's praise of his musical friend Casella.[73] This urbane poem, moving across the lines that divide the arts, languages, and political causes, contrasted strikingly with a biting sonnet of 1646 in which he answered criticisms of his prose treatises, which he dismissed as 'a barbarous noise . . . Of owls and cuckoos, asses, apes and dogs'. In another funny and deliberately ungainly sonnet he defended his choice of the obscure Greek musical term *Tetrachordon* as a title, insisting that it was no worse than the strange Scottish names now grown common in England: the poem allows him to rhyme

Tetrachordon with 'seldom pored on', 'what a word on' and 'Gordon' in a welter of deliberate and parodic badness.[74]

Later that year Milton wrote a poem confirming his disillusionment with the Presbyterians with whom he'd earlier ambiguously aligned himself, but whose growing dominance in Parliament revealed an authoritarian streak scarcely different from the Laudian desire 'To force our consciences that Christ set free'. It ended with the magnificently contemptuous line: 'New Presbyter is but old Priest writ large'. As well as confirming Milton's growing independence of belief, this line calls to my mind John Aubrey's report that Milton 'pronounced the letter R . . . very hard, a certaine signe of a Satyricall wit'.[75] On two occasions in 2008 I sat riveted as the poet Geoffrey Hill read Milton's poem against the Presbyterians aloud, and when he reached the last line – whether because he had Aubrey's description in mind, or from his own instincts – he rolled its repeated Rs out gloriously in his booming, slightly strangled voice: 'New Prrrrrresbyterrrrrr is but old Prrrrrrriest wrrrrrrit larrrrrrge'. Hill, known like Milton for his supposed gloominess, also shared this satirical wit: I met him once before his death, when he was sporting the Methuselan beard of his later years and seemed every inch the Miltonic prophet, and he told me with glee that his students in Boston had given him the nickname Santa on Crack, and roared with laughter. I still hear the poem in his voice when I read it to myself, and he's helped me recognise Milton's relish for the physical feel of this particular letter in the mouth: '*Vallombrrrrrosa*'; '*Parrrradise Lost*'.

Milton's activities in these years were varied, restless, a shuttling between acidic polemicist and urbane humanist poet. He returned to translating several of the Psalms into English, revisiting a preoccupation from his schooldays. He resumed correspondence with his Italian friends, sending affectionate letters to Carlo Dati. And, in a further plea for respectability, he sent his printed poems and collected prose writings to the Bodleian Library to be held for posterity, along with a Latin poem to the librarian, John Rous, claiming that the poems were written 'while he wandered in play through the shades of Italy and the green fields of England'.[76] This flitting between stern national prophet and playful, learned academician is perhaps unsurprising given both his personal circumstances and the wider backdrop. Mary had returned to live with him in 1645 following the rout of the Royalist army at Naseby. The Parliamentary victory began the end of the first Civil War; it was masterminded by Edward Fairfax, leader of the New Model Army, and his lieutenant general, Oliver Cromwell, who was quickly rising to prominence. Mary brought her family with her from war-torn Oxfordshire, and with them the mess of her father's financial affairs. Richard Powell died in 1646, and Milton's own father in 1647. As with his mother, Milton left no explicit testimony of how the death of this man, who had lavished him with music and money and indulged his private studies, affected him. He seems to have overcome whatever sexual problems might have led to his initial separation from his wife, since their first daughter was born in July 1646 and a second in October 1648. In some ways the violently focused energies that produced Milton's anti-episcopal and divorce tracts had dissipated, and his poems from this period seem to be divided between attending to the present and turning nostalgically to the past.

This changed again, along with the changes that would convulse English society for the remainder of the decade, and whose reverberations for Milton we'll continue to sense in the next chapter. The New Model Army that had been raised and deployed with miraculous speed and efficiency by Cromwell and Fairfax had now become a political force in its own right, far more radical and tolerant of extreme varieties of religious belief and practice than it was of the parliament whose war it had won. Charles had been taken captive in 1646 but escaped in 1647, shortly after the New Model Army marched on London and assumed control, Presbyterian opposition melting away before them. The king was imprisoned again on the Isle of Wight, and the second Civil War began in May 1648; but it was a much shorter (if no less bloody) affair, over before the end of the year, the same year that the Treaty of Westphalia was signed on the Continent, bringing to an end thirty devastating years of conflict. Charles was brought from his island prison to London, and in December Colonel Thomas Pride was instructed to arrest MPs who were seen as opposed to the army's cause as they entered Parliament. The remaining members, who came to be known as the Rump, agreed to the trial of the king, who was duly found guilty. On 30 January 1649, Charles, wearing an extra shirt so that he would not be seen shivering in the cold, was led onto a scaffold that had been constructed outside the banqueting house at Whitehall, where a large crowd had gathered. He gave a speech declaring himself innocent of the charges against him and calling himself a martyr of the people. He laid his neck on the block, told the executioner to wait for his signal, and gave it; with a single blow his head was struck from his body.

Milton, having somewhat withdrawn from public polemics following his flurry of activity in the first half of the decade, re-entered the fray following the death of Charles I. He first defended the regicide in *The Tenure of Kings and Magistrates*, in which he insisted that no ruler, however powerful, was exempt from punishment for crimes against his people: 'be he King, or Tyrant, or Emperour, the Sword of Justice is above him, in whose hand soever is found sufficient power to avenge the effusion, and so great a deluge of innocent blood.'[77] What gave him special prominence and notoriety in the aftermath of the king's death, however, was the response that he wrote to a book that was published soon after Charles's execution, and which claimed to contain the prayers and meditations with which Charles had consoled himself in the days and hours before he died. The volume became a sensation, focus both of the reverence that the king attracted as a martyr and of the hatred levelled at him as a deposed tyrant. As recognition for the alacrity and force with which he justified tyrannicide in *Tenure*, Parliament commissioned Milton to prepare a full rebuttal and discrediting of the book published under Charles's name. The king's book was called *Eikon Basilike*, the image of the king; Milton's response was the ominously titled *Eikonoklastes*.

Eikonoklastes allowed Milton to unleash once again the biting polemical skills that he had honed in his anti-episcopal tracts at the start of the decade, in a comprehensive deflating of the dead Charles's claim to virtue and piety. While I'll say more about his defences of the regicide in the next chapter, there's a single moment within this fiery text that stands out to me because it suggests another, less obvious connection with the concerns that, as I've been arguing, animated and sometimes deformed Milton's writings across the 1640s. A persistent concern both with the nature of true and false poetry, of wicked and virtuous books, and a connected preoccupation with the words and voices of women, a desire to lay claim to them and an anxious fear of being overcome by them.

From the moment it was published, the authorship of *Eikon Basilike* was a matter of sustained controversy: had the king really written it, or was it ghost-written by one of his fawning acolytes? The new prayers that continued to be added to the expanded editions that quickly appeared made the matter even more suspect. But it was Milton who first noticed that the problem of authorship went much deeper than this. One of the prayers published as the king's belonged neither to him nor his followers: it was lifted, almost without alteration, from the pages of Sir Philip Sidney's sprawling and famous sixteenth-century romance, *Arcadia*. In that work it's spoken by Pamela, a pagan princess who is taken captive by a wicked queen, Cecropia. Milton recognised her words instantly, and re-attributed them to their true author. It is, he wrote, 'a Prayer stol'n word for word from the mouth of a Heathen fiction praying to a heathen God; & that in no serious Book, but the vain amatorious Poem of Sr Philip Sidneys Arcadia, a Book in that kind full of worth and wit, but among religious thoughts, and duties not worthy to be named'.[78]

Milton's unveiling of whoever had compiled the king's book as not just a liar but a rank plagiarist was a killer blow.[79] It was a triumphant use of his years of wide and careful reading, now having a practical effect as it allowed him to deflate the dead Charles and humiliate his memory. But while spotting this piece of plagiarism was just one of the many strategies by which he skewered the king's inept admirers, I also think that debating this moment of heft resonated in deeper ways with his own ambitions and uncertainties at this point in his life. The displaced poetic energies of the anti-episcopal tracts; the anxious misogyny and desire for control over women's voices that raged in the divorce tracts; the concern with transformation and encounter that pulsed through *Of Education* and *Areopagitica*: all these converged around this moment of disputed literature as Milton continued to wrestle with what had made him a poet, with what he had made of himself up to this point in his life, and with what he might go on to do.

When Milton dismissed Sidney's *Arcadia* as a 'vain amatorious Poem', although he acknowledged its 'worth and wit', he was still disparaging a work that he much admired for its 'exquisite reasoning'.[80] His dismissal was tactical: he had to demean the work from which Charles or his ghost-writer had chosen to steal a prayer, by stressing its thorough impiety. But there's more going on here than meets the eye. The king, once Pamela's words were made his, took the place of Sidney's imprisoned princess; but this means that Milton, eavesdropping on Charles as he perpetuated his act of literary theft, took the place of Cecropia, the wicked queen who listens in on the prayer within Sidney's story. And it's not a comfort-able identification. Cecropia is not just a figure of fairy-tale wickedness; she's a demonic version of what a poet might be. She is the principal shaper and mover of Sidney's plot, determined to seize, transform, and make use of time, just as the poet does. She's also a version of a schoolteacher, the role in which Milton had spent much of the preceding decade. She refers to her persuasions of Pamela as 'lessons', and, when she fails to convince her, 'she having a rod in her hand . . . fell to scourge that most beautiful body'.[81] She beats her young charge much as Milton, to Mary Powell's horror, beat his own nephews. Sidney's wicked queen, lurking in the shadows of this argument over authorship, embodies the combination of identities that Milton had struggled to reconcile in the preceding decade.

This is the problem with inhabiting the minds and voices of women, as Milton so often sought to do, and as Charles's hagiog-raphers did too when they borrowed and redeployed Philip Sidney's words. These voices do not always obey; they bring with them more of their meanings, their associations and after-echoes, than the one who claims them tends to want. It becomes less and less clear, as is always the case for me when I read Milton, who is doing the claiming and who is being claimed. Who is spoken for, and who is spoken through.

IO

26 May 1658: 'A Universal Blank'

John Milton, six months short of his fiftieth birthday, sits at his desk in his pleasant house on Petty France, which opens straight onto the south side of St James's Park. At his elbow sits his assistant, a talented man and a kindred spirit a dozen years his junior named Andrew Marvell. The two men read and admired one another's poems before they ever met, and found much to talk of once they did. Few other men in England can follow Milton in his deft leaps between Latin and English and understand his allusions. Marvell has even spent time as a teacher, and so understands the pleasures and frustrations of passing on one's learning. Furthermore, especially now that the dead king's decadent rabble of followers have long fled, Marvell is one of the few men Milton knows who has experienced the delights of Rome, even its paintings and sculptures, and can reminisce with him about them.[1]

But their present conversation does not concern the arts; they are hard at work. Marvell is there for the most practical of reasons. When Milton took up his position – almost exactly eight years ago – as Secretary for Foreign Tongues to the Council of State, it was already clear that his vision was fading. As long ago as 1645, while still separated from his wife Mary, the sight in his left eye had begun to waver, and it was largely gone by 1648. Four years later, his right eye followed suit. His position – which required him to fashion the diplomatic letters with which the Council presented him in clear Latin, and render the letters they received from states across Europe quickly into English – would once have been a matter of ease; a return to his days at St Paul's when he flipped sentences effortlessly from Latin to English, and back. But blindness complicated things, even though his memory remained sharp, and he relied increasingly upon his assistants; he had requested Marvell four years previously, but the younger man had been approved only the year before. He was sorry that they had not worked together in the first half of the decade, when crafting letters to European luminaries and leaders, carefully repeating the rhythm of a Latin cadence and ensuring no more ambiguity than he intended, had been a thrill. It had felt like an apt reward both for his decades of absorbing Latin into the very tissues of his body, and for defending the killing of the tyrant King Charles when many were too timorous to do so. In those days, even as his sight fell dark, he remained convinced that he was doing God's work, helping the nation, and revisiting on his own terms the European landscape through which he had once travelled. He had even allowed himself, when crafting a letter to the Grand Duke of Tuscany at the start of 1652 which sought to establish 'commerce and mutual friendship' between the duke's territories and the Lord Protector's government, to slip in a personal detail. He had stressed that the traditionally admiring relationship between their nations 'is averred and confirmed not only by our merchants, who have traded in your ports for many years, but also by certain youths, the noblest and most honourable of our nation [*nostræ nationis nobilissimi atque honestissimi*], who either journey through your cities or sojourn there to improve their studies'.[2] He had smiled at the memories that leapt to his mind as he dictated these words.

Those days seemed far off. A few months before he wrote the letter to Tuscany his son and namesake had been born. The boy died a few weeks later, and his wife Mary had followed the child into the grave the following year, shortly after giving birth to their third daughter. By the middle of the decade the sense of infinite possibilities that had characterised its beginning was hardening into something more narrow and rigid. In 1655 came the devastating news that the Alpine lands in the northerly part of Italy – through which he had travelled in what he thought of as his last innocent days, before he learned of Charles Diodati's death – had become the arena for chilling atrocities. The Waldensian

Protestants who lived there, and who seemed to Milton like a remnant of a pure and original church that the papists had otherwise managed to extinguish, were brutally massacred by the Duke of Savoy. Milton had been moved to dictate to his assistant his first political sonnet for several years, asking God to 'Avenge . . . thy slaughtered saints, whose bones / Lie scattered on the Alpine mountains cold . . . Slain by the bloody Piedmontese that rolled / Mother with infant down the rocks'.[3] These faraway deaths melded in his mind with the death of his own infant and the tiny boy's mother.

Milton married his second wife, Katherine, in 1656, and their daughter was born soon after; but this baby too had lived only a matter of weeks. On this particular day in 1658 it was just three months since Katherine's body had also been committed to the ground. Marvell had covered for him during his time of mourning, but now Milton was returning to work, and history seemed swiftly and horribly to be repeating itself. Once again the Waldensians were in peril, the survivors of the previous massacre still hunted by the vile Duke of Savoy. Milton used to attend meetings of the Committee on Foreign Affairs, hear the words of ambassadors and men of state; now he preferred to stay at home, and have couriers bring the results of the committee's discussions for him to digest and translate.[4] He and Marvell's task for the day is to craft into Latin two letters that the Council of State has prepared – one to Louis XIV, the young king of France, the other to the leaders of the Swiss Cantons, imploring them to defend the Waldensians. He has Marvell read to him the next sentence, addressing the Swiss: 'But you, who not only lie so near adjoining, as to behold the Butcheries, and hear the Outcries and Shrieks of the Distressed . . .' Even with only half his mind on Marvell's recitation, the ideal Latin equivalent spills from Milton's mouth, its pieces fitting seamlessly together: '*Vos qui non modo fratrum cruciatibus ac pene clamoribus . . .*'[5] '*Cruciatibus?*' he hears Marvell ask as he scribbles down Milton's words, a slight sardonic edge creeping into the younger man's voice: is that not a little strong for 'outcries'? Yes, snaps Milton in reply, *cruciatibus*; torture, torment, racking anguish; this is what the innocent Waldensians have suffered; *this* is what he wants the word to say.

He speaks sharply in part because he is distracted, his mind cluttered and divided. The vision of those murders in the Alps, of blood flecking the snow, vies in his mind with other images. His dreams have been disturbed of late. Two nights before a woman visited him. He could not see her face, which was covered by a veil. At first he thought it must be Katherine, but there was something in her strong stance as she stood over his bed that reminded him of Mary. As she bent to embrace him he woke suddenly, to that terrible second when he could not work out why the darkness continued even once his eyes snapped open and he had to remember, all over again, that he could no longer see. He had emerged from the dream with most of a poem about it already formed in his mind, which would leave room for both of his wives within the apparition: he would simply call her 'my late espoused saint'. He would report the benevolent feeling that radiated from her despite her covered visage – 'Her face was veiled, yet to my fancied sight, / Love, sweetness, goodness in her person shined' – and he would end with the shock of multiple losses that he suffered when 'as to embrace me she inclined / I waked, she fled, and day brought back my night'.[6] Now all the poem needed was a middle.

This was not his only night-time visitation, however. Whereas he could easily recognise this figure, even if she seemed two in one, now the other voice returned with increasing frequency, and he had heard it again the previous night. For years now he would wake with a sense that a voice had been speaking to him, but he could rarely remember what it said or even what it sounded like. He could not even be certain that it was a woman's, though he thought so. Sometimes he would wake with a snatch of a phrase or a fading picture still in his mind. Recently, however, the voice seemed louder, more distinct. And suddenly last night's dream comes bursting back, a multicoloured memory. He had been standing on top of a mountain, looking out over a wide territory as a spectacle unfolded below. Someone seemed to be speaking, explaining what they were seeing, while another voice listened and occasionally responded: an angel and a man, he somehow knew; both seemed to be speaking with the same voice; the woman's voice and Milton's own voice, somehow all at once.

Far below he saw a group of people driving sheep and cattle; a group of giants abruptly appeared and began to slaughter them cruelly. He heard the voice narrate the horror: 'now scattered lies / With carcasses and arms the ensanguined field / Deserted'.[7] It must be the Waldensians, he thought, before realising that this was a people much more ancient. He saw the beleaguered group gather to defend themselves against the giants, but disagree violently on how best to go about it. And he saw a venerable man emerge and speak wisely to the crowd – this man 'spake much of right and wrong, / Of justice, of religion, truth and peace', the voice explained – but they nonetheless turned on him in fury and moved to kill him. Immediately Milton realised: this is Enoch, ancestor of Noah.[8] Milton had long been haunted by the unexplained fate of this man; the holy writ simply stated: 'And Enoch walked with God: and he was not, for God took him.'[9] Now in the dream he sees the reason for this eerie vanishing. A cloud descends and snatches the wise old man to Heaven before he could be killed. Milton in the dream is all these figures at once: the voice that whispers the story, the angel who retells it, the man who witnesses it, the mob who bay for Enoch's blood, the patriarch himself as he rushes through the heavens towards God. As he half woke from the dream Milton remembered St Paul's explanation of this moment: 'Enoch was translated that he should not see death; and was not found because God had translated him.'[10] To translate: *trans-latio*; to be carried over, to be carried between, to cross over; from dream to reality, from English to Latin, from Earth to Heaven. All this had faded when he woke; all of it flashes abruptly back as he sits at his desk, and he is able to hold onto its vividness.

Coming back to the present, he hears Marvell reading another sentence from the letter back to him: *Haec dum fraterne ac libere hortamur* . . . Enough, Milton butts in; write these words. And the words are still there, and they flow. Milton hears Marvell's nib scratch as he speaks: 'He looked, and saw wide territory spread /

Before him, towns, and rural works between / Cities of men with lofty gates and towers, / Concourse of arms, fierce faces threatening war . . .'[11]

◆

This scene is the latest of my attempts to place *Paradise Lost*; or rather, to continue circling around the fact that it cannot be securely placed in time. It's both certain that Milton planned the poem for decades, and uncertain exactly when he wrote it; it wasn't published until 1667, but it seems likely that the bulk of it was composed between the late 1650s and the early 1660s. I've already shown ways in which it seems to resonate with Milton's earlier experiences, from his encounters with Galileo and with Roman Catholic religion and architecture in Italy to his bitter wrestling with women's separateness in the divorce tracts. *Paradise Lost* seems to float over the entire latter half of Milton's life, while connecting with it at certain sharp and more clearly defined moments. And this is, in a sense, a mirror of my relationship with the poem. At times – reading a part of it slowly and with care, teaching it, trying to write about it – it lodges itself firmly in the forefront of my mind, consuming and exhausting my attention entirely. But parts of it – lines, phrases, mental pictures, memories of conversations – flash back at odder and less predictable moments, as if it's become just part of the clutter of my mind, enmeshed with my knot of rhythms.

I'm still not sure what it would mean to 'know' *Paradise Lost*: most obviously because it's too big, too dense with multiple suggestion at each moment; but also because of the sheer time that it takes to read and reread it, time that changes throughout the readings and between readings. In this chapter I aim to locate the poem amidst Milton's preoccupations in the 1650s, wagering that this was indeed when much of its writing was undertaken; but my deeper ambition is to try to describe in a more sustained way the kind of ongoing relationship – intoxicating, enthralling, frustrating – that this poem demands or solicits. The most honest account that I know of the demands of *Paradise Lost* comes from none other than Edgar Allan Poe, who acknowledges that it's impossible to reconcile 'the critical dictum that the "Paradise Lost" is to be devoutly admired throughout' with 'the absolute impossibility of maintaining for it, during perusal, the amount of enthusiasm which that critical dictum would demand'. For Poe, it's possible to enjoy *Paradise Lost* only 'as a series of minor poems': 'If, to preserve its Unity – its totality of effect or impression – we read it (as would be necessary) at a single sitting, the result is but a constant alternation of excitement and depression.'[12] Poe's point is that we can't easily read the poem all in one go, and that our experience of it must therefore involve a 'constant alternation' of responses – a rhythm, as I'd put it. The question of how to read and respond to *Paradise Lost* can't be answered singly and for all time, for any reader of the poem.

This is part of my motive for wanting to begin by placing at least part of the poem's composition in a scene that seems unsuited to it, the workaday world in which Milton spent much of the 1650s, translating letters in and out of Latin for the Cromwellian government. The leap that he made from civil servant back to epic poet is one of the most startling in a writing life that followed a remarkably tangled course of delays and changes of mind. I realise that I evaded this problem in my introduction by imagining Milton composing the poem in his last years, undistracted by other concerns, a prophet-poet and nothing more. But he must surely have been thinking the poem into being while he conducted his everyday governmental tasks. I can make sense of this up to a point – I've suggested above that Milton's continued movement between languages, and his confrontations with the bloody realities of religious persecution, might both have left their mark on his epic. But I don't want to imply that this in any way *explains* what *Paradise Lost* is like – quite the opposite. My interest lies rather in placing a moment from the poem in a possible scene of origin where I cannot make it smoothly fit. The question of how we imagine the beginnings of *Paradise Lost* is by no means incidental to how we understand the poem or its place in Milton's imaginative life. For this is a poem that is obsessed with beginnings – with what it means to begin creating, and with the challenges of relating oneself to beginnings that are unknown, beyond comprehension.

The most conspicuously strange feature of the opening of *Paradise Lost* itself is where Milton chooses *not* to start. His source material, the opening of Genesis, makes no bones about it: *b'reshit* in Hebrew, *in principio* in the Latin Vulgate, *in the beginning* in the English translations from Tyndale to King James, the Bible starts where all things start, and one might have expected Milton to do likewise. But he doesn't. After the opening invocation – to which I'll shortly return – he takes the reader instead to a scene that has no basis in scripture. This is initially the story not of the Creation or of the first human beings but of their tempter, 'Th'infernal Serpent', after he had been cast 'out from Heav'n, with all his Host / Of rebel Angels'. The first perspective that we occupy, the first glimpse we get of the world of the poem, is his. It's via 'his baleful eyes' that we peer as

>   *he views*
> *The dismal situation waste and wild,*
> *A Dungeon horrible, on all sides round*
> *As one great furnace flamed, yet from those flames*
> *No light, but rather darkness visible*
> *Served only to discover sights of woe . . .*[13]

There are few details, but that's the point. The wonderful oxymoron that I discussed in the introduction, 'darkness visible', encapsulates the scene: we see acutely that there's little to be seen. It's only at the end of this sequence, when we've spent some time sharing his view, that the figure is given his famous name, with deliberate belatedness: 'To whom th' Arch-Enemy, / And thence in Heaven called Satan, with bold words / Breaking the horrid silence thus began.' 'Thence' – meaning 'from then on' – is wonderfully ambiguous: it might mean, more generally, from the moment of his fall Satan assumed this name in Heaven; but there's the simultaneous suggestion that it means from *this* moment, taking on his true nature only at the very moment that we read these words.

The poem throws us into intimate proximity with Satan, seeing what he sees and feeling what he feels, and makes us stay there for hundreds of lines before we encounter a divine or human being. We soon feel the physical drag and heft of his huge body as he drags himself from the burning lake – lines that, as I discussed earlier, are studded with remembrances of Galileo and of Vallombrosa, as if Milton's mind returned to Italy when at its most arduously physical. Choosing this startling opening scene does several things at once. It tilts the reader's immediate sympathies in Satan's direction, as many readers have observed, in delighted and worried ways: William Blake, most famously, claimed that Milton 'was a true poet and of the Devil's party without knowing it', but every reader is in a sense of the devil's party even before they are exposed to his inner turmoil or his soaring rhetoric, by virtue of almost inhabiting his body. Beyond this troubling intimacy, it also makes clear that this is a poem that is going to do strange and bold things with its reader's sense of time. It will begin not at the beginning but with an unexpected part of the middle. And if Poe is right that it's hard to keep all of *Paradise Lost* in mind at once, this is partly because of its tangled, complicated plot. It begins in Hell and then, as we've earlier seen, moves across Chaos and past the Paradise of Fools, then to Heaven and finally to Eden; but the Angel Raphael then flashes back and tells Adam of the War in Heaven and of the creation of the heavens and of Earth, giving us the biblical beginning that we might have initially expected, but lodging it in the middle and relaying it via another's voice. Only thereafter do we witness the Fall and its aftermath. From its very beginning, Milton announces both that his poem will contain within itself many kinds of time and experiences of time – satanic, angelic, human, divine – and that it will ask its reader to experience time differently, to follow it through twists and reversals that, although the story has a foregone conclusion, make it genuinely uncertain what part of what happened will happen next, and how.

If Milton makes his poem's beginning into something of a surprise and a problem for the reader to wrestle with, he carries this problem of origins and starting points deep into the poem itself. In book 5, as Raphael retells Satan's fomenting of rebellion against God, he describes

Abdiel, the one virtuous and strident angel amongst thousands, who objects: 'Shalt thou give Law to God, shalt thou dispute / With him the points of liberty, who made / Thee what thou art, and formed the powers of Heaven / Such as he pleased, and circumscribed their being?' Satan's response to Abdiel's scolding is extraordinary:

> *That we were formed then sayest thou? and the work*
> *Of secondary hands, by task transferred*
> *From father to his son? Strange point and new!*
> *Doctrine which we would know whence learnt: who saw*
> *When this creation was? Rememberest thou*
> *Thy making, while the Maker gave thee being?*
> *We know no time when we were not as now;*
> *Know none before us, self-begot, self-raised*
> *By our own quickening power . . .*[14]

Satan's denial of ever having been created, his claim to have made himself, has attracted a degree of ridicule. C. S. Lewis scoffs that 'the being too proud to admit derivation from God, has come to rejoice in believing that he "just grew" like Topsy or a turnip.'[15] There is undeniably something comical about Satan's denial, which is reminiscent of those moments when small children struggle with, or are threatened by, the idea of a time before they were born, which can't have existed because they don't remember it. But, rather than this making Satan obviously ridiculous, the comparison might actually suggest that he's struggling with a real issue, a genuinely perplexing stage of individual development. There's real psychological penetration on Milton's part here. It's often been observed that Abdiel, 'the fervent Angel' who stood alone against Satan – 'his zeal / None seconded' – is a figure for Milton's sense of himself as a lone and heroic seeker for truth. But, as we've seen, his identifications are never straightforward, and Satan here also seems to represent a more troubling aspect of Milton's own imaginative inclinations. He's so sure of his own ability and potency, his own mighty capacity is so immediate and so tangible, that it seems easier to believe that he is somehow, in the face of logic, his own maker. The idea of having been created by someone else entirely is made to feel absurd, far-fetched. How could such a keenly felt individual existence be entirely dependent and reliant on another for its origins, or its continuation? Satan here is a kind of fantasy version of the Miltonic poet; the realisation of Milton's claim years earlier that a true poet 'ought him selfe to bee a true Poem'; that the poet, in making his works, makes and remakes himself. It is genuinely difficult – and Milton, I'm suggesting, felt this difficulty with extraordinary and productive force – to reconcile a sense of one's powerful individuality and separateness with the facts of one's own belatedness in time and dependence on others who come before. The answer that Satan provides may be wrong – logically, and, in Milton's view, theologically. But there's a quiet beauty in the line 'We know no time when we were not as now'. Many of Milton's sentences, famously, cascade across line breaks in their complicated unfolding. But this one, just as Satan aspires to do, stands alone, made up unusually of ten distinct monosyllabic words that quietly embody the separateness that he craves, even as this craving is already undermined by the repetition of *n* and *w* sounds that bind the words tightly together. In this moment the force of present certainty is all that seems to matter.

The fact that Satan can't recall or make sense of his origins makes his resemblance to the human reader of *Paradise Lost* greater than that of either Adam or Eve. Eve, as we saw in the last chapter, can recall and relate her first moments of consciousness when she saw her face reflected in the pool and heard the divine voice; the same is true of Adam, who relates his own first moments to Raphael. He begins with a disclaimer – 'For Man to tell how human life began / Is hard; for who himself beginning knew?' – but in the event it doesn't seem all that hard. He is able to recollect the first moments in which he awoke 'In balmy sweat, which with his beams the sun / Soon dried, and on the reeking moisture fed', and to relate the process by which he perused his own body, and the world around him.[16] Adam and Eve might not recall the act of creation itself, but neither are they haunted by a sense of having developed from a source, and in a manner, that they can only imperfectly recall and reconstruct. This is an aspect of human development that Satan experiences first, and that seems to begin for people only with the Fall. Only then does the question of how to begin when one has already begun, how to create freely when one is created, become a problem. But it's been a problem for the fallen reader of *Paradise Lost*, as I've already suggested, from its very beginning – not just via the choice to start in the middle of things with Satan, but via Milton's famous opening invocation. *Paradise Lost* gets underway like this:

> *Of man's first disobedience, and the fruit*
> *Of that forbidden tree, whose mortal taste*
> *Brought death into the world, and all our woe,*
> *With loss of Eden, till one greater man*
> *Restore us, and regain the blissful seat,*
> *Sing heavenly Muse, that on the secret top*
> *Of Oreb, or of Sinai, didst inspire*
> *That shepherd who first taught the chosen seed,*
> *In the beginning how the heavens and earth*
> *Rose out of chaos: or if Sion hill*
> *Delight thee more, and Siloa's brook that flowed*
> *Fast by the oracle of God, I thence*
> *Invoke thy aid to my advent'rous song,*
> *That with no middle flight intends to soar*
> *Above the Aonian mount, while it pursues*
> *Things unattempted yet in prose or rhyme.*[17]

There's much to say about these opening lines, but what's most important to me – what's easy to overlook, because they've become so famous – is their own conspicuous strangeness.[18] Even before we meet Satan, these lines make clear that this is a poem which has problems with its own origins, and wants to make them a problem for us. Milton's long and highly complicated sentence structure, his way of running the sense of the words across several lines, his stretching of the norms of English grammar to its limits: all are on conspicuous display. If these are part of what makes the poem difficult for its readers, I experience this opening difficulty differently when I connect it with Milton's obsession with origins and createdness later in the poem. These opening sixteen lines are a single sentence; if it's impossible to hold it together as one thought then this is our induction into the fact that, as Poe observed, this vast and complicated poem refuses to be experienced as a whole. And it seems to capture something both of Satan's proud insistence on singularity and Abdiel's insistence on dependence and indebtedness – a paradox captured by the fact that the sentence ends, as I observed in an earlier chapter, with a claim to originality that is borrowed from Galileo's favourite poet, Ariosto. The opening lines begin with marked strangeness – 'Of' is an awkward word with which to start a sentence – and exacerbate it by keeping us waiting a full six lines for the main verb that we know must be coming: 'Sing heavenly Muse'. But these words are a surprise of their own. The second word of the poem, 'man's', establishes a relationship with one of Milton's most important sources and models, Virgil's *Aeneid*, which begins '*Arma virumque cano*', 'I sing of arms and of the man', where '*virum*', 'of the man', is again the second word. But whereas Virgil's verb *cano* – 'I sing' – immediately makes his agency and his responsibility clear, Milton does not give us 'Of man's first disobedience . . . I sing', as we might expect. He eventually issues a call to his heavenly muse to sing, not a claim to be doing so himself. Responsibility for the poem's genesis is oddly shared, distributed. For all Milton's reputation for towering egoism, we do not read the word 'I' until the twelfth line.

It would be wrong, I'm suggesting, to assume that our aim in reading these lines should be to make sense of them, if this means becoming so familiar with them that we overlook their deliberate awkwardness and strangeness, their balance between indebtedness and originality, between claiming and disavowing a voice. We do better if we remember, behind their local intricacies and complications, a message at once simple and haunting: it is not, and should not be, easy to begin.

Paradise Lost was not the only work into which it is likely Milton poured his efforts during these years that remains difficult to pin down precisely in time, and that is preoccupied with the question of beginnings. In 1823 a document was discovered as part of a bundle of transcriptions of Milton's state papers in a cupboard in Whitehall: a long and unfinished theological manuscript written in Latin, divided into sections and with extensive marginal notes and corrections. It was quickly identified as Milton's own work. This was the text, thought lost, to which Edward Phillips referred in his biography of his uncle when, after describing his activities as a schoolteacher in the early 1640s, he wrote that Milton's 'next work . . . was the writing from his own dictation, some part, from time to time, of a Tractate which he saw fit to collect from the ablest of Divines . . . a perfect system of divinity'.[19] Debate has raged ever since about this work, which was given the title *De Doctrina Christiana*. First of all about whether Milton was, as is now generally accepted, its true author; and secondly over the extent to which the deeply idiosyncratic theology that the manuscript turned out to contain was reflected in his poetry, especially in *Paradise Lost*.

De Doctrina Christiana is not an easy read. It weaves together around eight thousand citations from scripture with Milton's own complicated scholastic Latin, and is clearly a work in progress. Milton probably began this project after he returned from his travels, inspired by the variety of theological opinion and error that he'd encountered in France and Italy. But it is staggering to imagine him continuing as he lost his sight, expanding and correcting the text with the help of the scribes and assistants in whose handwriting the surviving manuscript is written, and relying upon his own astonishing memory. If this work seems, like *Paradise Lost*, to float over many years of Milton's creative life, then this seems apt: the points at which the treatise and the poem resonate most excitingly with one another precisely concern the questions of creation, and of the place of creation in time, that I've just been suggesting are so insistently raised in Milton's poem.

One crucial point that emerges from *De Doctrina* is that Milton did not subscribe to the doctrine of the Holy Trinity in anything like the same manner as most Christians of his time, or indeed afterwards. According to most accounts of the Trinity, Father, Son, and Holy Spirit are distinct but equal aspects of a Godhead that is mysteriously both three and one at once. They are, crucially, *coeternal*, all held to exist beyond the vicissitudes of human time, and to have always done so. Time, according to most versions of this Trinitarian view, begins only with God's creation of the world. *In the beginning*, the opening words of Genesis, marks not only the beginning of creation but the beginning of the idea of beginning itself.

Milton views things very differently. For him, the Father precedes, and creates, the Son; the Son is perpetual – he will never cease to exist once created – but not eternal, or timeless. Those who argue otherwise, Milton insists, do so pointlessly, since 'in the whole of scripture they have been able to find no verse with which they might prove the Son's eternal generation'.[20] He, by contrast, is determined to ground his position in meticulous readings of biblical verses. He zooms in on the second of the Psalms, the texts that had attracted him since his schooldays, where God is quoted as saying 'Thou art my Son; this day have I begotten thee'; in Milton's Latin, '*Filius meus es tu, ego hodiè genui te*'.[21] In keeping with his insistent biblical literalism, Milton takes this verse, later cited by St Paul in his Epistle to the Hebrews, entirely at face value: the Son was begotten by the Father, rather than being coeternal with him; and, as the word *hodiè*, 'today', proves, this begetting happened at a particular moment in time. This, not the creation of the world, was when time must have begun. 'Therefore God begot the Son by his decree, and likewise in time [*in tempore genuit Deus Filium*]; for the decree must have preceded the decree's execution, as the added word "today" sufficiently declares.'[22]

This might not seem, to modern eyes, like an earth-shattering distinction. Two points, however, need to be made. The first is that, while problems with the orthodox doctrine of the Trinity – especially the flimsiness of its basis in scripture – had long been acknowledged (they were the basis of the co-called Arian Heresy in the fourth century CE), to deny it was still seen as among the most dangerous ideas that one could articulate in the seventeenth century. Among the dazzling variety of views espoused by the many religious sects and individuals who sprang into prominence in the revolutionary years of the late 1640s – and with whom Milton, as we saw in the last chapter, was sometimes associated on the basis of his views on divorce – anti-Trinitarianism was seen as one of the most dangerous. Particularly prominent were figures who were described as Socinians, followers of the Italian Fausto Sozzino, who had moved to Raków in Poland where his ideas flourished, and from where these ideas gradually made their way into the Netherlands and thence to England. The most prominent English Socinians, Paul Best and John Biddle, were repeatedly imprisoned for espousing these views, with many divines calling for their executions.[23]

Milton was not a Socinian, though he expressed ambiguous sympathy for their views, with which his had significant common ground. Socinians also brought God into closer contact with human time, though they went further, claiming that the freedom of the human will precluded God from certain knowledge of future events.[24] Milton may have been involved in licensing the most important of the Socinian writings, the Racovian Catechism, in the early 1650s, and certainly his governmental role seems to have brought him into contact with a wide range of radical religious writings.[25] He also owned a copy of the most controversial religious manuscript of the age, Jean Bodin's *Colloquium Heptaplomeres*, in which seven figures debate their respective outlooks: a Catholic, a Jew, a Muslim, a Lutheran, a Calvinist, a sceptic, and a figure close to deism or natural religion. This work was deemed to be so dangerous because of the views to which its participants gave voice and respectability, which included anti-Trinitarianism and the validity of divorce.[26] By writing his personal theology in learned and abstruse Latin, Milton was clearly closer to Bodin's kind of learned controversy than the vernacular pyrotechnics of sectarians like Gerrard Winstanley or Abiezer Coppe, but this doesn't change the fact that he held views that many of his contemporaries would have seen as shockingly radical.

Putting Milton's theological views in this context helps to clarify the stakes, but it doesn't explain what attracted him to this position; nor, more importantly, does it explain why I think that, for all their apparent abstruseness, these debates can help me understand the power that his works hold for me despite my not sharing any of his theological commitments. Why was anti-Trinitarianism such a dangerous, terrifying stance for so many people? One of the key reasons, I think, is that it drew the Godhead closer to the human world; it separated Christ from God, and, as we've seen, brought him closer to the contingencies of human time. It makes the distance between human and divine less absolute and uncrossable. To its opponents, this appears to be a slippery slope towards atheism and idolatry, to a confusion of divine and human that ends with the former being abolished. But for Milton, I think, this was its attraction. For all its apparent dryness, the theology of *De Doctrina* seems, to me, to represent an inseparable mixture of Milton's theological convictions and his personal obsessions. Here too he seems torn between assertions of absolute separateness and individuality, on the one hand, and possibilities of deep interconnectedness on the other. He objects to the identity of Father and Son in the simplest of terms: it is incoherent to claim that the Son is 'numerically of the same essence as the Father – in that case the Father and his Son would be the same person!'[27] Whereas orthodoxy would simply suggest that this mystery must be accepted as an article of faith, Milton bridles at such obfuscation. It offends his sense of the necessary integrity of the individual. The Son must be genuinely separate and distinct from the Father if he is to be anything at all.

And yet, precisely by effecting this separation, Milton makes the Son something like the highest point in the series that runs from God to humankind, rather than making him absolutely other in his divinity. And it is this that becomes clearer when we turn to the shape these ideas take in *Paradise Lost*. I showed in chapter 8 that Milton put into the voice of the Angel Raphael a view of Creation comprised of 'one first matter all / Indued with various forms, various degrees / Of substance', a vision that is at once hierarchical and molten, allowing for movement towards and away from the divine, and in which all the parts are integrally connected.

The Son as he appears in *Paradise Lost* is distinct from the Father, and functions more like the foremost of the angels, the very highest of the degrees of being below, and yet connected with, the Father. He takes on his true nature not all in one moment but gradually, over time: he is created, he is elevated to pre-eminence, and then he offers to become man so as to take the sins of humankind upon him. The closeness to the theology of *De Doctrina* is confirmed at the moment of his elevation, when God tells the angels: 'This day I have begot whom I declare / My only Son, and on this holy hill / Him have anointed, whom ye now behold / At my right hand.'[28] *This day*: the *hodiè* of Psalm 2 returns, confirming that we are witnessing not just a story told in time for the sake of our limited, mortal understandings, but the inception of time itself.

Milton, as I showed in chapter 4, launched his true poetic career with the Nativity Ode, in which he wrestled with the problem of divine timelessness and human time-boundedness, trying to cross the gap between them with the deft slipperiness of his language. While there's no reason to think that he was already harbouring unorthodox views on the Trinity at this early stage, we did see him, in that poem and in the unfinished attempt to confront the spectacle of the Passion, struggling to apprehend Christ in time and in language. *Paradise Lost* brings back this problem in a new and massive way. Here Milton has not just the Son but the Father in his story. Many readers – and I number among them – have struggled with the way in which he depicts God the Father as harsh, cruel, shrilly self-justifying. He is both certain that the Fall will happen, and certain that it is not his responsibility: 'So will fall', he pronounces of Adam, 'He and his faithless progeny: whose fault? / Whose but his own? Ingrate, he had of mee / All he could have.'[29] There have been many attempts to justify Milton's depiction, and many denunciations of it, most thunderously by William Empson, for whom the appallingness of Milton's God simply reveals and confirms the appallingness of its model: 'The Christian God the Father . . . is the wickedest thing yet invented by the black heart of man.'[30]

Although I've been aiming here to unfold some of the peculiarities of Milton's theological position and the way that it inflected
Paradise Lost, I'm ultimately less interested in judging whether he
succeeds or fails in his stated aim – to 'justify the ways of God' –
than in the struggle itself. This, for all the dry reason of *De Doctrina*
and the sinuous eloquence of *Paradise Lost*, is what I derive from
reading the two together – a sense of an individual mind struggling
to reconcile the traditions of belief that he has inherited with the
deep convictions that he has developed in the course of his life. It
is this sense of struggle itself, and the way in which it engages every
part of Milton's remarkable intellectual and imaginative capacities,
that I find most compelling. Both works provide the powerful sense
that to receive a tradition and to make it one's own is a difficult,
complicated, and protracted process. It requires – and I'll return
to this point – a seemingly paradoxical combination of the ability
to *receive* and the ability to *remake*, to suspend one's individuality
and to assert it.

The theology that Milton developed in the final years of his life
was so idiosyncratic that it's impossible to align him with any
broader Christian group or denomination – in fact, so novel was
his conception of the Father and the Son that it's debatable whether
he can be considered a Christian at all, in any of the conventional
senses. Yet it's precisely as a figure operating at the outer limits of
traditions he nonetheless struggles to make his own that I find
myself relating to him most strongly. My years of teaching Milton
have led me to the odd conclusion that being a fascinated outsider
to his ways of believing and imagining – both as an atheist and as
a Jew – makes it easier, rather than harder, to begin engaging with
them. This is because, I've found, the students whom I've taught
often have a vague sense of, for example, the doctrine of the
Incarnation or of the Trinity, but less of a sense that what a person
is being asked to believe by accepting these doctrines is in any way
strange or shocking. Indeed, admitting that a given belief might
seem strange or shocking might sound like an attack on that belief
or on the person who holds it. But this seems wrong to me. My
sense from my earliest years that believing in Jesus was *something*

that other people did – the fact that my grandmother was raised never to touch a New Testament; that a boy on her street told her at a young age that she killed Christ – have made me genuinely curious: *what would it mean to believe, really to believe, these wilfully strange things, to build one's life around them?* I found a cheerful insistence upon the necessary strangeness of Christian belief in a wonderful book by the scholar M. A. Screech, who was also an ordained priest, and who wrote that

> The Christian religion did seem particularly stupid and absurd to both the Jewish and the gentile worlds in which it first appeared. Two millennia of existence, marked by long periods of dominance, have blunted this stark fact. For Jews and for Gentiles the three basic doctrines of Christian belief were not merely unlikely, unproven or distasteful: they were daft. These doctrines are the Incarnation, the Crucifixion and the Resurrection of the body.[31]

St Paul claimed that 'the preaching of the cross is to them that perish foolishness; but unto us which are saved it is the power of God'; this is not just a dismissal of those too foolish to believe, but an acknowledgement that belief requires the acceptance of the apparently foolish – the daft, to use Screech's term. Belief in the seemingly foolish is not how we tend to understand faith, but Screech insists that we should. We've seen Milton struggle with the first two of these doctrines, the Incarnation and the Crucifixion, and we'll see at the end of the next chapter that he took an equally unique approach to the resurrection of the body. He does not seem to have found the central tenets of Christianity any easier to swallow than I do, in the form that he encountered them. But perhaps, I'm suggesting, it's the act of witnessing a genuinely complicated and vexed attempt to exist within a tradition that I do not share that helps me to think through my own complicated and vexed relationship to the traditions within which I do exist. Reading *Paradise Lost* involves a relationship much more complicated than simply sharing, or not sharing, the beliefs that it contains. It makes us confront at every turn the question of what we can make, for ourselves, of the ideas and beliefs that we receive.

I've once again found myself approaching Milton's struggles to make sense of the central tenets of his religion through my own position as a Jewish atheist. I also feel emboldened to make the connection here because it resonates in other ways with Milton's activities during the 1650s that formed the background to his theological and poetic creations. There was much interest in Jews in England in the 1650s, focused around the question of whether they should be officially readmitted to the country, having been expelled in 1290. As with modern forms of philosemitism among evangelical Christians, this was based less on any deep-felt respect for Jews qua Jews, and more on the widespread belief among various kinds of Puritan that their readmission was a necessary step towards the second coming of Christ, which was broadly anticipated. The most significant figure among these Puritan philosemites was Oliver Cromwell himself.[32] Milton, however, seems to have been less concerned with Jews who were his contemporaries than with the ways in which Jewish history offered both cautionary tales to the English as they rid themselves of their own king and resources for working out what they should do next. In *The Tenure of Kings and Magistrates*, published in the weeks after Charles I's execution, Milton claimed that 'generally the people of Asia, and with them the Jews also, especially since they chose a King against the advice and counsel of God, are noted by wise Authors much inclinable to slavery.'[33] Jews are orientalised, seen as intrinsically servile in the manner invariably ascribed to Asian people, and both groups contrast with the innate talent for freedom that the English must cultivate. This was part of a tendency, which stretches far beyond Milton, to divide the world into naturally free and slavish peoples, partly in order to justify the enslavement of the latter.[34] It's worth recalling here that Milton engaged with slavery in the abstract at the very moment when it was becoming an increasingly important basis of England's economic prosperity. His work for the common-wealth government coincided with the rise of sugar plantations in the West Indies, and a huge growth in the numbers of African slaves there. According to one estimate, the numbers grew from 11,200 white farmers and 5,680 black slaves in 1645, the year that Milton published his collected early poems, to 745 plantation owners and 83,023 slaves in 1667, the year that *Paradise Lost* was published.[35] This grim context enters Milton's writings in only the most fleeting and oblique of ways, even as he refers constantly to slavery as a fate that the English must avoid. In *Of Reformation* the worst fate he could imagine for enemies of the true Church was to be sent to Hell, where others among the damned would 'exercise a Raving and Bestial Tyranny over them as their Slaves and Negroes'.[36]

In the course of his political writings in the late 1640s and 1650s, Milton's discussions and uses of Jewish materials grew more complex. He was one of a number of scholars who began to read the Hebrew Bible not just as a repository of wisdom but as a form of political constitution, but he was unprecedentedly bold in his willingness to connect his readings of scripture with the politics of his immediate moment, and was the first writer to use it to make an overt argument against the institution of monarchy and unequivocally in favour of republicanism. Having emphasised the innate slavishness of the Jews in the *Tenure*, later in the same treatise he changed tack and suggested that God's anger with the Israelites proved to pious English people that 'he will bless us, and be propitious to us who reject a King to make him [i.e. God] onely our leader and supreme governor'.[37] Any people, Milton suggests – not just the original chosen people – can make God and not the supposed king their monarch, a revolutionary proposal indeed.

In the early 1650s Milton was sucked into another back and forth of polemical treatises, but this time on a European rather than national scale. The regicide had shocked rulers across the Continent, and defeated royalists sought to take advantage by commissioning the learned French Protestant Claude de Saumaise, known as Salmasius, to denounce it. Milton was asked to reply, and so began an exchange of bitter diatribes and ostentatious displays of learning with Salmasius and other antagonists, which produced Milton's first and second *Defences of the English People*. Here too the politics of the Hebrew Bible were violently contested. Milton's conclusion, when he re-entered the debate surrounding Deuteronomy and 1 Samuel against Salmasius, was that his opponent had been forced to 'admit that some of their rabbis deny that their fathers should have recognised any king but God, though such a king was given to punish them. I follow the opinion of those rabbis.'[38] Milton was the first Christian reader to interpret the Rabbis of the Midrash as arguing, absolutely and unequivocally, 'that it is a form of idolatry to ask for a king, who demands that he be worshipped and granted honours like those of a god'.[39]

If Milton turned to ancient and scriptural examples to justify republicanism in these years, he also looked to contemporary exemplars of political conduct, and especially to the figure of Oliver Cromwell himself. To admirers and detractors of his meteoric rise alike, Cromwell, riding at the head of the New Model Army, had become a personification of military efficiency, manly prowess, and dispassionate self-certainty. Milton recognised and described this in an unpublished sonnet 'To the Lord General Cromwell', which began: 'Cromwell, our chief of men, who through a cloud / Not of war only, but detractions rude, / Guided by faith and matchless fortitude / To peace and truth thy glorious way hath ploughed'.[40] By the time of his Latin *Defences* of the 1650s, however, Milton had shifted to offering a complex mixture of praise and cautionary advice to Cromwell, idealising him as a paragon of godly manliness – possessing expertise 'not just of military science, but of religion and piety' – but also warning him to 'suffer not that liberty, which you have gained with so many hardships, so many dangers, to be violated by yourself, or in any wise impaired by others'.[41] Paradoxically Cromwell's example threatened to destabilise the manly ideal that he embodied precisely by pushing it to an extreme. He seemed to his enemies – and, in time, to his erstwhile allies, including Milton – to possess masculine force to a kind of monstrous excess. This was especially the case as his own power grew. Cromwell was already the most powerful individual in the land following the execution of Charles I in 1649. He spent the next two years conducting brutal military campaigns, especially in Ireland, and upon his return he grew frustrated with the Rump Parliament's failure to pursue constitutional reform and pious reformation and dissolved it, with power passing to a new Council of State that he headed – a godly military coup. At the end of 1653 Cromwell was sworn in as Lord Protector, the role that he would hold until his death, but its nature was transformed in 1657 following a debate on kingship, resulting in the issuing of a 'Humble Petition' that made Cromwell king in all but name. When he was reinvested as Lord Protector he sat in the coronation chair that had been used ever since 1308, and wore a robe of purple velvet lined with ermine.

Milton's response to Cromwell is difficult to chart. Certainly in the early days of the English Republic – having been awarded his position as Secretary for Foreign Tongues, in twin recognition of his exceptional linguistic talents and his wholehearted defence of the regicide – he devoted himself fully to its service. One of his first assigned tasks was to draft some observations on the obstacles to peace in Ireland, to be printed as an appendix to the *Articles of Peace Made and Concluded with the Irish Rebels* that the committee were preparing to print in anticipation of Cromwell's campaigns there. Milton produced a depressing and often sickening document, using baroque details of the massacres committed by the Catholic rebels in the early 1640s – 'the bloud of more than 200000 . . . assassinated and cut in pieces by those Irish Barbarians' – to justify Cromwell's campaigns, which included the appalling massacres at Drogheda and Wexford.[42] A long-standing hatred of Catholics and willingness to take advantage of anti-Catholic panic in England made it easy for Milton to advocate and legitimise the most vicious forms of colonial violence.

While Milton had no problem justifying brutality in Ireland, however, he seems to have shared widespread concerns about Cromwell's colonial ambitions, but for practical rather than ethical reasons. As English strength at sea grew through the 1650s, the Lord Protector aspired to challenge Spain for gold and for territory in pursuit of a grand naval empire.[43] Some in England welcomed these ambitions as the realisation of England's divine mission. But others – especially those as well versed as Milton in the writings of Roman historians and their more recent Italian commentators – were more nervous.[44] In the early 1650s Milton had a scribe copy into his commonplace book a summary of Machiavelli's view that 'It is not for any state to expand the boundaries of its empire by war and to reduce other nations to its sway; indeed it is dangerous to do so unless that state be virtuously established [*probe instituta sit*].'[45] Both Cromwell's imperial ambitions and his ascent towards a more lavish form of pseudo-kingship by the late 1650s seemed to embody this risk. While Milton remained a loyal and diligent servant of the state, his own attitude to Cromwell seems to have shifted from the warnings and admonitions mixed into the praise of the Latin *Defences* to outright disillusionment as Cromwell became a king in all but name.[46]

For the remainder of this chapter I want to return to *Paradise Lost* via the feature of Milton's life in the 1650s that I have touched upon repeatedly but felt unable to inhabit, the aspect that is both the most famous and the hardest to understand: his blindness. It feels apt to ask how we approach Milton's blindness at this particular point, since its significance had been one of the issues that he and his opponents fiercely debated in the 1650s. Once his blindness became widely known following his defence of the regicide, every attack on Milton crowed that the loss of his sight was proof of divine judgement. The preface to *Regii sanguinis clamor ad coelum*, one of the attacks that prompted his Latin *Defences*, sought to meet Milton on his own learned territory, applying to him a verse from Virgil's *Aeneid*: '*Monstrum horrendum, informe, ingens, cui lumen ademptum*'; a horrifying monster, formless, huge, devoid of sight. Milton defended himself on two fronts: he cited reams of examples, classical and biblical, of virtuous blind figures; and he insisted that the loss of his sight was a necessary sacrifice in the service of liberty, and a willing one.[47] He knew that his sight was fading, and persisted regardless. Milton wrote a sonnet to his friend Cyriack Skinner marking three years since 'these eyes, though clear / To outward view, of blemish or of spot; / Bereft of light, their seeing have forgot'; his consolation, he explained, was 'to have lost them over-plied / In liberty's defence, my noble task, / Of which all Europe talks from side to side'.[48] A double consolation, in fact: the rightness of his cause, and his burnished Continental reputation.

Writing *Paradise Lost*, Milton would again take advantage of the long-standing association of blindness with inner prophetic illumination and poetic virtuosity. This is especially the case at the start of book 3, when, about to introduce God the Father as a speaking character, Milton again invokes the aid of a higher power, here described as 'holy light'. He can still, he insists,

> *feel thy sovereign vital lamp; but thou*
> *Revisitst not these eyes, that roll in vain*
> *To find thy piercing ray, and find no dawn;*
> *So thick a drop serene hath quenched their orbs,*
> *Or dim suffusion veiled.*

In lines of superb beauty and poignancy, he continues, still addressing the heavenly light:

> *Then feed on thoughts, that voluntary move*
> *Harmonious numbers; as the wakeful bird*
> *Sings darkling, and in shadiest covert hid*
> *Tunes her nocturnal note. Thus with the year*
> *Seasons return, but not to me returns*
> *Day, or the sweet approach of even or morn,*
> *Or sight of vernal bloom, or summers rose,*
> *Or flocks, or herds, or human face divine;*
> *But cloud instead, and ever-during dark*
> *Surrounds me, from the cheerful ways of men*
> *Cut off, and for the book of knowledge fair*
> *Presented with a universal blank*
> *Of nature's works to me expunged and raised,*
> *And wisdom at one entrance quite shut out.*

So much the rather thou celestial light
Shine inward, and the mind through all her powers
Irradiate, there plant eyes, all mist from thence
Purge and disperse, that I may see and tell
Of things invisible to mortal sight.[49]

Milton is more willing in these wonderful lines than he was while under attack in his political writings to admit to the losses of blindness, the lines rehearsing in their own tumbling beauty the sequence of phenomena that Milton can no longer experience. With characteristic virtuosity, as his sentences again stretch across several lines, he uses the line breaks to accentuate the experiences being expressed. Lamenting that he is 'from the cheerful ways of men / Cut off', the cutting of the line itself enacts an isolating lurch. Explaining that he experiences only 'a universal blank / Of nature's works', that hauntingly abstract phrase, 'universal blank', is made for a fleeting moment to hover at the end of the line before it is completed.

Even as he acknowledges these devastating losses, however, the lines as a whole offer the same logic of compensation that characterised his Latin *Defences* and the sonnet to Cyriack Skinner. Milton consoles himself once again by keeping in mind 'Those other two equalled with me in fate, / So were I equalled with them in renown, / Blind Thamyris and blind Maeonides, / And Tiresias and Phineus prophets old'.[50] While I am moved by these lines, they move within a logic of loss and recuperation that seems a bit too neat and tidy for the complicated ways in which, I think, Milton's blindness informs the poetry of *Paradise Lost*.

It's suggestive that Milton made mention in the sonnet to Skinner of the clear, unclouded appearance of his no-longer-functioning eyes, since this points towards his own interest in the physiological causes and nature of his blindness. So too does the phrase 'drop serene' in the lines quoted from *Paradise Lost*, which is equivalent to the Latin phrase *gutta serena*, the diagnosis that Milton believed applied to his blindness. In 1654 Milton wrote a letter to the Greek physician Leonard Philaras, giving a remarkably detailed description of his experiences as he went blind. What's striking, as with the physiological phrases in his poems, is the way in which he rooted these experiences in the entirety of his body and its condition. This is true not just of his remarkably kinetic and even sonic descriptions of his waning vision itself, and the way in which, 'as sight daily diminished, colours proportionately darker would burst forth with violence and a sort of crash from within'. The most surprising part of the letter from a modern perspective is Milton's observation that 'I noticed my sight becoming weak and growing dim, and at the same time my spleen and all my viscera burdened and shaken with flatulence.' He continued to link its progression to his eating habits: 'Certain permanent vapours seem to have settled upon my entire forehead and temples, which press and oppress my eyes with a sort of sleepy heaviness, especially from mealtime to evening.'[51] In linking his blindness to digestive disorders, Milton was following received medical wisdom. While seventeenth-century medicine was made up of an increasingly complex patchwork of theories, the ancient model of the body's balance of humours was still widely adhered to, and the notion that blindness could be caused by a build-up of bad humours in the body, eventually clouding the eyes, was far from outlandish.[52] But this common understanding takes on new significance. By connecting blindness to disorders attendant upon eating, Milton makes it part of his broader concern with the ways in which the individual encounters, takes in, and is transformed by the world, for better or worse, as we saw in chapter 8 with his interest in angelic digestion as a form of internal transubstantiation.

Rather than pursuing his blindness further in relation to seventeenth-century medicine, however, I find it more fruitful to take a broader view and approach Milton, once again, via one of his curious and passionate modern admirers – the unclassifiable Argentinian writer Jorge Luis Borges, fabulist, poet, and librarian, who himself went blind in later life. Borges's enthusiasm for Milton was lifelong – he claimed to have spent a family visit to France in his teens 'reading a copy of Milton's works . . . instead of seeing Paris', and, he insisted, 'I don't regret it.'[53] He returned repeatedly to Milton's writings, from an essay on the decision not to write

Paradise Lost in rhyme to his poem 'Una rosa y Milton', and he is another of the modern writers whom I've mentioned – like Joyce and Beckett – whose admiration for Milton was part of a writing life that hovered between languages and national traditions. It was in 1977, a decade before his death and two decades after he had first begun to lose his sight, that Borges delivered a lecture titled 'Blindness' in which he ruminated on his relationship with Milton at greater length. 'Milton's blindness', Borges claims, 'was voluntary. He knew from the beginning that he was going to be a great poet.' And, he continues, 'I too, if I may mention myself, have always known that my destiny was, above all, a literary destiny.'[54] Beyond these direct comparisons of vocation, however, Borges is more concerned to rethink what blindness means, and, in particular, to deny that it is anything as straightforward as a loss of *something*, that something being sight. Blindness, he insists, 'should not be seen in a pathetic way. It should be seen as a way of life: one of the styles of living.'[55]

At first glance this seems close to Milton's recuperation of blindness as part of his prophetic gift. It's a tempting way to think because it fits with our desire to see disability as more than a straightforward loss. It also chimes with Milton's invocation to Holy Light and with his most direct treatment of his blindness outside *Paradise Lost*, the sonnet that begins 'When I consider how my light is spent, / Ere half my days, in this dark world and wide', and which worries that this blindness is pure loss, the wasting of 'that one Talent which is death to hide / Lodged with me useless'.[56] Borges writes strikingly of the phrase from the second line of this sonnet – 'this dark world and wide', a characteristic Miltonic formulation in which the second of two adjectives is separated from its noun – that it is 'a line one can tell was written by a blind man . . . It is precisely the world of the blind when they are alone, walking with hands outstretched, searching for props.'[57] He's not the only modern writer to turn to this sonnet in creative ways. The contemporary poet Monica Youn has produced a wonderful series of ruminations on this sonnet, taking the words that end its fourteen lines as her starting point. In her comment on the line that Borges discusses she writes: 'The "wide" is always haunted by surprise. In a dark world, the "wide" is the sudden door that opens on unfurling blackness, the void pooling at the bottom of the unlit stairs. To be bounded is our usual condition; to be open is anomalous, even excessive.'[58]

What these writings, exploring the intricacies of blindness as Milton conveys it, have collectively brought home to me is that our senses and mental and physical faculties are not like a box of separate tools, from which one can be lost, leaving a simple gap. Rather they're intricately intertwined, as part of a way of being in and relating to the world, and to lose one aspect is necessarily to change the whole. This, I think, is what Borges means when he calls blindness 'one of the styles of living', and it also illuminates what at first seems like the very alien nature of Milton's self-diagnosis, blindness as digestive disorder, since this too roots the loss of sight in the entirety of his bodily being, its operations and its imbalances. In particular, Borges's habit of looking to Milton as an example helps me understand the ways in which blindness might involve a transformed relation to time, in a way which resonates with my experiences of *Paradise Lost*. It seems to me no accident that Borges shared Milton's acute sensitivity to the nature of time. In an essay written once his sight had already begun to fade, Borges articulated a divided view on time that closely echoes the ambivalence that I sense in Milton's poems. On the one hand Borges insists that 'there is no such thing as "the life of a man," nor even "one night in his life." Each moment we live exists, not the imaginary combination of these moments.' This notion of every moment as richly distinct, utterly singular, able to be grasped and shaped in a new way, is one that Milton also seems to have striven towards, and that the experience of reading his poems often offers. On the other hand Borges was forced to conclude, with magnificent bathos:

And yet, and yet . . . Time is the substance of which I am made. Time is a river that sweeps me along, but I am the river; it is a tiger that mangles me, but I am the tiger; it is a fire that consumes me, but I am the fire. The world, unfortunately, is real; I, unfortunately, am Borges.[59]

The moments add up to a whole that seems to exceed and run away from individual control. Time makes us into something rather than us making something of it. This is the same tension between activity and passivity, between control and surrender, that I find everywhere characteristic of Milton's imagination; but through Borges, I'm better able to see it as tied up with the 'style of living' that blindness involved.

Near the end of his lecture on blindness Borges states:

A writer lives. The task of being a poet is not completed at a fixed schedule. No one is a poet from eight to twelve and from two to six. Whoever is a poet is one always, and is continually assaulted by poetry. I suppose a painter feels that colours and shapes are besieging him. Or a musician feels that the strange world of sounds – the strangest world of art – is always seeking him out, that there are melodies and dissonances looking for him.[60]

What comes through here, and illuminates Milton's work, is the way in which blindness inculcates both a newly powerful sense of activity – an ability to use language and time more self-consciously, like tools – and an equally pronounced experience of passivity, illuminating the way in which the artist is always at the mercy of his or her materials, rather than master of them. These discussions resonate with the most detailed and penetrating modern account of the experience of blindness and going blind that I know, in which John Hull writes:

When you are blind, a hand suddenly grabs you. A voice suddenly addresses you. There is no anticipation or preparation. There is no hiding around the corner. There is no lying low. I am grasped. I am greeted. I am passive in the presence of that which accosts me. I cannot escape it. Normal people can choose whom they want to speak to, as they wander around the streets or the market-place. People are already there for the sighted person; they have a presence prior to their being greeted, and the sighted person can choose whether or not to turn that presence into a relationship by addressing an acquaintance. For the blind person, people are in motion, they are temporal, they come and they go. They come out of nothing; they disappear. St Augustine has a parable about the human soul. He says it is like a bird which bursts into a large building, flutters for a while, and then finds an escape and disappears. This idea of being visited, of being blessed by receiving a visitation, seems to me to be quite important in the blind experience of other people.[61]

This paragraph made me think differently about the long-standing connection, of which Milton himself makes much, between blindness and inspiration. Precisely because there's a long tradition of linking the two, all the way back to Homer and Tiresias, I realised, reading Hull's words, that I hadn't truly wondered why the connection might feel so obvious; what it said about the experience of blindness itself, not just as lack or privation but as a style of being. Hull, like Borges and Youn, beautifully captures the way in which blindness involves a new way of experiencing both space and time – the way in which experience, 'haunted by surprise', becomes a series of relatively unanticipated arrivals, visitations. Sensitive though his description is, however, Hull illuminates only one dimension of Milton's experience of his blindness. To understand this fully I need to return a final time to *Paradise Lost*, and Milton's writing of it in earnest at the end of the 1650s.

Milton does at times emphasise his own passivity in a way that resembles John Hull's words: 'I am passive in the presence of that which accosts me.' His willingness to be patient, to allow the world to arrive in a way that does not depend upon his busy and frenetic action, is a crucial facet of his mind in these years, most famously captured in the line that ends his sonnet on his blindness: 'They also serve who only stand and wait.'[62] Inspiration too, *Paradise Lost* often suggests, needs to be waited for patiently, and if it only arrives when Milton's muse visits him at night, this is partly because it is only then that his activity is stilled, and his mind is able to be purely receptive. In the invocation to book 7 Milton tells his muse – whom he calls, for want of greater certainty about her name, Urania – that he is

> *not alone, while thou*
> *Visitst my slumbers nightly, or when morn*
> *Purples the east: still govern thou my song,*
> *Urania, and fit audience find, though few.*[63]

These lines capture in tight compass the opposing tendencies of Milton's poetic sense of himself: on the one hand the desire to surrender entirely to a higher voice and force – 'still govern thou my song', he pleads – and on the other hand, in the line immediately following, the sense of his own specialness and singularity, the claim that he is an elite poet writing for a small and elite cadre of admirers. Self-deletion vies with self-assertion, a desire for total passivity tangled with ambitions of magnificent activity.

These tensions run electrifyingly throughout the poem, and indeed throughout his life. What makes Milton so compelling to me is that he exhibits this basic conflict in such extreme and vivid form and manages to make beautiful things out of it. The figures who populate *Paradise Lost* are divided according to how fully they are able to be receptive, to remain open to visitations and encounters that not only change them but reveal their incompleteness and their dependency. Adam and Eve, as we've seen, host the Angel Raphael even as human and angel struggle fully to understand one another's experiences and stories. This is just one example of the way life in the Garden of Eden is a perpetual encounter with forms of being that are never fully commensurate with one another, but can transform one another in a process of ongoing mutual perfection that is only interrupted by the Fall. This is true of Adam and Eve's relationship both with one another and with the natural world that they tend and upon which they labour, and it's true too of the creatures with whom they share the garden, like the sporting lion who 'ramped, and in his paw / Dandled the kid'.[64] All of these created beings, collectively derived from 'one first matter all', are incomplete in isolation; though originating with God's creative agency, they now need one another in order to flourish. An inclination towards self-sufficiency is what in Milton's view had to be forcibly overcome in Eve when she was first created, and it is what leads to Satan's downfall when he cannot accept the fact of having being made and being dependent for his origins upon someone other than himself. He articulates a different version of the same problem when he arrives in Eden, and the spectacle of beauty makes him fleetingly regret his delusional earlier attempt to

> *in a moment quit*
> *The debt immense of endless gratitude,*
> *So burthensome, still paying, still to owe;*
> *Forgetful what from him I still received,*
> *And understood not that a grateful mind*
> *By owing owes not, but still pays, at once*
> *Indebted and discharged; what burden then?*[65]

Though Satan quickly moves past this moment of wavering regret and steels himself for his nefarious mission, it's the most penetrating moment of insight that he achieves. He acknowledges here that he could previously understand his relation to God only as a debt of an economic sort – a debt of the sort taken on by usurers like Milton himself, and his father. A debt that can be measured and quantified, and that can and must be repaid. As he has now come to realise, however, we can owe things in different ways. What he owes God is not the endless repayment of an undiminishable debt, as if God were some kind of fearsome eternal loan shark. Instead he owes him, as we still say, a debt of gratitude.[66] This is the kind of debt whose endlessness is not a perpetual burden to the one who owes it, but rather the starting point for an ongoing relationship that can change and develop precisely because it can never and should never be paid off. And this too is why I find Milton's vision so compelling despite my own atheism. For Milton, it is not necessary or useful to see the ways in which we relate ourselves to God as different in kind from all of the other relationships that make up our lives. Our relationship with all kinds of other creatures can glow newly with meaning once we understand them as startling visitations that we cannot and should not anticipate or seek to control, and should instead be grateful for. Isn't this how we experience the other beings with whom our lives periodically intersect? Isn't this how we experience the people whom we love?

But this glorious sense of openness, this willingness to receive and to be visited, to offer hospitality to that which exceeds us and promises to transform us, is, as I've suggested throughout this book, only one side of Milton's imagination. The desire for absolute singularity, special uniqueness, that Eve and God and Satan in their different ways experience, also reflects a scarcely less powerful imaginative compulsion on his part. If, in reading *Paradise Lost*, we are frequently led to think of it as the passive acceptance of a visitation, we're also constantly aware of the herculean labours of scholarship and imagination that went into it: of the *effort* made and sustained by an extraordinary individual who is responsible for everything that we read. Both of these impulses – a talent for self-forgetting and for self-assertion – are necessary to make art; both are necessary to make and live a life. What distinguishes Milton for me is that he exhibits them both in a more extreme form than any other writer I know, and that he makes us feel the impossible co-presence of these impulses at every moment in our reading of the poem.

I'll close by turning to my favourite example. It is a wonderfully gratuitous passage that follows the construction of Pandaemonium, the demonic palace that may have been inspired by St Peter's in Rome. We probably weren't wondering about which specific devil was responsible for its architecture, but Milton – was he recalling his discussions with Henry Wotton about the finest architects that Italy had to offer? – feels the need to tell us anyway:

> *The hasty multitude*
> *Admiring entered, and the work some praise*
> *And some the architect: his hand was known*
> *In heaven by many a towered structure high*
> . . .

Nor was his name unheard or unadored
In ancient Greece; and in Ausonian land
Men called him Mulciber; and how he fell
From heaven, they fabled, thrown by angry Jove
Sheer o'er the crystal battlements: from morn
To noon he fell, from noon to dewy eve,
A summer's day; and with the setting sun
Dropped from the zenith like a falling star,
On Lemnos th'Ægean isle: thus they relate,
Erring; for he with this rebellious rout
Fell long before . . .[67]

Time is deeply out of joint in this passage. We're told of this architect that he was widely admired: 'his hand was known / In heaven', 'Nor was his name unheard' in ancient Greece. And yet these two uses of 'was' are utterly different: the first refers back from the moment being described to the time before the devils' fall; the latter refers to something that has not yet happened so long as we are in Hell, since ancient Greece will not exist for centuries. The first takes its bearings from the time of the poem's action, the second from the time in which the reader reads. Milton slides from one to the other, marking the oddity by a typically heavy use of multiple negatives which makes us question what exactly is being asserted: '*Nor* was his name *un*heard or *un*adored'. We move from the time of Hell to the time of later fables, the stories that will be told about these demons.

There are, I think, two ways of understanding this slipping of time. Or rather, there are two ways of experiencing it, but, rather than being asked to choose between them, we are compelled to experience them both at once. It's through this unique demand or appeal that *Paradise Lost* makes on us that, as I suggested above, its own difficulty and complexity starts to demand a special kind of receptivity, a willingness on the reader's part to host the alien and the strange. One way we might experience this passage is as the quintessence of Milton's desire to assert and wield his immense poetic power, over the materials at his disposal and the reader.

What he is doing, he claims, is revealing the truth that lies behind the fable. The Greeks, lacking divine revelation, had a dim notion of this figure, and they named him Mulciber, an alternative name for Hephaistos, or Vulcan, as he was known to the Romans. Milton, rather than dismissing this ancient myth as pure nonsense, takes it upon himself to reveal the kernel of truth that it contains, and restore its details. And he once again makes heavy use of a line break to reinforce his point: 'thus they relate, / Erring'.

It's important to grasp the magnitude of Milton's ambitions here, the extravagance of his poetic claim, since what he's ultimately trying to do is reshape our sense of time on the grandest scale. *Paradise Lost* is, on the one hand, self-consciously a late epic poem, perhaps the last true epic poem. As the references that I've mentioned suggest, and there are countless more, Milton saw himself as successor to Homer, Virgil, and the other ancient greats. But, on the other hand, he is trying to reverse this sense of himself as a late and belated participant in the writing of epic. Unlike these pagan geniuses, his words issue from a divine source. His muse did not dwell on Olympus or in the sacred spring of Helicon, but was 'heavenly born, / Before the hills appeared, or fountain flowed'.[68] This means that his muse came first, and, if *Paradise Lost* is largely hers, then *Milton* came first; his poem is the first epic, the only true epic, as well as the last, for where could one go from here? To experience the poem in this way is to recognise Milton turning the claim to poetic passivity, to inspiration, into the boldest of claims; it is to see him as believing himself able to reach into the minds of his readers and control their responses with surgical precision. He will give them just as much untruth as they need and can take, and then wipe away its effects with an abrupt and jarring gesture – 'thus they relate, / Erring' – and jolt them in an instant from falsehood to truth, making them chasteningly recognise the error into which they had fallen.[69]

And yet, other things happen when reading these lines – which are, as I already pointed out, entirely superfluous. If there is one kind of reshaping of time at work – in which Milton makes himself first and last, Alpha and Omega of epic poetry, almost in the manner of God himself – we're also exposed to another time that is not so easily wiped from our minds as mere error. This is the time of Mulciber himself, the time of fable, of the pleasure of poetry itself. Let me return to those gorgeous, gratuitous lines: 'from morn / To noon he fell, from noon to dewy eve, / A summer's day'. Why give a time at all to Mulciber's fall, if it is all mere fable? Why measure it in time so precisely? Why allow us a moment of freedom from the sweltering claustrophobia of Hell, and breathe the limpid earthly air? Why make us feel that we are fleetingly with Mulciber, tumbling in reverie through these spine-tingling lines as he was said to tumble through space? Why make the eve particularly dewy, or make the day a summery one? My experience of these details is not chastened: I do not find myself thinking yes, I was erring when I believed such fables, please restore me to truth. I do not sense at this moment Milton's mastery of his materials, of time, of me. I join him in an inexplicable, dilating instant for which I can be nothing but grateful. A dewy eve, a summer's day: the time, perhaps, of reading.

11

9 or 10 November 1674:
'Vain Monument of Strength'

A quiet, imperceptible moment, impossible to pin down in time: the death of John Milton.

An ill man sits sightlessly in a chair, silently enduring the pain from the gout that spasms through his legs, apparent only in the slight flexing of his calloused fingers as he grips the arms of the chair. Despite his various maladies his death is not expected, nor is it momentous. There are no children or admirers sitting at his feet, pen in hand, to capture any final words of wisdom. No crowd of weeping mourners around the deathbed, watching attentively for the moment when the chest no longer rises and falls. There are others in the room, but they are too busy with their own conversations and preoccupations to notice what has happened. One moment he is there; the next, simply, gone.

At the beginning of this book I found myself wanting to pin down the moment of Milton's birth with precision, even as I realised that it could tell me little about the person or the writer whom he would become. Likewise, there is a part of me that would like Milton to have had a momentous and noisy death. For him to have died thundering out lines from *Paradise Lost*, or singing a tuneful song in Italian, or cursing the king. I can recognise this desire for a death that seems fitting; that will be of a piece with, and give shape to, the life that preceded it.

In another sense, however, I have come to see the very quietness of Milton's death, and the difficulty of pinning down its exact moment, as entirely apt. Even the exact date is uncertain: it was definitely early November 1674, a month before Milton's sixty-sixth birthday, but even his earliest biographers are uncertain whether it was 'the 9th or 10th'. Another account, by one who may have been present at the time, claims that Milton 'dy'd in a fitt of the Gout, but with so little pain or Emotion, that the time of his expiring was not perceived by those in the room'.[1] A quiet, unobtrusive end; the crossing of the threshold from life to death invisible to those closest at hand. Even Milton's death, like so many other aspects of his life, seems to flicker in and out of time.

◆

There could be no greater contrast with this hushed, unspecifiable moment than the much noisier and more momentous death scene that Milton himself created in the greatest poem that he wrote in his final years: *Samson Agonistes*.

There we find no dignified and silent final moments. Instead we encounter hands pawing and scrabbling at the remains of a freshly dead body, a mass of pulp and mangled angles. A body recognisable only by its huge mass as its parts poke from the heap of limbs and rubble in which it is lodged. The hands prepare to scrape and swab the gore from the ruptured surface of the corpse, cleanse it with herbs that will banish the stench of catastrophe, separate it from the heap of death that it created.

This is the dead body made by Milton. Samson, his final great creation, the last of the prisms into which he directed the light of his imagination so that it might split into a rainbow spectrum of possibilities, from piercing brightness to murky shade. Samson, dead; crushed between the weight of the building that he has brought down on his own head, entangled with the bodies of the victims amidst whom he has met his end. His father Manoa is determined to extract him from the heap of corpses, take him home, and

> *build him*
> *A monument, and plant it round with shade*
> *Of laurel ever green, and branching palm,*

358

With all his trophies hung, and acts enrolled
In copious legend . . .[2]

To give Samson a monument is to give him a single, clear story; his acts were 'copious', but can be gathered, 'enrolled', within a single work, a 'legend'. To pull his mangled body from its place of death and plant it at the base of this imagined monument is to claim certain knowledge of what Samson's death, and the life that preceded it, meant. Monuments are constructed at a particular time and for particular reasons, but those who raise them aspire to timelessness. Building a monument is an act of collective remembrance that is also an act of collective forgetting: a forgetting of doubts, debates, conflicts, buried beneath a marble heap of apparent unanimity.

What is Milton showing us here? *Samson Agonistes* was published in 1671, just three years before his death. While it's possible that it was begun much earlier, the story of a blind, defeated, heroic figure rousing himself for a final act of divinely inspired revenge seems to chime almost too perfectly with Milton's frustrated hopes and his sense of himself in his final years. Does Milton, then, in his last great work, show us the beginning of Samson's transition from shattered corpse to stately monument because he wants us to approve Manoa's desire, because he hoped that he might receive the same treatment following his own death? It's certainly possible to find places in Milton's writings where he hoped that his achievements would lead to him being commemorated in this grand and static way. In the poem to Giambattista Manso, his host in Naples, in which he first announced his epic ambitions, Milton looked forward to a time 'when I had reached a ripe old age and paid my last debts to the grave', and hoped that a friend 'would stand by my bed with tears in his eyes', and perhaps later 'he might have my features carved in marble [*de marmore*]'.[3]

I began this book, however, by observing that while Milton has to some extent achieved this monumental status – routinely included on lists of great, austere, and significant historical figures – his own feelings about such monumentality, as on so many questions, were deeply mixed. Milton launched his literary career by proclaiming that Shakespeare needed no 'star-ypointing pyramid' in his honour, because his works were a monument in their own right.[4] And it would be tempting to say this of Milton too: that the man who wrote so thunderingly in *Areopagitica* that 'a good Booke is the pretious life-blood of a master spirit, imbalm'd and treasur'd up on purpose to a life beyond life' is best kept alive by being read, not by being enshrined in marble. I'll end up saying this myself, although perhaps not in the usual way.

It was a commonplace in Milton's day, especially among people well versed in the writings of the ancient Romans, that the ultimate aim of learning and wisdom was to achieve a good death; that to philosophise, as Montaigne put it in the title of one of his greatest essays, is to learn how to die. The poems that Milton produced in his final years meditate in different ways on this question. But the elusiveness of the exact moment of Milton's own death, the quietness of his passing, has come to feel to me oddly fitting, for he tends not to make death consolingly knowable – quite the opposite. Death is haunting, unclear, difficult to bring into focus. At least since the writing of 'Lycidas' decades previously, if not his university poems commemorating various luminaries, Milton had wrestled with whether and how death can be understood within the time of a life. In *Paradise Lost* he went further and depicted Death himself, son of Satan's incestuous union with Sin; or rather, *depicts* is exactly the wrong word, for what Milton shows us is that he cannot clearly show us. Death is introduced as 'The other shape / If shape it might be called that shape had none / Distinguishable in member, joint, or limb, / Or substance might be called that shadow seemed, / For each seemed either'.[5] The very categories of being – substance or shadow – seem to blur and bend here, like matter behaving strangely in the vicinity of a black hole. We can say nothing with certainty about Death – not that he has a shape, not that he doesn't. And, in this moment, we're experiencing what Adam and Eve will before long experience when they eat the forbidden fruit and realise that they did not fully grasp what God meant when he threatened them with death if they did so. They debate and discuss what death is and what it means in their first fallen hours, and painfully learn the difference between the sudden and peremptory death that Adam fears – arriving in 'one stroke' – and the worse reality of living death, of a life lived inexorably towards death, that they instead discover: 'endless misery / From this day onward, which I feel begun / Both in me, and without me, and so last / To perpetuity'.[6] In the final two books of the poem the Angel Michael arrives to give Adam a glimpse into subsequent human history, which is a lesson both in the gory reality of death – events appear to him as a relentless parade of slaughter – and its eventual divine overcoming and transformation. Michael also, however, provides his clearest guidance on how Adam is to pass his allotted time now that death is an inevitability. In the last chapter we encountered Milton's insistence in his sonnet that 'They also serve who only stand and wait', and Michael relays to Adam his own complex version of the same idea:

> There is, said Michael, if thou well observe
> The rule of not too much, by temperance taught
> In what thou eatst and drinkst, seeking from thence
> Due nourishment, not gluttonous delight,
> Till many years over thy head return:
> So mayest thou live, till like ripe fruit thou drop
> Into thy mother's lap, or be with ease
> Gathered, not harshly plucked, for death mature:
> This is old age; but then thou must outlive
> Thy youth, thy strength, thy beauty, which will change
> To withered weak and grey; thy senses then
> Obtuse, all taste of pleasure must forgo.[7]

These lines read like a compendium of Milton's deepest preoccupations. The concern with overabundant eating, which he saw as the root of his blindness, gives way to a moving account of the relatively old age that he was nonetheless able to achieve, and in which the senses of all people are destined to become as 'Obtuse' as his. Milton was continuing in these lines to develop and refine his thinking on the terrifying and elusive nature of death that had preoccupied him throughout his writing career. This is confirmed by the contrast between the gentle gathering of a mature death and the fear of being 'harshly plucked'. These words hark directly back to the opening of 'Lycidas' that I earlier found stuck in my head, and where Milton's own fear of failing to reach poetic maturity was summed up in the words: 'I come to pluck your berries harsh and crude.' Milton has shifted not just from a fear of the end to its gentle embracing, but, more deeply, towards new ways of lingering in the midst of life with this range of possible ends in mind.[8] Michael's words, it's also important to note, are yet another scene of teaching and learning.

Samson Agonistes, however, appears very different. There, death swiftly followed by the desire to erect a monument shows Milton's sharp awareness that death is only an ending of sorts; not just because, as we'll see that he believed, the body and soul that had died together would live together again when the Apocalypse came, but because a life that has ended not only means something to the one who dies, as Michael suggests, but fast becomes the concern and the property of others. Woven into new stories, ascribed new meanings. Milton himself, I think, was well aware that his late great works posed the question: what kinds of monument are these? And this in turn has inescapably become, for me, the question: what kind of monument does Milton demand, and deserve?

If questions of who is, and who deserves to be, remembered and who forgotten are raised by Milton's last great work, this reflects the fact that such issues had become inescapable in the last fifteen years of his life. Let's return briefly to the late 1650s, as the Restoration of the monarchy accelerated with extraordinary speed from a possibility to an inevitability, despite Milton's passionate efforts. Milton had continued his diplomatic services for the Cromwellian regime, despite his ever-deepening ambivalence about the pseudo-monarchical status and ambitions of the Lord Protector himself. He pursued this activity, as we saw in the last chapter, into the period of Cromwell's illness in 1658, by which time the latter had nominated his son, Richard, as his successor in the event of his death, a move which confirmed that the protectorate had morphed into a kind of monarchy, a role based on birth rather than merit or spiritual excellence. After Cromwell died, in September of that year, Milton's standing within the government was confirmed when he was granted funds to buy mourning clothes to be worn in Cromwell's funeral procession, along with his younger colleagues and fellow poets, Andrew Marvell and John Dryden. Perhaps it was one of their arms that Milton held for guidance as the convoy made its way to Westminster Abbey for Cromwell's interment. The Lord Protector's body would not remain buried for long.

Richard Cromwell was an unknown quantity when he stepped into his father's shoes, and the existence of an elaborate and well-organised state apparatus meant that his unsuitability for the role was not immediately apparent. Milton's own duties continued relatively unchanged, since the new regime needed to maintain functioning relations with the great powers of Europe, and his skills as a translator of diplomatic correspondence were much in demand. It was clear that a great change was in the offing, even if Milton, the government, and the country at large were collectively committed to maintaining the illusion of business as usual. He looked again towards the European Republic of Letters, and immediately following Cromwell's death – in a process that must have been maddeningly complicated for him and his amanuensis – Milton made various small changes to the third edition of his first Latin *Defence* and added a personal afterword. In it he expressed the hope that his successful defence of the English people in killing their king and establishing their own commonwealth would serve as an example to 'many other peoples, who had hitherto been deceived by shameful ignorance of their own rights and by a pretext of religion'. He was tempted to see this work, with its elegantly biting Latin polemic and its pan-European readership, as his lasting monument: 'Such as it is, this memorial, I see, will not easily perish.'[9]

If Milton remained focused on his European readership, however, the changes that began to unfold following Cromwell's death also prompted him, for the first time since his extraordinarily intense series of publications across the 1640s, to address his own nation in English prose. Suspicions that Richard Cromwell specifically favoured Presbyterianism in contrast to his father's inclination to tolerate a wider spectrum of religious views led to a renewal of debate about the proper nature and parameters of the national Church. Petitions were aimed at the new Lord Protector from all sides, most notably from George Monck, commander-in-chief of the army in Scotland, who had supported Oliver Cromwell but now waited for events to unfold before making his allegiance clear. Possible allegiances and alliances continued to shift, and when a new parliament was convened at the start of 1659 it confirmed how the landscape had changed. Andrew Marvell was now the MP for his birthplace, Hull, but probably more significant for Milton was the return to Parliament and to political life of Henry Vane the Younger. Vane had spent time in New England as governor of Massachusetts in the 1630s, and had emerged as a proponent of a strikingly capacious religious tolerance and a belief that the individual believer's conscience should be his or her guide. He had been a prominent figure during the revolutionary years but had spent much of the Protectorate in retirement, having clashed with Oliver Cromwell as the latter rose to individual dominance. Milton had written a sonnet to Vane before his fall from grace, praising him as an ideal statesman – 'young in years, but in sage counsel old' – particularly for his ability 'to know / Both spiritual power and civil, what each means, / What severs each'.[10]

Vane's return to political life suggested a new parliamentary audience for Milton's convictions, and he duly returned to English prose with his treatise *Of Civil Power in Ecclesiastical Causes*. This marked in some ways an uncanny return to the terrain of the 1640s: Milton arguing, against a background of dispute between Presbyterians and Independents, for toleration of a wide spectrum of Protestant belief while continuing to rigidly exclude Roman Catholicism, not to mention Judaism and all other faiths, from his apparently capacious vision. There were, however, significant changes. The sects who had proliferated and caused such excitement and consternation in the late 1640s – the groups sung about by Leon Rosselson in the songs that formed the soundtrack of my childhood, like the Diggers and the Ranters – had long been suppressed or disbanded. The most significant and successful of the radical groups who had emerged in their wake were the Quakers. Because the Quakers are the only group who emerged in this period to have survived as a denomination into the present day – and because they are most readily associated with gentleness, silence, pacifism – it's easy to forget how terrifying and dangerous they seemed to contemporaries in the seventeenth century, and with what hostility and violence they were often met. The individual's silent encounter with God, which could occur at any time or place and required no specific knowledge or ritual, left little place for an organised Church at all. Quiet acts undertaken with one's spirit and one's body still had the potential to turn the world upside down.

Milton was not a Quaker, though he shared several of their central convictions and, as we'll see, included some of their number among his close friends. By this point in his life, as we saw in the last chapter, he held beliefs that make it impossible to align him with any denomination or sect; he was a Church of One. But if the astonishingly creative development of his idiosyncratic convictions had percolated in private during the 1650s, known only to the amanuenses who helped him with the writing of *De Doctrina Christiana*, the change of regime in the late 1650s allowed him not yet to articulate these beliefs but to argue for the kind of commonwealth in which they could be safely articulated. While the tolerationist arguments that he put forward in *Of Civil Power* appear similar to those of *Areopagitica*, though without the soaring rhetoric of the earlier treatise, the precise fashion in which he made his argument for the range of beliefs that should and should not be tolerated was strikingly bold. His central claim – that all who practised true religion should be left to do so freely – was entirely uncontroversial, but his definition of what counted as true religion was remarkably broad. It effectively included any Christian who strove in good faith to derive their beliefs, by the exercise of reason, from the scriptures. But it was the genuineness of the striving, not the specific outcome, that mattered. 'To protestants therefore whose common rule and touchstone is the scripture,' he wrote, nothing can with more conscience, more equitie, nothing more protestantly can be permitted then a free and lawful debate at all times by writing, conference or disputation of what opinion soever, disputable by scripture: concluding, that no man in religion is properly a heretic at this day, but he who maintains traditions or opinions not probable by scripture; who, for aught I know, is the papist only.[11]

Roman Catholicism remains beyond the pale because it was to Milton effectively a form of political sedition rather than a religion, having abandoned the Bible as its sole touchstone. Heresy of this sort can be excluded, but within the true Christian community there can and must be relentless disagreement – 'debate *at all times*' – if the truth is to be found.

Milton would continue to argue along these lines for the remainder of his life, probably hoping that he could justify his own theological position as one that was wildly unusual but meticulously rooted in countless citations from scripture. In the late 1650s, however, events moved far too fast for his call to Parliament to have any effect. Richard Cromwell's total unsuitability for autocratic rule soon became painfully clear. By April 1659 he had been forced to resign, and the army now sought to turn back the clock to 1653 by restoring the Rump Parliament. Clashes between the restored Rump and the army as to whose leadership truly meant a return to the 'Good Old Cause' – a nostalgic description of the pre-Protectorate Republic that Vane had helped to popularise – made the establishment of a stable settlement impossible, and there was a further upsurge both of minor rebellions and of competing visions for the nation's future in which Milton took an active but increasingly desperate and belated part. In *Considerations Touching the likeliest means to remove hirelings out of the Church* Milton forgot his antipathy to the Rump in its earlier manifestation and addressed it as 'the authors and best patrons of religious and civil libertie, that ever these Ilands brought forth'.[12] In this tract he veered even closer to the Quaker position of indifference as to where worship took place, claiming that 'notwithstanding the gaudy superstition of som devoted still ignorantly to temples, we may be well assur'd that he who disdaind not to be laid in a manger, disdains not to be preached in a barn.'[13] But increasingly Milton was not just flattering the Rump but trying to see them as a sort of ideal safeguard of individual liberty despite, rather than because of, their actual actions. His plea to end the practice of tithing, for instance, was issued after the Rump had already resolved to continue it. Reality was refusing to behave.

The clashes between Parliament and army, and the proliferation of competing visions for Church and state, led many, including Milton, to fear that another civil war was imminent. Instead, events were driven from an unexpected direction. Late in 1659 General George Monck, having bided his time in Scotland and kept a careful eye on deteriorating events in London, led his forces south into England. His intentions were unclear and alarming. Monck had chosen his moment superbly; attempts to raise opposing forces were feeble, and in February 1660 his army arrived in London. It was still not clear what their arrival meant, and what Monck aimed to achieve, and Milton continued to dictate drafts for alternative strategies and systems of government. Perhaps recalling his own travels, he looked to the serene and unchanging government of Venice as a model for the kind of self-regulating and self-perpetuating republic, governed by an enlightened minority, that England might become.[14] While he worked on such proposals there were rumours that Monck would name himself Lord Protector, or even king. Milton put together the most developed version of his frantic political vision, *The Readie and Easie Way to Establish a Free Commonwealth*, frequently revising it in response to fast-changing circumstances and reworking it as a direct address to Monck himself – again calling for the establishment of a perpetual governing council on a broadly Venetian model. Reading these tracts, one can sense the desperate energies of Milton's mind as he tries to persuade himself and his contemporaries that a downwardly spiralling crisis was actually a moment of profound opportunity, a chance to make good on the missed opportunities of the early 1650s and create a republic with all the freedom and boldness of imagination that one might use in the writing of a great poem.

Instead, in February 1660 Monck allowed the Members of Parliament who had been excluded in Pride's Purge to return, effectively confirming that he endorsed the option for which they were sure to vote: the restoration to the throne of the executed king's son and namesake, who had spent the past decade in exile on the Continent waiting for an opportunity of this sort to present itself. On the 1st of May Parliament formally invited Charles Stuart to return as King Charles II. Despite Milton's tireless and frantic efforts, the nation had taken the decision that he found most loathsome and impossible to stomach: the deliberate, conscious choice to subject itself to the whims and uncontrolled powers of a monarch.

The Restoration of the monarchy involved a carefully choreographed mixture of vengeful remembrance and tactful forgetting. Charles issued a proclamation, the Declaration of Breda, in which he insisted that he wanted to assume the throne 'with as little blood and damage to our people as is possible', and to that end he granted 'a free and general pardon' so that 'henceforth all notes of discord, separation and difference of parties be utterly abolished among all our subjects'. There were, however, limits to this offer to consign most of the events of the past two decades to collective amnesia: all were to be forgiven, 'excepting only such persons as shall hereafter be excepted by Parliament'.[15] The tone was conciliatory, even as the door was left open for uncertain numbers of people still to be punished in unspecified ways. This same sinister balance was maintained by the 'Convention Parliament' that was elected in April 1660, and which in August passed the Indemnity and Oblivion Act, which confirmed the general clemency while making clear its exclusions: it did not apply to those guilty of murder, buggery, piracy, witchcraft, and above all to those directly responsible for, and implicated in, the regicide. But even the question of how direct responsibility was to be defined and how wide the net of punishment was to be cast was unclear, and hotly debated.

Unlike the men who were eventually excluded from the Act of

Oblivion and in most cases gruesomely executed, Milton had not signed the king's death warrant nor presided over his execution; but he had devoted the full weight of his learning and satirical skills to defending it, to a domestic and a European audience, and he was in considerable danger. He left his comfortable house on Petty France and went into hiding at a friend's house on Bartholomew Close, a little to the south of what is now Barbican tube station. Milton continued to be denounced in numerous lists naming the wickedest republicans, all of which agreed that his blindness was punishment for his sins. His books justifying the regicide were explicitly denounced and recalled by the Convention Parliament, and the gathered copies publicly burned by the hangman at the Old Bailey. Milton himself was ordered to be imprisoned, but could not be found. His burgeoning national and international reputation both inspired the actions against him and ultimately helped ensure Milton's personal safety. The restored regime was keen to begin broadcasting not just its mercifulness but its cultivation and sophistication, and this might not have been best served by executing a blind poet. The powerful connections that he had formed during his years as a public servant, with men who had a vested interest in ensuring that as few of the sins of the past were punished as possible, also helped: Edward Phillips wrote that 'the Act of Oblivion . . . proved as favourable to him as could be hop'd or expected, through the intercession of some that stood his Friends both in Council and Parliament; particularly in the House of Commons, Mr. Andrew Marvell, a member for Hull, acted vigorously in his behalf.'[16] Milton was confident enough to re-emerge from hiding, and though he was imprisoned in the Tower, it was only for a few weeks, and he was able to secure his release by paying a hefty fine of one hundred and fifty pounds. He moved house frequently during these scary and disorientating months, first to a house near Red Lion Fields in Holborn, then, following his imprisonment, to Jewin Street, near his previous residence in Aldersgate Street. Phillips claimed that Milton moved again, 'to a House in the Artillery-walk leading to Bunhill Fields' shortly after his marriage to his third wife, Elizabeth Minshull, in 1663, though it seems likely that this move took place later, after Milton's final and enforced departure from, and return to, London.[17]

When Sean and I set ourselves the task of walking the sites of Milton's London residences, we visited each of these places. When I planned our route in advance, it became clear that it was entirely impractical to follow the order in which Milton lived in each place, since this would involve a tiring and highly inefficient looping back to locations that we had already visited. We began – for logistical rather than symbolic reasons – at the end, meeting outside Moorgate tube station and making the ten-minute walk north to Bunhill Fields, near which had stood the last house that Milton occupied, and the one in which he died. We had chosen this starting point simply because it was the furthest east of Milton's London homes, and would allow us to spend the day walking westward, meandering our way around Bread Street and Aldersgate Street and making the longer walk to Petty France, where Milton had resided while working for the Protectorate. As with our trips to Horton and Ludlow, however, a lack of specific planning led us to encounter not just curious details but new ways to think, both about Milton's life and our relationship with it.

First of all, to walk in this way, to be guided by the conveniences of the map rather than the sequence of Milton's life, felt like a liberating alternative to the sheer sequential plodding of time. One thing that's struck me again and again as I've written this book is the number of ways – the range of speeds, the pirouetting variety of rhythms – through which time spent in Milton's company seems to move. There are periods and aspects of his life for which it seems utterly necessary to move in a linear fashion in order to understand them, and I've begun this chapter in roughly this way because the months before and after the Restoration were one such period. Milton's own writings and his activities were frenetic attempts to respond to, and to shape, the urgent contingencies of the moment in which he found himself, and works like *Of Civil Power* and *The Readie and Easie Way* can't be made sense of in any other way. I myself enjoy following the sheer gripping sequence of events, the granularity of their details, in my reading and in my writing. And yet when the Restoration came, and when it became clear that the causes to which Milton had devoted a decade and a half and the use of his eyes had been decisively defeated, he shifted into a new rhythm, a new relation to time. With one or two exceptions, his writings no longer sought to seize the charged moment of possibility and fashion something new from it.

Instead Milton continued in these years to work on the writings that, as I discussed in the last chapter, are difficult to locate precisely in time: *De Doctrina Christiana*, *Paradise Lost* itself, and, as we'll soon see further, *Samson Agonistes*, whose temporal origins are no less uncertain. In a strange way our non-linear walk, zigzagging between Milton's early and late homes in an order answerable to space rather than time, seemed like a fitting way to begin approaching these late, great works, a way that was less linear, less certain of itself. At the same time that he was working on these writings, Milton also began in other ways to loop backwards in time, to publish works which had largely been written much earlier, and which therefore allowed him to revisit his own past in new ways. In 1669 he published a book on Latin grammar whose subtitle aimed it at all who are 'desirous without more trouble than needs, to attain the Latin tongue'. His educational theories of the early 1640s returned in practical form, showing the basis on which he'd long argued that the fundamentals of a language could be learned quickly and pragmatically. A few months later his deep fascination with the history of the British Isles, which he'd once considered the most likely topic for his epic, gave belated rise to *The History of Britain*, published in 1670 but written much earlier; it gave a strikingly disenchanted account of the violence and savagery that this history had involved, not unlike the parade of brutality that is foreseen on a global scale in the final two books of *Paradise Lost*. Not until after Milton's death was a lengthy digression published that had been removed from the *History*. It confirmed his deep concern with the distinctiveness of the nation's past and future, even as he insisted upon the need for it to be shaped by porous contact with that which was foreign, as he himself had experienced. We're now better placed to understand the centrality to his mind of the words that I quoted in part in my introduction: 'the Sun which we want [i.e. lack]', he wrote in the digression, 'ripens Wits as well as Fruits; and as Wine and Oyl are Imported to us from abroad: so must ripe Understanding, and many civil Vertues, be imported into our minds from Forreign Writings, and examples of best Ages, we shall else miscarry still, and come short in the attempts of any great Enterprise.'[18]

These words may have resonated in a new way for Milton in the Restoration years, since, once it became certain that he was not to be executed or further punished, he was able to enjoy some of the fruits of his striving for a European reputation during the 1650s. Aubrey suggests that throughout his later years Milton was 'mightily importuned to go into Fr[ance] and Italie (foraigners came much to see him) and much admired him, and offered to him great p[re]ferm[en]ts. to come over to them'. Aubrey even claimed that the visitors 'would see the house & chamber where he was born' – a hint at the beginnings of a Miltonic tourist industry, and the enjoyable suggestion that Sean and I, in our wanderings, were following not just in Milton's footsteps but in those of these early, anonymous, European enthusiasts. Milton, Aubrey concluded, 'was much more admired abrode then at home'.[19] His blindness and worsening infirmities would have made a late journey to Europe of the sort to which his visitors urged him deeply impractical, but it nicely confirms my sense from the middle chapters of this book that being emphatically not at home in Europe was somehow where Milton was most at home, and I like to imagine that his stream of visitors stirred up memories for him as well as offering new opportunities for conversation.

It's easy, then, to create a relatively rosy picture of Milton's final years in the homes around whose locations Sean and I walked. He may have been more admired abroad, but Milton's reputation at home continued to climb. Edward Phillips claims that during these years the Earl of Anglesey 'came often here to visit him, as very much coveting his society and converse; as likewise others of the Nobility, and persons of eminent quality'.[20] The visits increased after *Paradise Lost* was published in 1667. Milton's poetic connections remained strong. Aubrey noted that John Dryden, Milton's one-time younger colleague in the Cromwellian administration and now Poet Laureate, 'who very much admires him . . . went to him to have leave to putt his Paradise-lost into a Drama in Rhythme: Mr. Milton received him civilly, and told him he would give him leave to tagge his Verses.'[21] The resulting – and not very good – outcome, *The State of Innocence*, was intended as the libretto for an opera, a form fast becoming fashionable in England, but it was never performed. It does suggest, however, the speed with which *Paradise Lost* was not just embraced but adapted in creative ways. Within a few years of its publication, 'halfe his Paradise lost' was translated into German – 'High Dutch . . . blank verse', as Aubrey put it – by Theodor Haak, fellow of the Royal Society and another of Milton's former colleagues in the Cromwellian administration.[22] In many ways these two early responses anticipate the poem's subsequent reception. On the one hand attempts to adapt it that ultimately fail: many in the twentieth century recognised the cinematic qualities of Milton's imagination, beginning with the great Russian director Sergei Eisenstein's claim that '*Paradise Lost* itself is a first-rate school in which to study montage and audio-visual relationships', but every attempt to produce a big-budget version of the film to date, most recently in the early 2000s, has foundered.[23] On the other hand its translation and circulation in other languages, which continues to this day: a recent volume of essays on Milton in translation includes chapters on Finnish, Persian, Korean, and many others.[24]

This would be a happy way to leave Milton, at home in his quiet final years prior to his equally quiet death, readying himself for his destiny as a poet of national and international renown. As I've already made clear, however, this narrative of immediate and obvious greatness is not one that interests me, for several reasons. Milton, as I discussed in the introduction has been far from universally admired, and for telling reasons. Furthermore my own relation to him, as I've made clear, is not one of straightforward affinity or admiration. And, while Milton's retreat from the forefront of public life means that I'll have less to say about the events that surrounded his final years, there is one domestic context that stands out for me and that complicates this apparent parade of admirers. I mentioned in the last chapter that Milton had three surviving daughters by his first wife, Mary Powell, and that by the Restoration he had married for a third time, his second wife having died without surviving children. These three daughters – Anne, Mary, and Deborah – begin to emerge in accounts of Milton's final years, although, like the other women who were integral to his life, they do so as elusive, shadowy presences, who seem to demand our imagination precisely because they elude our certain knowledge. They have reappeared in later works, from references in George Eliot's *Middlemarch* to Eugene Delacroix's painting of Milton dictating *Paradise Lost* to the trio. The evidence suggests tantalisingly that they were involved in Milton's reading and his writing, but in ways that are difficult to specify. Aubrey's account of the youngest daughter states: 'Deborah was his Amanuensis, he taught her Latin, & to read Greeke and Hebrew [Aubrey crossed through these two words and added a Q for 'Quare', reminding himself to discover whether it were actually true] when he had lost his eiesight.'[25] She would have been only around ten or eleven years old when *Paradise Lost* was finished, surely too young to have assisted with its transcription, but could in her teens have worked on *Samson Agonistes* and *Paradise Regained*. Aubrey's description of her as Milton's Latinate amanuensis makes this feel plausible. Edward Phillips, however, gives a very different account. He paints a scene not of genuine collaboration but of enforced labour and ignorance. The eldest daughter was excused on account of infirmities, he explains, but

> the other two were Condemn'd to the performance of Reading, and exactly pronouncing of all the Languages of whatever Book he should at one time or other think fit to peruse; *Viz.* the Hebrew (and I think the Syriac), the Greek, the Latin, the Italian, Spanish, and French. All which sorts of Books to be confined to Read, without understanding one word, must needs be a trial of Patience, almost beyond endurance; yet it was endured by both for a long time.[26]

Finally, Phillips claims, they did rebel, and broke away to take up occupations 'that are proper for Women to learn, particularly Imbroideries in Gold or Silver'. It's possible, then, that his daughters were no more than the latest and by no means the last victims of Milton's overbearing and diminishing attitudes towards women – made into tools for his learning, not partners in it. The case isn't certain, however. Phillips had his own agenda in his biography of his uncle, not least positioning himself as Milton's closest helper and truest intellectual heir. Wherever Aubrey derived the detail that Deborah actually understood Latin, it does suggest less total linguistic ignorance on the trio's part than Phillips implies; bluntly calling Deborah her father's amanuensis hints that she was more entangled in the making of his works than Phillips allows. This feels a fitting ending for the other side of Milton's home life with which I've wrestled throughout this book, striving to acknowledge his tendency to co-opt and stage-manage the women in his life and in his writings while also holding on to other possibilities, possibilities of collaboration where the power does not flow quite as clearly in one direction.

Turning away from the individuals who shared Milton's life in his final years, there was a second way in which, as Sean and I undertook our walk around their locations, the strange urge to stand near the sites of Milton's homes seemed to speak in a particularly apt way to his final writings. As I've already mentioned, none of Milton's London homes are still standing. We knew each time that we arrived at a new site that there would be nothing specific to witness, no hook on which to hang our desires and our interpretations. But our recurrent desire to visit Milton's homes, and our perennial disappointment, also led me back in a new way to the great triumvirate of his final poems, and especially the ways in which they end; ways that seem deeply connected with Milton's self-conscious sense of his own life having begun to end with the writing of these poems. *Paradise Lost* ends with Adam and Eve homeless and bereft, cast out of Eden. In lines whose tonal balance is extraordinary delicate, and which seem to sound different to different people – and different to me on each reading, dependent on my mood – he imagined their first experience of metaphysical desolation. Adam and Eve had been at home at all places and times within Eden; now it was uncertain that they would ever find a home again:

> *The world was all before them, where to choose*
> *Their place of rest, and providence their guide:*
> *They hand in hand with wandering steps and slow,*
> *Through Eden took their solitary way.*[27]

Nowhere is the interplay of possibilities in these lines, the simultaneous sense of appalling loss and just about possible consolation, more finely balanced than in the quiet contradiction of 'their solitary way', the poem's final words. The plural of the pronoun *their* pushes against the aching loneliness of the adjective, *solitary*: will they be together even when most alone, or alone even when most together?

When *Samson Agonistes* was published in 1671 it appeared as part of a strikingly odd diptych with *Paradise Regained*. As its title suggests, this was Milton's sequel to *Paradise Lost*, telling the story of Satan's failed temptation of Jesus in the wilderness and anticipating the redemption of the Fall that his first epic had detailed. These paired works contrast jarringly with one another: Old Testament versus New Testament, violence and destruction versus peaceful and detached triumph. The main point at which the pair seem calculatedly to be brought together by Milton, to speak directly to one another, comes at their respective endings. Manoa, as we saw, wants to make Samson a monument (in both senses), but not just anywhere: he specifically wants to take him 'Home to his father's house: *there* will I build him / A monument'.[28] A monument, yes, but an emphatically domestic one. At the very end of *Paradise Regained*, as the angels sing and feast in delirious triumph to mark Jesus's withstanding of Satan's temptation, their jubilation contrasts with the victor's much quieter behaviour: 'he unobserved / Home to his mother's house private returned'.[29] Three connected but very different endings: our first parents' first homelessness; Samson noisily dead and resplendently monumentalised at his father's house; Jesus inconspicuously at home at his mother's. This deep concern with being, and not being, at home that recurs in Milton's late great poems certainly made visiting the sites of his own homes seem newly fitting.

Of these three endings, the final moments of *Samson Agonistes* – with its combination of death, commemoration, and homecoming – seemed to resonate the most as we arrived at Bunhill Fields, since Milton's final residence stood a mere stone's throw away from a singularly interesting graveyard, full of monuments of its own. The very name of the place is likely a contraction of 'Bone Hill', reflecting the fact that it had been a burial place for centuries by the time Milton moved onto its doorstep. During his childhood, when Milton went to and from school each day, he would have seen in St Paul's Churchyard the old charnel houses which had contained the bones of the dead; by then many were rented out by stationers and book-sellers to store their wares. In the late 1540s, when King Edward had been determined to complete the reformation of the Church and reject the reverence for the dusty bones of one's forebears that had been such a mark of Roman Catholic piety, he had 'some thou-sandes of Carrie loades' of these bones carted from St Paul's and dumped to the east of the city – on Bone Hill.[30] Milton had moved to a place that bore beneath its soil the heaped fragments of the aggressively forgotten and displaced dead. While he was living there, however, it seemed that Bunhill would need to house heaps of the dead in much more fresh and horrifying fashion. In 1665, as the plague ravaged London, plans were formed to turn Bunhill Fields into a plague pit. Ultimately, for unclear reasons, this did not tran-spire. But the plans seem to have focused new attention on the status of this ancient burial site, which, although it was the resting place for countless bones that had originally been interred on consecrated ground, had never itself been consecrated. From the 1680s dissenting figures who rejected the rites of the re-Established Church began to take advantage of this fact and be buried there.

Walking around Bunhill Fields with Sean gave me a curious and powerful feeling: I wished Milton had been buried here. It's a wonderful spot, most of the graves inaccessible behind railings, but with views across the ripples and angles of the tombs and grave-stones, some beginning to sink slowly into the earth. A thick canopy of trees, the floor dappled with pools of sunlight on the day that we visited. A quiet, almost pastoral spot in the midst of a busy part of London, the sound of car engines and building sites fading into the background. But then, in the centre of the cemetery, a set of monuments, to three great nonconformist literary figures all buried nearby: John Bunyan, Daniel Defoe, William Blake. Blake in particular, the visionary admirer of Milton as his thunderingly prophetic precursor, lying beneath the earth a short way from the spot where Milton had breathed his last. If only Milton had lived a few years longer, I found myself wishing, until the time that dissenters began to be buried in Bunhill, he could have formed the fourth corner of a square of great writers. Some admirer would at some point have erected a monument in his memory, as had happened with the other three. My investigations and peregrin-ations would then have had a focal point, a place to which I could make quiet pilgrimages when I had time on my trips to London. I could sit on a bench near this monument, quietly read to myself the pocket copy of Milton's poems that I had bought in a charity shop in Ludlow, and Milton and I would both feel at home.

The moment passed, however, and so too did the feeling that I could after all envisage a monument for Milton that would do him, and my relationship with him, justice. Other ways of thinking re-asserted themselves as we walked westward and encountered the kinds of absence and oddly layered histories that were much more characteristic of my Miltonic excursions, and not just the half-hearted plaque on Bread Street. When we walked to Red Lion Square, near to which Milton had moved soon after the Restoration, Sean recalled that it had been the site of a demonstration against neo-Nazis in 1974 when a student named Kevin Gately had died, possibly as a result of police violence. Eventually we arrived at the church where Milton had in fact been buried, St Giles Cripplegate, now enveloped by the Barbican Centre. In another odd echo of Manoa's desire to take Samson home and bury him there, as one of the early biographies of Milton notes, when he died he 'happen'd to bee bury'd in Cripplegate where about thirty yeer before hee had by chance also interrd his Father'.[31]

This church is near homes that Milton occupied at two stages of his life – in the 1640s and again after the Restoration. When Sean and I visited we saw a modest plaque to Milton on one of the church's walls, dated 1793, and a life-size bronze statue of him from a considerably later date, with a score of Bach's music tucked into the crook of its arm by some wag. Milton monumentalised again, but yet again in what seemed like oddly muted tones. I knew that his body had been removed from its grave in this church more than a century after its burial there. I later learned that the reason for his disinterment in 1790 was that affluent members of the congregation planned to raise a monument in Milton's honour, and wanted to confirm his exact place of burial. Once the coffin was revealed, however, they could not resist opening it, and discovered fine strands of hair still poking from the top of the skull, matted and wet. A crowd of gawpers gathered: they tore off the hair in dank clumps, ripped teeth from the bony mouth, snapped away finger bones, even wrenched off a femur. Before long there was a lively trade in Milton relics around London.[32] Many people were horrified, including the poet William Cowper, who wrote a poem 'On the Late Indecent Liberties Taken with the Remains of the Great Milton', lambasting the 'wretches who have dared profane' the dead writer's 'dread sepulchral rest'.[33] The modest wall plaque that Sean and I saw was dated three years after these grisly events; presumably it was a belated, scaled-down version of the original plan, testimony to its bad planning. It seemed very apt that Milton's resting place was also the site of a failed attempt to make him a monument, just as our walk around his London homes had elicited in me both a deep desire for official forms of remembrance and the repeated feeling that something much more interesting happened when this desire was, repeatedly, disappointed.

I'll return to the question of the kind of monument that Milton might deserve, but I want now to go back to the work which inevitably haunted my mind as my walk with Sean became an encounter with the ways in which a life can end, be remembered, and be forgotten. There is an eerie extent to which these problems of whether and how Milton should be commemorated seem to have been played out in advance by him in *Samson Agonistes*. The uncertainty that I feel in trying to decide what monument, if any, Milton merits – the difficulty of ascribing a meaning to his death, and to the life that preceded it – are exactly the problems with which that work starkly leaves its readers in relation to its titular hero. It's certainly possible to read *Samson* as Milton constructing his own monument, writing his own epitaph. The story is taken from the Hebrew Bible, but Samson had often been interpreted by Christian scholars – a common strategy for domesticating the more unsettling stories of what they dubbed the 'Old Testament' – as a foreshadowing or an 'antetype' of Christ. Milton recast the story, as his prefatory note explained at length, on the model of a Greek tragedy, fashioning the plot after the example of 'Aeschylus, Sophocles, and Euripides, the three tragic poets unequalled yet by any, and the best rule to all who endeavour to write tragedy'. He also explained at length that because tragedy was 'the gravest, moralest, and most profitable of all other poems', it was ultimately not possible to distinguish it from sacred writings: one of the Church Fathers had written a tragedy on Christ's suffering, and St Paul himself 'thought it not unworthy to insert a verse of Euripides into the text of Holy Scripture, 1 Cor. xv. 33', a philological observation which eroded the division between pagan and pious wisdom.[34] Viewed from this perspective, the work becomes a telling of Samson's story that integrates various strands not just of Milton's learning but of his self: especially by being paired with *Paradise Regained*, this becomes a volume in which Hebraic, Christian, and classical elements flow together and complement one another. Even the strangeness of the verse in *Samson Agonistes* – often jagged and irregular lines of varying length, slipping in and out of rhyme and other kinds of regularity – seem to blend Hebraic and Greek rhythms while also harking back to the kind of shifting rhythmical experiments that Milton had undertaken in 'Lycidas'.

And most obviously, as I've already suggested, the Samson who first enters, blind and defeated, resembles Milton's state at the Restoration. His first words – 'A little onward lend thy guiding hand / To these dark steps' – recall both the routine assistance that the sightless Milton must have needed as he fled across London to avoid imprisonment and possible death, and the broader sense of stumbling into an uncertain future, the 'dark world and wide' that I discussed in the last chapter. Like the narrator of *Paradise Lost*, Samson is fallen on evil days and presented with a 'universal blank'. And yet both of these blind and beleaguered figures redeem themselves through great, heroic acts and construct their own monuments: Milton in the form of the epic poem that he wrote; Samson by the cataclysmic act of violence by which he revenges himself on his persecutors and captors, and in which he loses his life. Samson's final monument would, on this account, be multiple: the shattered temple and the heap of bodies that he created and into which he was subsumed; the one that Manoa planned to build, at home; and Milton's poetic account of the whole thing.

There's a lot that's plausible in this account. *Samson Agonistes* is certainly a work that – in its rich splicing of religious and literary traditions, its dazzling and rhythmically eccentric poetry, its unmistakable resonance with the dilemmas faced by Milton and other prominent defeated republicans – seems to demand to be read biographically. To be pinned to, and understood in terms of, the specific individual that produced it and the historical moment in which he did so. And yet, like those other works of Milton's that matter enduringly to me – the Nativity Ode and 'Lycidas', which seek to reshape and unsettle time even as they are superficially easier to place within it; *Paradise Lost*, which floats over and vibrates with the entire latter half of Milton's life – *Samson* seems to resist being pinned down in time in this fashion. The extent to which its hero seems to resemble Milton starts to feel like a trap laid for the aspiring biographer, a snare baited with the biographical temptation itself; the temptation of certainty, of knowability of a complex and long-dead individual. And, viewed from other perspectives, this knowledge is precisely what *Samson Agonistes* seems designed to thwart. Most strikingly, Manoa's desire to make a monument of his son is anticipated earlier in the work itself, when Samson resents having become 'to visitants a gaze, / Or pitied object, these redundant locks / Robustious to no purpose clustering down, / Vain monument of strength'.[35] He despises having become the wrong sort of monument, an object gazed upon for the worst of reasons. His words thereby insist that there are such things as bad monuments, vain monuments, and that we must be careful of the impulse to erect and marvel at them.

The sense that erecting and gazing at monuments is a problem and not just an ideal also comes from the basic form taken by the action – if action is the right word, since this is what *Samson* has often seemed to frustrated readers to lack. When we first meet the blind and defeated hero he has been shorn of his hair and his strength by Dalila – who Milton tellingly makes his wife, not just his lover – and forced to labour by the Philistines. He spends most of the narrative weakened and helpless, visited by a series of figures who seek in different ways to scrutinise him, to claim a version of him for themselves (the sequence of admiring visitors to Milton's Restoration homes horribly inverted, perhaps). And the majority of his words are spent resisting and rejecting these attempts, placing himself beyond them. Manoa wants to redeem him from captivity and care for him at home. So too does Dalila, who seeks to justify her behaviour at length, and who also wants to bring him home: 'though sight be lost,' she tells him, 'Life yet hath many solaces, enjoyed / Where other senses want not their delights / At home in leisure and domestic ease'.[36] The Philistine champion Harapha, whom Milton adds to the scriptural account, wants to crow over Samson's defeat and his unsuitability as an opponent. To these last two visitors Samson responds with fearsome threats of violence that he cannot and does not carry out. When Dalila begs him to 'Let me approach at least, and touch thy hand', Samson responds: 'Not for thy life, lest fierce remembrance wake / My sudden rage to tear thee joint by joint.'[37] When Harapha crows over the spectacle that Samson has become, the latter replies: 'The way to know were not to see but taste',[38] daring the Philistine giant to step close enough to test his strength. But nothing actually happens, or mean-ingfully changes, in any of these encounters.

When change does occur, it is necessarily invisible to the reader, for it takes place not through any of Samson's human interactions but via his sudden, inexplicable, and indubitable sense that God has singled him out and is inspiring him to great and terrible action. When he has been told that he will be paraded before the Philistine lords as part of their celebrations before their idol, Dagon, he suddenly tells the chorus: 'Be of good courage, I begin to feel / Some rousing motions in me which dispose / To something extraor-dinary my thoughts.'[39] He is willingly led away, and we later hear only from the messenger (as was standard practice in the Greek tragedies that were Milton's model) about the actions to which these 'rousing motions' prompted him: standing between the pillars of the Philistine temple, 'with head a while inclined, / And eyes fast fixed he stood, as one who prayed, / Or some great matter in his mind revolved.'[40] Finally he shook the pillars 'With horrible convulsion to and fro' until the temple came crashing down on the 'choice nobility and flower' of the Philistines, and 'Samson with these inmixed'.[41]

Everything hinges on how we understand the 'rousing motions' that Samson felt, what was going on 'in his mind' when he stood and wrenched down the pillars. Samuel Johnson complained, under-standably, that *Samson Agonistes* was 'lacking a middle, since nothing passes between the first act and the last, that either hastens or delays the death of Samson'.[42] This must be so, however, because the kind of transformation at which Milton hints – the feeling of rousing, divine motions within – is not something that can be narrated or explained. Such motions cannot be shared by those who have not experienced them. They do not come about through human effort or merit – they are visited upon Samson, or so at least he insists, in the midst of his passivity, just as Milton was visited by his divine muse. Until he feels these sudden motions, Samson is fixed in place; all he can do is rebuff those who seek to claim him or to demean him, until he can suddenly and terrifyingly do more.

Whether Milton must have, or could not possibly have, endorsed

Samson's act of violent slaughter has been one of the most contested questions in twenty-first-century discussions of his work. This was prompted in part when the eminent Milton scholar John Carey wrote an essay on the first anniversary of the attacks on the World Trade Center in September 2001, titled 'A Work in Praise of Terrorism?' Carey acknowledged the troubling resemblance between Samson's final act – indiscriminate violence carried out on a group, and on oneself, based on the inner conviction that one is divinely inspired – and the killings perpetuated by suicide attackers, but ultimately strove to distinguish them, insisting that 'Milton was a subtle-minded poet, not a murderous bigot'.[43] What's most telling to me about the debate that Carey's provocative claims began, nearly two decades later, is that it shows the extent to which, when it's argued what Milton must have meant or cannot possibly have meant in his poems, such judgements depend on our own idea of the poet and the person.[44]

I have no doubt that I am also doing a version of this when I read *Samson* neither as clearly endorsing nor criticising its hero's violent actions, but as something more like a case study in inscrutability, a brutal joke on the critic or the biographer who would claim certainty about the content of Samson's mind, or of Milton's. This is in part a product of its strange genre, which I haven't yet mentioned, and which is a particular challenge to modern readers. Though modelled on ancient tragedies, *Samson* was never meant to be staged; or rather, it is staged only in the mind of the reader. But it's worth remembering here that Milton scrapped his plan to write *Paradise Lost* as a play and gave us instead an epic poem with a powerfully involved narrator, who guides and influences the reader – although not, as I suggested in the last chapter, as securely as we might think. What we get in *Samson* is neither a physical spectacle – which would give us at least a specific performance, a set of embodied persons, on which to base our judgement – nor a narrator who could chime in and confirm the truly divine origin of Samson's inner impulse. Instead we must stage the scene in our mind, and therefore can never be certain whether the motions that he experiences were truly divine or not.[45]

There were many people in Milton's lifetime who were happy to justify extreme and exorbitant actions on the basis of an inner conviction that God had impelled them. There were also many who were panicked by the implications of such views, and the anarchy to which self-certain individuals might give rise. This was a central part of the longer legacy of the Reformation, whose leaders had sought to justify each individual interpreting scripture for him- (and occasionally her-) self, in accordance with the inner promptings of the spirit, but then had sought at every turn to restrict who in practice could do so, and what could be thought and said. We've seen a version of this contradictory dynamic emerge repeatedly in Milton's writings: an oscillation between a desire for open thought and imagination, and an opposing impulse to limit, restrict, exclude, violently castigate. It's certainly possible, encountering Milton at the pinnacle of his self-certainty and sense of his own specialness, to imagine him justifying almost anything to himself if he deeply believed it to be right. If this is an uncomfortable thought, that's because we are often unwilling to acknowledge the forms of violence woven into the religious, political, and intellectual traditions to which the Anglo-American world is heir. It's all too easy to think of violence as something happening elsewhere, perpetuated by those who are backward and alien. For me, one of the reasons to study the sixteenth and seventeenth centuries has always been to challenge this complacent view. Deciding in advance that Milton's subtlety as a poet automatically exonerates him from complicity with violence doesn't do justice to the very real and unsettling violence that I often encounter as one of the genuine expressions of his imaginative inclinations.

But this doesn't mean that I see him as endorsing Samson's gruesome act of mass violence and suicide. The reason that I focus not just on Samson's inward motions but also on Manoa's desire to take his dead son home and build him a monument, the reason that this has become one of the crucial moments in my own Miltonic canon, is that the tenor of *Samson Agonistes*'s ending changed significantly for me once I encountered this urge to approve and to memorialise. This might, I think, be a trick Milton borrowed from his beloved Shakespeare, whose influence is thick throughout *Samson* (most obviously and dazzlingly, Dalila's resplendent entrance borrows heavily from Shakespeare's descriptions of Cleopatra), and who, as we have seen, Milton insisted required no monument. Shakespeare would often end a play by having a character sum up the action and define its meaning in retrospect, but in a deliberately unsatisfactory way. The most obvious example is Horatio at the end of *Hamlet*, who promises to 'speak to the yet unknowing world / How these things came about: so shall you hear / Of carnal, bloody, and unnatural acts, / Of accidental judgments, casual slaughters, / Of deaths put on by cunning and forced cause'.[46] Horatio – who was not party to many of the central events of the play – makes its action sound like the kind of conventionally gory revenge play that *Hamlet* emphatically isn't. The ending of *Samson* can, I think, be read similarly: not as an endorsement of Manoa's desire to clean up his son's reputation along with his bloodied body, but rather as an insistence to the reader that building a monument is a way of assigning just one meaning to a life whose meaning and truth remain, to readers of Milton's last great work, maddeningly murky, perpetually beyond the reach of certainty. That even a memorial constructed by a grieving father for the noblest reasons might be a vain monument.

What then, if any, is the right kind of monument to Milton? I've suggested that *Samson Agonistes* ends by promising a monument that is deeply ambivalent, its validity impossible for readers to verify with any certainty. In a sense this rather well reflects the absences, false certainties, and awkward half-measures that I have encountered on my Miltonic journeys. I'll bring these journeys to an end by returning to the question of why Milton's homes came to the fore in my walk with Sean, and in his final works, in ways that are connected to the imperative to open oneself to strangeness that has been one of the central themes of this book.

In his final years Milton made one more move westward out of London, as he had in his twenties when he moved with his parents to Hammersmith and then to Horton. This was prompted by the epidemic of 1665 which nearly turned Bunhill Fields into a plague pit. Milton moved in July of that year with his household, including his third wife and his daughters, to the village of Chalfont St Giles in Buckinghamshire. He lived in a cottage which had been rented for him by the Quaker Thomas Ellwood, and the population of the village and area were predominantly Quakers. The move suggests the extent to which Milton's position on the sanctity of individual reason and the irrelevance of specific place to true worship had led him to overlap with this group, despite the continued differences in his idiosyncratic theology. Ellwood was a direct influence on Milton's work in other ways, since when Milton showed him the unpublished manuscript of his epic after arriving in Chalfont St Giles, Ellwood is said to have commented: 'thou hast said much here of *Paradise Lost*, but what hast thou to say of *Paradise Found*?' This may indeed have been the prompt for writing *Paradise Regained*. There Milton presents Jesus not as a figure of action but as one who withstands temptation and remains steadfast. While this completed a lifelong set of self-images that went back as far as the Lady in *Comus*, it may also have reflected his growing familiarity with the Quakers. *Samson's* violence was paired, in its first publication, with a resolutely passive and restrained Son of God, one who knows how to stand and wait.

The cottage at Chalfont St Giles is the only one of Milton's English residences to have survived, and it has become a museum to his memory, with a remarkable collection of books and objects relating to his life and writings. I visited it not with Sean but rather when I was making the radio programme that also took me to Italy, and was given a wonderful guided tour by a member of staff. As with the other moments that seemed to offer a direct and authentic connection to Milton – like my first encounter with the Trinity Manuscript of his writings – I experienced an almost superstitious tingle at the thought of standing in the rooms where Milton had breathed and slept and spoken and listened. I sought to honour this sensation by recalling the chair that I saw in the cottage in detail, and seating Milton in it, when I imagined him awaking to the composition of *Paradise Lost* in the opening words of this book.

When I left the cottage, I was greeted by two of its trustees, who were pottering in the garden there. It became clear that they'd heard a BBC Radio show was being recorded, and were keen to show me around the garden in which they took great pride. But they also wanted to show me connections to Milton and his work which went deeper than met the eye. Many of the plants there had been chosen because they were specifically mentioned in *Paradise Lost*. And then, towards the rear of the garden, they showed me the *pièce de résistance*: an apple tree with an artificial snake carefully arranged in its branches. The spectacle was amusing – harmlessly silly, as they seemed to acknowledge when they showed it to me – but by now it was more interesting to me as an impulse that I could recognise, and had identified in myself. The impulse to say, like the proprietors of the hotel in Florence or the monks at Vallombrosa, *Milton was here*, and his being here mattered, it helped and perhaps even caused him to imagine in the way that he did.

My travels in search of Milton had helped me to understand the ending of *Samson Agonistes*, and the ending of Milton's life which it seemed deliberately to anticipate, as genuinely torn between a desire for a monument that would give the final and definitive word, and a deep doubtfulness that such finality is desirable, or even possible. In the end I am glad that there is no definitive monument to Milton, even in Bunhill Fields; no single place to which one must go in order to capture or appreciate him. The fate of his body when it was removed from its grave in 1790, dispersed through London in macabre fragments, feels curiously apt. Milton remains best encountered as a series of scattered moments and encounters which do not, and need not, add up to a cohesive whole. This is what stops Milton, for me, becoming a monument of the wrong kind, the vainest kind: the kind of monument that, as Robert Musil realised, we no longer look at, because we think that we already know everything that there is to see.

I am nervous of concluding in light of these scattered encounters that the only true or proper monument to Milton is his writings. Of course as a professional teacher and scholar of literature, I would feel this, and it seems too sentimental and obvious to assert straight-forwardly. It is true that the manner in which I've sought in this book to follow and to inhabit the curious traces and absences of Milton's life bears a resemblance to the ways in which I seek to read and teach his writings, insofar as both eschew what I think is the wrong kind of monumentality, the kind that inhibits and stifles. But it is perhaps inevitable that a moment that sticks in my mind as representing the best monument to Milton occurred not when I was out and about in search of him, but in the quiet of a library. I had returned to Cambridge to visit Christ's College, where Milton studied. The librarian kindly took me up a winding staircase to the room containing the college archives, so that I could gawp at his signature in the matriculation records, although I had no good scholarly reason to do so. I also saw a variety of other intriguing Miltonic items, but what stood out was a copy of a work that had long fascinated me: the infamous edition of *Paradise Lost* that was produced in 1732 by a man named Richard Bentley.

Bentley spent thirty years in Cambridge as Master of Trinity College, and he was famous for his deep classical learning and infamous for his overbearing arrogance. He made his name as a scholar of difficult ancient texts, which often required ingenious conjecture to fill their gaps and correct errors of transmission. When Bentley read *Paradise Lost*, however, he was – like many readers through the centuries – troubled and even appalled by it, both theologically and poetically. But Bentley's response was different from most. He approached Milton's poem like one of his imperfect ancient texts; he concocted an entirely fictional scenario according to which the purities of the original had been corrupted by a sinister 'Editor', responsible for all the errors and solecisms. And he took it upon himself to correct them, deciding that he knew best how certain lines must have originally been intended by Milton.

For a long time Bentley's edition was dismissed as an oddity, representing the worst excesses of an arrogant crank. But some readers, notably William Empson, began to notice that there was a perverse brilliance to what Bentley was doing; that in aiming to 'correct' a line, he was often doing a better job of clarifying what made the poem's language genuinely strange, often stretched to the limits of sense, than those who simply admired it in fawning terms.[47] What Bentley confirms for me is the powerful way in which Milton can inspire conviction in his readers about what he must and must not have meant, what he must and must not have been like; and, while Bentley was clearly deluded in his creation of the 'Editor' responsible for the sins of the text, he helped me see the extent to which Milton's writings do often seem genuinely and fascinatingly split, riven by divided inclinations and convictions, almost as if there were two or more John Miltons.

Above all, Bentley confirmed to me that Milton is valuable and fascinating in part because, wherever we might be inclined to place him in the list of greatest poets (probably an unhelpful exercise), he certainly tops the list of English poets who have inspired the most passionate disagreements as to whether he is of value, and, if so, why. These disagreements are deeply instructive because they prevent him from ossifying into a monument. They are more valuable as ways of maintaining his books as 'the pretious life-blood of a master spirit, imbalm'd and treasur'd up on purpose to a life beyond life' than bland praise of his greatness or his universal relevance. When I opened up the copy of Bentley's Milton in Christ's, I discovered that it was itself a curious monument to this important fact. It had been owned by the poet William Cowper – whom I mentioned above, lamenting the raiding of Milton's grave – and he had filled it with marginalia, angrily rebutting Bentley's misreadings at every turn. When Milton wrote that 'the gorgeous East with richest hand / Showers on her kings barbaric pearl and gold', Bentley found the verb objectionable: if it were a shower, surely it would have splashed on to the king's subjects as well? Milton, he suggested, must have written 'sowed', a gentler verb. Cowper was irate, writing in the margin that 'The childish conceits of this note are below the dignity of a true critic.' The point is not a particularly crucial one; what I do find riveting is the sense, emerging in the century after Milton's death, that the precise appropriateness of every word that he wrote was open to debate, and worth getting worked up about. Immense and unremitting energy, even when expended in seemingly perverse or bad-tempered directions, sealed between the covers of a book: what better living monument could there be to Milton?

I am not ready, however, to leave behind Milton's homes for his poems quite so quickly or straightforwardly. I observed above that walking the sites of his London houses seemed oddly to resonate with his final works, which seem recurrently concerned with the losing and regaining not just of paradise but specifically of home. Samson in particular withstands Dalila's attempt to bring him home, and is claimed for home by his father only in death. I've suggested throughout this book that Milton was divided on the question of home, as he was on nearly every other question that I've encountered: mired in the parental home for an oddly protracted period, and then drawn to leave it behind for an extended encounter with the strenuously alien and challenging. It's perhaps this tension or contrast – rather than the excitement of his Italian experiences in and of themselves – that's led me to grant this period a prominent place in Milton's life. And what I've come to realise in my travels and ruminations around his final years is that this experience of alternating between being comfortably at home and exposed to the strange and even the repellent also echoes the rhythm of my experience in the years I have spent with Milton, as the pendulum has swung from the *tick* of easy intimacy to the *tock* of total alienation. This brings me back to the question I raised in the introduction, of whether the best model for relating to Milton is not quite friendship but perhaps, instead, hospitality.[48] To lose oneself in Milton's writing is to encounter and acknowledge its strangeness, even if we don't want to go as far as Richard Bentley; it is simultaneously to host, and to be hosted by, something that *should* retain a degree of strangeness. To accept the hospitality of Milton's writings, to accord them the hospitality of our time and our effort, are endeavours that don't require a relationship that is necessarily based on loving or even liking or agreeing with one another. This, I think, is the answer that the *experience* of reading and living with Milton and his writings offers, the closest to a consolation in light of the impossibility of being at home anywhere and everywhere that is occasioned by the Fall. It is why the writings of his final years return obsessively to the loss of home, and to the temptation of home as a place where problems will end and stories will become simple and single.

Let me end, then, by making Milton strange in one final way. I began this chapter by stressing the elusiveness of the moment of his death, and then linked this to the difficulty of pinning down death and its meanings in *Paradise Lost*. We can, however, ask what might seem like a strange question: what did Milton think about his own death? What did he think his experience of his own death would be? Among the various heretical opinions to which he adhered late in his life, along with his anti-Trinitarianism, Milton was a mortalist. While some mortalists denied the immortality of the soul altogether, Milton seems to have believed that after death the soul would persist, but it would not experience either punishment or bliss; instead it would sleep with the body until the Apocalypse, when soul and body would rise together, an indivisible whole. Like so many of Milton's core beliefs, this is an abstract argument that also seems to reflect his deep sense of inviolable individuality. He asked himself the question that he always asked: what would the experience of this be like? In *De Doctrina Christiana* he wrote that, for the one who dies, the long wait for resurrection would be no time at all. Unlike the in-between time of life, in which we need to learn and struggle to make something of it, this experience, even if separated by millennia, would be instantaneous for the individual: 'for those who have died, all intervening time will be as nothing, so that to them it will feel that they die and are with Christ at the same moment [*eodem fieri momento sentietur*].'[49] This is Milton's final reshaping of time, his sense of what would happen at his elusive end; he would close his eyes, open them in what would feel like the same instant, and be, at last, both out of time and at one with it.

Acknowledgements

This is a book partly about what it means to live with, to teach, and to be taught by a writer's work, and it is therefore both appropriate and delightful to be able to thank those who have lived with me, taught me, and been taught by me while it has come into being. Those who have lived with me the longest – my parents, Chana and Raf, and my siblings, Gabe and Ruby – are a seemingly bottomless well of inspiration and support, not least during a grim pandemic year when we have seen much less of one another than we would all like. I am always grateful to them, but particularly so in this case, where I have written more directly than before about how my experiences of growing up with them have shaped the ways in which I think and the person that I am. Thank you to them for reading and discussing with me those parts of the book and, in my mother's case, for reading much more of it and offering thoughtful suggestions.

I would like sincerely to thank my students – at Princeton, Cambridge, and Oxford – with whom it has been a privilege to discuss Milton and many other things. I have been fortunate indeed in my own teachers. I first taught Milton's work as part of a literature survey overseen by Jeff Dolven, and then at greater length beneath the benign gaze of Nigel Smith, who generously read the first parts of this book. A conference in honour of Leonard Barkan, who is certainly no *shmendrik*, gave me a first opportunity to speak in public about my relationship with Yiddish. All three have shaped my thinking in more ways than I can count. Among my earlier teachers I must mention Kevin Jackson, who died with shocking suddenness as the book was being completed. He never taught me

Milton, but meetings with him in Clown's and The Bun Shop, being boomingly recommended everything from Guy Debord to Nashville blues music, were deeply formative. My debt to Sean McEvoy is registered – though not adequately accounted for – in this book's dedication and in its pages.

I first grew convinced that I wanted to write a book about Milton when I was teaching in Cambridge, and I would like to thank my colleagues at Trinity College for support and stimulation. I would particularly like to thank Nicolas Bell, who opened up the treasures of the Wren Library for me – quite literally, when he and I looked together for the first time at the Trinity Manuscript of Milton's works, a moment I'll always remember.

The book was written after I moved to Oxford. I was fortunate to join University College, an environment where I have felt encouraged both to develop my ideas and to keep them connected with the wider world. For helping make it so I would like to thank Ivor Crewe and Valerie Amos, the Masters during my time at Univ; Andrew Bell, the Senior Tutor; Nick Halmi and Laura Varnam, my colleagues in English; and fellows across and beyond the humanities, particularly Polly Jones. I have felt privileged to be part of the Faculty of English, and have benefited from conversations with Matt Bevis, Nandini Das, Simon Palfrey, Emma Smith, and Adam Smyth about the kind of book I wanted to write. Will Poole, Miltonist extraordinaire, has not read any of this book, and I suspect my Milton is very different from his, but he has been unfailingly generous with the fruits of his formidable scholarship. The first people to read any of it were Lorna Hutson, Katherine Ibbett, and Katie Murphy; our work-in-progress group has been both joyful and inspiring, and their feedback a great help. Since my arrival in Oxford, Lorna has been a constant source of wisdom and encouragement as well as a model of open-minded conviction. Jack Parlett read the first half of the manuscript and offered generous feedback, and our shared adventures in reading have shaped it in numerous ways. I have learned a huge amount from talking and teaching with Bart Van Es, whose subtle and passionate thinking about what it means to read and to live with literature has been a constant impetus for my own.

I could not have completed this book had I not been the recipient of a Philip Leverhulme Prize in 2019, a life-changing and liberatingly open-ended award at a time when research feels at risk of becoming ever more instrumentalised and goal-driven.

I benefited greatly from Nick McDowell's and Regina Schwartz's early encouragement, and from several discussions in which I floated my ideas: the British Milton Seminar; the symposium 'On Difficulty in Early Modern Literature' at King's College London; the Oxford Centre for Life Writing; and the online meeting of the Renaissance Society of America. Thanks to Sarah Knight and Hannah Crawforth for organising the first two of these, and to Hannah for collaborating on the fourth, as well as for numerous inspirational discussions about reading and teaching Milton and other things.

Several dear friends read parts of the manuscript at various stages and offered valuable feedback: particular thanks to Namratha Rao and Mike Schoenfeldt for their comments. I *suppose* that the arrival of his daughter is a good-enough excuse for David Hillman not yet having read the whole thing but, as ever, our conversations and our friendship have left their mark on much of what I write.

I would like to thank the custodians of the various Milton-related locations that I visited in the course of writing this book, and others who shared their knowledge, especially: Brian Loomes; David Palmer; the staff of Milton's Cottage in Chalfont St Giles, the Museo Galileo in Florence, and the Villa Il Gioiello; the vicars of St Michael's Church at Horton and St Mary's Church at Langley; and the monks of the Vallombrosian order. Melissa Fitzgerald organised access to several of these places in the process of our putting Milton on the radio, and it was a pleasure to visit them with her. I would also like to thank the staff of the various libraries and coffee shops in which much of the research for this book was undertaken.

It was Tom Avery's contagious enthusiasm that first persuaded me that I should write something encompassing all of Milton's life. At Basic it has been a pleasure to work with Sarah Caro and Claire Potter. Sarah has been a remarkably engaged principal editor, playing a decisive role in the book taking its final shape. For her help with the production process it has been a breeze working with Caroline Westmore, and I am grateful to Hilary Hammond and Howard Davies for sharp-eyed copy-editing and proofreading, Juliet Brightmore for assistance with images, Caroline Jones for compiling the index, and to all those involved in production and publicity. Luke Ingram, old friend and exemplary agent, has acted as sounding-board and advocate with typically wry grace.

Alejandro and Beatriz were generously frank with their exasperation when they felt I was mentioning John Milton too often at the dinner table. While I have not met all of their narrative preferences – Ale would probably have preferred me to write a *Beano*-style comic, and I have still not fulfilled Bea's memorably surreal demand for a bedtime story 'with nothing and no one in it' – the big questions that I ask in this book have been animated and provoked by my love for them. To Rosa Andújar, who accompanied this book every step of the way, I am boundlessly grateful, as Milton's Adam is to Eve, for 'Those thousand decencies that daily flow / From all her words and actions'.

Picture Credits

Notes

Abbreviations

Milton's Poems

All references to *Paradise Lost* (abbreviated to PL) are given by book and line number and follow the 2nd revised edition of the text by Alastair Fowler (London: Longman, 2007). All of Milton's other poems are cited by line number from *The Complete Shorter Poems*, ed. John Carey, 2nd revised edition (London: Longman, 2007). I have used Carey's translations of poems from languages other than English, with some minor emendations.

Milton's Prose Works

CW   *Works of John Milton*, ed. Frank Allen Patterson, 18 vols (New York: Columbia University Press, 1931–8).

DDC   *The Complete Works of John Milton, Vol. VIII: De Doctrina Christiana*, ed. and trans. John K. Hale et al., 2 vols (Oxford: Oxford University Press, 2012).

MW   *The Complete Works of John Milton, Vol. XI: Manuscript Writings*, ed. William Poole (Oxford: Oxford University Press, 2019).

YPW   *Complete Prose Works of John Milton*, ed. Don M. Wolfe et al., 8 vols (New Haven, CT: Yale University Press, 1953–82).

Other Works

ABL   John Aubrey, *Brief Lives*, ed. Kate Bennett, 2 vols (Oxford: Oxford University Press, 2015).

EL   *Early Lives of Milton*, ed. Helen Darbishire (London: Constable, 1932).

Johnson   Samuel Johnson, 'Milton', in *The Lives of the Most Eminent English Poets*, ed. Roger Lonsdale, 4 vols (Oxford: Oxford University Press, 2006), vol. 1, pp. 242–95.

OHM   *The Oxford Handbook of Milton*, ed. Nicholas McDowell and Nigel Smith (Oxford: Oxford University Press, 2011).

Introduction: The Two John Miltons

1. These hints of visionary experience are collated from, among others, Abiezer Coppe, 'A Fiery Flying Roll', in *Ranter Writings*, ed. Nigel Smith (London: Pluto Press, 2014), pp. 73, 75. On the spiritual taste of the pineapple or 'West-Indian Piney' see Geoffrey Nuttall, *The Holy Spirit in Puritan Faith and Experience* (Chicago: University of Chicago Press, 1992), p. 139.

2. EL p. 33.

3. PL 7.216–17.

4. Augustine, *Confessions*, trans. Henry Chadwick (Oxford: Oxford University Press, 1991), p. 185.

5. 'Ad Mansum', ll. 30–4; translation of Ariosto from *Of Reformation* in *Complete Shorter Poems*, ed. Carey, p. 287.

6. See Christopher Ricks, *Milton's Grand Style* (Oxford: Clarendon Press, 1963), pp. 59–61.

7. Johnson, p. 242.

8. PL 7.27–8.

9. *Emerson in His Journals*, ed. Joel Porte (Cambridge, MA: Harvard University Press, 1982), p. 136.

10. *The Romantics on Milton*, ed. Joseph Wittreich (Cleveland, OH: Press of Case Western Reserve University, 1970), p. 92.

11. PL 2.176, 180, 218–20, 226–7.

12. PL 1.22–3.

13. Marcel Proust, *The Way By Swann's*, trans. Lydia Davis (London: Allen Lane, 2002), pp. 8–9.

14. Kim F. Hall, *Things of Darkness: Economies of Race and Gender in Early Modern England* (Ithaca, NY: Cornell University Press, 1995), pp. 1–2, citing YPW vol. 1, p. 568.

15. 'L'Allegro', ll. 33–4.

16. Italo Calvino, 'Lightness', in *Six Memos for the Next Millennium*, trans. Geoffrey Brock (London: Penguin, 2016), pp. 32, 18.

17. Johnson, p. 285.

18. He was born in 1626, when Milton was nearly eighteen, and died in 1676, two years after Milton. See the classic study by Gershom Scholem, *Sabbatai Sevi: The Mystical Messiah* (Princeton, NJ: Princeton University Press, 1973).

19. Terry Eagleton, preface to Catherine Belsey, *John Milton: Language, Gender, Power* (Oxford: Basil Blackwell, 1988), p. viii.

20. Thomas Grey, 'Elegy', ll. 5, 57.

21. YPW vol. 2, pp. 557–8.

22. James Holly Hanford, *John Milton, Englishman* (New York: Crown Publishers, 1949).

23. Tom Paulin, *Minotaur: Poetry and the Nation State* (London: Faber, 1992), p. 19.

24. YPW vol. 5, p. 450.

25. Franz Rosenzweig, *The Star of Redemption*, trans. William Hallo (Notre Dame, IN: University of Notre Dame Press, 1985), p. 302.

26. In what felt like a form of symbolic circularity, I would eventually go on to be taught as a graduate student by the leading authority on Abiezer Coppe and the Ranters, Nigel Smith. In 2014 life came full circle when I saw Nigel read from Coppe's writings at an event where Leon Rosselson played and sang this song.

27. Johnson, p. 293.

28. T. S. Eliot, 'Milton I', in *Selected Prose*, ed. John Hayward (Harmondsworth: Penguin, 1953), pp. 128–9, 148.

29. Matthew Biberman, 'T. S. Eliot, Anti-Semitism, and the Milton Controversy', in *Milton and the Jews*, ed. Douglas A. Brooks (Cambridge: Cambridge University Press, 2008), pp. 105–27.

30. Richard Wagner, 'Judaism in Music', in *Stories and Essays*, ed. Charles Osborn (London: Peter Owen, 1973), p. 27.

31. 'On Shakespeare', ll. 1–8.

32. Robert Musil, 'Monuments', in *Posthumous Papers of a Living Author*, trans. Peter Wortsman (Harmondsworth: Penguin, 1987), p. 61.

33. *Mark Twain's Speeches* (New York: Harper, 1923), p. 210.

34. https://www.gov.uk/government/publications/national-curriculum-
in-england-english-programmes-of-study/national-curriculum-
in-england-english-programmes-of-study. Accessed 1 March 2019.

35. Alexander Nehamas, *Only a Promise of Happiness: The Place of Beauty
in a World of Art* (Princeton, NJ: Princeton University Press, 2007),
p. 58.

36. T. S. Eliot, 'A Note on the Verse of John Milton' (1936), in *Selected
Prose*, ed. Hayward, p. 123.

37. Colin Burrow, 'Shall I Go On?', *London Review of Books*, 7 March
2013.

38. William Shakespeare, *Hamlet*, 1.5.172–3.

39. YPW vol. 2, p. 515.

Chapter 1: 9 December 1608: 'On Time'

1. John Stow, *A Survey of London*, ed. Charles Kingsford (Oxford:
Clarendon Press, 1908), vol. 1, p. 346.

2. Denise Levertov, 'Biography and the Poet', in *New and Selected
Essays* (New York: New Directions, 1992), p. 184.

3. Henry Vaughan to John Aubrey, 15 June 1673, Bodleian Library,
MS Wood F39, ff. 216–17.

4. PL 1.582–4.

5. Harry Rusche, 'A Reading of John Milton's Horoscope', *Milton
Quarterly* 13 (1979), pp. 7–8.

6. 'On Time', ll. 11, 21–2.

7. 'On Time', ll. 2–3.

8. PL 2.932–5.

9. Osip Mandelstam, *The Noise of Time*, trans. Clarence Brown
(London: Quartet, 1988).

10. Virginia Woolf, *A Room of One's Own and Three Guineas*, ed.
Hermione Lee (London: Vintage, 2001), pp. 4–5.

11. 'On Time', ll. 5–8.

12. ABL vol. 1, pp. 303–4.

13. ABL vol. 1, p. xl; Stuart Sherman, *Telling Time: Clocks, Diaries and
English Diurnal Form, 1660–1785* (Chicago: University of Chicago
Press, 1996).

14. See Carlo Cipolla, *Clocks and Culture 1300–1700* (New York: W. W. Norton, 2003).

15. Frank Kermode, *The Sense of an Ending* (Oxford: Oxford University Press, 2000), pp. 44–5.

16. Meric Casaubon, *A Treatise Concerning Enthusiasme* (London, 1655), p. 179.

17. *OED*, 'rhythm', 1a, 1d.

18. Émile Benveniste, 'The Notion of "Rhythm" in its Linguistic Expression', in *Problems in General Linguistics*, trans. Mary Elizabeth Meek (Coral Gables, FL: University of Miami Press, 1971), pp. 281–8, esp. pp. 281, 283.

19. See for example Frank A. Brown, Jr, 'Biological Rhythms in Integration', *International Journal of Chronobiology* 1 (1973), p. 8.

20. Tia DeNora, *Music in Everyday Life* (Cambridge: Cambridge University Press, 2000), p. 77.

21. Eliot, 'Milton I', p. 142.

22. Stéphane Mallarmé, *Œuvres Complètes* (Paris: Gallimard, 1945), p. 644; cited by Philippe Lacoue-Labarthe in 'The Echo of the Subject', in *Typography: Mimesis, Philosophy, Politics*, trans. Christopher Fynsk (Stanford, CA: Stanford University Press, 1998), p. 140.

23. Gerard Manley Hopkins, *Selected Letters*, ed. Catherine Phillips (Oxford: Oxford University Press, 1991), p. 87.

24. Hopkins, 'That Nature is a Heraclitean Fire and of the comfort of the Resurrection', ll. 1–2, in *The Major Works*, ed. Catherine Phillips (Oxford: Oxford University Press, 2009).

25. Hopkins, *Selected Letters*, p. 88.

26. Ibid., p. 107.

27. Ibid.

28. Ibid., pp. 108, 87.

29. *The Collected Works of Ralph Waldo Emerson, Vol. V: English Traits*, ed. Douglas Emory Wilson et al. (Cambridge, MA: Harvard University Press, 1994), p. 167; see Erik Gray, *Milton and the Victorians* (Ithaca, NY: Cornell University Press, 2009), p. 2.

30. Ralph Waldo Emerson, 'The Comic', cited by Matthew Bevis in *Wordsworth's Fun* (Chicago: University of Chicago Press, 2019), p. 194.

31. William Bunting, Calendar watch, *c.*1645–55, with spurious inscription of Milton's name, British Museum, https://www.britishmuseum.org/collection/object/H_1862-0801-1.

Chapter 2: 17 October 1614: 'At a Solemn Music'

1. *The Teares or Lamentacions of a Sorrowfull Soule: Composed with Musicall Ayres and Songs, both for Voyces and diuers Instruments. Set foorth by Sir William Leighton Knight . . . And all Psalmes that consist of so many feete as the fiftieth Psalme, will goe to the foure parts for Consort* (London: William Stansby, 1614), presentation copy to Charles Stuart, British Library class mark K.1.i.9; Verna L. Moore, 'Psalmes, Teares, and Broken Music', *Bulletin of the John Rylands Library* 46.2 (1964), p. 420.
2. Howard Mayer Brown, rev. Ian Woodfield, 'Chest of Viols', Grove Music Online, https://www.oxfordmusiconline.com.
3. ABL vol. 1, p. 660; EL p. 18.
4. 'At a Solemn Music', ll. 1–2.
5. Warwick Edwards, 'Consort', Grove Music Online; Richard Taruskin, *Music in the Seventeenth and Eighteenth Centuries* (Oxford: Oxford University Press, 2009), pp. 113–15.
6. Charles Rosen, *Piano Notes: The Hidden World of the Pianist* (London: Allen Lane, 2003), p. 4.
7. Elizabeth Hellmuth Margulis, *On Repeat: How Music Plays the Mind* (Oxford: Oxford University Press, 2014), pp. 62–7; DeNora, *Music in Everyday Life*, pp. 77–82.
8. Raymond Williams, 'The Creative Mind', in *The Long Revolution* (Harmondsworth: Penguin, 1965), pp. 40–1.
9. Marsilio Ficino, *Opera Omnia* (Basel, 1576), p. 651.
10. Plato, *Timaeus*, 47E; St Augustine, *On Music*, trans. Robert Catesby Taliaferro (Washington DC: Catholic University of America Press, 1947), pp. 370–1.
11. Thomas Browne, *Religio Medici*, in *The Major Works*, ed. C. A. Patrides (Harmondsworth: Penguin, 1977), pp. 149–50.
12. *The Closet of Sir Kenelm Digby Opened*, ed. Jane Stevenson and Peter Davidson (London: Prospect Books, 1997), pp. 205, 150.
13. See Paul Glennie and Nigel Thrift, *Shaping the Day: A History of Timekeeping in England and Wales 1300–1800* (Oxford: Oxford University Press, 2009), pp. 2–3.
14. Roger Mathew Grant, *Beating Time and Measuring Music in the Early Modern Era* (Oxford: Oxford University Press, 2014), pp. 23, 62.

15. Specifically, I have spent a significant amount of time listening and relistening to the pieces by John Milton senior on two CDs: *Sublime Discourses: John Milton and Martin Peerson, the Complete Instrumental Music* and *A Candle to the Glorious Sun: Sacred Songs by John Milton and Martin Peerson*, both of which I highly recommend.

16. I'm referring for convenience here to the modern arrangement of the piece by Richard Rastall, since bar divisions hadn't yet developed in the seventeenth century.

17. John Milton the Elder, *Complete Works, Vol. I: Vocal Music*, ed. Richard Rastall (Norwich: Antico Editions, 2011), p. iv.

18. ABL vol. 1, p. 660.

19. *Documents of the English Reformation*, ed. Gerald Bray (Cambridge: James Clark, 1994), pp. 344–5.

20. See Peter Le Huray, 'The Fair Musick that All Creatures Made', in *The Age of Milton: Backgrounds to Seventeenth-Century Literature*, ed. C. A. Patrides and Raymond Waddington (Manchester: Manchester University Press, 1980), pp. 241–72; Peter Le Huray, *Music and the Reformation in England, 1549–1660* (Cambridge: Cambridge University Press, 1978), esp. pp. 269–71, 388–90.

21. EL p. 51.

22. Taruskin, *Music in the Seventeenth and Eighteenth Centuries*, p. 114.

23. John Dod and Robert Cleaver, *A Godlie form of Household Government: for the ordering of private families* (London, 1612), sig. L4r; cited and discussed by Lorna Hutson, *The Usurer's Daughter: Male Friendship and Fictions of Women in Sixteenth-Century England* (London: Routledge, 1994), p. 20.

24. See Christopher Marsh, *Music and Society in Early Modern England* (Cambridge: Cambridge University Press, 2010), pp. 150–1.

25. *Peacham's Compleat Gentleman, 1634*, ed. George Stuart Gordon (Oxford: Clarendon Press, 1906), p. 100.

26. Thomas Dekker cited by John Gallagher, *Learning Languages in Early Modern England* (Oxford: Oxford University Press, 2019), p. 3.

27. On the group around St Paul's see Craig Monson, 'Thomas Myriell's Manuscript Collection: One View of Musical Taste in Jacobean London', *Journal of the American Musicological Society* 30.3 (1977), pp. 438–9. On foreign musicians see J. A. Westrup, 'Foreign Musicians in Stuart England', *Musical Quarterly* 27.1 (1941), pp. 70–89.

28. Christopher D. S. Field, 'Coprario [Coperario, Cooper, Cowper], John [Giovanni]', Grove Music Online.

29. John V. Cockshoot and Christopher D. S. Field, 'Ferrabosco Family', Grove Music Online.

30. Ben Jonson, 'The Houre-glasse', ll. 1–3; Edward Doughtie, 'Ferrabosco and Jonson's "The Houre-glasse"', *Renaissance Quarterly* 22.2 (1969), pp. 148–50.

31. Monson, 'Thomas Myriell's Manuscript Collection', pp. 429, 442.

32. See Gallagher, *Learning Languages*.

33. Thomas Nashe, *The Unfortunate Traveller and Other Works*, ed. J. B. Steane (Harmondsworth: Penguin, 1985), p. 345; cf. Edward Chaney, '*Quo Vadis?* Travel as Education and the Impact of Italy in the Sixteenth Century', in *The Evolution of the Grand Tour: Anglo-Italian Cultural Relations since the Renaissance* (London: Frank Cass, 1998), pp. 58–101.

34. Philip Stubbes, *The Anatomy of Abuses* (London, 1583), f. 110v; Linda Phyllis Austern, '"Alluring the Auditory to Effeminacie": Music and the Idea of the Feminine in Early Modern England', *Music & Letters* 74.3 (1993), pp. 343–54, esp. 350.

35. Tobias Hume, 'To the Understanding Reader', in *The first part of ayres, French, Pollish, and others together, some in tabliture, and some in pricke-song* (London, 1605), sig. B2v; Michael Morrow, Colette Harris, and Frank Traficante, 'Hume, Tobias', Grove Music Online.

36. See Vincent Duckles, 'The English Musical Elegy of the Late Renaissance', in *Aspects of Medieval and Renaissance Music: A Birthday Offering to Gustave Reese*, ed. Jan LaRue (London: Oxford University Press, 1967), pp. 134–53.

37. There is a recording available on CD: *The Triumphs of Oriana*, recorded by the King's Singers.

38. *Vita Edwardi Secundi: The Life of Edward the Second*, ed. Wendy R. Childs (Oxford: Clarendon Press, 2005), p. 29; see further John Boswell, *Christianity, Social Tolerance and Homosexuality* (Chicago: University of Chicago Press, 1981), pp. 252, 299.

39. Johnson, p. 248.

40. Browne, *Religio Medici*, in *Major Works*, ed. Patrides, pp. 149–50.

41. Roland Barthes, 'Listening', in *The Responsibility of Form*, trans. Richard Howard (Oxford: Basil Blackwell, 1985), pp. 246–7.

42. Bruce R. Smith, *The Acoustic World of Early Modern England:*

Attending to the O Factor (Chicago: University of Chicago Press, 1999), p. 55.

43. Ibid., pp. 51, 65.

44. J. Milton French, 'John Milton's Homes and Investments', *Philological Quarterly* 28.1 (1949), pp. 7–97; Gordon Campbell and Thomas Corns, 'John Milton and His Money', *Forbes*, 8 December 2008.

45. *An Annotated Bibliography on the History of Usury and Interest*, ed. John M. Houkes (Lewiston, NY: Edwin Mellen Press, 2004), p. 195; David Hawkes, 'Milton and Usury', *English Literary Renaissance* 41.3 (2011), pp. 519–20.

46. Craig Muldrew, *The Economy of Obligation: The Culture of Credit and Social Relations in Early Modern England* (London: Macmillan, 1998), esp. pp. 1–36, 123–95.

47. Mary Poovey, *A History of the Modern Fact: Problems of Knowledge in the Sciences of Wealth and Society* (Chicago: University of Chicago Press, 1998), p. 57 on mixed transactions; on the debates surrounding money and the commercial system in the 1620s see pp. 66–91.

48. Hutson, *Usurer's Daughter*, esp. pp. 41–2, 142; David Hawkes, 'Sodomy, Usury and the Narrative of Shakespeare's Sonnets', *Renaissance Studies* 14.3 (2000), pp. 344–61.

49. Conrad Russell, *Parliaments and English Politics, 1621–1629* (Oxford: Clarendon Press, 1979), p. 194.

50. Wye Saltonstall, cited by J. Milton French, *Milton in Chancery: New Chapters in the Lives of the Poet and His Father* (New York: Modern Language Association, 1939), p. 11.

51. Poovey, *History of the Modern Fact*, pp. 37–8.

52. MW pp. 186–7.

53. Hawkes, 'Milton and Usury'; David Hawkes, John *Milton: A Hero for Our Time* (Berkeley, CA: Counterpoint, 2009).

54. *The Letters of T. S. Eliot*, vol. 1, ed. Valerie Eliot and Hugh Haughton (New Haven, CT: Yale University Press, 2011), pp. 193–5; Wallace Stevens, 'Notes toward a Supreme Fiction', part 7. For Stevens's 'mischievous play with Milton's language' in his poems, see Eleanor Cook, *Poetry, Word Play and Word-War in Wallace Stevens* (Princeton, NJ: Princeton University Press, 1988); quotation at p. 252.

55. James Longenbach, *Wallace Stevens: The Plain Sense of Things* (Oxford: Oxford University Press, 1991), p. 113.

56. Jacques Attali, *Noise*, trans. Brian Massumi (Minneapolis: University of Minnesota Press, 1985), p. 22.

57. Ibid., pp. 19, 101.

58. Ibid., p. 142.

59. PL 3.38.

60. George Puttenham, *The Art of English Poetry*, in *Sidney's 'The Defence of Poesy' and Selected Renaissance Literary Criticism*, ed. Gavin Alexander (London: Penguin, 2004), p. 120.

Chapter 3: 8 April 1624: 'The Almighty's Hand'

1. 'Appendix B: Statuta Paulinae Scholae', in *The Admissions Registers of St Paul's School, from 1748–1876*, ed. Robert Barlow Gardiner (London: George Bell & Sons, 1884), p. 381; Donald Clark, *Milton at St Paul's* (New York: Columbia University Press, 1948), pp. 47–8. I have modernised the spelling of the statutes throughout.

2. Samuel Knight, *The Life of Dr Colet* (London, 1724), p. 375; Clark, *Milton at St Paul's*, p. 39.

3. Robert Alter, *Book of Psalms: A Translation with Commentary* (New York: W. W. Norton, 2007), p. 405.

4. Clark, *Milton at St Paul's*, pp. 119, 121, 145–7.

5. *Lily's Grammar of Latin in English: An Introduction of the Eyght Partes of Speche, and the Construction of the Same*, ed. Hedwig Gwosdek (Oxford: Oxford University Press, 2013), p. 200.

6. John Earle, *Micro-cosmographie* (London, 1628), sigs. I11r–K1r; Gallagher, *Learning Languages*, p. 26; Emily Cockayne, *Hubbub: Filth, Noise, & Stench in England, 1600–1770* (New Haven, CT: Yale University Press, 2007), p. 121; Smith, *Acoustic World*, pp. 60–1.

7. Mark S. R. Jenner, 'From Conduit Community to Commercial Network?', in *Londinopolis: Essays in the Cultural and Social History of Early Modern London*, ed. Mark S. R. Jenner and Paul Griffiths (Manchester: Manchester University Press, 2000), pp. 250–5.

8. Cockayne, *Hubbub*, p. 107.

9. John Bennell, 'Shop and Office in Medieval and Tudor London', *Transactions of the London and Middlesex Archaeological Society* 40 (1989), pp. 195, 199–200.

10. Stow, *Survey of London*, vol. 1, pp. 345–6; Bennell, 'Shop and Office', p. 195.

11. Alexandra Walsham, '"The Fatall Vesper": Providentialism and Anti-Popery in Late Jacobean London', *Past & Present* 144.1 (August 1994), pp. 36–87; Leo Miller, 'On Some of the Verses by Alexander Gil Which John Milton Read', *Milton Quarterly* 24.1 (1990), pp. 24–5.

12. French, *Milton in Chancery*, pp. 21–3.

13. One of Milton's more recent biographers gives an amusing account of the 'bizarre open-air ceremony' that took place when the plaque was unveiled on 14 July 2008, Bastille Day, and which was attended by the Lord Mayor of London and the Poet Laureate. (Neil Forsyth, *John Milton: A Biography* (Oxford: Lion, 2008), p. 15.)

14. 'Old Stone Signs of London', *Strand Magazine* (January 1891), pp. 487–8.

15. 'Statuta Paulinae Scholae', pp. 381, 388; on time and humanist education see Ricardo J. Quinones, *The Renaissance Discovery of Time* (Cambridge, MA: Harvard University Press, 1972), pp. 190–1.

16. 'Statuta Paulinae Scholae', p. 381.

17. Ibid., pp. 375, 376, 382.

18. CW vol. 8, p. 11; Clark, *Milton at St Paul's*, pp. 22–3.

19. *Collected Works of Erasmus* (Toronto: University of Toronto Press, 1974–), vol. 25, p. 194.

20. This account is indebted to Jeff Dolven, *Scenes of Instruction in Renaissance Romance* (Chicago: University of Chicago Press, 2007), ch. 1, esp. pp. 35, 37–8.

21. See Peter Beal, 'Notions in Garrison: The Seventeenth-Century Commonplace Book', in *New Ways of Looking at Old Texts*, ed. W. Speed Hill (New York: Renaissance English Text Society, 1993), pp. 131–47, esp. pp. 136–7.

22. Roger Ascham, *The Scholemaster* (London, 1570), p. 15; Dolven, *Scenes of Instruction*, pp. 42–4; John Sargeaunt, *Annals of Westminster School* (London: Methuen, 1898), p. 280.

23. Dolven, *Scenes of Instruction*, p. 48: 'The mind so represented is a timeless place.'

24. Patricia Parker, 'Virile Style', in *Premodern Sexualities*, ed. Louise Fradenburg and Carla Freccero (New York: Routledge, 1996), pp. 201–22; Lorna Hutson, 'Civility and Virility in Ben Jonson', *Representations* 78 (2002), pp. 1–27; Thomas Habinek, *Ancient Rhetoric and Oratory* (Oxford: Blackwell, 2005), ch. 4, esp. pp. 64–5; Maud W. Gleason, *Making Men: Sophists and Self-Presentation in Ancient Rome* (Princeton, NJ: Princeton University Press, 1995), esp. ch. 6.

25. Cicero, *De Officiis*, 1.12–9; Gleason, *Making Men*, p. 107.

26. Walter J. Ong, 'Latin Language Study as a Renaissance Puberty Rite', *Studies in Philology* 56.2 (1959), pp. 103–24; Thomas Elyot, *The Boke Named the Gouernour*, ed. Henry Herbert Stephen Croft (London: Kegan Paul, 1880), vol. 1, p. 35; Ascham, *Scholemaster*, p. 117.

27. YPW vol. 4, part 1, p. 612; EL pp. 18, 52.

28. *Erasmus Reader*, ed. Erika Rummel (Toronto: University of Toronto Press, 1990), p. 92.

29. For this version of Mulcaster see Alan Stewart, *Close Readers: Humanism and Sodomy in Early Modern England* (Princeton, NJ: Princeton University Press, 1997), p. 121.

30. ABL vol. 1, p. 631; ABL vol. 2, p. 1586.

31. ABL vol. 1, pp. 627–31.

32. Ben Jonson, *Time Vindicated to Himself and to his Honours*, ll. 116–18.

33. Michael McDonnell, *History of St Paul's School* (London: Chapman & Hall, 1909), p. 189; Clark, *Milton at St Paul's*, p. 97.

34. Eve Kosofsky Sedgwick, 'A Poem is Being Written', in *Tendencies* (Durham, NC: Duke University Press, 1993), p. 179.

35. Michael Wilding, 'Regaining the Radical Milton', cited in Mary Nyquist and Margaret W. Ferguson, introduction to *Re-Membering Milton: Essays on the Texts and Traditions* (London: Methuen, 1987), p. xv.

36. Lloyd DeMause, 'The Evolution of Childhood', in *The History of Childhood*, ed. Lloyd DeMause (New York: Psychohistory Press, 1974), p. 41.

37. Cited by Stewart, *Close Readers*, p. 88.

38. ABL vol. 1, pp. 629–30.

39. François Waquet, *Latin, or the Empire of a Sign*, trans. John Howe (London: Verso, 2001), p. 247.

40. Jennifer Richards, *Voices and Books* (Oxford: Oxford University Press, 2019), ch. 2, esp. pp. 76, 79–80.

41. Cicero, *De Officiis*, trans. Miller, 1.129; Quintilian, *Institutes*, 11.3.32, 40; Gleason, *Making Men*, pp. 107, 120.

42. Cicero, *Orator*, 18.59 (Loeb edition, pp. 348–9): 'nulla mollitia cervicum, nullae argutiae digitorum, non ad numerum articulus cadens'; Seneca, *Suasoriae*, 2.23 (Loeb edition, pp. 534–5): 'Quarum nimius cultus et fracta compositio poterit vos offendere'; Gleason, *Making Men*, pp. 107, 109; John Dugan, *Making a New Man: Ciceronian Self-Fashioning in the Rhetorical Works* (Oxford: Oxford University Press, 2005), pp. 267–79. Cicero and Seneca don't use the Greek term *rhythm* here but two of its Latin equivalents.

43. See Hutson, 'Civility and Virility in Ben Jonson'.

44. See Lynn Enterline, *Shakespeare's Schoolroom: Rhetoric, Discipline, Emotion* (Philadelphia: University of Pennsylvania Press, 2012), p. 18, for boys playing the parts of female personifications at St Paul's in 1527.

45. Erasmus, *De Conscribendis Epistolis*: 'epistolae ad exercitationem, vel ostentationem ingenii'. My translation: see, there's that late-acquired Latin being put to good use.

46. Petrarch, *Letters on Familiar Matters*, 3.212–13; cited by Colin Burrow, *Imitating Authors: Plato to Futurity* (Oxford: Oxford University Press, 2019), p. 150.

47. Daniel Boyarin, *Unheroic Conduct: The Rise of Heterosexuality and the Invention of the Jewish Man* (Berkeley: University of California Press, 1997), p. xiii; on Jewish male menstruation see James Shapiro, *Shakespeare and the Jews* (New York: Columbia University Press, 1996), pp. 37–8.

48. See Daniel Karlin's letter to the *London Review of Books* on his experiences of antisemitism at St Paul's School, 20 June 1996.

49. British Library (hereafter BL), MS Sloane 3722; MS Add. 46139, ff. 18, 134, 144, 167. See the excellent overview by William Poole, 'The Literary Remains of Alexander Gil the Elder (1565–1635) and Younger (1596/7–1642?)', *Milton Quarterly* 51.3 (2018), pp. 163–91.

50. Clark, *Milton at St Paul's*, p. 72.

51. See E. J. Dobson, *English Pronunciation 1500–1700* (Oxford: Clarendon Press, 1968), vol. 1, pp. 131–55, esp. p. 136.

52. Edmund Spenser, *The Faerie Queene*, 1.9.17.1.

53. YPW vol. 1, p. 321.

54. For discussions of this protracted process see Harris Fletcher, *The Intellectual Development of John Milton* (Urbana: University of Illinois Press, 1956), vol. 1, pp. 187–92, 283; on Gil's likely prowess in Hebrew and Aramaic see vol. 1, pp. 276–9.

55. YPW vol. 1, p. 816.

56. Joseph Justus Scaliger, 'Animadversiones in Prologum Hieronymi', in *Thesaurus Temporum Eusebii* (Amsterdam, 1658), vol. 2, p. 607; cited and translated by James L. Kugel, *The Idea of Biblical Poetry* (New Haven, CT: Yale University Press, 1981), pp. 256–7.

57. For Milton's attempts to replicate psalmodic rhythms see Mary Ann Radzinowicz, *Milton's Epic and the Book of Psalms* (Princeton, NJ: Princeton University Press, 1989), pp. 119–20.

58. For this Protestant ubiquity and the problem of voice see Hannibal Hamlin, 'My Tongue Shall Speak: The Voice of the Psalms', *Renaissance Studies* 29.4 (2015), pp. 509–30.

59. Philip Sidney, 'Defence of Poesy', in *Sidney's 'The Defence of Poesy' and Selected Renaissance Literary Criticism*, ed. Alexander, pp. 6–7.

60. See Christopher Hill, *The English Bible and the Seventeenth-Century Revolution* (Harmondsworth: Penguin, 1994), pp. 380–1.

61. Dante, *The Divine Comedy 2: Purgatorio*, trans. John D. Sinclair (Oxford: Oxford University Press, 1961), pp. 34–5. Sinclair mysteriously translates 'cento spirti' as 'a thousand spirits' – I have restored the original 'hundred'.

62. *Dantis Alagherii Epistolae*, trans. Paget Toynbee (Oxford: Clarendon Press, 1966), p. 199.

63. James Joyce, *Daniel Defoe*, ed. Joseph Prescott (Buffalo: State University of New York at Buffalo, 1964), p. 7.

64. James Joyce, *Ulysses*, ed. Jeri Johnson (Oxford: Oxford University Press, 2008), p. 651. Joyce follows the standard Roman Catholic ordering of the Psalms in calling this one 113, whereas for Protestants it was (and is) 114.

65. See, for example, Rabbi Nathan Goldberg, *Passover Haggadah* (New York: BN Publishing, 2005), pp. 48–9.

Chapter 4: 24 December 1629: 'But Now Begins'

1. My inspiration here is the rich setting of the scene for this poem's composition by Gordon Teskey, *The Poetry of John Milton* (Cambridge, MA: Harvard University Press, 2015), pp. 23–4.
2. 'Elegia Sexta', ll. 87–8.
3. Nativity Ode (henceforth NO), ll. 29–31.
4. NO, ll. 22–3, 85–7, 244.
5. Giorgio Agamben, *The Time That Remains: A Commentary on the Letter to the Romans*, trans. Patricia Daley (Stanford, CA: Stanford University Press, 2005), esp. pp. 62–5.
6. Martin Buber, *I and Thou*, trans. Ronald Gregor Smith (London: Continuum, 2004), p. 90; Rainer Maria Rilke, 'Fourth Duino Elegy', in *Selected Poems*, ed. Robert Vilain (Oxford: Oxford University Press, 2011), l. 73: 'im Zwischenraume zwischen Welt und Spielzeug.' See the wonderful discussion by Malcolm Bowie, 'Proust and Psychoanalysis', *Publications of the English Goethe Society* 68.1 (1998), p. 26.
7. NO, ll. 149–53.
8. Milton's younger contemporary, the poet Abraham Cowley, described God's *'Eternal Now'*, explaining that the philosophers Boethius, Aquinas, 'and all the *Schoolmen* . . . call *Eternity Nunc stans*, a *standing Now*, to distinguish it from that *Now*, which is a difference of *time*, and is alwaies *in Fluxu*': *Davideis*, 1. 26 and note, in *Poems*, ed. A. R. Waller (Cambridge: Cambridge University Press, 1905), pp. 251, 273.
9. NO, ll. 131–2.
10. NO, ll. 99–100.
11. NO, ll. 173–80.
12. NO, ll. 53–4.
13. Paul Goodman, *Speaking and Language: A Defence of Poetry* (New York: Random House, 1971), p. 15; cited by Christopher Ricks, *T. S. Eliot and Prejudice* (London: Faber, 1988), p. 175.
14. Galatians 4:4 (KJV).
15. Lancelot Andrewes, *Selected Sermons and Letters*, ed. Peter E. McCullough (Oxford: Oxford University Press, 2005), pp. 162, 164.
16. See Peter McCullough, 'Music Reconciled to Preaching: A Jacobean Moment?', in *Worship and the Parish Church in Early*

Modern Britain, ed. Natalie Mears and Alec Ryrie (Farnham: Ashgate, 2013), pp. 128–9.

17. Peter Lake, 'The Laudian Style: Order, Uniformity and the Pursuit of the Beauty of Holiness in the 1630s', in *The Early Stuart Church, 1603–1642*, ed. Kenneth Fincham (Basingstoke: Macmillan, 1993), pp. 161–85.

18. See Nicholas Tyacke, *Anti-Calvinists: The Rise of English Arminianism c.1590–1640* (Oxford: Clarendon Press, 1987).

19. See Martin Evans, *The Miltonic Moment* (Lexington: University Press of Kentucky, 1998), pp. 6–7.

20. David Como, 'Predestination and Political Conflict in Laud's London', *Historical Journal* 46.2 (2003), p. 275.

21. Ibid., p. 277.

22. On the challenges of interpreting texts written under these conditions see Annabel Patterson, *Censorship and Interpretation: The Conditions of Writing and Reading in Early Modern England* (Madison: University of Wisconsin Press, 1984).

23. YPW vol. 1, pp. 312, 314.

24. John Peile, *Christ's College* (London: F. E. Robinson & Co., 1900), p. 36; Quentin Skinner, 'The Generation of John Milton', in *Christ's: A Cambridge College over Five Centuries*, ed. David Reynolds (London: Macmillan, 2004), p. 48.

25. Skinner, 'Generation of John Milton', p. 29; William Costello, *Scholastic Curriculum at Early Seventeenth-Century Cambridge* (Cambridge, MA: Harvard University Press, 1958), pp. 13–14.

26. Cited by H. C. Porter, *Reformation and Reaction in Tudor Cambridge* (Cambridge: Cambridge University Press, 1958), p. 30.

27. William Empson, 'Warning to Undergraduates', in *The Complete Poems* (London: Penguin, 2001), pp. 49–50.

28. ABL vol. 1, p. 668.

29. Elegy 1, trans. Carey, 11–12; Elegy 4; YPW vol. 1, pp. 314–17.

30. David Cressy, *Dangerous Talk: Scandalous, Seditious, and Treasonable Speech in Pre-Modern England* (Oxford: Oxford University Press, 2010), p. 143.

31. Ibid., p. 145.

32. See Katherine Firth, *The Apocalyptic Tradition in Reformation Britain* (Oxford: Oxford University Press, 1979), pp. 216–29; Michael Murrin, 'Revelation and Two Seventeenth Century Commentators',

in *The Apocalypse in English Renaissance Thought and Literature*, ed.
C. A. Patrides and Joseph Anthony Wittreich (Ithaca, NY: Cornell
University Press, 1984), pp. 125–47; Kristine Haugen, 'Apocalypse:
A User's Manual: Joseph Mede, the Interpretation of Prophecy,
and the Dream Book of Achmet', *Seventeenth Century* 25.2 (2010),
pp. 215–39.

33. See John Rumrich, 'Mead and Milton', *Milton Quarterly* 20.4
(1986), pp. 136–41; Murrin, 'Revelation and Two Seventeenth
Century Commentators', p. 139.

34. Cited by Firth, *Apocalyptic Tradition*, p. 226.

35. Thomas Fuller, *The History of the Worthies of England* (London,
1662), p. 335.

36. Ibid.

37. Mede to Stuteville, 2 July 1625, BL, MS Harleian 389, f. 470r.

38. Mede to Stuteville, 11 November 1626, BL, MS Harleian 390,
f. 157r.

39. See John Twigg, *The University of Cambridge and the English
Revolution, 1625–1688* (Woodbridge: Boydell, 1990), pp. 11–41.

40. Mede to Stuteville, 9 December 1626, BL, MS Harleian 390,
f. 171r.

41. See Alexandra Walsham, 'Vox Piscis: or The Book-Fish: Providence
and the Uses of the Reformation Past in Caroline Cambridge',
English Historical Review 114 (1999), pp. 574–606, esp. p. 603.

42. See Margo Todd, 'Anti-Calvinists and the Republican Threat in
Early Stuart Cambridge', in *Puritanism and Its Discontents*, ed. Laura
Lunger Knoppers (Newark, NJ: Associated University Presses,
2003), p. 88.

43. See ibid. and also Ronald Mellor, 'Tacitus, Academic Politics and
the Regicide in the Reign of Charles I: The Tragedy of Dr. Isaac
Dorislaus', *International Journal of the Classical Tradition* 11.2 (2004),
pp. 153–93.

44. Thomas Hobbes, *Behemoth, or the Long Parliament*, ed. Paul Seaward
(Oxford: Clarendon Press, 2010), pp. 159, 179; Martin Dzelzainis,
'Milton's Classical Republicanism', in *Milton and Republicanism*, ed.
David Armitage, Armand Himy, and Quentin Skinner (Cambridge:
Cambridge University Press, 1998), pp. 3–4.

45. YPW vol. 1, pp. 240–1, 253–4.

46. See Ian Maclean, 'Language in the Mind: Reflexive Thinking in the

Late Renaissance', in *Philosophy in the Sixteenth and Seventeenth Centuries: Conversations with Aristotle*, ed. Constance Blackwell and Sachiko Kusukawa (Farnham: Ashgate, 1999), esp. pp. 315–16.

47. See John Hale, *Milton's Cambridge Latin: Performing in the Genres, 1625–1632* (Tempe, AZ : Arizona Center for Medieval and Renaissance Studies, 2005), esp. pp. 33, 86–90; N. K. Sugimura, *Matter of Glorious Trial: Spiritual and Material Substance in Paradise Lost* (New Haven, CT: Yale University Press, 2009), ch. 1.

48. YPW vol. 1, pp. 222, 228.

49. YPW vol. 1, pp. 246–7.

50. YPW vol. 1, p. 245.

51. *Complete Shorter Poems*, ed. Carey, p. 122.

52. PL 12.413–15.

Chapter 5: 10 August 1637: 'Yet Once More'

1. *The Diaries of Franz Kafka*, ed. Max Brod, trans. Joseph Kresh (Harmondsworth: Penguin, 1972), p. 146.

2. Oliver Sacks, 'Brainworms, Sticky Music and Catchy Tunes', in *Musicophilia: Tales of Music and the Brain* (London: Picador, 2007), p. 45.

3. Beckett to MacGreevy, 7 August 1634, *The Letters of Samuel Beckett, Vol. I: 1929–1940*, ed. Martha Dow Fehsenfeld and Lois More Overbeck (Cambridge: Cambridge University Press, 2009), p. 217.

4. Beckett to MacGreevy, 6 November 1955, *The Letters of Samuel Beckett, Volume II: 1941–1956*, ed. George Craig, Dan Gunn, Martha Dow Fehsenfeld and Lois More Overbeck (Cambridge: Cambridge University Press, 2011), p. 565.

5. 'Lycidas', ll. 1–5.

6. See the excellent discussion by James Rutherford, 'The Experimental Form of "Lycidas"', *Milton Studies* 53 (2012), pp. 17–37.

7. 'Lycidas', ll. 6–8, 15.

8. For the likely embarkation point and route see J. Karl Franson, 'The Fatal Voyage of Edward King, Milton's Lycidas', *Milton Studies* 25 (1989), pp. 67–88.

9. Jean-Yves Tadié, *Marcel Proust: A Life*, trans. Euan Cameron (London: Penguin, 2001), p. 321.

10. Johnson, pp. 278–9.

11. Johnson, p. 278.

12. Joyce, *Ulysses*, pp. 25-6.

13. Ibid., pp. 25–6. All punctuation, including ellipses, as per the original.

14. John Berryman, 'Wash Far Away', in *The Freedom of the Poet* (New York: Farrar, Straus, & Giroux, 1976).

15. 'Lycidas', ll. 50–5.

16. 'Lycidas', ll. 64–6, 70–6.

17. 'Lycidas', ll. 76–8, 81–2.

18. See John Leonard, '"Trembling Ears": The Historical Moment of Lycidas', *Journal of Medieval and Renaissance Studies* 21 (1991), pp. 59–81.

19. 'Elegia Sexta', ll. 53–64.

20. Whether or not Milton ever intended a vow of total celibacy, or only until marriage, is disputed: see John Leonard, 'Milton's Vow of Celibacy: A Reconsideration of the Evidence', in *Of Poetry and Politics: New Essays on Milton and His World*, ed. P. G. Stanwood (Binghamton, NY: Medieval and Renaissance Texts and Studies, 1995), pp. 187–202.

21. YPW vol. 1, p. 271.

22. YPW vol. 1, p. 267.

23. YPW vol. 1, p. 283; ABL vol. 1, p. 662.

24. PL 1.236–7; YPW vol. 1, p. 278.

25. 'At a Vacation Exercise in the College', ll. 1–4, 33–5.

26. YPW vol. 1, p. 266.

27. 'L'Allegro', ll. 26–7, 40; 'Il Pensoroso', ll. 12, 156, 165–6.

28. 'Lycidas', ll. 109–10, 112, 119.

29. 'Lycidas', ll. 123–9.

30. John Webster, *The White Devil*, 5.4.104–5.

31. See Christopher Kendrick, 'Anachronism in "Lycidas"', *English Literary History* 64.1 (1997), p. 15.

32. Elias Canetti, *Crowds and Power* (London: Phoenix, 2000), p. 93.

33. Ibid., p. 31. Emphases in the original.

34. 'Lycidas', ll. 154–60.

35. G. J. Toomer, *John Selden: A Life in Scholarship*, 2 vols (Oxford: Oxford University Press, 2009), vol. 1, pp. 388–437; James Muldoon, 'Who Owns the Sea?', in *Fictions of the Sea: Critical*

Perspectives on the Ocean in British Literature and Culture, ed. Bernhard Klein (Farnham: Ashgate, 2002), pp. 13–27.

36. Norman Postlethwaite and Gordon Campbell, 'Edward King, Milton's "Lycidas": Poems and Documents', *Milton Quarterly* 28.4 (1994), p. 107 n. 122; cf. Sharon Achinstein, 'Shipwreck is Everywhere: "Lycidas" and the Problems of the Secular', in *Milton Now: Alternative Approaches and Contexts*, ed. Catharine Gray and Erin Murphy (New York: Palgrave Macmillan, 2014), pp. 38–9.

37. Russell, *Parliaments and English Politics*, pp. 390–416, esp. pp. 407, 415; N. A. M. Rodger, *Safeguard of the Sea*: *A Naval History of Britain, 660–1649* (Harmondsworth: Penguin, 1997), pp. 391–4; Kevin Sharpe, *The Personal Rule of Charles I* (New Haven, CT: Yale University Press, 1992), pp. 97–104; B. W. Quintrell, 'Charles I and His Navy in the 1630s', *Seventeenth Century* 3.2 (1988), pp. 159–79.

38. 'Ad Patrem', ll. 20–1, 35–7.

39. 'Ad Patrem', l.17.

40. John Hollander, *The Work of Poetry* (New York: Columbia University Press, 1997), p. 3.

41. 'Elegia Prima', trans. Carey, ll. 37–40.

42. For the identification, initially made by Jason Scott-Warren, see Centre for Material Texts, https://www.english.cam.ac.uk/cmt/?p=5751. Accessed 11 May 2021.

43. 'Lycidas', ll. 165–71.

44. 'Lycidas', ll. 175–7.

45. 'Lycidas', ll. 182–3.

46. 'Sonnet VII', ll. 1–4.

47. 'Sonnet VII', ll. 9–12.

48. YPW vol. 1, pp. 319–20.

49. Peter R. Roberts, 'The Welshness of the Tudors', *History Today* 36.1 (January 1986), pp. 7–9.

50. Jeffrey Jerome Cohen, 'Hybrids, Monsters, Borderlands: The Bodies of Gerald of Wales', in *The Postcolonial Middle Ages*, ed. Jeffrey Jerome Cohen (New York: Palgrave, 2000), pp. 85–104; Christopher Hill, 'The Dark Corners of the Land', in *Change and Continuity in Seventeenth-Century England* (New Haven, CT: Yale University Press, 1991), pp. 3–47; Michael Wilding, 'Milton's "A

Masque Presented at Ludlow Castle, 1634": Theatre and Politics on the Border', *Milton Quarterly* 21.4 (1987), pp. 35–51; Philip Schwyzer, 'Purity and Danger on the West Bank of the Severn', *Representations* 60 (1997), pp. 22–48.

51. See Penry Williams, 'The Attack on the Council of the Marches', *Transactions of the Honourable Society of Cymmrodorion* (1961), pp. 1–22; Peter R. Roberts, 'The English Crown, the Principality of Wales and the Council of the Marches', in *The British Problem, c. 1534–1707: State Formation in the Atlantic Archipelago*, ed. Brendan Bradshaw and John Morrill (Basingstoke: Macmillan, 1996), pp. 118–47.

52. Francis Bacon, 'The Jurisdiction of the Marches', in *Works*, ed. James Spedding et al. (London: Longman, 1857–74), vol. 7, p. 587.

53. 'Comus', ll. 840–1.

54. 'Comus', ll. 349–50, 414–15, 419–20, 785–6, 796, 971.

55. See the outstanding account by Cynthia B. Herrup, *A House in Gross Disorder: Sex, Law, and the 2nd Earl of Castlehaven* (Oxford: Oxford University Press, 1999).

56. Leah Marcus, 'The Milieu of Milton's *Comus*: Judicial Reform at Ludlow and the Problem of Sexual Assault', *Criticism* 25.4 (1983), pp. 293–327.

57. 'Comus', ll. 710–17.

58. PL 7.485–6.

59. 'Comus', ll. 916–17.

60. Geoffrey Hill, *Scenes from Comus*, 2.3, in *Broken Hierarchies: Poems 1952–2012*, ed. Kenneth Haynes (Oxford: Oxford University Press, 2013), p. 432.

61. 'Comus', ll. 555–7.

62. 'Lycidas', ll. 186–93.

63. Thomas Laqueur, *The Work of the Dead: A Cultural History of Mortal Remains* (Princeton, NJ: Princeton University Press, 2015), p. 31.

64. Denise Riley, *Time Lived, without Its Flow* (London: Picador, 2019), pp. 13, 31.

65. Ibid., pp. 19, 52.

66. 'Lycidas', ll. 130–1.

Chapter 6: 19 May 1638:
'Your Thoughts Close, and your Countenance Loose'

1. YPW vol. 4, part 1, pp. 614–15.
2. Ian Atherton, *Ambition and Failure in Stuart England: The Career of John, First Viscount Scudamore* (Manchester: Manchester University Press, 1999), pp. 70–5.
3. Barbara Ketcham Wheaton, *Savouring the Past: The French Kitchen and Table from 1300 to 1789* (London: Chatto & Windus, 1983), pp. 43–4; Alberto Capatti and Massimo Montanari, *Italian Cuisine: A Cultural History*, trans. Aine O'Healy (New York: Columbia University Press, 2003), p. 41; Paolo Zacchia, *Il vitto Quaresimale* (Rome: Facciotti, 1636), pp. 238–9.
4. Kenelm Digby, *A Discourse Concerning Infallibility in Religion* (Paris, 1652), p. 3; *Letters Between The Ld George Digby and Sr Kenelm Digby Kt. concerning Religion* (London, 1651), p. 23.
5. John Milton, *Defensio Secunda pro Populo Anglicano* (The Hague, 1654), pp. 82–3; I follow the translation and the authoritative account of this period by Poole, MW p. 62 *et seq*.
6. Edward Jones, '"Filling in a Blank in the Canvas": Milton, Horton, and the Kedermister Library', *Review of English Studies* 53 (2002), pp. 31–60.
7. Cited ibid., p. 35.
8. YPW vol. 1, p. 328.
9. I borrow the use of this phrase from Hawkes, *John Milton: A Hero for Our Time*, p. 40.
10. See Gallagher, *Learning Languages*, for a discussion of the practical options.
11. Osip Mandelstam, 'Government and Rhythm', in *The Complete Critical Prose and Letters*, ed. J. G. Harris and C. Link (Ann Arbor: University of Michigan Press, 1979), p. 110.
12. Osip Mandelstam, 'Conversation about Dante', in *The Complete Critical Prose and Letters*, pp. 400, 399.
13. Marcel Proust, *In the Shadow of Young Girls in Flower*, trans. James Grieve (New York: Viking, 2002), pp. 370, 375.
14. Anne Carson, *The Albertine Workout* (New York: New Directions, 2014), pp. 6, 20.

15. John Shawcross, 'Milton and Diodati: An Essay in Psychodynamic Meaning', *Milton Studies* 7 (1975), p. 153.

16. Cited by Alan Bray, *The Friend* (Chicago: University of Chicago Press, 2003), p. 144.

17. See ibid. for a magisterial account of these complexities.

18. YPW vol. 1, p. 337.

19. Jennifer Sarha, 'Assyria in Early Modern Historiography', in *Beyond Greece and Rome: Reading the Ancient Near East in Early Modern Europe*, ed. Jane Grogan (Oxford: Oxford University Press, 2020), esp. 242, 250.

20. Alan Bray, *Homosexuality in Renaissance England* (New York: Columbia University Press, 1995), pp. 75, 134 n. 72.

21. See D. A. Miller, 'Secret Subjects, Open Secrets', in *The Novel and the Police* (Berkeley: University of California Press, 1988), pp. 192–220, on this category in relation to same-sex love and desire.

22. 'Lycidas', ll. 60–2.

23. Ovid, *Metamorphoses*, trans. E. J. Kenny (Oxford: Oxford University Press, 1986), 10.65–98.

24. E. K.'s note to Spenser's 'Januarye' eclogue in *Shorter Poems*, ed. Richard McCabe (Harmondsworth: Penguin, 1999), pp. 38–9. See in general Bruce Boehrer, '"Lycidas": The Pastoral Elegy as Same-Sex Epithalamium', *PMLA* 117.2 (2002), pp. 222–36.

25. Eve Kosofsky Sedgwick, *Epistemology of the Closet* (Berkeley: University of California Press, 1992), p. 53.

26. Theodor Reik, *Surprise and the Psycho-Analyst* (London: K. Paul, 1936), p. 119.

27. See Clay Hunt, *Lycidas and the Italian Critics* (New Haven, CT: Yale University Press, 1979).

28. YPW vol. 1, p. 339.

29. John Donne, 'To Sir Henry Wotton', l. 1.

30. See Melanie Ord, 'Returning from Venice to England', in *Borders and Travellers in Early Modern Europe*, ed. Thomas Betteridge (Farnham: Ashgate, 2007), pp. 155–71.

31. *Life and Letters of Sir Henry Wotton*, ed. Logan Pearsall Smith (Oxford: Clarendon Press, 1907), vol. 2, p. 201.

32. YPW vol. 1, p. 341.

33. YPW vol. 1, pp. 341–2.

34. *Life and Letters of Sir Henry Wotton*, vol. 1, p. 22.

35. Henry Wotton, *Reliquiae Wottonianae* (London, 1654), pp. 310–11.
36. See Ord, 'Returning from Venice to England', p. 164.
37. Digby to Hobbes, October 1637, in *The Correspondence of Thomas Hobbes*, ed. Noel Malcolm (Oxford: Clarendon Press, 1994), vol. 1, p. 51.
38. ABL vol. 1, pp. 663–4.
39. See Stephen Fallon, *Milton among the Philosophers: Poetry and Materialism in Seventeenth-Century England* (Ithaca, NY: Cornell University Press, 1991).
40. Richard Tuck, 'Grotius and Selden', in *The Cambridge History of Political Thought, 1450–1700*, ed. J. H. Burns and Mark Goldie (Cambridge: Cambridge University Press, 1991), p. 520; Richard Tuck, 'Hugo Grotius', in *Natural Right Theories: Their Origin and Development* (Cambridge: Cambridge University Press, 1979), ch. 3; Marco Barducci, *Hugo Grotius and the Century of Revolution, 1613–1718* (Oxford: Oxford University Press, 2017), pp. 54–6.
41. YPW vol. 4, part 1, p. 615.
42. See the excellent account by Victoria Kahn, *Wayward Contracts: The Crisis of Political Obligation in England, 1640–1674* (Princeton, NJ: Princeton University Press, 2004), pp. 33–41.
43. Torquato Tasso, 'Discourse on the Art of Poetry', in *The Genesis of Tasso's Narrative Theory*, ed. Lawrence F. Rhu (Detroit, MI: Wayne State University Press, 1993), p. 131.
44. Sidney, 'Defence of Poesy', in *Renaissance Literary Criticism*, ed. Alexander, p. 8; see the rich discussion of these ideas by Victoria Kahn, *The Trouble with Literature* (Oxford: Oxford University Press, 2020), p. 24 *et passim*.

Chapter 7: 20 July 1638: 'The Tuscan Artist'

1. Jonathan Rosen, 'The Enduring Relevance of John Milton', *New Yorker*, 26 May 2008.
2. Dan Brown, *Angels and Demons* (London: Transworld, 2000), pp. 249–51; quotation at p. 251.
3. YPW vol. 2, p. 538.
4. PL 5.261–3.
5. PL 1.287–9.

6. PL 3.588–90.

7. J. L. Heilbron, *Galileo* (Oxford: Oxford University Press, 2012), pp. 3, 8.

8. Eric Cochrane, *Florence in the Forgotten Centuries, 1527–1800* (Chicago: University of Chicago Press, 1973), p. 177; the poet was Curzio da Marignolle.

9. See Horst Bredekamp, 'Gazing Hands and Blind Spots: Galileo as Draftsman', *Science in Context* 14.1 (2001), pp. 423–62; Eileen Reeves, *Painting the Heavens: Art and Science in the Age of Galileo* (Princeton, NJ: Princeton University Press, 1997).

10. Galileo Galilei, *Due Lezioni all'Accademia Fiorentina circa la figura, sito, e grandezza dell'Inferno di Dante*, ed. Riccardo Pratesi (Livorno: Sillabe, 2011); Heilbron, *Galileo*, pp. 13–16; Mark A. Peterson, *Galileo's Muse: Renaissance Mathematics and the Arts* (Cambridge, MA: Harvard University Press, 2011), pp. 214–27.

11. Galileo Galilei, *Scritti Letterari*, ed. Alberto Chiari (Florence: Felice le Monnier, 1970), pp. 502–3; Jonathan Unglaub, *Poussin and the Poetics of Painting: Pictorial Narrative and the Legacy of Tasso* (Cambridge: Cambridge University Press, 2006), pp. 116–17.

12. Italo Calvino, *Six Memos for the Next Millennium*, trans. Patrick Creagh (London: Penguin, 2016), p. 52. See in general Crystal Hall, *Galileo's Reading* (Cambridge: Cambridge University Press, 2013).

13. William Poole, 'John Milton and Giovanni Boccaccio's *Vita di Dante*', *Milton Quarterly* 48.3 (2014), pp. 139–70, describes Poole's recent rediscovery of Milton's annotated copy and its significance.

14. PL 1.16; *Orlando Furioso* 1.2.2; Tobias Gregory, 'Milton and Ariosto', in *Ariosto, the Orlando Furioso and English Culture*, ed. Jane E. Everson et al. (London: British Academy, 2019), pp. 115–24.

15. John Evelyn, *Diary*, ed. E. S. De Beer (Oxford: Clarendon Press, 1955), vol. 2, p. 183; on this monument and the nature of Livorno in general see Molly Greene, *Catholic Pirates and Greek Merchants: A Maritime History of the Mediterranean* (Princeton, NJ: Princeton University Press, 2010), pp. 81–95, esp. pp. 82–3.

16. YPW vol. 4, part 1, pp. 615–17.

17. Robert Dallington, *The Survey of the Great Dukes State of Tuscany* (London, 1605), p. 9.

18. *Life and Letters of Sir Henry Wotton*, ed. Pearsall Smith, vol. 1, p. 395.

19. Ibid.

20. *Prose Fiorentine Raccolte dallo Smarrito Accademico della Crusca*, ed. Carlo Roberto Dati, 4 parts, 17 vols (Florence, 1716–45), 3.II.83–99 and 152–64, 3.I.81–104; Anna K. Nardo, 'Academic Interludes in *Paradise Lost*', *Milton Studies* 27 (1992), p. 213.

21. Cecil Grayson, *A Renaissance Controversy: Latin or Italian?* (Oxford: Clarendon Press, 1960). By a nice coincidence, the author of this work was the father of the vicar who showed me around the Kedermister Library.

22. Trans. Cowper, in *John Milton: The Critical Heritage*, ed. John Shawcross (London: Routledge, 1995), vol. 1, p. 59.

23. See Estelle Haan, *From Academia to Amicitia: Milton's Latin Writings and the Italian Academies* (Philadelphia: American Philosophical Society, 1998), pp. 13–19; A. M. Cinquemani, *Glad to Go for a Feast: Milton, Buonmattei, and the Florentine Accademici* (New York: Peter Lang, 1998).

24. YPW vol. 1, p. 330.

25. See Nick Haveley, '"Swaggering in the Fore-top of the State": Milton, the Prelates and the Protestant Dante, from *Lycidas* to *Of Reformation*', in *Dante and Milton: Envisioned Visionaries*, ed. Christoph Singer and Christoph Lehner (Cambridge: Scholars Publishing, 2016), pp. 15–40.

26. YPW vol. 1, p. 329.

27. YPW vol. 1, pp. 809–10.

28. Haan, *From Academia to Amicitia*, p. 19.

29. PL 8.618–20, 622–9.

30. C. S. Lewis, *A Preface to Paradise Lost* (London: Oxford University Press, 1942), pp. 112–13. See further Stephen Guy-Bray, '"Fellowships of Joy": Angelic Union in *Paradise Lost*', in *Queer Milton*, ed. David L. Orvis (Basingstoke: Palgrave Macmillan, 2018), pp. 139–50.

31. PL 8.601–2.

32. Jill Kraye, 'The Transformation of Platonic Love in the Italian Renaissance', in *Platonism and the English Imagination*, ed. Anna Baldwin and Sarah Hutton (Cambridge: Cambridge University Press, 1994), pp. 76–85.

33. PL 8.174.

34. PL 5.563–76.

35. PL 2.112–14.

36. PL 2.552–4, 557–9.

37. PL 7.229.

38. PL 3.58, 69–71.

39. PL 3.489–97.

40. PL 3.458–9.

41. John Leonard, *Faithful Labourers: A Reception History of Paradise Lost* (Oxford: Oxford University Press, 2013), ch. 11; Dennis Danielson, *Paradise Lost and the Cosmological Revolution* (Cambridge: Cambridge University Press, 2014), esp. pp. 118–20.

42. PL 1.301–4.

43. William Wordsworth, 'At Vallombrosa', ll. 9–10.

44. Mary Shelley, *Rambles in Germany and Italy* (London, 1854), vol. 2, pp. 137–8.

45. See Edward Chaney, 'The Visit to Vallombrosa: A Literary Tradition', in *Milton in Italy: Contexts, Images, Contradictions*, ed. Mario A. Di Cesare (Binghamton, NY: Medieval and Renaissance Texts and Studies, 1991), p. 130.

46. Quoted and translated by Walter Kaufmann, 'Nietzsche: Four Unpublished Letters', *Encounter* (October 1968), p. 6.

Chapter 8: 14 February 1639: 'Majestic Show of Luxury'

1. Pieter Rietbergen, *Power and Religion in Baroque Rome: Barberini Cultural Policies* (Leiden: Brill, 2006), pp. 263, 266.

2. Evelyn, *Diary*, vol. 2, pp. 364–5; Haan, *From Academia to Amicitia*, pp. 102–4; Andrew Dell'Antonio, *Listening as Spiritual Practice in Early Modern Italy* (Berkeley: University of California Press, 2011), pp. 44–7, 83–7.

3. Rietbergen, *Power and Religion*, p. 135.

4. PL 3.135–6.

5. George Sandys, *A Relation of a Journey* (London, 1615), pp. 253–4.

6. Giuseppe Galasso, 'Society in Naples in the Seicento', in *Painting in Naples 1606–1705 from Caravaggio to Giordano*, ed. Clovis Whitfield and Jane Martineau (London: Royal Academy of Arts, 1982), pp. 24–30; Andrew Graham-Dixon, *Caravaggio: A Life Sacred and Profane* (London: Allen Lane, 2010), pp. 334–8.

7. Galileo Galilei, *Opere*, ed. Antonio Favaro et al. (Florence: Edizione Nazionale, 1890–1909), vol. 10, p. 296; Massimo Bucciantini, Michele Camerota and Franco Giudice, *Galileo's Telescope: A European Story*, trans. Catherine Bolton (Cambridge, MA: Harvard University Press, 2015), pp. 83–4.

8. YPW vol. 4, part 1, p. 618; C. P. Brand, *Torquato Tasso: A Study of the Poet and His Contribution to English Literature* (Cambridge: Cambridge University Press, 1965), pp. 207–8.

9. 'Mansus', ll. 7–8, trans. Carey.

10. *Genesis of Tasso's Narrative Theory*, ed. Rhu, pp. 108, 139.

11. Ibid., pp. 140–1; Torquato Tasso, *Discourses on the Heroic Poem*, trans. Irene Samuel and Mariella Cavalcanti (Oxford: Clarendon Press, 1973), pp. 142–3; F. T. Prince, *The Italian Element in Milton's Verse* (Oxford: Clarendon Press, 1962), pp. 38–9; Brand, *Tasso*, pp. 252–5.

12. My thoughts about Milton and difficulty were developed in contexts arranged by Hannah Crawforth and Sarah Knight, to whom I'm most grateful.

13. *Genesis of Tasso's Narrative Theory*, ed. Rhu, pp. 104–6.

14. 'Mansus', ll. 78–84, trans. Carey.

15. For a loose translation see *Critical Heritage*, ed. Shawcross, vol. 1, p. 58.

16. *Genesis of Tasso's Narrative Theory*, ed. Rhu, p. 137.

17. 'Ad eandem', ll. 1–2, trans. Carey.

18. For connections between the painter and the poet see Elizabeth Cropper, 'The Petrifying Art: Marino's Poetry and Caravaggio', *Metropolitan Museum Journal* 26 (1991), pp. 193–212.

19. Graham-Dixon, *Caravaggio*, p. 276.

20. Ibid., p. 344; Walter Friedlaender, *Caravaggio Studies* (Princeton, NJ: Princeton University Press, 1974), pp. 207–10.

21. Cited by John Gash, review of Mina Gregori, *Come dipingeva il Caravaggio* (Milan: Electa, 1996), *Burlington Magazine* 140.1138 (January 1998), p. 41; Graham-Dixon, *Caravaggio*, pp. 247–8.

22. I draw here on the scintillating analyses by Michael Fried, *The Moment of Caravaggio* (Princeton, NJ: Princeton University Press, 2010), and Leo Bersani and Ulysse Dutoit, *Caravaggio's Secrets* (Cambridge, MA: MIT Press, 1998).

23. See Michael Fried, *After Caravaggio* (New Haven, CT: Yale University Press, 2016), p. 178.

24. Erich Schleier, 'The Bolognese Tradition and Seicento Neapolitan Painting', in *Painting in Naples*, ed. Whitfield and Martineau, p. 47.

25. Pierluigi Leone De Castris, 'Painting in Naples from Caravaggio to the Plague of 1656', in *Painting in Naples*, ed. Whitfield and Martineau, p. 43.

26. See Gabriele Finaldi and Jeremy Wood, 'Orazio Gentileschi at the Court of Charles I', in *Orazio and Artemesia Gentileschi*, ed. Keith Christiansen and Judith W. Mann (New Haven, CT: Yale University Press, 2001), p. 230.

27. *Paradise Regained* (hereafter PR), 4.421–2, 45, 58–60.

28. PR 4.109–11.

29. See Elizabeth Cary, Lady Falkland, *Lives and Letters*, ed. Heather Wolfe (Tempe, AZ: Arizona Center for Medieval and Renaissance Studies, 2001), p. 407.

30. See Stefania Tutino, *Thomas White and the Blackloists: Between Politics and Theology during the English Civil War* (Farnham: Ashgate, 2008), esp. pp. 43–4.

31. Edward Chaney, *The Grand Tour and the Great Rebellion: Richard Lassels and 'The Voyage of Italy' in the Seventeenth Century* (Geneva: Slatkine, 1985), pp. 244–51.

32. YPW vol. 4, part 1, p. 619.

33. PL 1.713–17.

34. Evelyn, *Diary*, vol. 2, p. 261.

35. PL 1.777–9, 789–90.

36. DDC pp. 749–51.

37. PL 5.434, 436–8, my emphasis.

38. PL 5.469–500.

39. See the excellent accounts by Regina Schwartz, *Sacramental Poetics at the Dawn of Secularism: When God Left the World* (Stanford, CA: Stanford University Press, 2008), esp. pp. 59–64, and Sophie Read, *Eucharist and the Poetic Imagination in Early Modern England* (Cambridge: Cambridge University Press, 2013).

40. Nicholas Davidson, 'Unbelief and Atheism in Italy, 1500–1700', in *Atheism from the Reformation to the Enlightenment*, ed. Michael Hunter and David Wootton (Oxford: Oxford University Press, 1992), pp. 55–85.

41. PL 1.768–71.

42. Evelyn, *Diary*, vol. 2, p. 261.
43. See Rietbergen, *Power and Religion in Baroque Rome*.
44. Frederick Hammond, *Music and Spectacle in Baroque Rome: Barberini Patronage under Urban VIII* (New Haven, CT: Yale University Press, 1994), pp. 23–4.
45. YPW vol. 1, p. 334; Rietbergen, *Power and Religion in Baroque Rome*, p. 272.
46. Dallington, *Survey of the Great Dukes State of Tuscany*, pp. 11–12; John Stoye, *English Travellers Abroad, 1604–1667*, revised edition; (New Haven, CT: Yale University Press, 1989), p. 71.
47. YPW vol. 1, p. 335.
48. YPW vol. 1, p. 334.
49. Tim Carter, 'The Seventeenth Century', in *The Oxford Illustrated History of Opera*, ed. Roger Parker (Oxford: Oxford University Press, 2001), pp. 18–19.
50. Margaret Byard, '"Adventrous Song": Milton and the Music of Rome', in *Milton in Italy*, ed. Di Cesare, pp. 305–28; Campbell and Corns, *John Milton*, pp. 122–3.
51. Argia Bertini and Susan Parisi, 'Leonora Baroni', Grove Music Online.
52. Roland Barthes, *Camera Lucida*, trans. Richard Howard (London: Vintage, 1993), p. 27.
53. Ibid., p. 96.
54. 'Ad Leonoram Romae canentem', ll. 4–8, trans. Carey.
55. See the summary of these readings in Carey's headnote: *Complete Shorter Poems*, p. 257.
56. PL 9.560, 10.508.
57. Sonnet 1, ll. 1–2, 5.
58. John Kerrigan, 'Milton and the Nightingale', in *On Shakespeare and Early Modern Literature: Essays* (Oxford: Oxford University Press, 2001), pp. 217–29; Mladen Dolar, *A Voice and Nothing More* (Cambridge, MA: MIT Press, 2006), p. 3.
59. Richard Wistreich, '"Inclosed in this tabernacle of flesh": Body, Soul, and the Singing Voice', *Journal of the Northern Renaissance* 8 (2017), https://www.northernrenaissance.org/inclosed-in-this-tabernacle-of-flesh-body-soul-and-the-singing-voice/.
60. For Milton's acquaintance with Doni see YPW vol. 2, pp. 765, 774.
61. Citations from Oliver Strunk, *Source Readings in Music History, Vol.*

3: The Baroque Era (London: Faber, 1981), pp. 3–5; see Claude V. Palisca, *The Florentine Camerata: Documentary Studies and Translations* (New Haven, CT: Yale University Press, 1989); Wayne Koestenbaum, *The Queen's Throat: Opera, Homosexuality and the Mysteries of Desire* (New York: Poseidon Press, 1993), pp. 179–83.

62. Translated in J. S. Shedlock, 'André Maugars', in *Studies in Music*, ed. Robin Grey (London: Simpkin, Marshall, Hamilton, Kent, 1901), pp. 226–7; on his visit to London and familiarity with Ferrabosco, see pp. 215, 224.

63. Catherine Clément, *Opera, or the Undoing of Women*, trans. Betsy Wing (London: Virago, 1989), p. 5; Stanley Cavell, *A Pitch of Philosophy: Autobiographical Exercises* (Cambridge, MA: Harvard University Press, 1994), p. 132.

64. Koestenbaum, *Queen's Throat*, p. 42.

65. EL p. 59; William Poole, '"The Armes of Studious Retirement"? Milton's Scholarship, 1632–1641', in *Young Milton: The Emerging Author*, ed. Edward Jones (Oxford: Oxford University Press, 2013), pp. 35–6.

66. Taruskin, *Music in the Seventeenth and Eighteenth Centuries*, pp. 15, 5–6, 8–9; Lorenzo Bianconi, *Music in the Seventeenth Century*, trans. David Douglas (Cambridge: Cambridge University Press, 1987), pp. 1–45; Gary Tomlinson, *Monteverdi and the End of the Renaissance* (Berkeley: University of California Press, 1987).

67. Peter Burke, 'Early Modern Venice as a Centre of Information and Communication', in *Venice Reconsidered: The History and Civilization of an Italian City-State, 1297–1797*, ed. John Martin and Dennis Romano (Baltimore, MD: Johns Hopkins University Press, 2002), pp. 389–419.

68. Deborah Howard, *Venice and the East: The Impact of the Islamic World on Venetian Architecture, 1100–1500* (New Haven, CT: Yale University Press, 2000).

69. See *Sarra Copia Sulam: Jewish Poet and Intellectual in Seventeenth-Century Venice*, ed. and trans. Don Harrán (Chicago: University of Chicago Press, 2009). Sulam died in 1641.

70. Marcel Proust, *The Prisoner and the Fugitive*, trans. Peter Collier (London: Penguin, 2002), p. 591.

71. See the excellent overview by William J. Bouwsma, *Venice and the Decline of Republican Liberty: Renaissance Values in the Age of the*

Counter Reformation (Berkeley: University of California Press, 1987), chs. 7–8.

72. Ibid., chs. 9–10.
73. *Life and Letters of Sir Henry Wotton*, vol. 1, p. 399.
74. David Wootton, *Paolo Sarpi: Between Renaissance and Enlightenment* (Cambridge: Cambridge University Press, 1983).
75. Nigel Smith, 'Milton and the Index', in *Of Paradise and Light: Essays on Henry Vaughan and John Milton in Honour of Alan Rudrum*, ed. Donald R. Dickson and Holly Faith Nelson (Newark, DE: University of Delaware Press, 2004), p. 101.
76. MW pp. 159, 170, 288–9.
77. MW p. 226.
78. Federico Barberiato, 'Paulo Sarpi, the Papal Index and Censorship', in *Censorship Moments: Reading Texts in the History of Censorship and Freedom of Expression*, ed. Geoff Kemp (London: Bloomsbury, 2015), pp. 63–70.
79. See Smith, 'Milton and the Index', pp. 106–7.
80. I draw in this paragraph on the seminal account by J. G. Pocock, *The Machiavellian Moment: Florentine Political Thought and the Atlantic Republican Tradition* (Princeton, NJ: Princeton University Press, 1975), esp. pp. 53, 84, 165, 185, 276.
81. Ibid., pp. 284–5.
82. Gasparo Contarini, *The Commonwealth and Government of Venice*, trans. Lewes Lewknor (London, 1599), cited in Pocock, *Machiavellian Moment*, p. 322.
83. Alberto Tenenti, 'The Sense of Space and Time in the Venetian World of the Fifteenth and Sixteenth Centuries', in *Renaissance Venice*, ed. J. R. Hale (London: Faber, 1973), p. 20.
84. 'Epitaphium Damonis', ll. 55–6, 113–15, trans. Carey.
85. 'Epitaphium Damonis', ll. 137, 182–3; YPW vol. 2, p. 763.
86. 'Epitaphium Damonis', ll. 212–13, 217–19, trans. Carey.
87. 'Epitaphium Damonis', ll. 170–1.
88. See Nicholas McDowell, '"Lycidas" and the Influence of Anxiety', in OHM p. 112.

Chapter 9: 10 August 1642: 'Knowing Good by Evil'

1. John Taylor, *The Carriers Cosmographie* (London, 1637), sig. B; Stow, *Survey of London*, vol. 2, p. 34.
2. ABL vol. 1, p. 671.
3. A. D. Nuttall, *Dead From the Waist Down: Scholars and Scholarship in Literature and the Popular Imagination* (New Haven, CT: Yale University Press, 2003), esp. pp. 111–12 on Mark Pattison (the main model for George Eliot's Casaubon), who suggested that 'Milton's young wife refused him the consummation of their marriage', which Nuttall interprets as a reflection of Pattison's own sexual fears and frustrations.
4. See Gray, *Milton and the Victorians*, esp. pp. 161–2.
5. ABL vol. 1, p. 671.
6. EL p. 62.
7. For the date and for these and other possible sources of inspiration see the definitive account by Poole, MW pp. 304–7.
8. MW p. 353.
9. ABL vol. 1, p. 670.
10. William Poole, *Milton and the Making of Paradise Lost* (Cambridge, MA: Harvard University Press, 2017), p. 49; Lynette Hunter, 'Sisters of the Royal Society: The Circle of Katherine Jones, Lady Ranelagh', in *Women, Science and Medicine, 1500–1700: Mothers and Sisters of the Royal Society*, ed. Lynette Hunter and Sarah Hutton (Stroud: Allan Sutton, 1997), p. 182.
11. Johnson, p. 248.
12. Ibid.
13. Dolven, *Scenes of Instruction*, pp. 239–57.
14. ABL vol. 1, pp. 669–70.
15. Hugh Trevor-Roper, 'Three Foreigners: The Philosophers of the Puritan Revolution', in *Religion, the Reformation and Social Change and Other Essays*, 2nd edn (London: Macmillan, 1972), p. 253.
16. See the thorough account by Poole, *Milton and the Making of Paradise Lost*, ch. 5: 'Milton's Curriculum', p. 51 on his 'extreme Italianism'.
17. YPW vol. 2, pp. 397, 382–3.
18. Helen Gardiner, 'The Chronology of Milton's Handwriting', *The Library* 14 (1934), 229–35; MW p. 64.

19. YPW vol. 2, pp. 402–5.

20. YPW vol. 2, pp. 366–7.

21. YPW vol. 2, p. 374.

22. YPW vol. 2, pp. 372–3.

23. YPW vol. 2, pp. 385, 386–7.

24. YPW vol. 1, p. 732.

25. YPW vol. 1, pp. 894–5.

26. YPW vol. 1, p. 572; Janel Mueller, 'Embodying Glory: The Apocalyptic Strain in Milton's *Of Reformation*', in *Politics, Poetics, and Hermeneutics in Milton's Prose*, ed. David Loewenstein and James Grantham Turner (Cambridge: Cambridge University Press, 1990), pp. 9–40; Nigel Smith, 'The Anti-Episcopal Tracts', in OHM, p. 163.

27. YPW vol. 1, p. 581.

28. YPW vol. 1, p. 524.

29. See the excellent account by Smith, 'Anti-Episcopal Tracts', pp. 159–62.

30. Spenser, *Faerie Queene*, 1.1.18.6, 3.9.

31. Julie Spraggon, *Puritan Iconoclasm during the English Civil War* (Woodbridge: Boydell, 2003), p. 257.

32. Philip Schwyzer, 'John Milton and the Reception of Reformation Iconoclasm', in *Memory and the English Reformation*, ed. Alexandra Walsham, Ceri Law, Brian Cummings and Bronwyn Wallace (Cambridge: Cambridge University Press, 2020), pp. 238–54.

33. YPW vol. 1, pp. 808–16.

34. YPW vol. 1, p. 890.

35. Sonnet 8, ll. 1, 7.

36. YPW vol. 2, pp. 249–50; see Annabel Patterson, 'No meer amatorious novel?', in *Politics, Poetics, and Hermeneutics in Milton's Prose*, ed. Loewenstein and Grantham Turner, pp. 85–101.

37. YPW vol. 2, p. 249.

38. YPW vol. 2, pp. 589–90; Stephen M. Fallon, *Milton's Peculiar Grace: Self-Representation and Authority* (Ithaca, NY: Cornell University Press, 2007), pp. 113–32.

39. YPW vol. 2, p. 258.

40. YPW vol. 2, p. 326.

41. Johnson, p. 276. Johnson's orientalism on this point is conventional but also an inaccurate simplification – Ottoman Muslim women, for

example, retained ownership of their property even after marriage, unlike women in Milton's England.

42. Sandra M. Gilbert and Susan Gubar, *The Madwoman in the Attic: The Woman Writer and the Nineteenth-Century Literary Imagination* (New Haven, CT: Yale University Press, 1979), p. 188.
43. PL 2.650–3, 656–9.
44. PL 10.924, 935.
45. EL p. 66.
46. PL 4.299.
47. See Mary Nyquist, 'The Genesis of Gendered Subjectivity', in Nyquist and Ferguson, *Re-Membering Milton*, pp. 99–127.
48. Genesis 1:27.
49. Genesis 2:18, 21–3.
50. YPW vol. 2, pp. 598, 246.
51. PL 4.741–3; for extensive discussion of the problem see James Grantham Turner, *One Flesh: Paradisal Marriage and Sexual Relations in the Age of Milton* (Oxford: Clarendon Press, 1987).
52. PL 9.209–12.
53. PL 9.220–4.
54. PL 9.247–8.
55. PL 8.403–7.
56. PL 4.464–5.
57. PL 4.478–80, 488–91.
58. See Jason Rosenblatt, *Torah and Law in Paradise Lost* (Princeton, NJ: Princeton University Press, 1994), pp. 97–112.
59. See the excellent account by Sharon Achinstein, '"A Law in this Matter to Himself": Contextualising Milton's Divorce Tracts', in OHM pp. 174–85.
60. YPW vol. 2, p. 229.
61. Ann Hughes, *Gangraena and the Struggle for the English Revolution* (Oxford: Oxford University Press, 2004), pp. 244–5.
62. For more on Mrs Attaway see the *Oxford Dictionary of National Biography* entry by Ariel Hessayon.
63. YPW vol. 2, p. 345; Achinstein, 'Contextualising Milton's Divorce Tracts', p. 180.
64. See Nigel Smith, '*Areopagitica*: Voicing Contexts, 1643–5', in *Politics, Poetics, and Hermeneutics in Milton's Prose*, ed. Loewenstein and Grantham Turner, pp. 103–22.

65. YPW vol. 2, pp. 492–3.
66. YPW vol. 2, pp. 514–16.
67. Christophe Tournu, 'John Milton, the English Revolution (1640–60), and the Dynamics of the French Revolution (1789)', *Prose Studies* 24.3 (2001), p. 28.
68. *The Declaration of Independence: The Evolution of the Text*, ed. Julian Boyd (Princeton, NJ: Princeton University Press, 1994); YPW vol. 3, pp. 198–9; Tony Davies, 'Borrowed Language: Milton, Jefferson, Mirabeau', in *Milton and Republicanism*, ed. Armitage et al., p. 261.
69. See J. M. Coetzee, *Giving Offence: Essays on Censorship* (Chicago: University of Chicago Press, 1996), p. 10.
70. YPW vol. 2, p. 565.
71. YPW vol. 2, pp. 557–8.
72. Davies, 'Borrowed Language', p. 257.
73. 'Sonnet XIII. To Mr H. Lawes, on his Airs'.
74. 'Sonnet XII. I did but prompt the age to quit their clogs', ll. 3–4; 'Sonnet XI. A book was writ of late called *Tetrachordon*', ll. 4–5, 8.
75. ABL vol. 1, p. 663.
76. 'Ad Joannem Rousium', ll. 7–8, trans. Carey.
77. YPW vol. 3, p. 93.
78. *The Complete Works of John Milton, Vol. VI: Vernacular Regicide and Republican Writings*, ed. N. H. Keeble and Nicholas McDowell (Oxford: Oxford University Press, 2013), p. 292.
79. It was so perfect that there's a long-standing conspiracy theory claiming that Milton added the prayer himself to make the king look bad: see the judicious discussion by Nicholas McDowell, 'Milton, the *Eikon Basilike*, and Pamela's Prayer: Re-Visiting the Evidence', *Milton Quarterly* 48.4 (2014), pp. 225–34.
80. MW p. 12.
81. Ronald Levao, *Renaissance Minds and Their Fictions: Cusanus, Sidney, Shakespeare* (Berkeley: University of California Press, 1985), pp. 237–41; Dolven, *Scenes of Instruction*, p. 201.

Chapter 10: 26 May 1658: 'A Universal Blank'

1. Nigel Smith, *Andrew Marvell: The Chameleon* (New Haven, CT: Yale University Press, 2010), pp. 53–62, 106, 123–4, 136–7; Estelle Haan, '"The Adorning of My Naked Tongue": Latin Poetry and Linguistic Metamorphosis', in OHM pp. 56–7.
2. YPW vol. 5, part 2, p. 558; CW vol. 13, p. 48.
3. Sonnet XV, ll. 1–2, 7–8.
4. See Barbara Lewalski, *The Life of John Milton: A Critical Biography* (Oxford: Blackwell, 2000), p. 279.
5. CW vol. 13, pp. 362–3.
6. Sonnet 19, ll. 1, 10–11, 13–14.
7. PL 11.653–5.
8. PL 11.652–67.
9. Genesis 5:24.
10. Hebrews 11:5.
11. PL 11.638–41.
12. Edgar Allan Poe, 'Theory of Poetry', in *Essays and Reviews*, ed. Gary Richard Thompson (New York: Viking, 1984), p. 71.
13. PL 1.34, 37–8, 57, 59–64.
14. PL 5.821–5, 853–61.
15. Lewis, *Preface to Paradise Lost*, p. 98. Topsy is the slave girl in Harriet Beecher Stowe's *Uncle Tom's Cabin* who professes ignorance of both God and a mother, saying 'I s'pect I growed. Don't think nobody never made me.'
16. PL 8.255–6.
17. PL 1.1–16.
18. See the fine reading by Tzachi Zamir, *Ascent: Philosophy and Paradise Lost* (Oxford: Oxford University Press, 2017), pp. 19–21.
19. EL p. 61.
20. DDC vol. 1, p. 129.
21. DDC vol. 1, p. 130.
22. DDC vol. 1, pp. 132–3.
23. See Nigel Smith, '"And if God was one of us": Paul Best, John Biddle, and Anti-Trinitarian Heresy in Seventeenth-Century England', in *Heresy, Literature, and Politics in Early Modern English Culture*, ed. David Loewenstein and John Marshall (Cambridge: Cambridge University Press, 2006), pp. 160–84.

24. H. John McLachlan, *Socinianism in Seventeenth-Century England* (London: Oxford University Press, 1951), p. 186.

25. Stephen Dobranski, 'Licensing Milton's Heresy', in *Milton and Heresy*, ed. Stephen B. Dobranski and John P. Rumrich (Cambridge: Cambridge University Press, 1988), pp. 139–58; Martin Dzelzainis, 'Milton and Antitrinitarianism', in *Milton and Toleration*, ed. Sharon Achinstein and Elizabeth Sauer (Oxford: Oxford University Press, 2007), pp. 171–85.

26. Lewalski, *Life of John Milton*, pp. 351, 406; Poole, '"Armes of Studious Retirement"', pp. 39–40.

27. DDC vol. 1, p. 133.

28. PL 5.603–6; see Poole, *Making of Paradise Lost*, pp. 271–2.

29. PL 3.95–8.

30. William Empson, *Milton's God* (London: Chatto & Windus, 1961), p. 251.

31. M. A. Screech, *Erasmus: Ecstasy and the Praise of Folly* (Harmondsworth: Penguin, 1988), p. 19.

32. See Achsah Guibbory, 'England, Israel and the Jews in Milton's Prose', in *Milton and the Jews*, ed. Brooks, pp. 13–34.

33. YPW vol. 3, pp. 202–3.

34. See Mary Nyquist, *Arbitrary Rule: Slavery, Tyranny, and the Power of Life and Death* (Chicago: University of Chicago Press, 2013).

35. Eric Williams, *Capitalism and Slavery* (London: André Deutsch, 1964), p. 23; Maureen Quilligan, 'Freedom, Service and the Trade in Slaves: The Problem of Labor in *Paradise Lost*', in *Subject and Object in Renaissance Culture*, ed. Margreta de Grazia, Maureen Quilligan and Peter Stallybrass (Cambridge: Cambridge University Press, 1996), pp. 220–1.

36. YPW vol. 1, p. 617.

37. YPW vol. 5, p. 236.

38. YPW vol. 4, part 1, p. 366.

39. I draw in this and the previous paragraph on the remarkable account by Eric Nelson, *The Hebrew Republic: Jewish Sources and the Transformation of European Political Thought* (Cambridge, MA: Harvard University Press, 2010), esp. pp. 37–44.

40. 'To the Lord General Cromwell', ll. 1–4.

41. YPW vol. 4, part 1, p. 668; Laura Lunger Knoppers, *Constructing*

Cromwell: Ceremony, Portrait, and Print 1645–1661 (Cambridge: Cambridge University Press, 2000), pp. 93–5.

42. YPW vol. 3, p. 308.

43. See Carla Gardina Pestana, *The English Conquest of Jamaica: Oliver Cromwell's Bid for Empire* (Cambridge, MA: Harvard University Press, 2017).

44. See David Norbrook, *Writing the English Republic: Poetry, Rhetoric and Politics, 1627–1660* (Cambridge: Cambridge University Press, 1999), pp. 302–3.

45. MW p. 286.

46. See Austin Woolrych, 'Milton and Cromwell: "A Short but Scandalous Night of Interruption?"', in *Achievements of the Left Hand: Essays on Milton's Prose*, ed. Michael Lieb and John T. Shawcross (Amherst: University of Massachusetts Press, 1974), pp. 200–9; Blair Worden, *Literature and Politics in Cromwellian England* (Oxford: Oxford University Press, 2007), ch. 11.

47. See Poole, *Making of Paradise Lost*, pp. 130–1.

48. Sonnet 22, ll. 1–3, 10–12.

49. PL 3.22–6, 37–55.

50. PL 3.33–6.

51. YPW vol. 4, part 2, p. 869.

52. See Michael Schoenfeldt, *Bodies and Selves in Early Modern England* (Cambridge: Cambridge University Press, 1999).

53. *Borges at Eighty: Conversations*, ed. Willis Barnstone (Bloomington: Indiana University Press, 1982), p. 106; see the excellent discussion by Angelica Duran, 'Three of Borges's Miltons', *Milton Studies* 58 (2017), p. 183.

54. Jorge Luis Borges, 'Blindness', in *Seven Nights*, trans. Eliot Weinberger (London: Faber, 1984), p. 116.

55. Ibid., p. 114.

56. Sonnet 19, ll. 1–4.

57. Borges, 'Blindness', p. 117.

58. Monica Youn, *Blackacre: Poems* (Minneapolis: Graywolf, 2016), p. 69.

59. Jorge Luis Borges, 'A New Refutation of Time', in *Selected Non-Fictions*, trans. Esther Allen, Suzanne Levine and Eliot Weinberger (London: Penguin, 2000), pp. 322, 332.

60. Borges, 'Blindness', p. 120.

61. John Hull, *On Sight and Insight: A Journey into the World of Blindness* (Oxford: Oneworld, 1997), p. 87.
62. Sonnet 19, l.14.
63. PL 7.28–31.
64. PL 4.433–4.
65. PL 4.51–7.
66. I am indebted to and grateful for the sensitive discussion by Zamir, *Ascent*, esp. pp. 123–4.
67. PL 1.730–33, 738–48. Like all who admire this passage, I'm indebted to the inimitable discussion by Geoffrey Hartman, 'Milton's Counter-Plot', *English Literary History* 25 (1958), pp. 1–12.
68. PL 7.7–8.
69. I am paraphrasing here the famous and influential account of the experience of reading *Paradise Lost* developed by Stanley Fish in *Surprised by Sin: The Reader in Paradise Lost*, 2nd edn (Cambridge, MA: Harvard University Press, 1997).

Chapter 11: 9 or 10 November 1674:
'Vain Monument of Strength'

1. EL p. 33.
2. *Samson Agonistes* (hereafter SA), ll. 1733–7.
3. 'Ad Mansum', ll. 85–91, trans. Carey.
4. 'On Shakespeare', l. 4.
5. PL 2.666–70.
6. PL 10.810–13. See the excellent discussion by Emily Wilson, *Mocked with Death: Tragic Overliving from Sophocles to Milton* (Baltimore, MD: Johns Hopkins University Press, 2004), ch. 8.
7. PL 11.530–41.
8. See the wonderful account by Patricia Parker, *Endless Romance: Studies in the Poetics of a Mode* (Princeton, NJ: Princeton University Press, 1979), ch. 3, esp. pp. 150–1.
9. YPW vol. 4, pp. 536–7.
10. 'To Sir Henry Vane the Younger', ll. 1, 9–11.
11. YPW vol. 7, p. 249; see Campbell and Corns, *John Milton*, p. 283.
12. YPW vol. 7, p. 274.

13. YPW vol. 7, p. 304; see Campbell and Corns, *John Milton*, p. 289.

14. YPW vol. 7, p. 336.

15. *Constitutional Documents of the Puritan Revolution 1625–1660*, ed. Samuel Rawson Gardiner (Oxford: Clarendon Press, 1906), pp. 465–6.

16. EL p. 74.

17. EL p. 75.

18. YPW vol. 5, part 1, p. 450.

19. ABL vol. 1, p. 663.

20. EL p. 75.

21. ABL vol. 1, p. 663.

22. ABL vol. 1, p. 665; Nigel Smith, 'Haak's Milton', in *Milton in the Long Restoration*, ed. Ann Baynes Coiro and Blair Hoxby (Oxford: Oxford University Press, 2016), pp. 379–96.

23. Sergei Eisenstein, *The Film Sense*, trans. Jay Leyda (New York: Meridian Books, 1958, p. 58; see in general Eric C. Brown, *Milton on Film* (Pittsburgh, PN: Duquesne University Press, 2015).

24. *Milton in Translation*, ed. Angelica Duran, Islam Issa, and Jonathan R. Olson (Oxford: Oxford University Press, 2017).

25. ABL vol. 1, p. 661.

26. EL p. 77.

27. PL 12.646–9.

28. SA, ll. 1733–4.

29. PR 4.638–9.

30. Stow, *Survey of London*, vol. 1, p. 293.

31. EL p. 34.

32. Lorna Clymer, 'Cromwell's Head and Milton's Hair: Corpse Theory and Spectacular Bodies of the Interregnum', *Eighteenth Century* 40.2 (1999), pp. 103–4.

33. William Cowper, 'On the Late Indecent Liberties Taken with the Remains of the Great Milton', ll. 15–16.

34. *Complete Shorter Poems*, ed. Carey, pp. 357, 355.

35. SA, ll. 567–70.

36. SA, ll. 914–17.

37. SA, ll. 951–3.

38. SA, l. 1091.

39. SA, ll. 1381–3.

40. SA, ll. 1636–8.

41. SA, ll. 1649, 1654, 1657.

42. *The Yale Edition of the Works of Samuel Johnson: The Rambler*, ed. W. J. Bate and A. B. Strauss (New Haven, CT: Yale University Press, 1969), p. 376.

43. John Carey, 'A Work in Praise of Terrorism?', *Times Literary Supplement*, 6 September 2002.

44. The most penetrating and judicious overview of the debate is given by Feisal Mohamed, *Milton and the Post-Secular Present: Ethics, Politics, Terrorism* (Stanford, CA: Stanford University Press, 2011), though ultimately I disagree with his conclusion as to Milton's endorsement of Samson's actions.

45. I agree about the ultimate and deliberate undecidability of the question with Ross Lerner, *Unknowing Fanaticism: Reformation Literatures of Self-Annihilation* (New York: Fordham University Press, 2019), ch. 4.

46. William Shakespeare, *Hamlet*, 5.2.358–62.

47. William Empson, *Some Versions of Pastoral* (London: Chatto & Windus, 1935), ch. 5.

48. This thought is developed at length in relation to Milton by Zamir, *Ascent*.

49. YPW vol. 6, p. 410. I have chosen Carey's more elegant translation of this passage; for comparison see DDC vol. 1, p. 457. See the discussion by William Kerrigan, 'The Heretical Milton: From Assumption to Mortalism', *English Literary Renaissance* 5.1 (1975), p. 147.

Index

Page numbers in *italic* refer to figures.

441